To Clive

With every good wish

David Walsh

Christmas 2020

Public Schools and the Second World War

To our parents and the example given by their wartime generation. Remembering three members of that generation who have been a particular inspiration to us – Lord Bramall, Leonard Cheshire VC and Professor Sir Michael Howard.

Public Schools and the Second World War

David Walsh and Anthony Seldon

Pen & Sword
MILITARY

First published in Great Britain in 2020 by
Pen & Sword Military
An imprint of
Pen & Sword Books Ltd
Yorkshire – Philadelphia

ISBN 978 1 52675 039 6

Typeset by Mac Style
Printed and bound in the UK by TJ International Ltd,
Padstow, Cornwall.

Pen & Sword Books Limited incorporates the imprints of Atlas,
Archaeology, Aviation, Discovery, Family History, Fiction, History,
Maritime, Military, Military Classics, Politics, Select, Transport,
True Crime, Air World, Frontline Publishing, Leo Cooper, Remember
When, Seaforth Publishing, The Praetorian Press, Wharncliffe
Local History, Wharncliffe Transport, Wharncliffe True Crime
and White Owl.

For a complete list of Pen & Sword titles please contact

PEN & SWORD BOOKS LIMITED
47 Church Street, Barnsley, South Yorkshire, S70 2AS, England
E-mail: enquiries@pen-and-sword.co.uk
Website: www.pen-and-sword.co.uk

Or

PEN AND SWORD BOOKS
1950 Lawrence Rd, Havertown, PA 19083, USA
E-mail: Uspen-and-sword@casematepublishers.com
Website: www.penandswordbooks.com

Contents

Acknowledgements

We would like first to give a very sincere thanks to all the people and schools who have made this book possible. The bedrock has been material supplied in the questionnaires, and in much supplementary form, by school archivists. They are an under-recognised part of school life and we would like to thank them very much indeed, particularly those who have responded many times to what must have become tiresome requests for information. We hope that schools will continue to value their archivists and recognise the importance of acknowledging and prioritising their heritage.

Those archivists whose help has been well beyond the call of duty include Sarah Wearne (Abingdon), Jeremy Bromfield (Bancrofts), Karen Ward (Bradfield), Catherine Smith (Charterhouse), Bill Richards (Christ's Hospital), Jane Teal (Christ's NZ), Calista Lucy (Dulwich), Toby Parker (Haileybury), Timothy Leary (Hampton), Julia Hudson (Highgate), Mary-Louise Rowland (Hurstpierpoint), Peter Henderson (King's, Canterbury), John Allinson (Leighton Park), John Weitzel (Loughborough GS), Grainne Lenehan (Marlborough), Peter Elliott (Mill Hill), Angela Kenny (North London Collegiate), Yvette Gunther (Nottingham HS), Jackie Sullivan (Roedean), Chris Nathan (St Edward's), Howard Bailes (St Paul's Girls'), David Jones (The Perse), Rachel Hassall and Patrick Francis (Sherborne), John Brown (Taunton), Bev Matthews (Tonbridge), Jerry Rudman (Uppingham), Caroline Jones (Wellington), Elizabeth Wells (Westminster), Suzanne Foster (Winchester) and Carrie May (Wycombe Abbey). Sarah Wearne's own book on school memorials of the Great War is hugely moving and inspiring and should be in every school library.[1]

We would like to thank all those schools who have given us access and allowed us to quote from school magazines, school histories and war memorial books, which are listed in the bibliography. These have provided much of the subject matter in the book.

We are also very grateful to the governors and heads of the following schools for allowing us to quote from official papers in their archives or supplying us with photographs which we have used: Bishop's Stortford, Charterhouse, Christ's College NZ, Christ's Hospital, Cranleigh, Durham, Elizabeth, Eton, Hampton, Highgate, King's School Canterbury, Leighton Park, Marlborough, Merchant Taylors', Queen Anne's Caversham, Roedean, St Paul's Girls', Sherborne, Tonbridge, Wellington, Winchester and Wycombe Abbey.

Henry Wilson and Matt Jones at Pen & Sword have again been an invaluable source of advice and has shown great forbearance in answering every question we have raised, as has our inestimable editor for the second time, George Chamier.

William Richardson, former General Secretary of the Headmasters' Conference (HMC), has been enormously supportive and helpful over aspects of HMC policy and wider political issues in this period. Nick Hillman, Director of the Higher Education Policy Institute, has also given us freely of his time and offered valuable insights and advice on the public schools in the Second World War and beyond. Robin Brodhurst, Joe Davies, Christopher Everett, Peter Henderson, Penny Lenon, Bill Purdue and Alan Smithers have kindly read through the whole book or various chapters and offered valuable comments. We have also benefited from the wise counsel of distinguished academic historians in John Bew, David Edgerton, Brian Harrison, David Kynaston, Leo McKinstry, Charles Messenger, Kenneth Morgan, Dominic Sandbrook, Richard Thorpe and David Turner.

We are very grateful to the late Field Marshal Lord Bramall, who wrote the foreword for the book. His was the generation immediately affected by both world wars, and his own gallant war record as a young officer in the Normandy and North-West Europe campaign was the prelude to a highly distinguished military career. Lord Bramall personifies the quality of duty before self, and there has been no finer servant of his country in the seventy-five years since the war ended.

Ours was the first generation not to have fought a major war, for which we are profoundly thankful. Anthony's grandfather, Wilfred Willett, was badly wounded near Ypres in 1914, while David's great-uncle was killed at Arras in 1917. Our fathers both fought in the North African and Italian campaigns, and David's uncle, Edward Jourdain, a Stowe contemporary of Leonard Cheshire, was killed at Dunkirk in 1940. His memorial book, passed on to David by his grandmother, is one of his most prized possessions. We spent our childhoods surrounded by family members and friends whose vivid and often distinguished war experiences would occasionally emerge from the reticence that marked their generation.

In the course of teaching history together at Tonbridge, we led a series of battlefield trips, one of which was a charity walk for several hundred boys, staff and parents along the Somme front line in aid of Leonard Cheshire's Memorial Fund for Disaster Relief. This raised a substantial amount of money, which we presented personally to him. There is no greater figure to emerge from the Second World War than Leonard Cheshire; his life has been an inspiration to us, as to so many others, and profits from this book will go to Leonard Cheshire Disability. If this book portrays to the young of today something of what Cheshire's generation endured and achieved, then we feel content.

David Walsh and Anthony Seldon

Foreword

Field Marshal The Lord Bramall
KG, GCB, OBE, MC, JP, DL

I am delighted to write a foreword to this well researched book by David Walsh and Anthony Seldon on the key contributions of the public schools to the outcome of the Second World War, because it reflects many of my own recollections and experiences. Warfare completely dominated my upbringing and indeed my whole life. I was born in the shadow of the First World War in which my father served and suffered. By its end my own school, Eton, had sustained 1,157 fatal casualties, almost a complete school generation, and I believe that this casualty rate was reflected in other public schools proportionate to their size.

When I entered Eton in 1937, I was quickly swept up in the approach of the Second World War. The Provost and Headmaster refused to evacuate the school, and I remember watching the Battle of Britain being fought immediately overhead and experiencing at first hand the Blitz, with fire and high explosive bombs landing on the school itself. At seventeen I joined the school contingent of the Home Guard (in which I was made a sergeant), with special responsibilities for containing enemy parachute landings threatening Windsor Castle. I was also a member of the school's Officer Training Corps, which on the outbreak of war was taken very seriously indeed. We were instructed on weapon training and tactics by regular Guards NCOs stationed nearby at Windsor and had to pass certificates on military organisations, tactics and junior leadership, an invaluable first step to what lay ahead.

When I left school at eighteen, I had no hesitation in putting aside the place I could have had at Oxford and joined the army as soon as possible. The actual battles that I experienced as a twenty-year-old commander of a mechanised infantry platoon of the King's Royal Rifle Corps were to be somewhat different from what my fellow Etonians had experienced in the First World War, although in places the casualties would not be too dissimilar. In 1914–18 most of the set-piece battles had been fought over a relatively confined area, while those in 1939–45 were conducted over a broader canvas. When my platoon landed on 7 June on Juno beach in Normandy, I found myself engaged in no ordinary battle, the biggest amphibious and airborne operation ever attempted. The British and Canadian forces in the east of the Normandy bridgehead held down and degraded the most battle-hardened German divisions, making it easier for the Americans to break out and envelop the German forces in western Normandy and then move across the Seine into Belgium and Holland.

Not until early March 1945 did the assault across the Rhine bring the final advance to the Elbe to link up with the Russians. I was closely and violently involved in all this and ended the war in the devastated city of Hamburg. From it I would not only take with me many emotive memories, but would also learn some profound lessons about the whole nature and future of conflict which were to impinge on my own profession of arms as I rose through the ranks to become Chief of the Defence Staff and head of the armed forces. What had struck so many of us who had been fighting through North-West Europe was that we had come face to face with all the worst manifestations of total war – the bombing of every German city to utter destruction, the ghastly crimes against humanity on an unprecedented scale, the millions of displaced persons drifting across Europe without food or shelter and the growing numbers of casualties on all sides, which, by the time Japan surrendered, totalled no fewer than sixty million.

All this was to give me in my professional life a compelling and enduring belief that total war could no longer be considered by any government as a rational extension of foreign policy by other means. If military force ever had to be used in future, it would have to be in a more selective and subtle form, more consistent with available resources and the rapidly changing threats. I am glad to know now that the school generations of my father and myself were to be the last to experience total war, and I commend this book for revealing vividly and movingly what my public-school generation experienced in the second of those catastrophes.

Introduction

Public Schools under Attack

Public schools have become a public enemy. Unloved by governments of both main parties, by the press and by commentators, they have sunk to perhaps the lowest level of public estimation in their history.

The perception that Britain has a public-school 'problem', with the schools enhancing a two-tier society embedding privilege, can be traced back to the Second World War. The 1960s, not least with the election of the Labour government in October 1964, saw the schools come under an even more intense spotlight. In that new age of egalitarianism and modernisation, these very traditional schools were regarded as holding Britain back and responsible for many of the failures of the past. This included the way in which indifferent public-school toffs contributed to the callous slaughter of hundreds of thousands of working-class soldiers in the First World War.

The last decade has seen an intensification in the criticism of public schools. Three of the most articulate books to have been published are: Alex Renton's *Stiff Upper Lip. Secrets, Crimes and the Schooling of a Ruling Class* (2017); *Posh Boys. How English Public Schools Ruin Britain*, by Robert Verkaik (2018); and *Engines of Privilege: Britain's Private School Problem*, by Francis Green and David Kynaston (2019). These point to the entrenched privilege, sexual corruption, arrogance and sense of entitlement which have all been part of the public-school story, without always recognising the positive contribution that the schools have made to the country, and the values of public service that they have tried to instil.

Had Jeremy Corbyn won power in the December 2019 general election, Britain would have had a Labour government more committed to taking on public schools than any since the Labour governments of the 1960s and

1970s. His defeat, however, does not mean any reprieve for the schools. The Boris Johnson government is no friendlier to public schools than its recent Conservative predecessors. Johnson, like David Cameron before him (Prime Minister 2010–16) attended Eton College (as did nineteen of the fifty-five who have occupied that position), and defending privilege was the last thing its two most recent alumni PMs wanted to be seen to be doing. Margaret Thatcher, grammar-school educated, was the last Conservative Prime Minister to be well-disposed towards public schools.

Against this background, it has been hard, and remains so, to assess the contribution of public schools to the history of the twentieth century, most specifically the two world wars. Our two books, *The Public Schools and the Great War* (2013) and now this volume, are therefore works against the grain, attempting to assess the impact of those wars on public schools and their place within the education system, and at what public-school alumni contributed to both wars, in the hope of achieving a more rounded historical understanding.

The Influence of Public Schools on their Alumni

It is impossible to know definitively how the character, outlook and skills of alumni were forged by the public schools they attended. That the Battle of Waterloo was 'won on the playing fields of Eton', as the Duke of Wellington is alleged to have said, was of course a glib statement, referring not to games pitches but to the bare-knuckle fights which regularly took place in corners of College Field. The assumption rests unchallenged that the school forged the warlike qualities demanded by the battle. But many other factors were at play in shaping officers and soldiers in the Napoleonic wars, as in both world wars. One important influence in the twentieth century was Christianity, both in the schools but also independently of them. The universities that alumni attended also framed their outlooks, although the culture of Oxford and Cambridge, heavily dominated by public-school alumni, resembled that of their schools, at least until the 1960s. The ethos of the armed forces and other professions, as well as family background, played their part too. Even if one accepts the importance of the public-school ethos in shaping the character and outlooks of alumni, including such values as service and team spirit, the culture and influence of wider society cannot be disregarded.

Ultimately, all we can assert with confidence is the proportion of the key decision-makers in each war who attended public schools, remarkably high in both, and across every facet of war service. It was not surprising that the military leadership in all three services should have come almost exclusively from a public-school background, or that the Oxbridge-dominated higher ranks of the Civil Service also emanated from that stable. More surprising is the conclusion of the historian David Edgerton, that 'most of the important Second World War scientists had been to public school', since one of the strongest criticisms of those schools has been of their slavish commitment to a classical education.[1] Whatever the role of later university, career and other social influences on alumni, we conclude that the ethos and influence of their schools was significant, and all the more so because, in the first half of the twentieth century, their educational experience was far more likely than today to have been one of all-consuming, seven-day-a-week boarding schools.

Public Schools and the Great War

Our earlier book, published on the eve of the centenary of the Great War, was the first to be dedicated exclusively to the subject, perhaps surprisingly, since it has often been regarded as the 'public-school war'. The social elites from the schools took the principal political and military decisions and were identified in its cultural legacy as responsible for callously sending so many to death in futile battles. The pointedly anonymous 'old card' of 'The General' in Siegfried Sassoon's 1917 poem had, we assume, not attended his local state school. From here it was a short journey to the savage attack on the public-school officer class in Joan Littlewood's seminal musical *Oh! What a Lovely War!* (1963), and later in the 1990s in *Blackadder Goes Forth*. The recently departed Michael Howard, in his foreword to our first book, qualified this criticism by pointing out that, for the military leadership, the new industrial war of 1914

> demanded a new kind of professionalism that could master the complex interaction of weapons, many of which had only just been

invented, and that professionalism could only be learned by a ghastly process of trial and error. Without it, the heroic courage instilled into the pupils of public schools was simply suicidal, and to demand it of troops under their command all too often murderous.[2]

It is that 'murderous' element which has prevailed in public perception.

It was also a 'public-school war' in the sense that the ethos schools imbued in their pupils of duty, endurance and sacrifice fitted the conditions in which the war was fought and explains at least some of the reasons for the eventual victory. We set out to examine whether the portrayal of the political and battlefield leadership as the villains of the piece was in fact justified by the facts. Were public-school alumni the cowards hiding behind the front line or the heartless red-tabbed incompetents portrayed in poetry and theatre?

We examined in detail for the first time, through research in individual school archives, the scale of public-school losses. We found that they stood at 19 per cent of those who served, just short of double the national average; so no shirking of responsibility can be asserted by examining that evidence. Courage and selfless duty were evident, we argued, in the battlefield leadership and sacrifice of the younger junior officers, who comprised 90 per cent of public-school casualties. Clearly there was military incompetence, so that charge holds, though this was not confined to Britain, and the most senior officers who were responsible for these flawed decisions were arguably conditioned far more by long years in the military than by the more recent experience of their schools.

The centenary events that ended in 2018 may not have changed wider cultural interpretations, but they have challenged perceptions of a 'futile war' and drawn attention to what the officer class, including the much maligned generals, contributed by their example and leadership to a crushing military victory in 1918, in which British troops took a more dominant role than in 1945.

The Public Schools' Predicament in 1940

The Second World War was also a 'public-school war' in that the political and military leadership continued to come as significantly from that background, but it is more commonly labelled as the 'People's War'. It was first given that moniker by Winston Churchill in a broadcast on 14 July 1940. He called it 'the war of the unknown warriors ... not only soldiers but the entire population, men, women and children'.[3] In the shocked Britain which faced defeat between 1940 and 1942, the ideology of the 'People's War', with its mantra of a democratic and classless sense of community, was seriously at odds with the public-school claim to social exclusiveness and privilege.

At no point during the First World War had there been any comparable questioning of the ruling elites or the status of the schools which had educated them. But the spectre of defeat in 1940 brought political threats to public schools. They were too closely associated with those who had brought Britain to her knees in 1940, fingered in the anonymous polemic *Guilty Men* (written by three former public schoolboys, including Michael Foot). Their targets were the pre-war politicians of the Conservative Party, such as Neville Chamberlain, Stanley Baldwin and Lord Halifax, educated almost exclusively at elite boarding schools like Eton and Harrow, who had not only failed to prevent war, but taken Britain into it so unprepared.

The start of the war caught the public schools at a particularly low ebb. The world outside their gates had witnessed rapid political and social change between the wars, but their ethos and traditions had remained redolent of the Victorian age. Their finances in the Depression years of the 1930s had been weakened by falling numbers, particularly in boarding schools. The leaders of the Headmasters' Conference (HMC), the umbrella organisation for public-school heads, even opened negotiations with the Board of Education to see if government money could be provided to prop them up, in the form of either state scholarships or income tax relief on school fees. Only in their response to the plight of European Jewry, by offering education and shelter to refugees from Nazi-occupied Europe in the late 1930s, were there the beginnings of a greater sense of altruism, and this little-recognised aspect of their history has been researched for this book.

The events of 1939 and 1940 exacerbated the already precarious situation of many schools. Several were forced to evacuate their premises in September 1939 after military or civil authorities forcibly requisitioned them. Then came Dunkirk, the threat of invasion and the Blitz which not only rapidly increased the number of schools evacuating, but also saw pupil numbers drop further across the whole sector as taxation was raised. It would have been no surprise if more schools had closed, as Weymouth College did in 1940, although the Board of Education was prepared to go beyond its remit in looking for ways to alleviate the threat.

The Contribution of Public Schools to the Second World War

Research for this book shows similar conclusions emerging from the 1939–45 war as in our first book. Casualties among public-school alumni were again close to double the national average and, in numerical terms, not that far short of the 1914–18 figures; junior officers again provided the biggest element, and this in a war where overall British military casualties were less than half those of the First World War. School rolls of honour show large losses of alumni in the Royal Air Force, especially Bomber Command, and in front-line combat units in campaigns like Normandy, where the daily casualty rate was comparable to the Somme. Battlefield leadership by junior officers on the ground, at sea and in the air was just as crucial to success as it had been in 1914–18.

The Second World War was of course won by the courage and sacrifice of millions. There were crucial battlegrounds where public-school alumni played little part, such as service on the merchant ships bringing food across the Atlantic. There were also men in high office like Ernest Bevin, his education ending at the age of eleven, whose contribution to the work of the Wartime Coalition was as important as that of his public-school colleagues. The pioneer of radar, Robert Watson-Watt, found his ladder of opportunity to university and lasting distinction from a Scottish state school, Brechin HS. The contribution of men like Bevin and Watson-Watt begs the question of how many others there might have been from less privileged backgrounds who, with a more egalitarian educational system, could have taken on crucial wartime roles.

There were, however, certainly roles in which the public-school contribution can be said to be critical, and out of all proportion to the size of the sector, such as the military high command and officer corps, the intelligence services and government. Four out of five members of Winston Churchill's War Cabinet appointed in May 1940 came from public-school backgrounds, while 84 out of 110 others who held ministerial roles during the war came from the same stable, twenty-eight from Eton alone. The top levels of the Civil Service were also dominated by public-school alumni, including Churchill's two most important advisers, Edward Bridges (Eton), the Cabinet Secretary, and General 'Pug' Ismay (Charterhouse), his military assistant.

That contribution can be illustrated by identifying the key decision-makers present on 28 May 1940, when Churchill met with the War Cabinet and then with a wider group of ministers of Cabinet rank who supported him in his determination to reject any accommodation with Germany and to fight on. Over three-quarters of those present at these meetings came from a public-school background, as did the main spokesman for accommodation with Germany, Lord Halifax. Clement Attlee, the Labour leader educated at Haileybury, gave Churchill strong support, and it was another Labour minister, Hugh Dalton, himself an Etonian like Halifax and eleven others present, who recorded the way in which Churchill phrased the passion and moral right behind the critical decision: 'If this long island story is to end at last, let it end only when each one of us lies choking in his own blood upon the ground.'[4]

Max Hastings has observed that one of the main reasons for Allied success was that 'they empowered many of the brightest people in their societies to deploy their talents, with an imagination which the dictatorships never matched.'[5] Public-school alumni were significantly over-represented in roles like the intelligence services and scientific research and development, including medicine. Quantifying this contribution can only be imprecise, but Oxbridge, from where much of the intellectual galaxy came, was overwhelmingly dominated by public schools. At Lincoln College, Oxford, one of the less patrician colleges, Brian Harrison says that four-fifths of undergraduates between the wars came from this background.[6]

Intelligence operations contributed much to ultimate victory, in breaking German codes at Bletchley Park and in other clandestine organisations like the Special Operations Executive (SOE). By their very nature, and by the urgent demands of war, these relied for recruitment on familiar school and Oxbridge networks. When the first official history of

SOE was published in 1966, some reviewers protested at the space taken up by the names of the schools and universities which key personnel had attended. M.R.D. Foot, the historian and himself at Winchester, defended this by explaining that England at the time was

> run almost entirely by an educated governing class drawn from Headmasters' Conference public schools. Among these schools there was a pecking order, endlessly contested in detail but well known in outline to everyone concerned; to know which school a man had been at was to know something about his probable competence and character.[7]

Not all agree. Dominic Sandbrook questioned this supposed link between school and character, saying that it 'tends to matter only to insiders, the public at large finding such debates utterly baffling'.[8]

Character proved anyway to be a double-edged sword, since those same intelligence services recruited by these networks men from elite schools who betrayed their country. When Kim Philby (Westminster) was recruited to the Secret Intelligence Service in 1940, the deputy head of SIS, who had known Philby's father when they were both colonial officials in India, vouched for him in these terms: 'I was asked about him and said I knew his people.'[9] Philby used his Cambridge networks in the 1930s to recruit to the Communist cause Guy Burgess (Eton), Donald Maclean (Gresham's) and Anthony Blunt (Marlborough), the 'Cambridge Spies'. Another product of a prestigious school, Oswald Mosley (Winchester), leader of the British Union of Fascists, spent half the war in prison after the Home Secretary reported to the War Cabinet in May 1940 that MI5 believed that '25 to 30 per cent of the BUF would be willing, if ordered, to go to any lengths on behalf of Germany'.[10]

The professional officer corps of all three services in 1939 were the products of military colleges also overwhelmingly dominated by public schools, comprising 85 per cent of entrants to Sandhurst and Woolwich between 1920 and 1939, and 90 per cent at RAF Cranwell. While the war's demands of necessity diluted and, to a lesser extent, democratised officer selection, that public-school influence remained strong in the battlefield leadership of junior officers in all three services. This was not confined to men, for the expansion of the women's uniformed services allowed alumnae from girls' schools opportunities for vital roles from Bletchley Park to the Air Transport Auxiliary. Whereas the public-school contribution in 1914–18 is primarily remembered as leadership and sacrifice in the war of attrition on the Western Front, its contribution in 1939–45 is more diverse and reliant on intellect and imagination. In both world wars Britain was essentially led by a public-school-educated elite in the political and military spheres. The fact that victory came in both wars, and that Britain emerged from those wars in a better state than most other protagonists, with its democracy intact and its economy at least surviving, suggests that the public-school governing elite was at least competent. Whether a more open, meritocratic elite would have done better is an interesting counterfactual question.

The Opportunity Lost

The end of the war brought the opportunity for boarding public schools to end their social exclusiveness and open their doors to pupils paid for by the state. Public schools were excluded from the provisions of the 1944 Education Act which reformed state secondary education, but R.A. Butler (Marlborough), the President of the Board of Education, sought in another way to draw them into closer ties with the state system. In 1942 he set up the Fleming Committee, whose report in 1944 recommended a way in which public schools could be more closely integrated with state education, with schools allocating 25 per cent of boarding places to pupils paid for by the state, recommendations which were accepted at the first post-war HMC Annual Meeting in January 1946. Detractors suggested that schools were merely seeking to secure their financial future, but by 1945 their numbers and finances had begun markedly to improve, so they had less need of state help.

The landslide victory of Labour in the July 1945 General Election initially sparked fear in public schools. Labour's National Executive in 1943 had resolved effectively to abolish them by requiring all children to attend state schools, but Labour in power, with other pressing priorities, showed no wish to abolish public schools or even coerce them. The key ministers were moderate social patriots, who had served alongside Churchill through the war and valued Britain's institutions. Prime Minister Clement Attlee was fond of Haileybury and believed that not allowing schools to exist outside the state system was incompatible with his notion of freedom. His government allowed individual local authorities to pay for places at boarding schools along the lines of Fleming's recommendations, but no national system emerged, causing the scheme to wither on the vine. The cost to the state of these places could not easily be justified in straitened times, while the difficulty of establishing criteria for selection of candidates also proved a stumbling-block.

The public schools themselves, sensing the dwindling interest from Labour in the Fleming scheme and no longer in need of state money, which had anyway threatened their independence, moved on to securing their own futures and prospered under the improved economic conditions of the 1950s. Fleming, coming as it did on a tide of popular wartime support for a more equal society never likely to be as strong again, represented the best opportunity since 1945 to make progress on the issue. Social historian Anthony Sampson, commenting in 1962 on the significance of the timing, wrote that the common danger of 1940 produced 'an intense interest in the future ... but the post-war years have had a tragic sense of bathos ... the social ferment has subsided, the public schools have prospered as never before, and Oxford and Cambridge have re-fashioned their gilded cages.'[11]

Public schools were helped to prosper by the comforting cultural memory of the Second World War and by perceptions that this time they had enjoyed a 'good war'. The heroes in cultural terms came mainly from the officer class, now portrayed in lastingly popular 1950s war films like *The Dam Busters*. Their codes of honour, dismissed by First World War critics as anachronistic and sentimentalised, now provided admired leadership in moving films about the triumph of British arms and intellect, with more cerebral and complex heroes like Alan Turing (Sherborne) also later honoured. The star actors mostly came from public-school backgrounds and had fought in the war themselves, including Richard Todd (Shrewsbury), Anthony Quayle (Rugby) and Kenneth More (Victoria, Jersey). Contrast this with the cultural legacy of the First World War, when officers had been lampooned. Captain Edmund Blackadder and General Melchett in *Blackadder Goes Forth* were portrayed as the epitome of their decadent class. By contrast, in the most popular comedy series about the Second World War, *Dad's Army*, it is the class-conscious Captain Mainwaring, from the local grammar school, who is the main butt of the humour, while the public-school educated Sergeant Wilson, an officer in the First World War, is kindly, effortlessly charming and more in touch with the needs of his men.

The survival and flourishing of public schools since 1945 owe much to the British experience in the war. Recollections of the war remained rose-tinted as the nation basked in the aura of a job well done. Churchill's state funeral in 1965, one of the great public ceremonies of history, elevated him to certain immortality in the minds of millions of Britons for whom he was a heroic figure. The reputation and value of Clement Attlee in wartime and in shaping the peace has also been enhanced in more divisive political times. Nothing much has happened since to change perceptions of the war in general, and the year 1940 in particular, as the most sublime moment in the nation's history. Among the beneficiaries of this comforting nostalgia have been our traditional institutions, including public schools, from where Churchill, Attlee and so many other war heroes came.

Public schools have moved on a long way since 1945. Rebranded in the 1980s as 'independent schools', they have improved the education they offer, now emphasising academic rigour, creativity and social responsibility as well as the more traditional training of character. 'Broadening access', along the lines Fleming recommended, may be the dominant strategy of many public schools today, although now largely with funds raised themselves, but the hopes raised by his report of bringing state and independent sectors of education closer together remain elusive. Boris Johnson's drive since the 2019 General Election to 'level up' and increase social mobility in schools is a recognition of how little has changed since 1945. Post-war Britain would have been a very different place if the spirit of the 'people's war' had translated into a 'people's peace' in education. This book explains how far the Second World War was a 'public-school war' and why it was also followed by a 'public-school peace'.

Postscript

When the writing of this book was already complete, coronavirus struck our nation and its educational system. Independent schools face greater challenges than at any time since 1940. Economic and social disruption, like wars, are history's greatest impetus to change. This crisis provides an opportunity to re-think the relationship between the wider educational system and these schools, whose independence and excellence are so important in meeting the challenges ahead. An opportunity was lost in the wake of the Second World War to create a national scheme for opening independent schools to a wider social base. A new opportunity now presents itself to open up places at a cost to the state no greater than it pays for them in the maintained sector. Schools and government need both compromise and creative thinking to ensure that the opportunity is not again lost.

Part I

The Opportunity Opens

Twice within twenty-one years, public schools have found their existence and educational purpose, along with the lives of their pupils and alumni, dominated by world war. The Great War cast a long shadow over the schools in the 1920s and, as it passed from the living memory of schoolchildren in the 1930s, so the spectre of another war loomed. This war was to be very different, the Home Front as dangerous as the fighting front in its first two years, and public schools not only found their physical survival at stake but also experienced serious questioning of their privileged status.

Chapter 1

The Long Shadow of the Great War

The Great War cast a long shadow over public-school life. The schools emerged from it with a strong sense of pride in what their boys had achieved and sacrificed, along with clear expectations of the next generation. On Haileybury's memorial was written:

> In proud remembrance of 577 Haileyburians who served in the Great War and were found faithful unto death ... Ye who come after them forget not their sacrifice, claim as your heritage a portion of their spirit and, in peace or in war, take up their sword of service. So shall the living and the dead be for all time bound in one fellowship.

The belief was strong in schools in the immediate aftermath of the war that continuity of tradition would validate what these Haileyburians and others had died for.

Such belief could not easily survive pressure for change from the world outside. The games-dominated rigour of the character training which had prepared young men to administer the Empire and lead their platoons over the top was less suitable for the very different cultural and political challenges of the post-war world. Already cracks had appeared in the edifice of the British Empire, which had been 'the single greatest driver determining the character of the public schools between the 1870s and 1930s'.[1] Rampant nationalism and the rise of extremes on both right and left undermined democracy across Europe. In Britain, women had been given the vote, two inter-war Labour governments and the General Strike of 1926 bore witness to an upsurge in worker power and class consciousness, and the world of communication and entertainment was revolutionised by the wireless, popular music and mass cinema audiences.

For the first two decades of the twentieth century 'the public schools were secure in their rural seclusion from the vulgar gaze of socialists and proletarians'.[2] Now they began to face accusations of social exclusiveness in a country where, despite Lloyd George's promise to create a land fit for heroes, the education system continued to reinforce class divisions and predetermined chances in life. The toxic political issue which public schools were to become had its beginnings in these inter-war years, as Labour replaced the Liberals as the main opposition to Conservatives and criticism of class-based privilege sharpened.

Change did come to schools in the inter-war years, but it was slow and grudging. Public schools continued to look back too much to the models of the past, even to Victorian times. Although they were used to producing the leaders of the nation, they lacked, in the inter-war years, strong headmasters with the boldness to promote across the sector visionary new educational ideas and practice, although new schools founded in the inter-war years like Stowe and Bryanston could shed some of the baggage of the past. Alec Waugh's 1917 accusation that tradition and convention had replaced ideals in public schools was still valid in 1939, for the inter-war years were a torpid era on which the sector cannot look back with much satisfaction.[3]

In the 1930s political and cultural criticism merged with serious financial pressures to threaten the future of public schools. The Depression brought a fall in pupil numbers and consequent financial problems, as schools were exposed to adverse market forces for the first time. Weymouth College closed in 1940, and other more famous schools came under threat, as the leaders of the sector went with a begging-bowl to government. None of these problems had been resolved by the time the next war started, the outbreak of which was broadly anticipated and provoked none of the jingoism of 1914. Tommy Macpherson, just leaving Fettes in 1939, wrote that 'the politicians kept saying war would not happen, but every dog in the street knew it was coming and that there was very little we could do about it.'[4]

The Legacy of the Great War

Frank Fletcher was sixty-five years old in 1935 and had been headmaster of Charterhouse since 1911, having previously been headmaster of Marlborough. A distinguished classical scholar, notably formal in his approach, he was the leading head of his generation and had been Chairman of the Headmasters' Conference (HMC) in eight separate years, including 1914 and 1915. His headmasterships were dominated by the Great War and its aftermath. In May 1915 a grieving parent wrote to him: 'I have often thought of schoolmasters during this war and think that their sorrows must be next to the parents, as they know the boys so well.'[5] The three schools at which Fletcher had taught – Rugby, Marlborough and Charterhouse – suffered the loss of over 2,000 boys in the war, mostly well known to him.

That memory of the Great War hung over public schools as the post-war generation grew up in the shadow of death. About one in every five public schoolboys who served was killed, double the national average. Casualties tended to be higher in the more socially exclusive boarding schools with strong Officer Training Corps (OTC) contingents, as a higher proportion of their pupils were commissioned in front-line infantry regiments as subalterns, the most dangerous rank in the army. Eton, the biggest school in 1914, lost 1,157 boys, followed by Marlborough with 749, 90 per cent of them junior army officers. Marlborough's Senior Prefect in summer 1914, Harold Roseveare, left school on 30 July 1914 and was dead on the Aisne by mid-September. His successor, Sidney Woodroffe, left that December and won a posthumous Victoria Cross at Hooge in July 1915. Charles Douie wrote that of the fifty-six boys in his boarding house at Rugby in 1910, twenty-three died in the war, a figure of over 40 per cent. He wrote that 'we who have lost our friends know well that much of the richness and beauty of life passed with them for ever'.[6]

Schools in the post-war years were physically and emotionally shaped by the war memorials which they built to commemorate their dead. These memorials represented ideals of duty, sacrifice and pride in the school's contribution to the national cause. Few doubted that 'public-school spirit' had played an important part in the victory, the Dean of Canterbury telling his audience on speech day at King's in 1920 that the public schools had 'risen to the test in a manner which was to their lasting honour and the honour of the country'.[7] The Harrow chapel was 'virtually a mausoleum', with almost every modern furnishing 'a memento of a dead army or navy Harrovian'.[8] When Stanley Baldwin opened the Harrow War Memorial building in 1926 he dedicated it to the fallen of the past. For him and so many others within the public-school system, victory 'confirmed the superiority of the English way of educating its leaders', Harrow's self-image shaped by its experience of the war.[9] At the unveiling of the statue of a dying Highland officer in the main quad at Fettes in 1921, General Macpherson told the assembled school that they should hold the memory of the dead and their gallant deeds in trust: 'Duty and sacrifice are the foundations on which patriotism, justice and freedom, the birth-right of every citizen in our great empire, are firmly and everlastingly fixed.'[10]

At every school, teaching staff who returned from the war exerted a profound influence. The ranks of HMC headmasters in 1939 included eighteen who had been decorated with either the DSO or MC or both in the Great War and many others who had fought. Hugh Lyon, head of Edinburgh Academy and then Rugby, was a published war poet. When the Reverend Ernest Crosse left his teaching post at Marlborough to become head of Christ's College in New Zealand, he took with him to hang in the chapel the Union flag he had used to cover the coffins of those whose burial services he had taken at the front.[11] At Sherborne in 1929 five out of six bachelor housemasters had served on the Western Front, with two MCs and a DSO between them; the sixth had been rejected on medical grounds and felt it deeply. Sherborne in the inter-war years was 'a very monastic establishment and still deeply influenced by traditional values which had been reinforced by first-hand experience of the First World War on the part of many masters'.[12] Survivors' guilt affected senior housemasters at Charterhouse who were 'agonisingly aware of their own unworthiness, compared with friends who had fallen, and haunted by memories of a land of lost content'.[13]

Tragedy could easily follow. Ronald Gurner was one of twelve Marlborough masters who went to war in 1914; only five survived. Gurner was badly wounded at Arras, winning the MC, but his nerves were in a delicate state when he returned to Marlborough after the war. One friend recalled that 'in the middle of a conversation, his florid face would go blank, his eyes would glaze over and he would appear to be far away.'[14] He became headmaster of King Edward VII, Sheffield, and of Whitgift, and he had many qualities of educational leadership – a first class degree, an imposing physical presence and a reputation as a reformer

– but his behaviour at Whitgift in the 1930s became increasingly erratic. Financial problems followed, and he killed himself in 1939 by drinking a bottle of corrosive disinfectant. Delayed war trauma contributed to this final, terrible act, according to his family, for he often felt that he had let down his friends by not dying with them on the battlefield. In an autobiographical novel, *Pass Guard at Ypres*, published in 1929, Gurner wrote of what haunted him:

> Ypres rises mystic in the sunset glow,
> The Menin Road winds where the waters flow,
> And those strange ghosts that ever come and go
> Speak to me sometime.[15]

Public-School System and Ethos

Public schools trace their history from the Middle Ages. In the three centuries following the Norman Conquest, advanced schooling available to the public was supervised by the Church or overseen by other bodies such as boroughs or by the local lord. From the 1380s new schools, endowed by patrons, spread education more widely and catered to a new rural gentry class. They included Winchester, founded in 1382, and Eton, in 1440. These schools were 'public' in the sense that places were not the preserve of trainees for the Church, and most pupils paid fees.

The term 'public school' emerged into common parlance in the early nineteenth century. This presaged a remarkable expansion in the Victorian era, fuelled by the growing prosperity of the business and professional classes who wanted a quality education for their sons which the state could not provide, and by the expansion of railways. What all these schools had in common was independence of state control and income from payment of fees. For boys and girls in state schools, education ended in their elementary schools at the age of twelve before 1918, unless they were clever enough to win a scholarship to continue at a grammar school. New public schools emerged almost annually, their systems and ethos modelled on the ideas of the greatest reforming headmaster, Thomas Arnold of Rugby School (1828–41). They included boarding schools like Marlborough (1843) and Radley (1847), but also day schools like Glasgow Academy (1845). This Victorian expansion was replicated in the self-governing Dominions of Australia, New Zealand, South Africa and Canada. King's Parramatta was the first to be founded in Australia, in 1831, by an old boy of Kings, Canterbury. Governing and business elites, together with the Christian churches, founded schools to give their children an education like their contemporaries in Britain. They recruited teachers, particularly headmasters, from Britain and sought to maintain British standards and customs.

In 1869, responding to fears that their independence was under threat from government following the Public Schools Act of 1868, Edward Thring, headmaster of Uppingham, asked fellow headmasters to meet at his house to consider the formation of a 'School Society and Annual Conference'. This created the 'Headmasters' Conference' (HMC), which became the organisational umbrella for public schools, although it was the individual headmasters who were members, rather than their schools. Numbers steadily rose from 114 in 1914 to 220 in 1939, swelled by overseas schools, new school foundations between the wars and by the election to membership of heads from the state-maintained sector. HMC, through its officers and committee, acted as spokesman for the sector in negotiations with other bodies, notably the responsible government department, the Board of Education.

There was a recognised pecking order of public schools, powered by the social background of pupils and alumni and by prowess at sport. For some, public schools just meant Eton and Harrow, as universities meant Oxford and Cambridge. Others widened it to the 'Clarendon nine', so-called because they were the nine schools examined by the royal commission on public schools in 1864 chaired by the Earl of Clarendon.[16] The sporting hierarchy was revealed by which schools competed in the Ashburton Shield for shooting, the Henley Royal Regatta and prestigious cricket matches at Lord's, where Eton had first played Harrow in 1805.[17] Academic success played a lesser part in distinguishing the more from the less glamorous schools, but Oxbridge scholarships were prized and publicised, with some schools helped by 'closed scholarships' for their pupils at certain colleges, and Oxbridge entrance was overwhelmingly dominated by public schools. Alumni associations, which flourished from the nineteenth century, bound former pupils to their schools and to each other, creating extensive and powerful 'old boy networks' across every facet of university, social and business life in Britain and abroad, marked by the 'old school tie' which made its wearer part of an instantly recognisable network.

Although the term 'public school' became, in the eyes of the public, synonymous with the more socially prestigious boarding schools, the sector was more complex. The major public schools were charities, but there also existed a network of 'private schools' run for profit, including prep schools owned by a proprietor but also boys' and girls' secondary schools of doubtful educational standards. Not all 'public schools' were fully independent of the state, with more than half receiving state assistance in some form. Membership of HMC was one way of judging a school's status, but its members in 1939 ranged from Eton to Carlisle GS. In that year, 189 British-based HMC schools educated 65,000 pupils – 27,000 in fully independent schools, almost all boarding, and 38,000 in schools receiving grants from either central or local government.[18] Their heads were admitted to HMC membership if the committee was satisfied on the general question of their independence, and they included powerful academic day schools like Manchester GS, KES Birmingham and Magdalen College School, but also schools with higher proportions of boarders like Framlingham and Barnard Castle. Direct grant schools were chosen by middle-class parents who wanted an affordable school, one less socially exclusive and more deeply rooted in the communities from which they came. Their independence was more limited than most boarding schools, since LEAs or the Board of Education were entitled to places on their governing bodies. Direct grant schools had little in common with Eton, while the differences between them and state grammar schools were minimal, usually just in the balance between pupils whose fees were paid by parents and those paid by local authorities. Wilson's School in Camberwell, a state grammar school founded by royal charter in 1615, historically relied for income on its endowment and fees paid by some pupils, but the 1902 Education Act provided for grants from the Board of Education and London County Council which 'brought it more and more within the public system of education'.[19] Wilson's was not a member of HMC, but its ethos was similar to public schools' – a house system, the OTC, an alumni association and a school song – and in the mid-1930s it put more elite public schools in the shade by having eleven science scholars in residence at Oxbridge. In practice, there was very little difference in the social composition of the pupil body between a state grammar school like Wilson's and direct grant grammar schools within HMC.

Co-education barely existed before 1939, although Bedales, founded in 1893, had established itself as a progressive co-educational school for liberal parents. Girls' schools could not be members of HMC but had their own organisation founded in 1874, the Association of Headmistresses. Whereas Eton and Harrow were undoubtedly 'upper-class' schools, such distinction existed less in girls' schools. Many upper-class girls were educated by governesses at home and 'finished abroad'. Middle-class girls went to schools modelled on boys' public schools like Cheltenham Ladies' College, founded in 1853, which was the second biggest boarding school in the country after Eton, and to other schools founded before the First World War like Roedean (1885), Wycombe Abbey (1896) and St Paul's Girls' (1904). After the First World War there was a welcome expansion as greater importance was placed by parents on the education of their daughters. Academically selective schools like Bromley High School, founded in 1883, had 184 pupils in 1908, growing to over 400 in the 1920s. Major new boarding schools were founded, including Benenden in 1923 and Westonbirt in 1928, while a plethora of smaller private girls' schools opened in places like Eastbourne, where there were twenty-three, Bexhill, thirty-two and Malvern, twenty-two.[20]

Field Marshal Lord Plumer, who had been at Eton in the 1870s, expressed a common view that the style of education was more important than the content, when he said to a group of Etonian officers in 1916: 'We are often told that they taught us nothing at Eton. It may be so, but I think they taught it very well.'[21] Public schools put considerable emphasis on intellectual development but even more on the development of character and leadership, fitting pupils for a life of public service into which the majority went. Duty, loyalty, stoicism and conformity were expected of them, while their characters were shaped largely by the traditions and customs of schools – twice-daily services in Chapel to teach boys the self-denial and sacrifice implicit in the Christian faith, the spartan living conditions and punishments which bred toughness, the prefect system to teach leadership and the strong, even obsessive games culture played for their moral value as much as physical exercise.

The public-school ethos and traditions had come under attack in *The Loom of Youth*, written by Alec Waugh and published in 1917, just after he had left Sherborne for the trenches. He questioned the merits of the system and quality of the product, sensationally highlighting the presence of homosexuality but more damningly arguing that the wider aims of education had been compromised by too much focus on development of a narrow type of character. The timing of the publication, when so many young men from these schools were sacrificing their lives, brought a furore of opprobrium on Waugh's head from those who saw him as a traitor to his caste, but the substance of his arguments struck a chord with those who saw a system which had grown complacent and out of touch with a changing world.

Despite Waugh's attack, little immediately changed after the war. Hugh Trevor-Roper, the historian, who went to Charterhouse in 1927, felt that 'there was something dead about the school itself. Little had altered there since the mid-nineteenth century, though the world outside had changed beyond recognition.'[22] Development of character continued to trump intellectual excellence in the purpose of public schools. Parents continued to send their sons to gain self-confidence and learn to be gentlemen, a status defined by class but also by a shared identity and a moral code encouraging fair play, manliness, and emotional detachment. The ethos remained one of compulsion, conformity and team spirit, along with blind loyalty to the school and house. It was a segregated world, obsessed with hierarchy and tradition, in which a boy could pass from public school through other institutions in adult life without ever having to mix closely with different classes of people. For the defenders of this ethos, tradition, 'playing the game' and spartan austerity were a validation of what so many had died for, and they perceived the war's lessons as the need to learn duty and endurance. Many heads in post in the 1920s had been appointed before the war and remembered so many of the young men killed. They would have agreed with Henry Kendall at St Edward's, Oxford, that 'it had never been the school's object to foster love of ease and comfort. Life's realities were hard.'[23] Or as future Cabinet minister, Derek Walker-Smith, said of Rossall in 1931: 'Public schools were based on the assumption that anything sufficiently unpleasant is sure to be good for the boy.'[24]

Markers of Change

Some signs of change appeared in the schools of the 1930s as the war, and all it had stood for, receded into the distance. At Westminster School, change was described as moving 'from tradition, conformity, classics, narrowness of vision coupled with the unquestioned exercise of authority by boys over other boys, towards the arts, independence of mind and action, internationalism or at least political interest of a national and European kind'.[25] Not all in the sector would have seen things this way, and the pace of change could anyway never match what was happening in the world outside, as greater material hedonism, a revolution in transport and communications, and growing political radicalism affected new generations of pupils and parents.

Such changes to ethos and tradition can be perceived more easily with the benefit of hindsight, for the daily lives of boys in the inter-war years remained very similar to that of their pre-1914 forebears. They were dominated by austere living conditions, compulsory team sport, daily Chapel and group conformity. Tradition meant that arcane rules, dress and slang distinguished one school's customs from another, while every little advance in seniority within a school earned an extra privilege, often petty but jealously guarded from those lower down the pecking order. The domination of classics within the curriculum persisted in most schools as heads fought a rearguard action to preserve it against encroachment by subjects like science and modern languages. In 1922 the HMC annual conference passed a motion making it 'incumbent on headmasters to take all possible steps in their own schools to strengthen and promote the study of classics'.[26] Critics within HMC argued that this implied a value in classics not given to other subjects and signified a lack of educational progressiveness in a world where science and technology had assumed a greater importance; but most of the cleverer boys, particularly in more traditional boarding schools, continued to be directed towards classics, and this was reinforced by the disproportionate numbers of classics scholarships at Oxbridge. Newer subjects like history, science and modern languages all increased in popularity, but at Eton in 1936 there were still thirty-nine masters teaching classics, sixteen teaching maths and just nine teaching science.[27]

When Hugh Trevor-Roper intimated to Frank Fletcher at Charterhouse that he would like to specialise in mathematics in the sixth form, he was told, 'Clever boys read classics', and Fletcher showed him the door. Trevor-Roper reflected that the one element lacking in his education at Charterhouse was 'thought', the emphasis being rather on 'the discipline of language and mathematics and building up a repository of factual and linguistic knowledge, the essential tools for later exploration'.[28] There were teachers in public schools prepared to give clever boys more creative latitude. At Tonbridge in the late 1930s, Sidney Keyes started writing poetry and short stories when he was about fifteen, encouraged by his teacher, Tom Staveley, who recognised that 'it was the work of genius'. When he reached the sixth form, Staveley had an arrangement with Keyes that if some moment of inspiration occurred in the middle of a lesson, he could give a signal and leave the room while he tried out his idea.[29]

Tradition also meant survival of the authoritarian and often sadistic disciplinary regime, with a range of powers delegated to prefects. At Bradfield in the 1930s, 'the prefects had absolute power and there was a whole hierarchy of petty authority which could and often did deteriorate into tyranny.'[30] Peter Townsend recalled the cruel initiation ceremonies for new boys and the several beatings, accompanied by sadistic rituals, he had to endure from prefects in his first two years at Haileybury, a process which led Ludovic Kennedy, at Eton in the 1930s, to follow in later life Goethe's precept to 'distrust all those in whom the urge to punish is strong'.[31] The traditions of schools prevented heads from interfering in the work of housemasters, and housemasters from reining in their prefects or taking sufficient steps to stop bullying. The perpetuation of such powers owed much to the acceptance by boys that, if they endured long enough, the same powers would be theirs. Public schools were aware of parental concerns, and the reputational damage which could ensue. At the HMC conference in 1934, the Revd Cuthbert Creighton, head of King's, Worcester, raised the question of prefect power, following correspondence with the head of a large preparatory school:

Parents are increasingly pre-occupied with the question of the powers of prefects in public schools, they viewed with increasing

trepidation the sending of boys into their public schools and they
were afraid to talk to headmasters about it.[32]

The underlying traditions and ethos may have only slightly shifted, but
certain markers of change can be identified. One was in the leadership
of schools, as a new generation of heads emerged. By the time he retired
in 1935, Frank Fletcher's commitment at Charterhouse to classical
orthodoxy, the value he put on spartan austerity and his lack of interest
in contemporary politics were being challenged by a new guard of pupils
and teachers who put less value on the traditions of old. Robert Birley,
his successor, had been too young to fight in the Great War, had been a
charismatic teacher of history at Eton, actively involved as a councillor
in Slough in relieving distress in the homes of the unemployed and
was directly in touch with anti-Nazi intellectuals in Germany and
Czechoslovakia.

With new heads came an influx of younger masters readier to challenge
conventional opinion, like Brian Hone at Marlborough or the more
radical Terence Worsley, who took on the strangling conservatism of the
Wellington common room. Hone became one of the most innovative and
inspiring headmasters of the post-1945 era at Cranbrook and Melbourne
GS in Australia. Many of these young staff were on the political left,
more receptive to new ideas and more critical of tradition, while a new
generation of pupils looked for greater political awareness and debate
than earlier generations had been allowed. At Westminster in 1931, John
Bowle, a young history teacher, founded the Political and Literary Society,
whose speakers in its early years included Mahatma Gandhi, Clement
Attlee and Bertrand Russell.[33] John Freeman, who left Westminster in
1933, believed that it taught him the 'civilising values of tolerance and
courtesy, but also awakened political and social consciousness'.[34] He
joined the Labour Party in 1932 after witnessing the hunger marchers
massing outside the Westminster School gates, writing that 'the school
heard the voice of England's forgotten people'.[35] At Eton the Political
Society received men of various political persuasions and the sessions
could be lively. When Sir Oswald Mosley came to speak in the 1930s,
Michael Astor asked him, 'Will you tell us, Sir Oswald, whether you
chose black for the colour of your party's shirts for motives of economy?'

Mosley lost his temper, and the cause of fascism was lost at Eton for good.[36]

One key post-war battleground within schools was the OTC, which had not surprisingly been of the highest importance during the war. In the early 1920s remembrance of the war continued to sustain the institution; at Harrow in 1921 the governors formally recognised the OTC as compulsory for all boys over fifteen, with parades twice a week and endless polishing of kit. Boys regarded it in the same way as other compulsory school activities, reviled but accepted as part of school life, but such militarism of action and spirit became increasingly hard to sustain as the war receded into increasingly distant memory, especially for boys unborn during its course.[37] As pacifist sentiment increased in the late 1920s, more boys came to see the OTC as out of kilter with a world in which war, as the League of Nations proclaimed, was a folly of the past. James Eccles, head of Gresham's, revealed in 1930 that he had received frequent letters from parents objecting to the OTC.[38] At Harrow Terence Rattigan led a 'boy mutiny' in 1928 against excessive drill and pervasive militarism which was well publicised in the *Daily Express* and supposedly brought a telegram to the Harrow head from the Eton OTC offering to march to his assistance. One boy pointed out pertinently in *The Harrovian* that the government was spending £100,000 on the League of Nations but £150,000 nationally on the OTC.[39] At the 1930 HMC conference there was a long discussion about the future of the OTC, because the Labour government was threatening to withdraw its supporting grant, and because the very concept of military training in schools was under increasing attack from the vociferous pacifist lobby. Staff commitment was a further problem, with George Turner, Marlborough head and decorated war veteran, concerned that his OTC was being propped up by older men with war service and that younger staff were increasingly reluctant to become involved.[40]

Even at Wellington, one of the most traditional Army schools, militarism was under challenge. There was a sharp decline between 1924 and 1934 in the numbers joining the Army as a career, while the Oxford Union 'King and Country' debate in 1933 affected the standing of the OTC. When the school debating society addressed the same motion, headmaster Frederick Malim noted with concern in his diary that '44 boys at debate voted they would not fight for their King and Country', enough of a minority to render senior officers on the governing body apoplectic. The Romilly brothers, Esmond and Giles, nephews of Winston Churchill, refused to join the OTC, inserted pacifist leaflets into the college hymn book on Armistice Day 1933 and then ran away from school to launch their own communist newspaper. Despite such outbursts of rebellion, the OTC continued to be a mainstay of public-school life in the 1930s, increasingly important as the decade progressed, and many were to be thankful for the basic training it gave. Esmond Romilly, like other public-school rebels of the 1930s, joined up in 1940 and was killed in action over Germany while serving with the Royal Canadian Air Force.

Another battleground within schools was between traditional group conformity and increasing individualism. John Le Mesurier, Sergeant Wilson of *Dad's Army*, said of Sherborne in the 1930s that 'more than anything else, I resented Sherborne for its closed mind, its collective capacity for rejecting anything that did not conform to the image of manhood portrayed in the ripping yarns of a scouting manual.'[41] In 1921 at Sedbergh, perhaps the most spartan of all public schools, new boy Freddie Spencer Chapman was beaten by his head of house four days running for refusing to play cricket, until his housemaster intervened, allowing him to miss cricket provided he did not waste his time. Freddie was allowed to go climbing, poaching, and ferreting on the fells above the school, a friend writing of 'his determination to seek recognition of himself as an individual, freedom to pursue ends which he himself valued, and a refusal to conform unthinkingly to an imposed regime'.[42] In schools obsessed with sport, a taste for art and beauty was one of the main ways in which dissent and individualism could be expressed. At Marlborough in the 1920s, aesthetes who hated games were sufficiently numerous to constitute a self-supporting group. John Betjeman, Anthony Blunt and Louis MacNeice were almost exact contemporaries, distinguishing themselves 'in forms of defiance which ranged from straightforward protest to ironic self-mockery'.[43] Their antics included playing conspicuously on the cricket field with a big rubber beach ball, but they also founded an art society, approved by their headmaster who agreed to be its president.

New schools not constrained by old traditions introduced fresh ideas and a more civilising influence. Rendcomb, founded by Noel Wills in 1920 to provide a boarding school for boys from the elementary schools of Gloucester, tried to educate boys 'in a family atmosphere and in beautiful surroundings'.[44] Bedales was joined as a pioneer of co-education by Frensham Heights, founded in 1925, another school with strongly liberal principles encouraging mutual respect between pupils and staff. The new school with the biggest impact on the establishment was Stowe, founded in 1923. Its first headmaster, J.F. Roxburgh, wanted to create an institution which promoted individualism and freedom of expression, for he was convinced that the mass slaughter in the trenches, which he had experienced, was caused by slavish conformism drilled into the public-school officer class. He shrewdly engaged with the spirit of the Enlightenment which had imbued Stowe House in the eighteenth century, and 'wanted this spirit of critical enquiry to permeate the school'.[45] He encouraged boys to explore the grounds and temples of the 800-acre estate, and hoped that the beauty of the house and gardens would rub off on them and build a strong tradition in music and art. In his first address in 1923 he said that 'every boy who goes out from Stowe will know beauty when he sees it for the rest of his life'.[46] He also liberalised the curriculum by allowing a wide variety of sixth form specialisation; by 1930 there were just twenty classicists and over sixty taking maths and science. Roxburgh was, however, shrewd enough to realise that Stowe should not be branded as too liberal or progressive a school, for he wanted to attract the parents who might also consider Eton and Wellington, so OTC and team sports received his full backing.

Stowe produced one of the cult figures of left-wing political dissent between the wars. John Cornford survived his contact with the public-school system he despised largely through the tolerance of Roxburgh, who wrote in his reference to Cambridge: 'I cannot keep pace with him at all in his views on politics, economics or literature ... though he disapproves entirely of the public-school system, he takes no active steps to interfere with its workings at Stowe.'[47] At Cambridge, Cornford joined the Communist Party (CPGB), along with his Roedeanian lover Margot Heinemann, and spent much of his time as an organiser for the party before becoming one of the first of the International Brigade volunteers in Spain. Noel Annan, a fellow Stoic, remembered him at Cambridge organising a demonstration: 'He emitted power, energy and conviction. His mission was to convince … He believed in the Communist Party with all the ardour a young priest feels for the church on being ordained and able to say mass.'[48] Cornford was killed in Spain in December 1936, becoming for his fellow-travellers on the left the martyred poet-intellectual of the war against fascism.

Public schools have always had 'an historic ability to contain and self-mythologise acts of individual rebellion. The paralysing mystique surrounding the traditions of Eton, Harrow and the rest meant that most of the rebels were half in love with the things they were complaining about.'[49] Much rebel activity was about the striking of attitudes. Richard Hillary's housemaster at Shrewsbury wrote of him that 'he seemed to dislike the conventional view of things merely because they were conventional', but he never really wanted to develop coherent alternatives to the conventions he opposed and in his deepest beliefs did not seriously differ from others of this age.[50] Patrick Leigh Fermor, who enjoyed his time at King's, Canterbury from 1929 to 1931, was less a rebel than a free spirit who could not resist taking on authority. Suspended once, he had a total disregard for punishment and described his increasingly wild behaviour as 'a bookish attempt to coerce life into a closer resemblance to literature'.[51] One of the last reviews written by George Orwell, a serial critic of public schools, was of a book about Eton, which he praised for its tolerant and civilised atmosphere, allowing each boy the chance of asserting his individuality. Eton in the inter-war years demonstrates the difficulty of labelling the 'public-school product', since it produced war heroes and adventurers like Ian and Peter Fleming, Fitzroy Maclean and Wilfred Thesiger, but also artistic and literary figures like Oliver Messel, James Lees-Milne and Anthony Powell.

The system generally bent more freely to the individual in the 1930s, and many of the rebels and wild spirits of the 1930s became war heroes. John Hopgood had a blazing row with his housemaster as he left Marlborough in July 1939 about the way 'his system favoured the goodies and the gutless'; less than four years later, he died over the Moehne Dam.[52] Hallam Tennyson, at Eton in the 1930s, was not forced to join the OTC and was allowed to sell *Peace News* in Eton High Street. He became a conscientious objector in the war, serving with the Friends' Ambulance, but lost both his brothers in action. When his brother Penrose was killed in the war, their father wrote: 'I do not think there are many schools where a boy would have been allowed such freedom of expression; where his disregard of discipline and convention would have met with such indulgence.'[53]

Competition and Criticism

Public schools first surfaced as a toxic political issue in the early 1930s, coinciding with the supplanting of the Liberals by Labour as the main party of opposition, the emergence of a more class-based politics and the influence of a left-wing intelligentsia mostly educated themselves at public schools. In 1914 public schools had been self-confident in their traditions and social exclusiveness, even assertively so, and they paid little heed to what politicians might think of them or whether their social exclusiveness might be regarded as harmful to the nation. By 1939 they were on the defensive, financially under pressure, politically under scrutiny, no longer confident of what they stood for and identified as a source of class division. There had been warnings from within the sector. At the 1915 HMC conference, Charles Lowry, the Tonbridge headmaster, spoke of the inevitable sweeping away of class differences after the war.[54] At the first post-war conference, Frank Fletcher told heads that their duty was to introduce new social classes to their schools so that a wider spectrum of society could benefit from the public school virtues of self-discipline and service, and he met with the President of the Board of Education, H.A.L. Fisher, in an unsuccessful bid to move this forward.[55]

Lowry and Fletcher were both harking back to an era when schools used their endowments to fund places for poorer local scholars, but they were lone voices in a sector increasingly dominated by class and wealth. Schools were now, however, more under threat from circumstances outside their control. The 1918 Education Act established the basis, through local education authorities, of a system of compulsory education for children aged five to fourteen, the school leaving age having been raised from twelve. This was a limited reform, and a more radical restructuring of secondary education had to wait until 1944, but over the next two decades there was an increase in the number of state secondary schools and pupils attending them – from 1,027 schools and 187,000 pupils in 1913 to 1,397 schools and 485,000 pupils in 1937.[56] However, the system was a long way from being a national one. The often inadequate 'all-in' elementary schools were still where 75 per cent of England's children experienced the whole of their education, and 'state secondary education' before 1944 'meant in effect grammar school education, necessarily confined to a small number of children'.[57]

The stirrings of debate over state secondary education were to reinforce the public-school image as that of 'a closed private system, running parallel with the national system but having few points of contact with it'.[58] The Teachers' (Superannuation) Act 1918 delivered a serious financial sting to public schools in imposing minimum salaries for teachers in the state system and giving them a pension for the first time, forcing public schools to follow suit to compete for the best teachers and increasing their costs. It was during the implementation of this Act that the public schools, through Fletcher, offered 'free places' in return for their teachers getting the same pension entitlement as those in state-aided schools, but the offer was rejected by Fisher and the Board of Education.[59]

State grammar schools outside HMC, which charged fees to a proportion of their pupils until 1944, provided competition as a free or cheaper alternative. They mimicked the public-school model, unsurprisingly, since the most influential figures in state education in the 1930s were Henry Pelham (Harrow) and Maurice Holmes (Wellington), Permanent Secretaries at the Board of Education and described by a school inspector as 'entirely without first-hand acquaintance with the proletarian class whose education they control'.[60] Malcolm Muggeridge, at Selhurst High School in Croydon during and just after the First World War, remembered the four houses there, 'Alpha, Beta, Gamma, Delta, as well as prefects, colours and other trappings reminiscent of *Tom Brown's Schooldays*. We had a Latin motto '*Ludum Ludite*' or 'Play the Game', invented, I suppose, by one of the masters.'[61] The pupils in these schools absorbed public-school codes from children's magazines like *Boy's Own Paper*, and from novelists like Frank Richards with his stories about Billy Bunter at Greyfriars School, which distorted school traditions into myth, conditioned the imagination of a generation of state-educated children and possibly increased the aura of boarding schools as a closed society with adults as remote authority figures.

Public schools in the inter-war years were out of step culturally with a country which saw itself as increasingly modern. The biggest division within public schools was not between schools which were fully independent and those which were in some way state assisted, but between city day schools and the more prestigious boarding schools. The traditions and ethos of the latter, according to the historian Dominic Sandbrook, 'seemed Victorian in outlook and image when there was a general backlash in the first half of the twentieth century against fusty and backward Victorianism.'[62] It was these more socially exclusive schools, especially Eton, whose alumni dominated elite positions in the state. The sense of entitlement of the elites came under attack from public school-alumni within the intellectual left. W.H. Auden, at Gresham's just after the First World War wrote: 'The public schoolboy's attitude to the working class and the not-quite-quite has altered very little since the war. He is taught to be fairly kind and polite, provided of course they return the compliment, but their lives and needs remain as remote to him as those of another species.'[63] The most articulate critic was R. H. Tawney, who had been at Rugby and, as a sergeant in the Manchester Regiment, was badly wounded on the first day of the Somme. After the war he became Professor of Economic History at the London School of Economics, as well as being active in the Labour Party in drawing up educational policies. In 1931 he turned his fire on the public-school system: 'The English education system will never be, what it should be, the great uniter, instead of being, what it has been in the past, a source of disunion, until children of all classes in the community attend the same schools.'[64] Tawney quantified the advantage public-school alumni enjoyed in their dominance of elite positions, claiming that 76 per cent of those in leadership positions in church, state and industry had been at public schools, and 63 per cent at just twelve schools. Over 25 per cent of Conservative MPs between 1920 and 1940 were Etonians.

Public schools found it difficult to respond to such criticism. The new guard of heads lacked visionary leaders of the earlier calibre of Edward Thring of Uppingham or Frederick Sanderson of Oundle. Robert Birley was an exception, a great teacher and man of political vision who was to represent HMC on the Fleming Committee in 1942. His political views brought him the nickname 'Red Robert', but he was 'more of a nineteenth century liberal with a passionate belief in academic freedom'.[65] His influence on Charterhouse was one of moderate progressiveness, modernising some of its practices, civilising it and encouraging wider intellectual questioning, rather than introducing radical changes in its system or mission. Elsewhere there were few signs between the wars of heads identifying what needed to change or of leading others in educational innovation, while HMC itself was chronically incapable of giving a lead or taking even minor collective decisions.

One of Thring's successors at Uppingham was John Wolfenden, appointed in 1934 at the very young age of twenty-eight after being a don at Oxford. Wolfenden had the intellectual stature to give leadership to the system in the inter-war years, but he was described as 'an ascetic, unsophisticated man with a good mechanical brain but little imaginative flair'.[66] He was to be Chairman of HMC in the important years after the war. Another don turned headmaster was Claude Elliott, appointed to Eton in 1933, an able administrator but lacking the vision to be a great headmaster. When he was knighted in 1958 'for services to education', at Eton it was considered 'an irony considering that few headmasters have been so determinedly not educationalists'.[67] The highest-profile head of these years was Cyril Norwood, head in turn of Bristol GS, Marlborough, then Harrow from 1925 to 1934, and the educational pundit to whom R.A. Butler turned in 1941 for a report on the secondary school curriculum. Norwood in 1909 had been critical in print of public-school elitism, but during his time at Harrow he accepted 'the moral and social superiority of the public-school system' and shied away from the kind of changes which might have set the school and sector on a more progressive and visionary course.[68]

Financial Threat

Public schools had undergone rapid expansion in the 1920s. The war enhanced their reputation and popularity, and most schools saw numbers rise substantially, Sherborne increasing in size from 287 in 1918 to 413 in 1929. Then the 1930s Depression hit public schools hard and profoundly affected their self-confidence. Numbers fell in all but a few schools, exposing their susceptibility for the first time to market forces. Higher taxation, an uncertain international climate, competition from the state sector and a falling birth rate threatened even worse in the future. Schools had shot themselves in the foot by borrowing to expand in the 1920s and were hit in the mid-1930s by loss of fee income and increasing debt interest. Harrow had grown in numbers from 515 in 1918 to 669 in 1931, but by 1939 was down to 515 again. Admissions to Harrow between 1934 and 1939 collapsed by 37 per cent, masters were laid off and one house closed. By January 1939 Harrow had a school account deficit of £27,000 on a turnover of £100,000 and debts and overdraft of nearly £200,000. The very existence of the school was threatened, leading it to appeal to the loyalty and generosity of Old Harrovians.[69] At King William's, Isle of Man, the situation was desperate in 1933, with only thirty-six new pupils compared to ninety-eight in 1919, a growing overdraft and a borrowing limit reached. Grant aid was accepted from the Tynwald, and the governance of the College was restructured to reflect its reduced independence.

In 1938 the threat to the financial security of public schools brought discussions with the Board of Education about what could be done to help. Writing about this in 1947, Spencer Leeson, head of Winchester and chairman of HMC throughout the war, summarised the motives behind these discussions:

> By 1938 the prosperity of the years immediately following the previous war had passed into eclipse, another war was believed by many to be approaching, the school population was falling and a further decline was expected. Some schools were already in difficulties, others saw difficulties but a short way ahead. It was not economic anxieties that first awoke the minds of those in the schools to the unfair anomaly that the benefits they could offer were confined to expensively trained scholars and those whose parents could afford to send them as fee-payers. We had inherited social and financial divisions in our schools, as in our national life, but for at least twenty years many have felt unhappy that it should be so. Apprehension for the future in 1938 stirred us to attack all those difficulties, and great numbers of people came to see that the admission of boys from public elementary schools would not only fill vacant places but was right in itself.[70]

Leeson's conversion to a policy of broader access, and the motive he identified for engagement with the state, might be viewed with some scepticism, but there were powerful voices in the Board who had no wish to see the public-school system founder under the weight of financial problems. It is striking how senior officials at the Board, almost all public-school educated themselves, went well beyond their direct remit in seeking ways to help, and discussions with HMC were continuous from 1938 until the end of the 1940s. In October 1938 Maurice Holmes, the Permanent Secretary, wrote to Leeson offering support but suggested it would be better if HMC approached the Board rather than the other way around.[71] Another senior official, Geoffrey Williams (Westminster), principal assistant secretary in the Secondary Branch and a strong influence on the policy outlooks of Holmes and later R.A. Butler, was highly protective of public schools and was to become the main conduit between the Board and HMC. Williams in late 1938 believed that the amalgamation of schools might be a way of dealing with the problem, quoting the example of a half-full Lancing being only a short distance away from Ardingly and Hurstpierpoint.[72]

   The threat to many individual schools, and therefore to the wider health of the sector, was very real. Cyril Norwood, now President of St John's, Oxford, used his influence to plead with the Board for help in October 1938: 'Headmasters are literally spending half their time in commercial travelling and touting on prep school doorsteps.'[73] Standards, he claimed, were declining and disaster threatened, although he implied this would be a disaster for the wellbeing of the nation and not limited to public schools themselves. The HMC conference in December 1938 was dominated by discussions about the fall in demand. The headmaster of Dover, a school particularly threatened, spoke about the nervous strain induced on heads by falling numbers and increased competition. HMC was forced to warn its members against 'competitive advertising, ill-concealed bribery by means of reduced fees and other methods of attracting parents and boys which would be distasteful in the highest degree'.[74]

Divided Response

The response to this financial threat, and to wider political and cultural criticism, exposed divisions within the sector. The perception of public schools in the outside world, and of HMC itself, was dominated by the boarding schools. These, especially the biggest and wealthiest, provided, in the words of Cyril Norwood, 'a social badge and rights of entry to circles which people do very much want to enter'.[75] The decision-making officers and committee of HMC came almost exclusively from these grander boarding schools. Between 1919 and 1939 the chairmen of HMC came from Charterhouse seven times, Wellington three times, Harrow, Eton, Rugby and Shrewsbury twice each and Winchester once; only KES Birmingham in 1922 and 1929 broke the boarding-school domination. The HMC committee in 1939 comprised the heads of Eton, Winchester, Rugby, Cheltenham, Charterhouse, Uppingham, and Repton, along with Manchester GS and Leeds GS.[76] The first seven were among the most socially exclusive schools, charging the highest fees, and none of them admitted pupils paid for by the state, but the strongest bridges between public schools and wider society were built by city day schools, more mixed in social background but still not penetrating far into the working class. HMC had become more internationalist in the inter-war years, admitting to membership thirty-one heads of schools from Australia, Canada, New Zealand, South Africa and West Indies.[77]

The idea of a royal commission into the condition of the sector was first floated in late 1938 in discussions between HMC and the Board, as the chairman of HMC feared that 'a war to the knife was inevitable with only the fittest surviving'.[78] Geoffrey Williams, the Board of Education spokesman for secondary education, wrote to another official in February 1939: 'As I see it, the position in some of the public schools is now so precarious, and likely to become more so, that the government would be incurring a heavy responsibility in declining to set up a royal commission if formally asked by HMC to do so. It is a problem which needs tackling and tackling quickly.'[79] The Board was keen to set up a royal commission, and Williams went as far as drawing up possible terms of reference, but headmasters made clear they would have to consult with their governing bodies. By May 1939 there was no majority within governing bodies for the commission, because they feared encroachment on their independence, a fear particularly strong in schools established and effectively owned by London livery companies.[80]

James Higgs-Walker, head of Sevenoaks, was particularly trenchant in his opposition to a commission, convinced that the request was occasioned solely by the decline in numbers at larger schools: 'I do not see how a Royal Commission can increase the birth-rate or the dwindling number of parents ready to pay £200–250 a year per boy.' He believed the larger schools had only themselves to blame, having charged high fees in the boom period of the 1920s and borrowed to build expansively, and commented that 'headmasters of smaller, less expensive and therefore solvent schools fear that some of the hard-hit larger schools are hoping that a royal commission can be used to reduce our power to compete against them.'[81] For the time being that is how matters rested, the government having too many other pressing problems in 1939 to give much attention to public schools.

The Shadow Lengthens Again

In March 1935 Robert Birley was appointed headmaster of Charterhouse at the age of thirty-two. Shortly afterwards, he wrote to his predecessor, Frank Fletcher: 'You guided the school through the last war. I shall have to guide it through the next.'[82] His prescience was based on a lecture tour he had made to Berlin in the winter of 1933–4 and his background as a historian, the first non-classicist to be headmaster of Charterhouse. As the memory of one war faded, so schools were faced with the approach of the next.

By 1936 events in Germany were of increasing concern, but it was the start of the Spanish Civil War in the same year which first engaged public schools and their alumni, revealing stark political divisions across Europe and in Britain. The military revolt by Franco against the Republican government was supported by Spain's Catholic Church and assisted by the forces of fascism in Italy and Germany, only partly counter-balanced by the engagement of the USSR on the republican side, while France and Britain pursued a policy of non-intervention. Within the schools themselves, most sympathies were with the Republicans, but many Catholic public schools like Beaumont and St George's Weybridge supported Franco. The editor of *The Georgian* wrote in 1936 of his pride in 'that little band of Old Georgians who boldly protest against the injustice of the British press in siding with the scum of the earth against the patriots of Spain'.[83] One Old Georgian, Marques Carlos de Silvela, was murdered with his wife by the communists in Madrid in 1936.

Ideologically committed public-school alumni fought in Spain, not all of them on the republican side. When the teenaged Julian Amery, son of the Secretary of State for India, went to Spain on Franco's side in 1938, he found himself sheltering from gunfire in a ditch alongside another young man in the uniform of a monarchist volunteer. After greeting the other in French, German and Spanish without getting any reply, his companion introduced himself: 'Kemp. Wellington and Trinity. How do you do?' and Amery replied, 'How do you do? Amery. Eton and Balliol.'[84] The republican side had the greater support of young men and women who served in the International Brigades. About 2,300 came from Britain, most of them from working class backgrounds, but also many from public schools. Tom Wintringham (Gresham's), an early member in 1923 of the CPGB, who originally went to Spain as a journalist for the *Daily Worker*, eventually commanded the British battalion of the International Brigades and was twice wounded in 1937. Julian Bell (Leighton Park), nephew of Virginia Woolf and a pacifist from his Quaker school background, enlisted as an ambulance driver and died of wounds in 1937. Lewis Clive, an Etonian who had won an Olympic gold medal for rowing in 1932, resigned his commission in the Grenadier Guards in 1937 to become a Labour councillor in Kensington and then commanded a company of the British battalion fighting Franco and was killed in August 1938 on the Ebro. Fighting for a moral and universal cause had more appeal for politically aware idealists in 1936 than taking up arms for king and country. Even such a peaceable man as Walter Oakeshott, Winchester teacher in 1936 and later its head, said at the end of his life that he would have gone to fight in Spain in 1936 if he had had the guts and had not had a wife and family: 'Certainly those who did so were some of the best people I knew.'[85]

Concerns about German rearmament and the threat of mass bombing had become more urgent by 1937. Official estimates of 60,000 casualties per day from air attack now seem absurd in relation to German bomber capability, but the fear existed, and the HMC conference of December 1937 was addressed by a Home Office official about Air Raid Precautions (ARP) and the need for city schools to have evacuation plans ready. Not all within the sector thought that this applied to them. In December 1937, Old Harrovians Samuel Hoare, the Home Secretary, and the Marquess of Zetland, Secretary of State for India, overruled the Secretary of State for Air to prevent, in the grounds of Harrow, the deployment of a balloon barrage depot with its unsightly hangars, Hoare describing it as 'a catastrophe for Harrow'.[86] The days of such cosy patronage were now over as the Air Raid Precautions Act was rushed into law in January 1938, giving the government emergency powers to overrule local objections.

There is little evidence that financially constrained schools did much to prepare until Munich in the following September. Geoffrey Bell, head of Highgate, was one who had the foresight to undertake a reconnaissance to Devon in April 1938, making a formal request to his governors to consider evacuation plans, but they shelved the matter because they did not wish to spend money on something which might not happen. Bell persisted and sent two masters to Devon in September to reserve accommodation at hotels. On 28 September, the day before Chamberlain was due to meet Hitler at Munich and with war looking likely, Bell ordered evacuation, the junior school going to Totnes and the boarders to Ilfracombe and Westward Ho. The senior day boys were about to follow when Chamberlain returned from Munich with an agreement, and the Highgate boys returned to London.

Munich brought fierce debate in schools. At Westminster in October 1938 the motion to approve Chamberlain's Czech policy was defeated by fifteen votes to seven, Francis Noel-Baker, the future Labour MP, arguing that Munich had greatly strengthened Hitler's position and set him on the road to domination of Europe.[87] At Marlborough the debating society split almost evenly in February 1939 in supporting a motion that 'this house deplores the government's foreign policy'.[88] Robert Birley at Charterhouse had invited a professor from Prague University to speak to senior boys in summer 1938, but Munich came as a terrible shock, and Birley could not feel the sense of relief of the general population at what he saw as the betrayal of the Czechs. He excused himself from school matters for a couple of days and went to London, where he ran into the Carthusian MP, Ronald Cartland, who reassured him that Britain would go no further along the road of appeasement. Birley returned to school to prepare for what he knew would now come; staff were given ARP training and air-raid trenches were dug. When the Germans marched into Prague in March 1939, Birley explained its significance to the school in chapel and then invited them to stay and listen to the organ voluntary by the Czech composer, Smetana.[89]

The problems heads could face with their governors over ARP plans became apparent when Walter Oakeshott took up his appointment as head of St Paul's in January 1939. In the previous September, before Munich, he had discovered that the Mercers' Company, the school governors, had done nothing to prepare for war, and during the Munich Crisis their only plan was to close the school and let parents take up government evacuation offers. Astonishingly, the minutes of the governors' meeting on 18 November 1938 again contain no mention of any discussion about war emergency plans. Only when Oakeshott took over in January 1939 did he also discover that the school was likely to be requisitioned in the event of war, but he still found the Mercers' Company obdurate about considering evacuation. In early February he was at last given permission to seek premises for evacuation, provided it did not cost too much. After many inquiries, Oakeshott settled on Wellington College, prepared to share teaching and games facilities, with accommodation at a nearby mansion, Easthampstead Park, and the plans were grudgingly approved by the Mercers.[90]

At Eton, an unseemly row ensued between headmaster Claude Elliott and the Provost, Lord Hugh Cecil.[91] Elliott pressed Cecil and the governors to provide the school with adequate ARP protection, but Cecil declared after Munich, 'I do not think a war in the next few years at all likely.' He went on to suggest that Eton would only be bombed by accident or oversight, that it was not practical to take precautions against remote dangers and that Eton's financial state was too parlous. On 21 February 1939 Cecil was outvoted at a meeting of the Fellows; the cost of ARP was to be met by a charge on school bills and work began on 1 March. Even then, shelters were barely ready for the start of the war, and masters were recalled early to finish filling sandbags.[92]

That last peacetime summer term of cricket and exams can now be seen in an ethereal light as international tension built and many schools frantically tried to speed up ARP preparations. The Military Service Act was passed in May, introducing conscription for the first time in peace and welcomed as fair and sensible by headmasters who would no longer have the responsibility of being deluged with applications for commissions, as they had been in the mass volunteering spirit of 1914. The War Office also decreed that public schoolboys with OTC experience would no longer receive any special privileges and would have to prove their worth with an initial spell in the ranks before applying for officer training. OTC Camps in late July and early August were cancelled by the War Office, but the first Air Training Section camp for school OTCs went ahead at Norton Priory airfield near Chichester. Two hundred and fifty cadets attended from thirty-five schools, and they were given an exceptional experience in the week's camp, including visits to Hornchurch to inspect Spitfire and Hurricane squadrons and addresses by senior RAF officers, including the Chief of the Air Staff, Sir Cyril Newall.

As the camp broke up on 5 August, school summer holidays began. Within a month, and before the start of the next term, Britain had declared war on 3 September. The Bloxham headmaster, Valentine Armitage, received his Army call-up papers in August and left for good. London schools generally complied with government evacuation policy. Geoffrey Bell, who had acted with such foresight in 1938, put into action the plans he had carefully prepared for Highgate. On 24 August an advance party left for Devon and a notice was published saying that the school would open there on 28 August. By 3 September 356 senior boys were at Westward Ho and 109 juniors at Hartland Abbey. At Westward Ho the school had to lease a dozen houses and hotels, more than a mile apart, the Sunshine Café on the beach serving as a classroom.

At St Paul's Girls' School, Munich had alarmed parents to such a degree that only five girls, instead of the usual seventy, sat the October 1938 entrance exam. Miss Strudwick, the headmistress, had to argue forcefully to prevent the school governors, the Mercers, taking the nuclear option of closing the school if war broke out. She pushed them to agree that the school should move to the country and eventually secured a deal with Wycombe Abbey.[93] There the school went on 3 September with 183 girls, mostly accommodated in town billets which Miss Strudwick assiduously visited each evening. Half the girls from North London Collegiate School left for Luton on 1 September, the other half remaining in Edgware, which was outside the evacuation zone. Thelma Woolford was billeted on four sisters in Luton who had just had their dog put down for fear of bombs, and she reflected that a spotty adolescent girl was poor exchange for a beautiful red setter.[94]

On the last day of term in late July, Geoffrey Wellum, cricket captain at Forest School, processed out of chapel with other monitors after the prophetic final hymn, *God Be With You Till We Meet Again.* Only vaguely that day was he aware of the impending crisis. On 3 September he reported to Desford Flying Training School in Leicestershire, where he and other trainee pilots sat round the radio listening to Chamberlain's declaration of war. He recorded, 'There is silence at first, then someone says quietly, "Well, that's that".'[95] This matter-of-fact response was very different from the patriotic excitement of 1914. The First World War had been a 'public-school war' in that it had presented itself as an extension of the ethos of duty, endurance and sacrifice, and in its appeal to imperial glory and 'playing the game'. This second war appealed to basic instincts of national solidarity in the face of destruction and was to be more populist and democratic, victory justifying a whole nation and not just one set of class values. Those leaving school in 1939 had no illusions about the nature of modern industrial warfare. There was for them a sense of resignation, of uncertainty and foreboding, a more pragmatic, unromantic and measured view of what was required, but also a sense of common purpose and patriotism no less deeply felt than that of 1914, if differently expressed. For the schools themselves, beset by financial concerns, problems were about to multiply.

Chapter 2

War Comes to the Public Schools

T he coming of war caught public schools at a moment of economic vulnerability and divisions within the sector. These problems were made worse by the immediate requisitioning of some schools and a more general decline in pupil numbers and finances as the dislocation of war made itself felt. Gone from schools were the confident pride, sense of excitement and patriotic certainties of 1914. Harold Nicolson, an Old Wellingtonian MP, summed up in his diary the prevailing mood in the country: 'The curious contrast with August 3rd 1914. Then there was a sense of exhilaration. Today we are merely glum.'[1]

The year 1940 was to become the most significant one in the history of public schools. Never had their existence been threatened on such a scale, nor had the lives of their pupils been put in such danger as they were between late May and December 1940. The disaster of Dunkirk made the threat of invasion and bombing an overwhelming reality, and heads had to take decisions about the safety of their pupils which might have to be reversed at a moment's notice. Evacuation became the norm for most schools in the south-east, creating a fresh set of problems. For schools which remained in the most dangerous areas, school routines were submerged beneath the rigours and dangers of Home Guard duty, fire-watching and long periods spent in air-raid shelters.

It was also a year when public schools faced significant political dangers. Dunkirk brought a reaction against those 'guilty men', mainly conservative politicians from elite schools, who had taken Britain into war unprepared. The 'People's War' emerged as the signifying concept of the Second World War on the home front. The prevailing assumption, identified by historian Paul Addison, was that 'the war was being fought for the benefit of the common people, and that it was the duty of the upper classes to throw in their lot with those lower down the social scale.'[2] That 'People's War' ideology of social cohesion and a democratic sense of community was at odds with the public-school claim to social exclusiveness and privilege, and its sense of shared sacrifice would fuel demand for equality of entitlement when peace came.

As the 'guilty men' departed, their place was taken by Winston Churchill, educated at Harrow, a man steeped in the history of Britain and her institutions and devoted to her Empire. He became the fuser of national unity, the voice which reached out to millions to rally them to the nation's 'finest hour'. The political price which had to be paid in 1940 was a shift leftwards, as Churchill enlisted the support of Labour for the Wartime Coalition and harnessed the power of the working classes and popular opinion for the national war effort. The machinery of government and civil service remained, however, largely in the hands of public-school educated men.

Public schools had to accommodate themselves to this new national consensus and emerging political reality. The Winchester headmaster and Chairman of HMC, Spencer Leeson, wrote of the year 1940:

> The war has brought a deeper reality and purpose into our life and work. Many old barriers are being broken down, a sense of isolation that it was difficult to escape in peacetime is being dispersed by circumstances and general goodwill, and Winchester, together with the other public schools of England, is seeing a new vision of the service she can offer.[3]

Leeson's complacency about the future was not widely shared, but it reflected the new reality of the more hostile political environment in which public schools had now to operate, with their chances of survival resting on a greater sense of readiness to serve the wider community.

Guilty Men

The outbreak of war had the immediate effect of increasing costs for schools and worsening their wider financial plight. Evacuated schools had to hire new premises and thus forfeited much of their attraction to parents, particularly prospective ones. The problem was worse for schools like Highgate with a majority of day boys which lost touch with their local

base of support. The general uncertainty and dislocation of war brought
a further fall in numbers and fee income across much of the sector.
Tonbridge, not evacuated but in a danger area, closed one boarding house
in early 1940 as the number of boarders dropped from pre-war 364 to 225
in 1941, at which point it closed another house. Weymouth College, a full
member of HMC, closed its doors entirely in 1940, and Imperial Service
College was forced into a merger with Haileybury in 1942. Harrow in late
1939 even used Stanley Baldwin, alumnus and former Prime Minster, to
approach the Board of Education unsuccessfully for a financial grant to
save the school from closure.[4] Maurice Holmes, Permanent Secretary at
the Board and an Old Wellingtonian, feared that requisitioning would be
the last straw for many schools and argued in a paper to the Cabinet for a
special compensation scheme to support them.[5]

As in 1914, the loss of young masters brought many problems for
heads, but there was now a more orderly process to joining up. The
confusions and injustices of the volunteer system in 1914, with teachers
not knowing where their duty lay, was replaced by the wider obligations
of the National Service Act, whereby schoolmasters over twenty-five
were regarded as being in a reserved occupation. Young staff inevitably
departed, as did others with special military skills. Merchant Taylors',
Northwood, lost its bursar, eleven teachers and eleven non-teaching staff,
while Winchester lost five staff immediately in September 1939 and six
others within a term or so. Conscription also brought a more meritocratic
system for boys.

In April 1940 threadbare British forces failed to prevent the German
invasion and occupation of Norway. The government of Neville
Chamberlain was brought to account in a debate in the House of
Commons on 8 and 9 May, not only for its lack of leadership, but for
its failure both to prevent war and to prepare for it. The War Cabinet
formed on the outbreak of war had nine members, all Conservatives,
and all except Churchill members of the pre-war Cabinet. Eight of the
nine had been to elite boarding schools, two each to Harrow (Churchill
and Samuel Hoare) and Rugby (Chamberlain and Maurice Hankey), and
one each to Eton, Fettes, Dartmouth and Clifton (Lord Halifax, John
Simon, Lord Chatfield and Leslie Hore-Belisha). Kingsley Wood alone
was educated at a London state school, Central Foundation Boys' School
in Islington, where his father was Methodist minister.[6]

The Norway debate was one of the most dramatic moments in parliamentary history, in a House of Commons dominated by members from public schools. The ethos of loyalty learned at school was put to the test as Conservative rebels gathered for the kill. Lord Lloyd (Eton), normally unremittingly loyal to his party, wrote to his son fearing that the subservient Conservative majority would leave 'Chamberlain at the head of affairs until some further blunder brings fresh humiliation and disaster to our armies'.[7] The most electrifying intervention was by Leo Amery, invoking Oliver Cromwell's words against Chamberlain: 'You have sat here too long for any good you have been doing. Depart, I say, and let us have done with you. In the name of God, go.' Amery wanted Churchill to be Prime Minister and needed to avoid damaging him politically, but they also had history. Contemporaries at Harrow, the new boy Churchill had pushed the second-year Amery into the swimming pool.[8]

The fall in Chamberlain's majority from two hundred to eighty was the equivalent of a defeat. Forty-one Conservatives voted against their own government and about sixty abstained. It was a fratricidal contest, unleashing a flood of vitriol. John Profumo (Harrow), only recently elected, was one of those to vote against the government and was carpeted the next day by David Margesson, the Harrovian Chief Whip, rather as if he had just been summoned to the prefects' room at Harrow: 'And I tell you this, you utterly contemptible little shit. On every morning that you wake up for the rest of your life you will be ashamed of what you did last night.' Alec Dunglass (Eton), Chamberlain's Parliamentary Private Secretary, watched as many from his school joined the opposition – Harold Macmillan, Anthony Eden, Quintin Hogg, Robert Boothby, Duff Cooper. Fourteen of the Conservative dissidents were serving officers in uniform, including another Etonian, William Anstruther Gray, who in his Coldstream Guards uniform led his group into the 'No' lobby as if marching four abreast. Hugh Dalton, an Etonian Labour MP, witnessed him, 'a young officer in uniform, who had been for long a fervent admirer of Chamberlain, walking through the Opposition lobby with tears streaming down his face'. How many of these young men, he wondered, were exercising the last Parliamentary vote they would ever give – for their country and against their whips.[9] On 10 May the Germans invaded France, Holland and Belgium, and Winston Churchill became Prime Minister.

In July 1940 three journalists working for Lord Beaverbrook published, under the pseudonym 'Cato', a political pamphlet, *Guilty Men*. All three of the authors had been at public school – Michael Foot (Leighton Park), Frank Owen (Monmouth) and Peter Howard (Mill Hill). Their publisher, Victor Gollancz (St Paul's), creator of the Left Book Club, had been sacked in 1918 from his teaching job at Repton for disseminating subversive material. The targets of *Guilty Men* were those politicians, mostly public-school alumni themselves, who had taken Britain unprepared into war and were held responsible for Dunkirk. *Guilty Men* had a sensational impact, selling 200,000 copies in a few weeks. Its popularity, in explaining the military catastrophe, lay in showing that there was nothing wrong with the British people, only with those from the social and political elites who had been in power in the 1930s and had let the people down. Harold Nicolson had sensed this coming and wrote in his diary on 13 January 1940, 'A great and angry tide is rising against the governing classes.'[10]

Born in that summer of 1940 was the 'People's War'. This was the people rescuing the nation from the elites, a war of national unity and social cohesion in which class differences all but disappeared. The 'people' had gone across to Dunkirk to rescue the Army, using in the words of J.B. Priestley, the influential broadcaster, 'the little holiday steamers which made an excursion to hell and came back glorious'. They had joined up in their millions in the Home Guard to defend their land, 'ploughman and parson, shepherd and clerk, turning out at night, as our forefathers had before us, to keep watch and ward over the sleeping English hills and fields and homesteads'. Priestley also recognised the political consequences of this huge collective effort: 'We're actually changing over from the property view to the sense of community, which simply means that we realise we're all in the same boat'.[11] Churchill, in his broadcast of 14 July, took up the theme:

This is no war of chieftains of dynasties or national ambition; it is a war of peoples and of causes. There are vast numbers not only in this island but in every land, who will render faithful service in this war, but whose names will never be known, whose deeds will never be recorded. This is a war of the unknown warriors.[12]

To the 'people's war' could be added the 'Dunkirk spirit', which also became evident that summer. That spirit was about courage, unity and belief in the face of adversity, the British people pulling together and refusing to accept defeat. 'Very well, alone', proclaimed the soldier in David Low's famous cartoon of that year. It was evident at Dunkirk itself, a defeat hailed as a victory, and in the Battle of Britain and the Blitz. Churchill's rhetoric through that summer appealed to basic instincts of national solidarity, a new national spirit of populism, democracy and consensus. But who was to blame for the danger the country was in? *Guilty Men* provided some of the answers by blaming the politicians, but others blamed the public schools which had educated such an out-of-touch and arrogant elite. Terence Worsley, Marlborough boy and Wellington master, wrote in 1940: 'We are where we are, and shall be where we shall be, owing, largely, if not wholly, to the privileged education which the ruling classes have received in the last forty years.'[13]

The problem was even recognised by the boys of Sherborne two months before Dunkirk. An editorial in the *Shirburnian* in March 1940 claimed that 'the public schools are attracting a very severe flood of criticism, some of it deserved and accurate' and went on to state that 'Sherborne, like the majority of the more fashionable foundations, has been accused of a lack of social responsibility which is all the more serious when one remembers that the public schools have as their professed *raison d'être* the production of the nation's leaders.'[14] This criticism of a lack of social responsibility, from within as traditional a school as Sherborne, strikes at the heart of the dilemma for public schools in the new circumstances of 1940. In the First World War, the struggle could be visualised in terms of public-school ideals. Duty, patriotism, self-sacrifice constituted those ideals, together with an expectation of social deference and an assumption that battlefield and political leadership should be in the hands of the ruling elites, as they had been throughout British history. Because those same elites were now blamed for the mess in which the country found itself, public schools suffered by association, and the charge that they lacked social responsibility required them to respond by full engagement in the spirit of national consensus and the 'People's War'. As a Charterhouse boy put it in June 1940, 'Some of us perhaps are glad, some perhaps sorry that England has awakened to the realisation of the war, but whether it is a cause for anxiety or relief, it is a cause for readjustment of values.'[15]

Wartime Government and Civil Service

The government which Churchill formed in May 1940 has been represented as one group of public-school alumni replacing another, but it was a coalition more representative of the nation's struggle, with Conservatives joined by Labour ministers like Clement Attlee, himself educated at Haileybury, and Ernest Bevin, who had left his elementary school at Crediton in Devon at the age of eleven to become a farm labourer.

The public-school grip on government, however, can barely be said to have shifted. Of ten members of the War Cabinet appointed during 1940, six had been to public schools (Churchill, Attlee, Chamberlain, Halifax, Anderson and Eden), three to state schools (Wood, Bevin and Greenwood), and Lord Beaverbrook was educated in Canada. Arthur Greenwood had won a scholarship to Bewerley Street School in Hunslet at the age of thirteen and had only been able to pay for his education there, and later at the tertiary Yorkshire College, by becoming a pupil teacher.[16] John Anderson, from George Watson's College in Edinburgh, has been described by Peter Hennessy as 'the greatest administrative genius ever produced by the British Civil Service', giving his name, as Home Secretary in the War Cabinet, to the air raid shelter which adorned most British back gardens from 1939.[17] Of six other later appointments to the War Cabinet, five went to public schools (Oliver Lyttelton, Stafford Cripps, Lord Moyne, Richard Casey and Lord Woolton); Herbert Morrison had left St Andrew's, an elementary school in Lambeth, at the age of fourteen. In Churchill's wider wartime government were 110 others who held some form of ministerial position; eighty-four of these went to public schools, twenty-eight to Eton and eight to Harrow.[18]

Ernest Bevin was a giant of the coalition who, from his solid base of power in the trade union movement, became Minister of Labour, producing for the War Cabinet within three days of taking office 'a bold programme of action, the essence of which was Bevin's claim to unify responsibility for all manpower and labour questions under his own authority'.[19] The contrast is stark between what he achieved after his negligible education and the lesser achievements of most of the privileged ministers above, begging the question of how many other Ernest Bevins might have been produced by a more egalitarian educational system.

Public-school alumni also dominated the top levels of the Civil Service, shaping and implementing government war policy. The big Whitehall beasts in 1939 were the Permanent Under-Secretaries at the Treasury, Foreign Office and Home Office, along with the Admiralty and War Office. Only Horace Wilson (Kurnella School, Bournemouth) at the Treasury did not come from public school, but he was succeeded in 1942 by Richard Hopkins (KES Birmingham).[20] Alexander Cadogan (Eton), Under-Secretary of State at the Foreign Office from 1938 to 1946, acted as principal adviser to government on every key foreign policy issue. At the Home Office it was Alexander Maxwell (Plymouth College), while the War Office was headed by Lord Croft (Eton and Shrewsbury) and Edward Grigg (Winchester), and the Admiralty by Richard Carter (Eton).

The ranks of the Civil Service were to expand very rapidly in wartime, as Hitler's threat meant that new men and methods had to be found almost overnight from school and university networks. The mixture of career regulars and outside irregulars, blended between 1939 and 1945, represented, according to historian Peter Hennessy, 'the high point of achievement in the history of the British Civil Service'.[21] The influx of irregulars had been planned as early as 1936, when Warren Fisher (Winchester), head of the Home Civil Service 1919–39, and Maurice Hankey (Rugby), Cabinet Secretary, had anticipated future challenges by forming a committee, with university vice-chancellors, to find university academics to fill the new government departments needed in war. Into the Ministry of Supply in 1938 came academics like Oliver Franks (Bristol GS), Professor of Moral Philosophy at Glasgow University who, according to Paul Addison, proved to be 'the outstanding temporary civil servant of the period, with not only an outstanding talent for manipulating a large organisation, but a rare intuition into the psychology of colleagues'.[22] Henry Tizard (Westminster), Rector of Imperial College, compiled a list of science and engineering dons and took a key role himself in the Air Ministry. Hugh Gaitskell (Winchester), head of the political economy department at UCL, joined the Ministry of Economic Warfare, while his fellow Wykehamist, Douglas Jay, Fellow of All Souls, joined the Ministry of Supply. By November 1940 there were seventy-two mostly public-school educated Oxford dons employed as temporary civil servants, including several who played an active role in foreign policy. Isaiah Berlin, the philosopher and political theorist, whose journey from the chaos of 1917 Russia to education at St Paul's School and an All Souls fellowship is a story in itself, worked in the British embassy in Washington, sending a stream of much valued analyses to Churchill on American politics.[23]

Churchill realised that the overriding imperative in wartime was 'to solve problems and implement solutions thoroughly and swiftly'.[24] His main support within the Civil Service was the Cabinet Secretary, Edward Bridges, son of the Poet Laureate, Robert Bridges. After a stellar academic career at Eton and a first in Greats at Oxford he was badly wounded in 1917, winning the MC. After the war he gained an All Souls Fellowship in 1920 and entered the Civil Service, succeeding in 1938 Maurice Hankey as Cabinet Secretary, a role Hankey had held since the establishment of the post in 1916. The Cabinet Office, run by the Cabinet Secretary, was 'the glue binding together often very diverse Whitehall departments in the massively expanded post-1918 government'.[25] In 1938 Chamberlain split the Cabinet Office into civil and military sides, Bridges taking the former role and General Hastings 'Pug' Ismay (Charterhouse) the military side. Jock Colville (Harrow), one of Churchill's private secretaries, summed up their relationship: 'They galloped side by side, in perfectly matching harmony … Ismay was nearer to being indispensable to Churchill than any other man, but Sir Edward Bridges followed close behind.'[26] Colville, who knew the difficulties of reining in Churchill's sometimes erratic initiatives, concluded that 'without the unruffled competence of the Cabinet Office, which became, under Sir Edward Bridges, the powerful organisation it has since remained, and the patient diplomacy of General Ismay's office of the Ministry of Defence, the machinery of government would have broken under the strain.'[27]

Bridges was present at War Cabinet on perhaps the most critical day of the war, 28 May 1940, when the success of the Dunkirk evacuation and Britain's fate still hung in the balance. The War Cabinet met an unprecedented nine times in three days to consider Lord Halifax's proposal to approach the Italians to mediate between Britain and Germany and explore what terms might be offered.[28] Things were beginning to move Churchill's way when, on 28 May, the War Cabinet was briefly adjourned and twenty-five other ministers, of Cabinet rank but outside the War Cabinet, filled the room to provide a spontaneous surge of support for fighting on. One of them was Hugh Dalton, who had been appointed Minister of Economic Warfare. He recorded the 'magnificence' of Churchill's performance that day with 'loud cries of approval around the table, in which I think Amery, George Lloyd [Eton] and I were loudest'. Churchill's own words to the ministers caught the mood of the nation in its determination to fight through to the end:

> I am convinced that every man of you would rise up and tear me down from my place if I were for one moment to contemplate parley or surrender. If this long island story of ours is to end at last, let it end only when each one of us lies choking in his own blood upon the ground.[29]

The War Cabinet met again briefly, and it was Chamberlain, hitherto more sympathetic to Halifax's position, who moved to support Churchill's determination to fight on. No other moment in the war better illustrates the unique influence of Churchill and the grip of the wider group of public-school alumni on key decision-making; more than three-quarters of those present at the meetings were from that background, thirteen from Eton alone, and they routed their isolated fellow Etonian, Lord Halifax.

Threat of Invasion

On the night of 7 September 1940 Bernard Garside, senior history master at Hampton Grammar School by day and Home Guard soldier by night, was orderly officer for his platoon at Hampton Court Bridge. Garside, a veteran of the Great War, had trained them in attacking German tanks with Molotov cocktails. He wrote:

> That night, a man on a motor-bike roared up to the bridge with a message that I was to double the sentries … this was the real thing and I was to be right on the alert. To my company commander I wrote back: 'My total force here is eleven men and two NCOs. Is this sufficient for any real enemy encounter?' The message came back:

'Thanks for message. Force adequate. Good reserve is at the drill hall.' We looked for German parachutists to appear at any moment but, by the mercy of God, nothing happened. As we know now, the Germans did not come, but I shall never forget those long hours, with eyes and nerves stretched on the bridge over the Thames.[30]

This story echoes similar episodes that summer and autumn as German invasion became likely and teachers and pupils by day became soldiers by night. The war was not some remote event in France but one which now threatened directly every school and every pupil. In 1940 national survival was at stake and with it the institutions which underpinned the nation. The threat of invasion forced all heads of schools remaining in the south-east of England to consider their positions. A German invasion force might land anywhere between Ramsgate and Southampton, virtually without warning, accompanied by glider and parachute landings further inland, and heavy bombing of military targets and airfields. On the presumption that the coast could not be defended for long, further stop-lines would have to be established south of London, using rivers like the Medway and the Wey, which became heavily fortified. Schools in London had mostly already been evacuated, but twenty-six boarding boys' public schools remained in Kent, Sussex, Surrey and Hampshire, as well as a multitude of girls' schools and prep schools.

Eastbourne College in late May 1940 could hear the artillery fire in Calais and see the smoke from burning oil installations at Dunkirk drifting down the Channel. One Sunday in early June, a rumour reached Eastbourne that German parachute troops had landed near Dover, and an emergency housemasters' meeting debated what to do. The rumour proved baseless, but staff and senior boys were called to patrol Beachy Head with loaded rifles. This situation was untenable to the Eastbourne governors, who met on 17 June and agreed to evacuate the school to Radley for what became five years of exile.[31] The collapse of France and the possibility of invasion similarly affected Roedean, making 'us realise that before the autumn our position on the cliffs would become untenable and that at any time the authorities might find it necessary to ask us to leave'.[32] One of the girls, Barbara Kenyon, wrote to her mother in late May: 'It's terribly exciting. We can hear the guns on the French coast.'[33]

On 20 June an invitation came from the National Council of Education in Canada for fifty Roedean girls to travel there, leaving the school only the briefest time to consider this proposal and find girls whose parents wanted them to go. In the next six days frantic activity ensued with passports and finding berths on ships, the group sailing on 26 June and arriving in Montreal on 4 July.

At Tonbridge prayers for the deliverance of the Army were offered in Sunday chapel on 26 May, when General Ironside, Old Tonbridgian CIGS and a current parent, told the headmaster that there was little hope of saving much of the BEF. Troop trains carrying exhausted soldiers back from Dunkirk passed through Tonbridge on the main line, and boys who could speak French were sent to the station to help with French soldiers or to hand out tea and cigarettes to haggard men in blood-soaked bandages. If more evidence was needed of crisis, Tonbridge itself became heavily fortified, with the River Medway designated a key line of defence if the Germans invaded. Pill-boxes, gun emplacements and anti-tank obstacles sprouted across the school and its surrounding area. Tonbridge head, Eric Whitworth, who had won a Military Cross in 1917, feared a sudden panic-driven evacuation and in late June spent thirty minutes with Ironside, now C-in-C Home Forces, who told him: 'Have everything ready to go at twenty-four hours' notice, but don't go. If I have reason to change my mind, I will let you know.' No word came, and Tonbridge saw out the summer term under that deadline.[34]

At Charterhouse, fevered discussions were also taking place. In late May, just before Dunkirk, the headmaster, Robert Birley, was at a governors' meeting at the London Charterhouse when he was drawn aside by the Archbishop of Canterbury, the chairman: 'I have just been having lunch with Anthony Eden. You know the situation is desperately serious. It looks as though the British Army may well be surrounded.' Parties of boys helped dig slit trenches in house gardens and anti-tank ditches in the Wey Valley, one of the hastily prepared positions running within a few hundred yards of the school. A staff officer came to the school with the instruction that, if the Germans landed, Birley was to march the boys to Aldershot, at which Birley asked, 'And the wives and children?' Charterhouse stayed put. In September, 130 boys in the OTC and Home Guard, along with members of staff, were armed and ready, having come back for a week during the summer holidays to undertake military training, prepare fortifications and guard the school. Birley noted the historical significance of these events when he pointed out that this was the first time in the history of the school that its members had formed part of an actual military organisation, equipped for active service in time of war.[35]

Merchant Taylors' School in North London realised the situation was serious when Army lorries drove into the quad in early June and took most of the rifles from the school's armoury. The headmaster, Norman Birley, who had won the DSO and MC in the First World War, made an impassioned speech to the whole school, telling them that, in the event of invasion, the OTC would defend the school to the last man and the last round, which would be fired by his own revolver from the roof of the Great Hall. The OTC guarded the school night and day with loaded rifles, until a boy on guard duty outside the school fired a warning shot, nearly killing a visiting parent who had failed to stop his car. The school buildings formed part of the defensive ring round London, with a concrete machine-gun post over the porch of Great Hall manned by the school OTC, while the playing fields were covered with anti-tank ditches, tree trunks and cricket sightscreens to prevent enemy gliders landing.[36]

The threat of invasion brought fierce debate about evacuating children to the USA and Canada. The government introduced an official evacuation scheme for all parents who wanted their children to go, countering the accusation that only the rich could buy safety. Over 200,000 applications were received in the summer of 1940, some of them from Jewish families alarmed at the likely consequences of German occupation. Under the government scheme about 2,500 children were evacuated, mainly to Canada, but over 14,000 made private arrangements. The wealthier evacuees included the Roedean girls, future politician and St Paul's Girls' pupil, Shirley Williams, and John Julius Cooper, the prep school son of Duff Cooper, Minister of Information. Whatever their motivation, this reeked of the kind of privilege which schools were now desperate to avoid by association.

Parental opinion was divided. At St Paul's Girls' one mother wrote to a fellow parent on 28 May: 'I am not a defeatist by any means, but we have to face facts. As things now stand, an invasion of England is no longer outside the range of possibility … Parents should withdraw their girls and engage some responsible teachers to take them to Canada.' Her correspondent entirely disagreed: 'The issue is now joined for every man, woman and child in Britain and the only proper thing is for us all – without any privileged exceptions whatever – to stand by our country and face it out.'[37] One young pupil from Lady Eleanor Holles School, Barbara Fairhead, whose parents had sent her to Canada, was drowned, along with eighty other children, when the SS *City of Benares* was sunk by a U-boat in the Atlantic on 17 September 1940.[38] This terrible tragedy, affecting both government evacuees and children travelling on private arrangements, effectively brought the government scheme to an end. At the HMC Annual Meeting in December 1940, Spencer Leeson, the Chairman, reflected the majority view:

> Many of us felt that once a boy had entered his public school, he had, in a sense, taken his place in the firing line, and that, while so many of his contemporaries were employed in national service … it was not right that those, who hereafter might be called to be leaders, should be encouraged to find security for themselves at the expense of their duty.[39]

Requisitioning and Evacuation

Requisitioning of school buildings and grounds by government and military authorities was unprecedented in British history. Schools had little or no choice in the matter, for the Civil Defence Act of July 1939 gave the government and local authorities extensive powers to requisition. The purpose was to provide a safe place for government departments, hospitals and other public bodies, away from danger areas. The records of such departments, all in paper files, needed to be preserved if the administration of the country was to proceed smoothly. Requisitioning could happen in any part of the country, and among those taken over were Ashville College in York by the Air Ministry, Bromsgrove School by the Ministry of Works and Kingswood School in Bath by the Admiralty. Malvern College was requisitioned twice, first by the Admiralty on the outbreak of war and then in May 1942 by the Telecommunications

Research Establishment (TRE), which used it for research on radar and electronic warfare. Malvern moved to Blenheim Palace in September 1939, returned to Malvern in July 1940 and then had to move out again in 1942, finding a home at Harrow School. Around twenty-five boarding schools for boys and girls were directly requisitioned, and the War Cabinet briefly considered in 1940 wholesale use of school premises for the expansion of the Army. Evacuation had a lasting effect on many schools, Clifton's experience at Bude becoming 'a time of jettisoning outmoded customs that had no visible purpose'.[40]

Wycombe Abbey received a letter in March 1942 to say that the school would be requisitioned at only sixteen days' notice as the headquarters of the US Army 8th Air Force. Since notice was so short and vacant premises unavailable, the Council took the decision that the school should be closed for the war's duration and the girls dispersed to other schools. It was forbidden by the censor to give the reason for closure, so parents were left bewildered and indignant, but the headmistress, Miss Crosthwaite, managed to find places for everyone. She stayed on at the school, maintaining contact with staff in twenty-five different schools and girls in as many as forty schools, as far apart as St Leonard's in Fife and Benenden, which was itself now in Cornwall. These years in which Wycombe was only a theoretical entity could have been terminal for the school, but it survived to reopen in 1946, when only six of the original girls returned. The financial cost was huge, with the War Office only paying rent and taking no account of loss of income.[41]

It did prove possible for some schools to fight off the threat of requisitioning, thanks to friends in high places. Robert Birley of Charterhouse stopped an attempt by the Admiralty to take over the buildings in autumn 1940 by dashing to London to see the chairman of governors, who was the Archbishop of Canterbury. 'This is out of the question', said the Archbishop, 'I shall see Anthony Eden at once.'[42] He did see Eden, and the Admiralty's claim lapsed. In 1942 the Ministry of Aircraft Production wanted to take over Marlborough, but resistance was orchestrated by two Old Marlburians – Rab Butler and William Jowitt, future Labour Chancellor. Jowitt saw the Minister and wrote to the headmaster that 'he was hopeful that what I have said has not been without influence'. Butler was more direct, speaking to Churchill himself and pointing out that the evacuated City of London School would also be displaced if Marlborough had to leave; unsurprisingly, Marlborough stayed put.[43]

At least ninety boys' and girls' public schools were evacuated either permanently or temporarily during the war, along with an unknown number of state schools and preparatory schools. For non-requisitioned schools, the safety of pupils was the overriding concern, but also the integrity of the school as an institution. German invasion in term-time would have brought panic-led evacuation, joining columns of destitute refugees on the road to supposed safety, as the British Army had witnessed in France in May 1940. Over sixty schools acted as host to those evacuated, while the rest established themselves in a variety of stately homes, hotels and any other premises they could find. Resourcefulness and improvisation were the watchwords. One headmaster's wife in search of safer quarters found the hotels further west 'full of lean and hungry schoolmasters with harassed expressions on their faces and leaping into their cars whenever a suitable house in the district became available'.[44] By 1941 over eighty prep schools in Kent and Sussex had scattered to new homes across the country, some of them never to return.

King's, Canterbury, under Canon John Shirley as headmaster, was only ten miles from the most vulnerable section of the Kent coast. At the time of Munich, Shirley and the governors considered plans for evacuation to either Cornwall or Scotland, but then shelved them. The fierce fighting which broke out in France on 10 May convinced Shirley of the urgent need to move the school, more from fear of bombing than a belief in possible invasion. His memo to the governors on 11 May read: 'Now that the Germans have invaded the Low Countries the situation is different. It is also widely known that German aircraft have flown over East Kent this week and dropped five bombs near Chilham. Parents have been busy on the telephone and by telegram.' Four days later, he warned parents of the likelihood of evacuation, and on 18 May governors gave Shirley financial authority to negotiate a lease of accommodation in Cornwall for the duration of hostilities. The next day, 19 May, the decision to evacuate was given to the school and by letter to parents. Norman Scarfe, a senior boy, wrote home: 'Apparently we have been given orders to leave Kent as soon as possible, although I think there is no imminent danger as everyone will be occupied on the western front for a while yet.'[45] Shirley moved swiftly to lease the Carlyon Bay Hotel near St Austell, together with a smaller hotel, two large Georgian houses three miles apart and about ten other houses. The boys were given instructions to go home for a seven-day break and then to catch the night train from Paddington on the eighth day. Senior boys and staff helped to pack up furniture, books and equipment and load it on railway vans and lorries. Shirley took with him to Cornwall the senior and junior schools of King's, the Cathedral Choir School and the senior and junior schools of St Edmund's, Canterbury.

This massive logistical exercise saw the schools reassemble at Carlyon Bay by Thursday 6 June. There were no classrooms, no laboratories and no playing fields, and in the first summer all the teaching was done out of doors, but a major effort was made to replicate familiar routines. The house system was maintained even though most of the 'houses' were just a floor of the hotel. Uniforms were kept, and on Sundays the scholars processed in their surplices to the 'cathedral', which was a converted garage. Boys continued to take School Certificate and Higher School Certificate, but it was hard to focus on exams when boys were called up immediately on leaving school. Education in a wider sense gained, with flourishing music and other societies and an intensity of experience in unfamiliar circumstances, as the war widened perspectives. Fourteen-year-old John Dalrymple remembered being allowed by his father to travel for the summer holidays to his home in Surrey by bicycle, which took him four days.[46] Shirley's decision to move the school was fully justified when fifteen high explosive bombs fell on the cathedral precincts in the Baedeker raid of 1 June 1942 which destroyed one-fifth of the old part of Canterbury.

Westminster School, so close to the centre of government, evacuated their 300 boys in September 1939, mostly to Lancing College, but with some accommodated at Hurstpierpoint College a few miles away. The split arrangement proved difficult to manage, as well as financially costly, and during the spring of 1940 discussions took place between the headmaster, John Christie, and the governors about reuniting the school in one place. The majority of governors favoured a return to Westminster as soon as possible, Lord Davidson writing hopefully that 'the defences of London are increasing in strength every day, and unless the Hun goes completely mad, it seems incredible that he would be so foolish as to attempt large-scale bombing', but at the end of May the school was still at Lancing. On 20 June the Regional Defence Commissioner gave both Lancing and Westminster a week's notice to leave the area. Westminster boys with bicycles were instructed, in the event of an enemy invasion, to travel towards Horsham with light luggage and a groundsheet, then to bear west and make for Exeter, avoiding towns and main roads. In the event, the whole school was taken by special train to Exeter for accommodation at the university.

Exeter could only be a temporary refuge until the university returned, so in early July the governors decided that Westminster would return to London for the autumn term, a prospect for which the staff felt nothing but apprehension. The reason for the governors' decision was financial; only thirty new boys were registered to enter in September, and twelve of those would only come if the school was in London. In August all the school furniture was moved back to Westminster, as well as hundreds of yards of blackout curtains made by masters, wives and boys. On 6 September the last bed was moved in, only for the bombing of London to start the next day. Some informal effort was made to teach the day boys, but most days and nights were occupied with fire-watching or sheltering in cellars, while the headmaster and senior staff scoured the country for new premises. Financial problems worsened, and the possibility of closing the school for the rest of the war seemed the only way to avoid complete insolvency. Accommodation was finally secured in a dispersed group of farms and houses around Bromyard in Herefordshire. Negotiations with the owners were fraught, but eventually 250 boys moved there in early November with the warning 'not to bring tail-coats as the local peasantry will be somewhat startled'. It was not a moment too soon, for in October the Busby Library at the school was destroyed by an incendiary bomb and the headmaster's secretary was killed in an air raid while sheltering in Church House, a building earlier identified as ideal protection for the school.[47]

Two public schools in great danger in the summer of 1940 were Victoria College, Jersey, and Elizabeth College, Guernsey. On 15 June, nearly two weeks after Dunkirk and with France visibly crumbling under the German onslaught, Churchill decided that the Channel Islands could not be defended. The collapse of France came as a huge shock to all the inhabitants and elicited a variety of responses as they waited for the Germans to occupy the islands. In Jersey the great majority of the islanders chose to stay, with only 6,600 evacuated out of a total population of about 50,000, a contrast with Guernsey, from where 5,000 schoolchildren and 12,000 adults were evacuated out of a population of 42,000. Some boys from Victoria College were in England at the time and established a wartime base at Bedford School, but on Jersey the majority who remained were forced to relocate to other premises, as the Germans took over the college buildings for their headquarters. With a backdrop of increasingly repressive occupation laws, Victoria provided an example of what might have become the fate of every public school if an invasion of Britain had succeeded.

The experience of Elizabeth College provides one of the epics of 1940. Until June school life had not been seriously affected by the war. Some work had been done digging air raid shelters and blacking out the buildings, but as late as 6 June the headmaster took a phone call from England asking about a boarding place. The full extent of the danger began to be realised when on 15 June the last British military units left Guernsey, and two days later France asked the Germans for an armistice. Henry Milnes, head of Elizabeth, had only taken up his post in September 1939. A veteran of the Royal Flying Corps with an MC, he had come from Uppingham, whose head had written in his reference that 'few events in school life, whether they were emergencies or matters of routine, could find him unprepared'.

Milnes set himself to arrange the evacuation of his school. He had little help from the Guernsey authorities but agreed, by telephone to London, a tentative plan for a ship to pick them up, although without any certainty that one would be available. At one stage, when he could hear explosions from Cherbourg, he almost gave up hope of rescue and booked passages for his wife and family on the mail boat, resolving himself to stay with his school. On 18 June each boy took home a note stating that the college was going to leave the island if possible and that all who received the necessary permission from their parents would be taken. More than 90 per cent of parents signed the form and they were given a list of articles for each boy to take – change of clothes, satchel of books, rug, rations for 24 hours, mug, plate, knife, fork and spoon. It was deemed wise to dispose of all OTC uniforms and weapons before the Germans arrived.

No guarantees could be given from England that any ship would be forthcoming, but on the evening of 19 June it was reported that one would be arriving early the next day. Accordingly, after morning assembly on 20 June, the boys were sent home to fetch their luggage and say goodbye to their parents. They waited at school through most of that day, until at 9.30 pm they received word to proceed down to the docks in a long column of 150 boys of all ages. For those in charge there was the added burden that they had no idea of where they would land in England, or where they would then go. There had not been time to make any advance arrangements about reception or accommodation, the English authorities being overwhelmed by the returning Army and by rapidly escalating events.

By the time they reached the docks it was dark, and no ship was in sight, but soon the *Batavia IV*, a Dutch cargo ship, hove into view and quickly berthed. They all filed on board, moving into whatever space could be found, mostly in the dark holds from which any escape would have been very difficult if the desperately overcrowded ship was attacked. Those on deck kept anxiously scanning the sky and horizon for enemy ships and aircraft, while hoping that no minefields had been laid across their track. At dawn Portland Bill was sighted, and they disembarked in Weymouth, where harassed officials spent several hours considering the status of the party, a unique combination of refugees, but British ones, before deciding to send them to the North of England. Buses were waiting when they arrived at Oldham early the next morning. They were taken to the Co-operative Society hall for refreshments and mattresses on the floor, their first proper food and sleep more than forty hours after that last assembly in front of the college.[18] Later they moved to a new home in Derbyshire, where they spent the next five years.

The Experience of War for State Schools

The problems of evacuation and requisitioning faced by public schools paled in comparison with those experienced by many state schools and local authorities. In the first week of the war, under the official government evacuation scheme, chaos ensued when the main railway companies carried 1.3 million children, accompanied by their teachers, from the cities to reception areas in the country. At one point in 1940 the London suburb of Croydon had 20,000 children scattered in over a hundred towns and villages from Penzance to Newcastle-upon-Tyne. Schools now unoccupied in the cities became ARP posts or other military installations, but this caused problems as evacuees started to drift back during the Phoney War and education had to be provided for them and those who had never left, a problem particularly acute in London, where other obstacles included a shortage of teachers. The system did recover briefly, but the Blitz from September 1940 sent city education again into chaos. In London more than two hundred schools were wholly or partly damaged, and attendance in secondary schools varied from 10 to 50 per cent according to area. Educational provision in other cities also suffered. When the Board examined, in the winter of 1940–1, the situation in Portsmouth, it was found that over half the children were receiving no education at all and only a third were attending full-time.[49]

It was easier for single, independent public schools to make suitable arrangements for education under the pressure of evacuation than it was for state schools, who had to rely on overwhelmed state bureaucracy while also dealing with the vast range of socio-economic classes, the most deprived suffering most. Public schools also had their history and tradition to keep them together, whether evacuated or not, along with the support of parents and alumni. Where such traditions existed in the state sector, it was easier for schools to adapt. This applied mostly to the long-established state grammar schools, which were in some cases helped by public schools in evacuation areas. Rye GS, evacuated to Bedford, was given access to the gymnasium, swimming pool, science labs and workshops of Bedford School, while Sevenoaks School became the refuge for Shooter's Hill GS from London.

Wilson's School, a selective state grammar school founded in Camberwell in 1605 by royal charter, showed how tradition and a strong sense of school identity could overcome adversity. On 1 September 1939 a party of 300 Wilson's boys, some with brothers and sisters whom families wanted to keep together, along with masters and their wives, left London by train. They alighted at Eynsford, sitting for five hours by the roadside before heading by coach for Tonbridge. All the billets here were taken, so they were sent to Farningham, but this was a village with no accommodation, so they moved on to Swanley where, after two days of arduous travel, they found themselves in unsuitable billets and only just outside the London balloon barrage area already designated as unsafe. London County Council unhelpfully declared that once a school left London it was no longer responsible, so the headmaster took the initiative and they moved further out into Kent, first to a holiday camp on the coast near Deal and then to Ashford Grammar School. Finally, in April 1940, the head was directed by the Board of Education to a newly built camp school near Horsham, cedar wood huts on concrete foundations in thirty acres of ground. Such camp schools had been built before the war to offer temporary and very basic accommodation for school field trips. Wilson's adapted to circumstances very well, effectively transforming itself into a boarding school for the duration of the war. It was helped by nearby Christ's Hospital, which allowed use of its playing fields, swimming pool and assembly hall on a regular basis, while Wilson's staff and senior boys served in the Christ's Hospital OTC. Numbers at Wilson's rose from 248 in 1940 to 333 in 1944 and the school emerged from the war stronger for its experience 'with not only the tradition but the efficiency of the old school successfully transplanted'.[50] The key to that success was the same strong sense of school identity that allowed independent schools to survive the difficulties of 1940.

The Home Front

In the First World War the only common ground between the highest and lowest social classes was in the trenches, sharing the same dangers. On the home front there was little danger, and few concessions were made to draw the working class and their political representatives into a shared war effort. In the Second World War it was the experience of life on the home front which drew social classes together. Churchill contrasted the two wars thus: 'The fronts are everywhere. The trenches are dug in the towns and streets … The front lines run through the factories.'[51] Only by responding positively to this shared sense of crisis and demand for national unity could public schools hope to justify their existence in 1940 and beyond. They found ways to share the dangers and hardships, in the process achieving a more profound understanding of the country in which they lived.

Public schools demonstrated their commitment to the war effort and social cohesion in various ways. At Glasgow Academy six hundred local people would come into the school by night to use the trenches and shelters within the school grounds. The school recruited their own air-raid marshals to bring order to the process, issuing tickets for the shelters to local families. When the King came to visit the severe bomb damage in Bristol in November 1940, civil defence units paraded for him on the playing fields of Bristol GS, with the bombed-out prep school in the background; Bristol GS took pride in refusing to evacuate and staying where it belonged at the heart of the city, much of whose historic centre lay in ruins. St Benedict's in Ealing became the base for the National Fire Service, the playground filled with parked fire engines and teaching compressed into one large residential building. Brighton College, steadfastly refusing to evacuate from the south coast, developed an engineering scheme in 1942 by which staff and boys used the school workshops as a production unit to manufacture parts for wartime munitions. Early problems of lack of quality were overcome and the production line became increasingly efficient as boys mirrored the shifts and work practices of factories.

At Hurstpierpoint College, the headmaster, Walter Dingwall, previously bursar of St Edward's, Oxford, where he had paid Douglas Bader's fees out of his own pocket, was determined to keep the school programme going but was also aware of his wider social responsibilities. At night he commanded the Home Guard platoon of senior boys, masters and local volunteers manning road-blocks, setting up radio communication and training in how to use Molotov cocktails to disable enemy tanks. He expanded contacts with the local village by offering the OTC band for events and helped to raise money for campaigns like 'War Weapons Week'. He turned over playing fields to growing food, tended by boys and staff, and made sure that boys gave up some of their summer holidays on farming and forestry camps in Sussex, taking part in them himself. They cut timber, weeded crops and carted and threshed wheat, supplied with their meals by Mary Dingwall and other staff wives. It was no wonder that Dingwall wrote to a friend in August 1943: 'I cannot cope with this. I am too worn out with the struggle of wartime difficulties. My average for the last eight days of term was getting to bed between 2.30 and 3.00 am, finishing up with an all-night show with the Home Guard just before the farming camp.'[52]

Agricultural and forestry camps filled the summer holidays of most schools after the 1940 HMC conference was addressed by Walter Smith from the Forestry Commission, who stressed the national importance of the work. Such voluntary work had happened in the First World War, but now it was on a much larger scale. In August 1940 a party from Stowe travelled to the Lake District, where they camped for a month and worked seven days a week, eight hours a day, felling 180 acres of woodland, then trimming the timber for pit-props. Washing only in a stream and enduring all manner of weather conditions, it was hard, back-breaking work with heavy saws and axes. Closer to home in those same summer holidays, other Stowe boys came back to school to help bring in the harvest on local farms for sixpence an hour. One boy wrote that 'stacking flax was the hardest job as the bundles stuck to each other and it was difficult to separate them and throw them on the elevator'.[53] Virtually every public school had a similar story to tell. Thirty-three boys and a master from Hampton School clocked up over 5,000 hours at Cholsey in summer 1941 working in the fields and camping out in a local village school. The girls of Lady Eleanor Holles went to camps in Hertfordshire, stooking and carting corn, gathering pea crops and sleeping outside on straw mattresses. The spirit of practical co-operation which prevailed across very different communities made boys and girls more aware of their social responsibilities.

Heads recognised the extra work being asked of their pupils and the consequent fatigue. Henry Flecker, head of Christ's Hospital, testified to this: 'Apart from classwork, the OTC demanded of senior boys larger and more strenuous parades. They spent one afternoon per week digging a field to help our food supply by growing extra potatoes. They had Home Guard parades every Sunday, and on one weekday, and fire-watching once a week.' All boys over fifteen were also expected to spend three weeks of their summer holidays working on local farms, as well as cultivating the school fields for vegetables. 'It was wrong', said Flecker, 'to accept the sacrifice of the lives of thousands of merchant seamen who were bombed or torpedoed when bringing us our sustenance from overseas, and make no personal effort to relieve them of at least some part of their burden by growing food.'[54]

The core component of many local Home Guard units in 1940 consisted of staff and senior boys from public schools, alongside men from all walks of life. One Stowe master who commanded a Home Guard section recalled 'the night exercises when tea had to be brewed at midnight on forced marches across the countryside, and a comradeship in arms was forged between educated boys of seventeen and much older farm-hands, hedgers and ditchers, road men, ground staff and poachers.'[55] A boy at Wellington gave his take on the contrast in ages and the qualifications necessary for command in an area full of retired soldiers: 'No. 2 Platoon (Wellington College) of our battalion, average age seventeen and a half; qualifications necessary to become an NCO, to be Dormitory or College Prefect. No. 1 (Crowthorne) Platoon, average age sixty-eight, qualifications to become an NCO, must be a retired Brigadier.'[56]

The priceless commodities which schools had to offer, in those days when any weapon could be called into service, were the rifles from the school armoury and trained military personnel on their staff who were too old for the army.[57] Headmasters and senior staff with military experience sometimes assumed command of local units. William Marsh, headmaster of St Alban's, combined his school duties with commanding a local company of the Home Guard, advising the Royal Naval Signals School and setting up the Sea Cadet Corps. Merchant Taylors' headmaster Norman Birley, who had reached the rank of lieutenant colonel in 1918, served in the Merchant Taylors' platoon of the Hertfordshire Home Guard as a sergeant. For boys the Home Guard was an exciting adventure, especially in the heady days of 1940, but, as the war went on and the danger of invasion receded, it could become a burden, especially to those older men who had done a full day's work. One, contemplating his own battalion in 1942 with its companies of elderly estate workers, unfit schoolmasters and callow schoolboys, was profoundly grateful that it was never ordered into action against enemy infantry and armour.

The change in social attitudes was noted by John Christie, Westminster head-in-exile in Wales:

The war really did bring us down to earth, all of us, one class with another, the old with the young. We ceased to expect any privileges … In evacuation Westminster boys had to make the best they could of living in dilapidated houses and grew more dependent on themselves. Constantly they found men with far less formal education than their own to be so much better with a rifle or a hoe or a tractor. Boys will always give their admiration to a master of his craft, and some of them discovered for the first time that the art of the scythe was comparable to the art of the cricket bat, and far more useful just then.[58]

The Blitz

The danger to schools, particularly those in the south-east, escalated during the summer holidays of 1940. J.F. Hough, headmaster of Brentwood School, gave an account of what this meant as the drama unfolded around him:

> There were some indications that the invasion was about to take place in the third week of July. We sent the boarders home in a hurry so that the beds and bedding could be used for the wounded … We had half a dozen big air battles above and around Brentwood … Then came the great attacks on London and we saw the whole western sky lit up with what seemed one vast fire. I had intended to open our term on 13 September but the government said no, for fear of invasion … We opened on 23 September with 575 boys instead of our usual 750; the others had gone to safer parts. I could not tell parents that Brentwood is a safe place because it is not, but I do say 'reasonably safe' and we take precautions.[59]

By the time schools came back for the autumn term, the Blitz had started in earnest. From 7 September London was bombed on fifty-seven consecutive nights, and attacks continue through to May 1941. These spread to other major cities, with Birmingham, Glasgow, Southampton, Bristol, Hull, Coventry, Liverpool, Portsmouth and Plymouth particularly badly hit. About 43,000 civilians were killed, roughly half of them in London, where more than a million houses were destroyed or damaged. Not until late 1942 did British uniformed casualties outstrip civilian ones.

The impact on London schools was reduced by evacuations, but school property suffered. Thirty-three fires in school buildings at Harrow were started by incendiary bombs on the night of 2 October, destroying the roof of the Speech Room; one fell directly in front of the headmaster as he entered the ARP control room. Dulwich College, which had stayed in London, escaped major damage, but the school looked like a fortress under siege, anti-aircraft shrapnel littered the rugby field and sirens could go off seven or eight times a day. One boy wrote: 'When the banshee howls, we double to and fro in apparent chaos between dusty underground cellars, equipped with benches made by experts in the art of torture, and classrooms whose boarded windows shed only a dim religious light.'[60]

St Paul's Girls' was hit on the night of 17 November, when twenty-seven incendiaries were dropped on the school and in the grounds. Winifred Pasmore, art mistress, was one of those staff who fought the fires:

> The raid began and was very heavy. I opened one of the fireproof doors and saw the whole building lit up with brilliant white lights and small fires. We donned overcoats and outdoor shoes, picked up shovels, buckets of sand and stirrup pumps and sallied forth. We put out the incendiaries up the passages on either side of the baths and made our way to the playground, when Groves shouted, 'get down' and everybody fell flat on the ground as a string of bombs whizzed overhead. By this time little fires were burning all over the place, but we grabbed the fire hose, which I had been taught to handle as a warden and aimed it first at the hall roof. As I looked up into the sky the planes were moving about, the shells were exploding, and searchlights were weaving their giant arms about the sky.

The school was badly damaged but back in operation a week later.[61]

In other cities public schools fought their own battles for survival. The autumn term at Bablake in Coventry saw air raids grow in frequency and intensity. On 12 October a 500lb bomb wrecked the school pavilion. Two nights later, unexploded bombs brought the closure of the school for five days. Then came the devastating attack on the city on 14 November which killed 568 people, injured 1,100 more and destroyed countless buildings. Bablake's history records that terrible night:

> The school library was completely burned out and its contents destroyed. Incendiaries fell into the preparation rooms but were quickly brought under control. It was a direct hit with an oil bomb which destroyed the library. Although school hoses were run out, no water was available … With all its precious contents the library was consumed completely and in the morning was so much level ash. Ironically, the only thing recognisable was a page from a German dictionary.[62]

No boy or member of staff had been killed, but the homes of many had been destroyed and the school itself badly damaged. It was decided that evacuation was the only sensible course, but movement around the city was very difficult and it took a week to gather the boys together and evacuate them to Lincoln on 23 November. They did not return to Coventry until the summer of 1943.

Smaller towns and their schools also suffered from bombing. At Sherborne on the afternoon of 30 September several hundred bombs were jettisoned over the town and its surroundings by about 150 German bombers. They had been attempting to destroy the Westland aircraft factory at Yeovil when they were intercepted by a squadron of Spitfires. By coincidence, the Spitfires were under the command of an Old Shirburnian, Peter Devitt, who later wrote:

> I saw their bombs falling away from beneath their bellies. On looking down to see what the target was, to my horror I saw the old School Courts, which I knew so well. I could not see much of where the bombs fell, as I was too intent on what was going on around me. I did, however, see in one instant a great deal of smoke round the old buildings and knew there must be some hits and damage and probably casualties.

Incredibly, no member of the school or staff was killed, but there were eighteen fatalities in the town, including several children.

The most significant school casualty of the Blitz was Bobby Longden, headmaster of Wellington College. An Eton scholar and Oxford don, he was only thirty-three years old on his appointment in 1937, bringing to what was a stuffy and traditional school strong personal qualities and a modernising agenda. On 8 October 1940 an air raid alert sounded at 7.30 pm and Longden visited boys in the shelters before returning to his house for dinner. Soon after 8.00 pm a bomb fell between the chapel and the laundry, and Longden went to his front door to see if any damage had been caused. At that moment a second bomb, jettisoned randomly by a German bomber, fell in the forecourt of the house, followed by another bomb and two incendiaries. Christopher Wright, in his first term at the school, and in the shelter only fifty yards from Longden, remembered 'the most almighty explosion'.[63] Longden was killed instantly, the heavy porch collapsing on top of him, and it was some time before his body could be dug out. The college suffered many broken windows and shattered ceilings and the head's house was badly damaged, but Longden was the only casualty. A young Wellington souvenir hunter wrote home that 'the Master has been killed but I have got a piece of shell and about six pieces from the chapel windows.'[64]

At Tonbridge the diary of Donald Birrell gives a graphic account of what it was like to live at school through the Blitz, as German bombers passed nightly over the town following the main railway line to London. Between 27 September and 1 October Birrell lists twenty-four separate alarms, five or more a day, and the daylight hours and whole nights he had to spend in the shelter. He writes of a burning Blenheim bomber crashing just north of the school, with pieces of the plane hitting the sanatorium. Schoolboy trivia is mixed with serious events, such as the diary entry for 28 November – 'Saw an ME109 shot down during the afternoon. The pilot baled out. Went to tutor with Mr Thomas in the evening.'[65] The school was lucky in that only one bomb landed within the estate, burying itself in the ground near the chapel and shattering many windows, but hundreds fell on Tonbridge and neighbouring parishes. On clear nights a red glow could be seen in the north as London burned, while staff and senior boys took turns fire-watching, armed with sand, water and stirrup pumps.

Schools could contribute to the spirit of the Blitz in other ways. Harrow organised a concert tour in the Midlands in September 1940, the school orchestra playing in state schools and in institutes and factories. Henry Havergal, Harrow's Director of Music, wrote that 'in school after school we found an audience tired after nights spent in shelters, but eager to hear and quick to respond to the exhilaration of music.'[66] At Bradfield between October and December 1940 the school gave rest and recuperation to small parties of Londoners, mainly civilian emergency personnel like firefighters and ambulance drivers. They usually stayed for a week recovering from their ordeal, sleeping in the sanatorium and being looked after by boys. Here in the rural Berkshire calm, some, when they first arrived, dared not walk to meals without their helmets. One attended every Chapel service and said on leaving, 'If only every ship and every regiment and every factory could start with prayers as this school does, what a difference it would make.'[67]

At the end of that momentous year, in December 1940, Winston Churchill went back to his alma mater, Harrow, for School Songs and to speak to the pupils. Earlier that year, he had been asked how the public schools were faring in the war and had quipped: 'Much as usual. Harrow has Amery, Gort and myself, Eton has the King of the Belgians and Captain Ramsay, and Winchester has Oswald Mosley to their credit.' It was a good joke, since Ramsay and Mosley had been locked up as Nazi sympathisers, and the King of the Belgians was believed to have capitulated too easily. His speech reminded his audience that they were fortunate to be living at such an historic hour, not encouraging the illusion that all was well but making people determined never to give in. He sang lustily with the boys, was greatly moved to find that extra lines about himself had been added to one of his favourite Harrow songs, but told the boys that he wanted to make a small change:

> It is in the line 'not the less we praise in darker days the leader of our nation'. I have obtained the headmaster's permission to alter 'darker' to 'sterner' ... These are not dark days, they are great days, the greatest days our country has ever lived.[68]

By the end of 1940, Britain and her public schools had survived those 'sterner days'. Some headmasters had shouldered heavy responsibilities, balancing the safety of their charges with worries about the future survival of their schools. Many schools faced daily and nightly physical danger from air attack, while trying to keep a semblance of normality in educational routine. Pupils could be children by day, soldiers and fire-watchers by night. Staff became exhausted by the emergency work thrust upon them. Evacuated schools had to improvise in numerous ways. In the process, public schools and nation had entered a period of togetherness based on shared dangers and community spirit on the home front, while alumni took on varied wartime roles across the globe.

Part II

Winning the War

The contribution made by the alumni of public schools in the Second World War was both global and multi-dimensional. Junior Army officers in campaigns like Italy and Normandy fought battles similar to their predecessors on the Somme, but public-school alumni served in much greater numbers in the irregular forces and in both the Royal Navy and Royal Air Force, with casualties in the latter forming a substantial proportion of rolls of honour in most schools. Public-school alumni, both men and women, also made important contributions to the winning of the war in the intelligence services and in scientific research and development.

Chapter 3

Air and Sea

On the Air Forces Memorial at Runnymede are commemorated 20,000 airmen with no known grave, lost without trace in the sea, buried unfound in the earth or consumed by fires which engulfed their aircraft. Here are not only pilots of the Battle of Britain and the missing of Bomber Command, but many other aircrew who flew long, lonely vigils over the Atlantic for Coastal Command and those killed in Fighter Command's later war, carrying out offensive missions over Europe in support of ground forces. Every public school will have boys named here, probably in greater numbers than on any war memorial outside school grounds.

The global nature of the war, and the need for Britain to protect her imperial and mercantile interests, meant that the war at sea and in the air assumed a much greater importance than in 1914–18. Both services therefore had to expand way beyond the public-school dominated professionals of the inter-war years, and women played an important role in that expansion. Public-school alumni not only constituted the vast majority of the pre-war professional officer corps in both the Royal Navy and Royal Air Force, but also joined both wartime services in much greater numbers than in the Great War. To give just one example, in 1914–18 only 5 per cent of those who served from Dulwich College were in the Navy and 7 per cent in the Royal Flying Corps (RFC); in 1939–45 the Dulwich figures are 13 per cent in the Navy, and 28 per cent in the RAF.

A myth developed in the war that the RAF, and especially Fighter Command in 1940, was composed mainly of wealthy, wild-spirited young men. This was not so, but flying, from its inception just before the First World War, was for some time a rich man's sport. The RAF's Second World War leadership was dominated by the products of public schools who had flown in the RFC over the Western Front, while most officers trained in the inter-war years went to the RAF College at Cranwell from public schools. It was the rapid expansion of the service from the creation of the Royal Air Force Volunteer Reserve (RAFVR) in 1936, the 'citizens' air force', which brought dilution of that public-school influence.

The historical relationship between the public schools and the Royal Navy was more semi-detached but similarly based on class and wealth. Since the nineteenth century, potential officers had experienced a four-year education, from the age of thirteen, at the naval colleges of Osborne and Dartmouth, and then two years further training at sea as midshipmen.[1] The navy, like the Jesuits, perceived advantage in catching boys young and instilling naval tradition into them at an impressionable age. Some boys went to mainstream public schools for a couple of years up to the age of thirteen or fourteen, but most came to naval college from prep schools. Osborne and Dartmouth were essentially part of the public-school system, specialised boarding schools recruiting pupils from the same social class, and both were members of HMC from 1909. As the fees at these colleges equalled those of public schools, the pre-war officer class, and therefore the dominant element in the wartime senior leadership of all three services, continued to come from that background. Dartmouth, like public schools, found a ready market in the children of service families.[2] One such was the future Admiral Sir Henry Leach, First Sea Lord in the Falklands War. When he was just ten years old in 1933, his naval father (later killed in 1941 when captaining the battleship *Prince of Wales*) came to his room to say goodnight, and then left. In an afterthought, he pushed the door open again and said quickly to his son, 'I take it you have no objection to joining the Royal Navy.' He then closed the door without waiting for a reply, went downstairs and said to his wife: 'I've discussed things with the boy and he has agreed.' The young Henry dutifully went off to Dartmouth, reflecting fifty years later that he could find no objection to his 'careers interview'.[3]

Public Schools and the Royal Air Force in the Inter-War Years

The RFC in the First World War was monopolised by officers from public schools, and it was the survivors who filled the upper ranks of the RAF in the inter-war years. The wealthy classes dominated the early days of flying before 1914 because of the cost of learning to fly and the leisure time needed to gain the coveted Royal Aero Club Certificate. The early holders of this were therefore gentlemen of means like John Moore-Brabazon (Harrow), who served in Churchill's wartime government, or serving officers in the Army or Navy, among them Hugh Dowding (Winchester), future head of Fighter Command. Because the RFC remained part of the Army until 1918, the selection of men for wartime training as pilots and observers was in the hands of senior Army officers from public schools. When Cecil Lewis, seventeen years old and at Oundle, applied to join the RFC in 1915, he was interviewed by an Etonian staff captain, Lord Hugh Cecil, an interview focused on his school – 'So you were at Oundle under the great Sanderson?' – and on the sport he played – 'Fives you say you play, so you should have a good eye then.'[4] This approach ensured that most chosen were public-school educated officers, until the heavy losses of 1916 brought a widening of the net. Virtually all those in senior RAF command in the Second World War had come from public schools to serve in the RFC, including Dowding, Sholto Douglas (Tonbridge), Arthur Harris (Allhallows), Charles Portal (Winchester), Arthur Tedder (Whitgift) and John Slessor (Haileybury).

Hugh Trenchard commanded the RFC through most of the war and then became Chief of the Air Staff (CAS) from 1918 to 1930. His education was at private crammers, but every subsequent CAS until 1976 went to a major public school. Those who immediately succeeded Trenchard were John Salmond (Wellington), Geoffrey Salmond (Wellington), Edward Ellington (Clifton), Cyril Newall (Bedford) and, in the war years, Portal. They had all taken a chance on a new service at a time when air fighting was even more dangerous than staying in the trenches, but they were excited by the possibilities inherent in this new form of warfare and less inhibited by the historically more stifling traditions of their Army and Navy contemporaries. They were also in many cases more broadly educated than their Army equivalents – senior commanders like Portal, Douglas, Tedder and Trafford Leigh-Mallory (Haileybury) had all been to Oxbridge.

The establishment in 1920 of the RAF College at Cranwell ensured that the RAF's future officer corps would be trained in a college to rival Sandhurst, Woolwich and Dartmouth. In 1919 Lord Hugh Cecil chaired a committee which defined the qualities needed by future RAF officers as 'a high standard of courage, self-control and honourable conduct, and seemly manners', along with evidence of responsibility held at school and sporting ability, character traits valued by public schools for decades.[5] As a new service in a more democratic age, the committee stated a wish for the RAF to be open to all talents and backgrounds, but in practice the RAF leadership believed that public schools still provided the right type of future officer, and HMC was regularly consulted on issues related to education and training at Cranwell. Even during the war, the RAF remained prejudiced in favour of privately-educated aircrew drawn from the British upper middle-class; an Air Ministry memorandum of 1942 complained that the squadrons 'are not getting a reasonable percentage of the young men of the middle and upper classes, who are the backbone of this country, when they leave their public schools.'[6] In a service where technology and navigation skills were important, candidates for Cranwell had to pass School Certificate in eight subjects, with a pass in maths essential and science desirable, restricting the pool of candidates even further. The final clincher favouring public schools was that parents had to pay fees comparable to those at a boarding public school for their sons to attend Cranwell's two-year course. A few prize cadetships were offered to those who could not afford the fees, but these often went to the sons of impoverished officers who had already benefited from generous bursaries at public schools, like Douglas Bader from St Edward's, Oxford.

The entrance exam for Cranwell was competitive, offering the same papers as Sandhurst and Woolwich but with a higher pass mark. It was difficult for state schools, or even smaller public schools, to compete with those major schools which already had the means in place, the army class, to prepare boys for the Cranwell exam. Ninety per cent of schoolboy entrants to Cranwell between 1920 and 1939 came from public schools, mostly from those schools with both an army class and a strong parental military background – Wellington with fifty candidates, Cheltenham, twenty-eight, Tonbridge and Imperial Service College, twenty-two, Marlborough, Eton and Haileybury, twenty each.[7] The only concession to meritocracy came in the ten or so cadets per year who entered via the RAF's engineering apprentice college at Halton, including Frank Whittle (Leamington College), the inventor of the jet engine. The course at Cranwell followed many of the public-school traditions of sport and spartan living, but was distinctive in that cadets went there because they were attracted by the thrill of flying and the risks implicit in it.[8] Peter Townsend's passion for flying was encouraged by his Haileybury housemaster, who drove him to an RAF base for his first flight, aged fourteen: 'That flight decided me: I would become a pilot.'[9] When he reached Cranwell, flying 'offered the highest form of adventure; it was dangerous, unfamiliar, thrilling and it meant risking your neck.' A mid-air collision he witnessed killed two instructors and two cadets – 'bodies torn apart and mutilated were recovered from trees and neighbouring fields to be re-assembled for burial. There was not one of us who did not think "this could happen to me" and tried not to believe it.'[10]

In December 1936 Sir Edward Ellington came to address HMC's conference at Ampleforth. For the Chief of the Air Staff to attend was a sign of how important the RAF believed the public schools to be in its future expansion, but Ellington was blunt about the dangers facing the country and the need rapidly to treble the RAF's size.[11] These words, and the creation of the RAFVR in the same year, challenged for the first time the assumptions by which the British military establishment had traditionally chosen its officers in peacetime. The Army and the Navy had yet to open their doors more than a fraction to potential officers from outside public schools, but the RAF, to find the numbers needed to prepare the service for war, established merit, not social background, as the criterion for officer selection, and the main beneficiaries were products of smaller public schools and the state grammar school system. The RAFVR was created in July 1936 to be open to the 'whole middle-class in the widest sense of the term, namely the complete range of the output of public and secondary schools'.[12] Its creation 'hastened the transformation of the Air Force from a tiny elite dominated by the comfortably off and privately educated into a mass organisation drawn from every level of Britain's sharply stratified society.'[13]

Separate from Cranwell-trained professionals, and before the creation of the RAFVR, two other forms of entry to the RAF favoured boys from public schools and strengthened the belief that flying was an upper-class preserve. Trenchard wanted close links between the RAF and the universities to stimulate the study of aeronautical engineering and to build a lobby for the service among future ruling elites. The means to this end was the establishment of university air squadrons (UAS) at Oxford and Cambridge in 1925, to be followed by London University in 1935. At Cambridge the RAF supplied officers and ground crews to teach undergraduates to fly at nearby Duxford, the numbers set at seventy-five, increasing to one hundred in 1938. Cambridge reciprocated by funding a professorship of aeronautics. Most of these cadets came from public schools, as that was still the overwhelmingly greatest source of Oxbridge undergraduates.

For the undergraduates themselves, it functioned as a pleasurable flying club with friends, for which the government paid. Among those in the Oxford UAS in 1937 were Leonard Cheshire (Stowe) and Melvin Young (Westminster), future bomber pilots in 617 Squadron, and Richard Hillary (Shrewsbury), author of *The Last Enemy*. Hillary came to Oxford from Shrewsbury and personified intellectual vision and the romanticised approach to flying scorned by the more hard-bitten professional RAF officers. In a fighter plane, he believed, 'we have found a way to return to war as it ought to be, war which is individual combat between two people in which one either kills or is killed.'[14] As they began their wartime training, regular RAF men mocked the undergraduates as 'weekend pilots' or 'long-haired boys'.[15]

The other socially exclusive source of pilots was the Auxiliary Air Force (AAF). The RAF's equivalent of the Territorial Army was first formed in 1925 with four squadrons – Nos. 600 (City of London), 601 (County of London), 602 (City of Glasgow) and 603 (City of Edinburgh). The pilots flew at weekends and at annual camps, their planes maintained by RAF ground crews. Trenchard saw them as an important part of a reserve of pilots and thought they would be a success 'if it was as much of an honour to belong to one as it is to belong to a good club or university'.[16] The social exclusivity certainly applied to 601 Squadron, known as the 'millionaires' squadron', which was conceived in White's Club by Lord Edward Grosvenor and his mainly Etonian friends, including Sir Philip Sassoon, society host at Port Lympne and Under Secretary for Air from 1931 to 1937. University-trained men found their way into the AAF to continue flying, like Max Aitken (Westminster), son of Lord Beaverbrook, who joined 601 in 1935. Further AAF squadrons were formed in the 1930s, but access was limited to a certain class; when Johnnie Johnson, later the RAF's top ace and from a respectable school, Loughborough GS, tried to join a squadron in the 1930s, he was convinced his rejection came 'when the interviewing officer discovered he was not a fox-hunting man'.[17] When war broke out, the AAF was absorbed into the RAF, with fourteen AAF squadrons taking part in the Battle of Britain.

The creation of the RAFVR did not do much to change the nature of the RAF leadership at the start of the war, which was officered at every level mainly by public-school alumni from Cranwell, or by men from the UAS and AAF taking up permanent or short service commissions. This could not last, as the expansion of the service, along with casualties, meant that the RAF as a mass wartime organisation became a broader church. When battle was joined, so complete was the amalgamation of professionals and amateurs, public school and grammar school, that 'the distinctions of peacetime between the component parts ceased to be discernible and the memory of them failed to have any significance.'[18]

Public Schools and the Royal Navy

Osborne and Dartmouth were public schools in all but name, maintaining strong links with the system through their recruitment of staff. Senior naval officers commanded the colleges, but civilian headmasters were in charge of the academic programme and were usually drawn from public schools. Headmaster of Osborne from 1905 until it closed in 1921 was a former head of maths at Winchester, Charles Godfrey, and headmaster of Dartmouth from 1905 to 1927 was Cyril Ashford, former head of science at Harrow, succeeded from 1927 to 1942 by Eric Kempson, head of science at Rugby. The academic education differed from that of public schools in putting more emphasis on maths and science, and in immersing boys in seagoing life and traditions, but the institutions copied the pastoral attitudes and often brutal disciplinary systems of public schools, and valued character in the same way. Just as there was pressure on public schools to mitigate their social exclusivity, so the Navy was encouraged to widen access to Dartmouth. This was difficult without the support of the Treasury, as Dartmouth charged cadets similar fees to public schools and, in straitened times, the Treasury was reluctant to subsidise them. The Royal Navy was also as resistant as the Army to social engineering, believing that it risked undermining the shared identity of the officer corps, so the numbers becoming officers from outside a restricted social class were small. Only in 1955 did Dartmouth transform itself from public school to tertiary college, with all the entry coming in at the age of eighteen.

The alternative to Dartmouth, as a way into the Navy for an officer, was the Special Entry scheme set up in 1913. This allowed boys, again mostly from public schools, to apply for entry at the age of seventeen and undergo a year's course of sea training. Forty-one were successful in the first year, but by 1937 this had increased to over 100, compared with 145 joining the Navy from Dartmouth in that year. The schools clearly favoured it over Dartmouth because it allowed them to keep those boys for four years, as with candidates for Sandhurst and Woolwich, and they could be taught within the same army class. From 1925 to 1929 the public schools producing ten or more Special Entry cadets were unsurprisingly led by Portsmouth GS with eighteen. Cheltenham was close behind with seventeen, Eton fifteen, Plymouth fourteen, Bedford and Christ's Hospital thirteen each.[19]

In 1937 the government had belatedly provided the funds to expand the fleet, so only in 1939 did the Royal Navy step up plans for an increase in personnel. In January 1939 it had 10,000 officers and about 110,000 men, barely enough to man the existing fleet, but by 1944 this had increased to 863,000 officers and men, including over 70,000 women in the Women's Royal Naval Service (WRNS). The means of expansion was the Royal Naval Volunteer Reserve (RNVR), 'amateur' sailors, many of them well-heeled yachtsmen who gave up their spare time for sea training and brought to the service an enthusiasm at odds with the stiff hierarchy characterising Dartmouth. As early as 1942, RNVR officers formed half the Navy's total officer corps, the new intake particularly vital to the manning of the smaller frigates and corvettes needed for convoy duties in the Atlantic and Arctic. One such officer was Nicholas Monsarrat (Winchester), who joined the RNVR early in 1940 and wrote a compelling novel about his experiences in *The Cruel Sea*. Edward Young (Highgate), pre-war designer of the covers for Penguin Books and amateur yachtsman, became the first RNVR officer to command a submarine.[20]

The most highly decorated RNVR officer was Lieutenant Commander Robert Hichens, who personified the 'enthusiastic amateur'. At Marlborough in the 1920s, and then as a solicitor in Cornwall with a family house at Flushing, his spare time was full of action – competitive sailing in the Fastnet Race, rowing at Henley, motor racing at Le Mans and a commission in the RNVR. He completed his war training in six weeks in October 1939, serving in a minesweeper at Dunkirk and going ashore several times to organise the transfer of troops into small boats, for which he was awarded the DSO. He transferred to the command of a motor gunboat in coastal forces at Felixstowe and in September 1941 was given command of 6th MGB Flotilla, the first RNVR officer to achieve this level of command. They were regularly involved in high-speed actions with German ships off Holland and the French coast, sinking several of them and earning Hichens a total of two DSOs, three DSCs and two Mentions in Dispatches, before he was killed on the night of 12 April 1943 in another Channel engagement. Men like Hichens, whose sense of duty took them regularly into extreme danger, made a crucial difference to the way in which the worth of 'amateur' officers in the RNVR was perceived by the wider Navy.[21]

Both wartime First Sea Lords, Dudley Pound and Andrew Cunningham, had passed out of Dartmouth in the 1890s, the pre-1914 training school for every top naval commander in the Second World War. Before Dartmouth many of them attended the most navy-orientated prep school, Stubbington House, then near the Solent. Cunningham's classmate at Stubbington was Admiral Sir James Somerville, who commanded Force H from 1940 to 1942 and the Eastern Fleet from 1942 to 1944. Admiral Sir Bruce Fraser, C-in-C Home Fleet responsible in December 1943 for sinking the German battlecruiser *Scharnhorst*, was unusual in the top command of the Navy in having spent two years at Bradfield before going to Dartmouth at the age of fourteen.[22] Those coming through the RNVR or the Special Entry scheme found promotion to higher ranks slower. Not until 1945 did the first Special Entry cadet reach the rank of rear admiral: Geoffrey Oliver, who had joined the scheme from Rugby in 1915. The future Admiral Sir Varyl Begg, who joined from Malvern in 1926 as a Special Entry, was a lieutenant commander when war broke out, and still only a commander in 1945. The main contribution of these officers was therefore at lower operational levels, men such as Peter Roberts (King's, Canterbury), who joined under the scheme in 1936 and won the VC in 1942 for dealing with two unexploded bombs lodged in his submarine's deck casing.[23]

The Battle of Britain

The pilots of the Battle of Britain, 'the Few', enjoy mythic status in British history. That myth extends to popular perception that they were mostly 'young lords', rich young men from the major public schools. The truth was revealed by Churchill himself in a conversation recorded by his private secretary in October 1940: 'He told us that Beaverbrook had produced figures to show that only about thirty per cent of RAF pilots came from public schools, the remainder being products of elementary schools and professional classes. It was striking that none of the aristocracy chose the RAF – they left it to the lower middle class.'[24] The Battle of Britain may have conferred glamour on pilots, but Churchill was certainly partially correct in suggesting that the RAF as a pre-war service was largely middle and upper middle-class and had only limited appeal to 'toffs' as compared with smarter Army regiments.

Churchill's figure of 30 per cent was broadly accurate; 2,917 men were awarded the Battle of Britain clasp for flying at least one authorised sortie with Fighter Command between 10 July and 31 October 1940, of whom 544 lost their lives in the course of the battle, as did another 795 in other later theatres of war.[25] Research and analysis show that 614 Battle of Britain pilots can be positively identified as coming from British or Dominion public schools, 21 per cent of the total of 2,917; but, if one excludes the 283 pilots from the USA and mainland Europe, mostly Poles and Czechs, and the 602 gunners and radio operators in the larger Blenheims and Defiants also deployed in the battle, the identified figure for British and Dominion pilots is right on Churchill's estimate of 30 per cent public-school alumni.

At the start of the battle on 10 July, the public-school presence in the RAF's order of battle was proportionately higher, for the main source of pilots at this stage was commissioned officers from the regular pre-war RAF and the AAF, including those coming from the university air squadrons. Casualties among this group, and the newly trained replacements coming to the squadrons from the RAFVR, steadily diluted that proportion. Even in as socially exclusive a squadron as 601 (County of London) AAF, whose order of battle in July 1940 was dominated by the products of the more famous public schools, including eight Etonians and four Harrovians, only five pilots remained from the squadron's pre-war strength by October 1940, and sixty-one had passed through, including RAFVR sergeant pilots, Poles and Czechs.[26]

Eton, belying Churchill's jibe about the social class of pilots, contributed the largest number of Battle of Britain pilots from a single school, with thirty, the majority from the AAF and university air squadrons. It was followed by Harrow and Wellington with seventeen, Stowe with sixteen, four schools with fourteen (Cheltenham, Dulwich, Haileybury, Tonbridge), Winchester and Marlborough with thirteen, Charterhouse and Sherborne with twelve, Malvern and Shrewsbury with eleven.[27] The contribution of Dominion public schools was also important, headed by two New Zealand schools in King's Auckland and Wanganui Collegiate School with five pilots each, and Bishop's in Cape Town with four. Eton lost the most pilots killed in action during the battle with eight, including Richard Kay-Shuttleworth, who had succeeded his father as Lord Shuttleworth in 1917 when the latter was killed in action.[28]

One of the Etonians was Willie Rhodes-Moorhouse, whose story has special pathos. On 6 September 1940, 601 Squadron was heavily engaged over the skies of Kent at a crucial moment of the Battle of Britain, with Rhodes-Moorhouse in the thick of the battle, as he had been since Dunkirk. This time his luck ran out as his Hurricane was shot down and dived vertically into the ground near Tunbridge Wells. His father, also called William, had flown to France with the fledgling Royal Flying Corps (RFC) in August 1914, just five months after his son was born. Eight months later, he carried out a bombing raid against German troops at Courtrai where, flying at only 300ft, he was badly wounded by ground fire. With blood pouring from his wounds, he somehow managed to fly the plane back to his base, where he died the next day. In May 1915 he was awarded a posthumous Victoria Cross, the first ever given to an airman.

His son was brought up at Parnham House in Dorset, the home of his grandparents, where his father had been buried in 1915, the authorities still allowing repatriation of bodies at that time. The father was at Harrow, but Willie went to Eton, where he had private flying lessons and gained his pilot's licence at the age of seventeen in 1931. He inherited his father's estate worth a quarter of a million pounds in 1933 and used some of it to make himself a top-class skier, qualifying for the British Winter Olympics team in 1936. In 1937 he joined 601 Squadron AAF, where one of his fellow pilots was his brother-in-law and fellow Etonian, Stephen Demetriadi, who flew and died with him in the battle. Willie's body was recovered and cremated, his ashes buried alongside his father at Parnham House.[29]

Squadron life during the battle remained based on the public-school atmosphere prevailing in the small world of the regulars in the 1930s – close friendships, school slang and nicknames, with the officers' mess providing the shared fun of the boarding house. Nicknames included 'Stuffy' Dowding for his alleged lack of humour and 'Prof' Leathart because he was one of the few to have gone to university. Dangers had to be understated and brushes with death treated as a joke. George Barclay (Stowe) of 249 Squadron recorded in his diary that when 'Butch' Barton was shot down in a fight with German bombers in August 1940 and had to bale out, 'Everyone just stood and laughed when the Army brought Butch back, taunting him with the jibe "shot down by a bomber".'[30] Drinking sessions fuelled the jollity and helped stressed pilots to forget the dangers, its effect on battle performance largely unremarked. Geoffrey Wellum (Forest) of 92 Squadron, eighteen years old, recalled his flight commander, Brian Kingcome (Bedford), organising an outing to the White Hart at Brasted after a day of fierce action at Biggin Hill: 'I think a pint or three will do us all a world of good. Transport leaves the Mess at 8.30. Don't be late, anyone, and Geoffrey, don't drink more than three pints and get tight again because we shall have to call you the "Boy Drunkard" if you do.'[31]

Geoffrey Wellum was one of the youngest Battle of Britain pilots, his age and cockiness earning him the nickname 'Boy'. When he joined the squadron in May 1940 he had never seen a Spitfire, let alone flown in one, so he had to watch other pilots taking off to patrol over Dunkirk: 'By the end of that first day we'd lost five people, four of whom I'd met the night before in the officers' mess. I thought, "Hold on a minute, this is bloody dangerous".'[32] Aerial fighting he depicted as confused, brutal and highly dangerous, only his instinctive flying ability saving him when he had an Me109 on his tail: 'I've been bounced from behind … an Me109 is sitting on my tail not thirty yards away as I hear hits somewhere down the fuselage. I hear myself say "Oh God, I'm going to be killed"… I know the meaning of the word "fear", real stark staring fear, the sort of fear that few people possibly ever experience.'[33] He survived the battle, and combat in Malta, before he finally broke down, suffering from combat exhaustion aged only twenty, and never flew again.

Flying a modern fighter in combat was a young man's game. Of thirteen Marlburians who flew in the battle, the youngest was twenty-one, the oldest twenty-nine. Flying ability had to be instinctive, eyesight and reflexes very sharp and tactical awareness crucial, and that was just to survive. Pilots needed time to learn combat skills and, to gain time, they needed luck. One writer compared it to 'passing your driving test and entering a Grand Prix the next day, knowing that somewhere among the competitors are the best drivers in the world'.[34] One of the Tonbridge pilots was Arthur Rose-Price, who joined the RAFVR in 1937 and spent the first year of the war as an instructor. He joined 501 (County of Gloucester) Squadron on 2 September at Gravesend, twenty-one years old and with plenty of flying experience but none in combat. A fellow pilot recalled him arriving at lunchtime that day

> in a beautiful Riley car and, as it stopped and we looked in, we saw a squash racket and some golf clubs, as if he planned a long stay. The CO told the newcomer: 'Grab yourself some food, but forget sleeping quarters for now, we'll do that later. We're on readiness in a quarter of an hour, so you've just got time to grab something to eat. We lost three blokes today so you're on.' 'Yes sir', replied Rose-Price. I shall always remember his face as he said that. We took off on patrol about two o'clock and he was dead by a quarter past, shot down off Dungeness.[35]

Guy Mayfield (Lancing), serving as a chaplain at RAF Duxford during the battle, found it difficult to comfort young men when they came to talk to him about death:

I am thankful to be trying to do something as a priest, but that it should be telling young men of twenty, real good young men, how to die, and why there is nothing to be afraid of (except the pain which we don't mention) … Peter has been talking today about not wanting to die yet. He wants more from life than he fears he will have time to get. The heartache is to see these young men waiting to have their lives cut short.

He reflected that fighter pilots were often explosively high-spirited: 'They tend to live violently and enjoy themselves violently, for everything may be for the last time.'[36]

Over a quarter of public-school pilots who fought in the battle were unsurprisingly concentrated in the fourteen squadrons of the AAF (out of seventy-one Fighter Command squadrons in all). The relationship between them and the rest of the RAF was not always easy. 616 (South Yorkshire) Squadron was one of the last to be formed, in 1938, the year that Hugh Dundas left Stowe and joined while training to be a solicitor: 'There can seldom have been a body of men more outwardly confident and pleased with themselves than the pilots of the AAF. We wore big brass 'A's' on the lapels of our tunics … the regulars insisted that they stood for "amateur airmen" or even "argue and answer back".'[37] To Dundas it was like a very special club. The pilots were lawyers and farmers, stockbrokers and journalists, and had two things in common: a passion for flying and 'a fierce determination that anything the regulars could do, the auxiliaries could do better'.[38] Confidence could easily turn into arrogance. When petrol rationing came in, threatening the use of cars by the well-heeled pilots of 601 Squadron, Willie Rhodes-Moorhouse went out and bought a garage. When it became clear that it would still be difficult to get deliveries of petrol, another pilot remembered he was a director of Shell, and within days a tanker delivery had replenished stocks.[39]

Hugh Dundas vividly describes the moment that he came face-to-face with the reality of war. His first taste of combat was over Dunkirk, his desire to engage the enemy being trumped by a desire to stay alive and, as he landed, he recalled: 'I was transformed, Walter Mitty-like: now a debonair young fighter pilot, rising twenty, proud and delighted that he had fired his guns in a real dogfight, even though he had not hit anything, sat in the cockpit which had so recently been occupied by a frightened child.'⁴⁰ A brutal ordeal followed when 616 moved down from the north to Kenley on 19 August to join the front line of the battle. First Dundas himself was shot down by an Me109 he had not even seen, baling out with cannon shells in his leg and a dislocated shoulder. Then in the next eight days five pilots were killed and another five wounded, about half the pre-battle squadron. His older brother John, who had gone from Stowe to Oxford and a first in history, fought all through the battle and was killed that November.

It would be wrong to assume that all pilots from public schools who fought in the battle were university-educated gentlemen amateurs. Regular RAF officers, mostly Cranwell-trained, formed the core of every squadron, Douglas Bader (St Edward's, Oxford) being one of them. He had left Cranwell in 1930 and then lost both his legs in a low-level flying accident in 1931. He talked and proved his way back into the RAF on the outbreak of war, quickly rising to command 242 Squadron through the battle, by which time he was thirty years old and something of a father figure to his younger pilots. From St John's College in Johannesburg came Caesar Hull, who boxed for the South African team in the 1934 Empire Games and then joined the RAF in 1935, becoming one of its top aerobatic pilots at air displays. Wounded in the Norway campaign, he took command of 43 Squadron on 30 August, shooting down six German planes in six days before falling victim himself on 7 September, very experienced but still only twenty-six. Men like Bader and Hull helped the less experienced survive.

Johnnie Johnson, top-scoring RAF pilot of the war, came from a different kind of background. His father was a police sergeant, and Johnnie's boarding fees at Loughborough GS were paid by an uncle who saw potential in him. His school career was chequered, with academic and sporting successes outnumbered by the many breaches of the school rules which led to his finally being asked to leave when he was seventeen. He never held this against the school and was subsequently very generous to it in time and money. Johnson graduated from Nottingham University as a civil engineer in 1937, started taking flying lessons at his own expense and applied to join the AAF but was turned down, for what he felt were class reasons. Only in August 1939 was he accepted by the RAFVR and moved on to Spitfires in August 1940, but an old rugby shoulder injury made flying fighter aircraft very painful, and he only flew one operational patrol in the Battle of Britain before having an operation. He came back to action in 1941 and quickly proved his skills, finishing the war with thirty-eight victories and the rank of Group Captain.

One of the Dominion pilots was Percy Burton, who came from Bishop's in Cape Town to Oxford to read law in 1937, learning to fly with the Oxford UAS. He was called up in October 1939 and joined 249 Squadron at Church Fenton. On 16 August he was flying with James Nicolson (Tonbridge), when the latter won the only VC of the battle for 'continuing to engage the enemy after he had been wounded and his aircraft set on fire'. This may have had a bearing on why Burton was not also awarded the VC for the action in which he was killed on 27 September. Pursuing a Bf110 north of Hailsham, he appeared to run out of ammunition in the chase and, probably already mortally wounded, dived at great speed and deliberately rammed the tail unit of the German aircraft, sending both planes and both pilots to their deaths. His fellow pilots believed Burton should have been awarded a posthumous VC, but he received only a Mention in Dispatches, possibly because Nicolson's VC from the same squadron was already in the pipeline.[41] Of the four pilots from Bishop's who flew in the battle, three died in action, a higher rate of loss than any school in Britain or the Dominions.

The Battle of Britain continued to deliver moving stories well after the war ended. Michael Doulton, of Westminster School and 604 Squadron, was shot down on 31 August, and no trace of him was found. His American wife of a year, Carol, was two months pregnant when he died, and she returned to the USA to have the baby, named Paul, but came back to England in 1944 so that Paul could be brought up where his father had lived and died. She took a job teaching at Vinehall prep school in Sussex, and Paul in due course followed his father to Westminster. In 1984 the crash site of Michael Doulton's Hurricane was located near Romford, his body still in the cockpit, the gun button set to fire and the throttle fully open. Carol and Paul were both present when Doulton was finally cremated that same year.[42]

WRNS and WAAF

The Women's Royal Naval Service (WRNS), which had been formed in 1917 but disbanded in 1919, re-formed in 1939. War service for women in the First World War was mainly restricted to mundane roles in factories and public services vacated by men going into the Army, or in nursing, but in 1939 a much wider range of work opened for women, and with significantly greater responsibilities. In 1941 war service of some kind became compulsory for all single women between twenty and thirty. Roedean was one school with a substantial presence in the services – a hundred in the WRNS and ninety in the WAAF. 'Join the WRNS – free a man for the fleet' ran one of the recruiting posters, and by 1944 there were 73,000 WRNS working in a wide range of land-based jobs including radio operator, cypher clerk and naval intelligence staff. Twenty girls from St Paul's served in the WRNS, although the school's most memorable link with the Navy was arguably old girl Celia Johnson starring in the patriotic 1942 war film, *In Which We Serve.* Dame Marion Kettlewell (Godolphin, Salisbury), who went on to become Director of the WRNS in 1967, joined the service in 1941 as the driver for Admiral Max Horton but was commissioned in 1942 and commanded a WRNS unit at Harwich preparing landing craft for D-Day. Margaret Cooper (St Mary's Wantage) was one of many Wrens serving at Bletchley Park, her role as assistant to Frank Birch, head of the naval decoding section.

The Women's Auxiliary Air Force (WAAF) was formally created in June 1939. One volunteer was Felicity Peake, educated at St Winifred's in Eastbourne, one of the many seaside girls' boarding schools now long closed, who learned to fly in 1935 and joined the WAAF in 1939. Throughout the Battle of Britain she commanded the 250-strong WAAF contingent at Biggin Hill, including the vital plotters in the air defence command structure. For her courage and conduct in the devastating bombing of the airfield on 30 August, which cratered the airfield and killed thirty ground personnel, she was awarded the MBE, and two of her NCOs, the Military Medal. This episode put an end to any fears among RAF commanders that WAAFs would go to pieces under fire. Peake moved later to senior staff roles at Bomber Command and in Mediterranean Command and achieved, as the last Director of the WAAF, the post-war transition to the WRAF in 1949.[43]

Separate from the WAAF, but just as important to the war effort, were the intrepid women pilots of the Air Transport Auxiliary (ATA). This was a civilian organisation set up in 1939 to ferry new and repaired aircraft from factories to airfields. Over 300,000 aircraft of 147 different types were ferried in this way, and 108 of the pilots were women. The women's branch of the ATA was established by Pauline Gower (Beechwood Sacred Heart), who had first flown in the late 1920s with Alan Cobham, the long-distance aviation pioneer. She recruited the women pilots, among whom were Margaret Fairweather (Notting Hill HS), who became the first woman to fly a Spitfire; Helen Harrison-Bristol (St Mary's Calne), who in 1943 ferried a Mitchell bomber across the Atlantic; and Lettice Curtis (Benenden), who became the first woman to ferry a Lancaster bomber. Diana Barnato Walker, a 1936 debutante who had been to Queen's College in London, was one of the first to join. She had such a natural aptitude for flying that she went solo in 1936 after only six hours dual instruction. By the time the ATA was disbanded in 1945 she had flown eighty types of aircraft, delivered 260 Spitfires, and in 1963 became the first woman to break the sound barrier in a Lightning jet.

Bomber Command

The sheer size of Bomber Command meant that the diversity of aircrew was more pronounced than in Fighter Command, although it was still public school and Cranwell-educated pre-war regulars who filled senior ranks in both squadrons and staff posts. Bomber Command had 125,000 aircrew, of whom 55,000 were killed, an attrition rate of 44 per cent, by some way the highest of any of the services in the war and a worse chance of survival than an infantry officer's on the Western Front. In the spring of 1943 less than one man in five was completing an initial tour of operations, comprising thirty trips. By contrast, fewer than 3,000 pilots flew in the Battle of Britain, and during the whole war about 4,000 Fighter Command personnel were killed.

It is therefore not surprising that in most public schools Bomber Command aircrew make up a substantial element in rolls of honour. Bishop's Stortford College is one, with ninety-three war dead in the Second World War compared with sixty-one in the First. This rise, with no corresponding increase in overall pupil numbers between 1919 and 1939, is explained by the school's fifty-four RAF casualties, nearly 60 per cent of the total, of whom twenty-five died in Bomber Command's strategic air offensive over Germany. Most of those were pilots, but they included all the other roles in a bomber – navigator, wireless operator, air gunner, flight engineer and bomb aimer – and fifteen were commissioned officers, ten sergeants. The men of Bomber Command were all volunteers, and even in the years of greatest losses there was still a surplus of them. In a command prioritising technological skill, those volunteers, funnelled through the ever-expanding RAFVR, mostly came from the more educated sector of the population, public and grammar schools and every university. Wilson's School, then in Camberwell, a selective state grammar school, has roll of honour statistics very similar to Bishop's Stortford, with half their war dead in the RAF, and half of these in Bomber Command, although with the balance of ranks reversed, commissioned officers being in a minority.[44]

RAF bomber crews were a mixture of commissioned and non-commissioned ranks, but the Canadians in 1942 put forward the belief that 'all pilots, navigators and air bombers are of equal importance, and all of them have an equal claim to a commission.' At the heart of this were issues of equal pay, sharing of messes, status and class. The official RAF response reflected different beliefs going back into the public-school traditions of the service: 'A commission is granted in recognition of character, intelligence (as distinct from academic qualifications) and capacity to lead, command and set a worthy example. Many aircrews, though quite capable of performing their duties adequately, have no officer qualities.' The RAF was speaking the language of a small regular service recruited in a country where inequalities of this kind found readier acceptance than in the younger Dominions, but their position resulted in the not uncommon absurdity of a sergeant-pilot commanding an aircraft in which officers were in a subordinate position.[45] Pilots and navigators were more likely to be commissioned, because they came from more educated backgrounds than air gunners.

Since a bomber's aircrew were dependent on each other for survival in a way only matched in tanks and submarines, class issues for them were of secondary importance. One man, who had left school at fourteen, desperately wanted to be a bomber pilot and was worried that snobbery and a lack of education would count against him: 'Could it be that becoming one of these pilot types required a university education or even an old school tie? This was far from true ... The war brought opportunity and the great British class system counted for surprisingly little. I saw nothing of it at all in my RAF days.'[46] Denholm Elliott (Malvern), the future actor, volunteered for Bomber Command on his eighteenth birthday and was of the same mind:

> I was mixing for the first time with many different types of men from different strata of society and I found that I was getting on really quite well with them. I had been living in a fairly monastic world since the age of nine, in prep and public schools ... I found myself making great mates with all sorts of people I would probably never have met had it not been for joining up to meet the national crisis.[47]

Elliott served as a sergeant wireless operator in a mixed crew of officers and NCOs and was shot down close to the German coast in 1942, becoming a prisoner.

By mid-1942 most of the pre-war generation of Bomber Command aircrew had been killed, made prisoner or promoted to non-operational staff posts. Their places were filled by the wartime volunteers emerging from Operational Training Units (OTUs), where the appalling accident rate could be as high as 25 per cent.[48] They deployed to bleak airfields along the east coast, living in cold Nissen huts and hoping that they could beat the odds. Fatalism was widespread as losses mounted, with one pilot writing that 'if you live on the brink of death yourself, it is as if those who have gone before have merely caught an earlier train to the same destination.'[49] Experience was no panacea. Gray Healey (Tonbridge), close friend of Guy Gibson in 106 Squadron, was well into his second tour of operations with an equally experienced crew when he was shot down on 19 January 1943. Gibson wrote to Healey's mother saying that he had been killed by flak: 'It must have been a direct hit and I am quite certain that he and the rest of the crew suffered no pain.' He probably knew that Healey's Lancaster had been attacked by a night-fighter on the way to Essen, setting two engines ablaze. As Healey fought to keep his doomed and burning plane in the air, a running battle developed between the fighter and Healey's gunners, who continued to retaliate until they hit the ground in a fireball.[50] It was not just the likelihood of death which kept young airmen awake in their billets, but the method of it.

Issues of rank, class and educational background can be explored in the personnel of 617 Squadron, the Dam Busters. Their action on the night of 16 May 1943 was the most famous bombing operation of the war. It was led by Guy Gibson (St Edward's, Oxford), described later by Ralph Cochrane, his 5 Group commander, as 'the kind of boy who would have been head prefect in any school'.[51] In fact, his school career was relatively undistinguished: he never rose above house prefect, his academic record was mediocre, and in rugby he was second XV. He joined the RAF at the second attempt in 1936 on a short service commission and was classed average as a pilot after training but, unlike many of his contemporaries, he survived long enough to complete over 170 operations, winning the VC, DSO and Bar and DFC and Bar. The choice of him to lead the Dams Raid was down to 'his single-minded determination to complete whatever task he had been given and to drive everyone around him to do likewise'.[52] His own crew exemplified the British class structure and the Empire beyond – two Canadians, an Australian, a flight engineer who had only been to elementary school, a wireless operator from Liverpool Institute (where Paul McCartney later went), and a commissioned rear gunner from Wellington College, Richard Trevor-Roper, cousin of the eminent historian Hugh, who admired his war record and described him, perhaps slightly jealously, as 'a wild boy, expelled from Wellington for running a gambling syndicate'.[53]

Gibson had the ability to inspire those around him and never asked others to do what he would not do himself, but he had a lack of sympathy for aircrew who showed weakness in the face of the enemy and could be brusque with NCOs from a different class. He was only twenty-four at the time of the raid and found it difficult to live with the huge public acclaim which came with it. Soon after the raid he kept a promise to visit St Edward's, now with his VC on his tunic. Derek Henderson, head boy at the time, remembered him dining with the Warden and then being asked to make a speech to the boys which lasted for less than one minute: 'Most chaps when they come back say they didn't work at all. Well, all I can say is, don't believe them, I worked like hell.' With that simple advice, he walked out.[54] In his memoir, *Enemy Coast Ahead*, he revealed sensitivity to the human consequences on the ground: 'The fact that people might drown had not occurred to us … Nobody likes mass slaughter, and we did not like being the authors of it.'[55] Gibson may not have inspired much affection from those he worked with, but he had their respect and has kept his image as a great leader and warrior, clean of the stain that followed revelations about the strategic bombing campaign.

Of the ten British pilots who flew on the raid, nine had been to public schools, a higher percentage than usual in Bomber Command squadrons.[56] It is probably no coincidence that they mostly came from the boarding school background with which Gibson was most comfortable. Most of them were very young to be carrying responsibility for the success of the mission and the lives of their crews; Bill Ottley (Hurstpierpoint) had only left school at Christmas 1940 and was just twenty, but had already completed thirty operations. The core of the squadron under Gibson were his official deputy, John Hopgood (Marlborough), and his two flight commanders, Henry Maudslay (Eton) and Melvin Young (Westminster and Kent, Connecticut). All except Gibson perished that night. Young was comparatively old at twenty-seven, from a wealthy Anglo-American background and an Oxford rowing blue in 1938. Hopgood had only left Marlborough in July 1939, and not until 1941 did he first fly on operations, joining Gibson at 106 Squadron, where they became friends, leading to his being personally invited to join 617 Squadron. Hopgood had already won the DFC and Bar, but the strain of forty-seven completed operations was increasingly obvious. When his half-sister saw him for the last time in April 1943 at his second DFC investiture, the boy she remembered looked 'pale and very drawn and was smoking heavily'.[57] He had a premonition before the raid of what veterans called 'the chop', saying to a fellow pilot, 'I think this is going to be a tough one, and I don't think I'm coming back.'[58] Second to attack the Moehne Dam after Gibson, his aircraft was hit as he came in, but even as the flames spread and death beckoned, he managed to climb 500ft to allow two of his crew to escape before M-Mother exploded in mid-air. Henry Maudslay was even younger, only twenty-one at the time of the raid and one of the relatively few Etonians in Bomber Command, most of his contemporaries preferring smart infantry regiments. Henry had been Captain of Boats and Athletics at Eton before joining the RAF in 1940. He was described as 'a classic product of Britain's upper-middle-class, with its courtesy, sense of duty, and acceptance of responsibility'.[59]

The other icon of Bomber Command was Leonard Cheshire, a more cerebral and sensitive man than Gibson and more understanding of those around him, but just as tough and determined. J.F. Roxburgh at Stowe struggled to find portents of his later fame:

> As a schoolboy Leonard was very successful in the ordinary sense of the word – that is he became Head of House, a School Prefect and Captain of Lawn Tennis – but I cannot remember that he made more impression on his generation than several others did … There was something about him – was it perhaps a kind of moral dignity? – which made it inconceivable that he would think or do anything that was below top level.[60]

At Oxford, work took a back seat to more worldly pleasures and involvement in the university air squadron, but he made friendships easily with people from different classes, and one family friend remembered 'a withdrawn quality about him, a secret self-sufficiency'.[61]

Cheshire joined Bomber Command in June 1940 and had already completed his first tour of thirty operations by January 1941. He completed two more tours commanding 76 Squadron, where his warmth and humanity impressed everyone on the squadron, as did the personal example he set and his fierce determination to press home attacks. Taken off operations after his third tour, with ninety operations, three DSOs and one DFC already to his name, he became a station commander in Yorkshire, but in September 1943 took command of 617 Squadron. Here his leadership of the squadron, still with many from the Dams raid suspicious of newcomers, the risks he was prepared to take and the techniques he developed to mark targets at low level brought him the VC in September 1944. This was a unique award in that the 'date of bravery' was given as 1940–1944, four years of sustained courage over his operational career, rather than for any specific action. After the war his compassionate charitable work, together with his wife Sue Ryder, eclipsed even his outstanding war record, bringing him the Order of Merit and a peerage and confirming the moral dignity Roxburgh had seen in the schoolboy.

Gibson heard of Cheshire's VC when he was a base staff officer, the RAF refusing to let him return to operations after the Dams Raid. Barred from operations, he seemed like a lost soul, his energetic, mercurial temperament unsuited to the safety of a desk. News of Cheshire's VC made him more aware of his irrelevance, spurring him to demand a return to operations and the destiny he perhaps craved. He was reluctantly allowed to be controller of a raid on 19 September 1944, and his Mosquito was shot down on the way home over Holland. Barnes Wallis, who was devastated by his death, wrote of him:

> Facing death had become his drug. He had seen countless friends and comrades perish in the great crusade. Perhaps something in him even welcomed the inevitability he had always felt that, before the war ended, he would join them in their Bomber Command Valhalla. He had pushed his luck beyond all limits and he knew it. But that was the kind of man he was … a man born for war but born to fall in war.[62]

By the nature of their war, many of the airmen and seamen who perished have no known grave. There are memorials at all the towns hosting major naval bases on which the names of those who died at sea are inscribed. Runnymede does the same for airmen, whose graves can also be found in large numbers in the Dutch and German cemeteries along the route the bombers took to their targets. John Hopgood and his crew are in Rheinberg, Guy Gibson at Steenbergen, Gray Healey at Apeldoorn, where every year children place flowers on the graves of him and his crew. Such memorials remind us of the cost of the war. Public-school losses in all commands of the RAF, particularly in Bomber Command, constitute half the total killed from many schools, and not below a third in most. Tonbridge had 301 killed in the Second World War, 144 of them in the RAF, of whom sixty were killed in action with Bomber Command and another twenty-five in training accidents.[63] Lancing's figures are similar, with 140 killed, fifty-nine of them in the RAF, thirty-three in Bomber Command.[64] At Taunton School and Loughborough GS, RAF losses constitute 60 per cent of the roll of honour. Overall, public-school deaths in the Second World War are close to those of the First, and in some schools exceed them. For an explanation of that, RAF losses are one side of the coin. The other side largely comprises junior Army officers who, like their fathers before them, faced battlefields demanding leadership, endurance and example in land campaigns as ferocious if not as interminable as those of 1914–18.

Chapter 4

War on Land

There was a deluge of rain when we took over there at night from the Cameronians. Their slit trenches on a forward slope had become filled to the top with water, so they were simply standing in the darkness beside them when we arrived. We baled out these two-man slit trenches all through the night with our mess tins or steel helmets, for we had to stay underground all day, as we were under observation on a forward slope ... Two mortar bombs landed near me in the same slit trench as two guardsmen. The first broke one man's leg and the next bomb blew the other's head off. I was glad the night was dark when I removed what was left of one man in order to get the survivor on a stretcher.

Readers may think that this describes the later stages of the Passchendaele battle in November 1917, but it actually relates to an action near the River Garigliano in Italy in January 1944. Its author is Archie Elliott, twenty-one years old, Eton-educated wartime subaltern commanding a platoon in 2 Scots Guards.[1]

The Second World War may have lacked the endless attrition of trench warfare on the Western Front, but the effects of artillery were equally devastating, the sharp end of war could be just as intense and brutal, and the battlefield leadership of platoon and company officers was as crucial to success as in the earlier conflict. Overall war deaths in the British Army may have been much fewer than those of the First World War, but this reflected a different level of wartime engagement. There were battlefields in Italy, Burma and North-West Europe where casualties reached the same level as the Somme, not least among the same junior officers who had died in the trenches at a faster rate than any other rank. Those junior officers in front-line combat units in 1939–45, whether pre-war regulars or wartime conscripts, came from an officer corps still dominated by public-school alumni. This, along with the high RAF casualties, explains why Second World War casualties were in most schools not very different from the 1914–18 figures, and once again twice as high as the national average.

The sharp end of war on the ground also embraced the more daring enterprises of irregular warfare behind enemy lines, where the public-school officer presence in formations like the Special Air Service, the Commandos and the Chindits was disproportionately high. Free spirits from the inter-war public schools, especially those regulars and wartime officers frustrated by lack of conventional military action in northern Europe after 1940, entered enthusiastically into unconventional operations more exciting and elitist than the soldiering their fathers had experienced in Flanders. Irregular warfare diverted precious manpower and was generally disliked by the Army high command, but it was enthusiastically backed by Churchill and allowed Britain to pursue creative and aggressive tactics at a time when conventional campaigns had been pushed by necessity to the periphery of strategic thinking.

The British Army in the Second World War had more men taken prisoner than killed, while the sailors and airmen added to that number meant that there were more prisoners of war than in the First World War. Films and television series about Colditz and other camps in Europe and the Far East cannot begin to record the grimness of imprisonment for active young men, so the comparisons with boarding school life, which are sometimes made in jest, do both institutions a disservice. Imprisonment for officers in Europe brought years of boredom and often tough conditions, but thoughts of escape kept the most adventurous occupied. In the Far East the prisoner experience was very much harsher, the conditions, especially on the Burma railway, a story of ghastly suffering without any hope of escape except death.

There is much for public schools to discover about their Second World War generation. The military historian Brian Bond has concluded that 'in proportion to the numbers in the front line, British casualties in the two world wars were about equal.'[2] The suffering was equal too. In October 1943, at Termoli on the Italian Adriatic coast, Cedric Prowse (Tonbridge), consultant physician in Sussex before the war, was commanding 18th Casualty Clearing Station. He was based in a school, treating not just wounded soldiers but those with various kinds of sickness, including venereal disease and malaria, and the more harrowing injuries of Italian children who had stepped on mines. Shellfire had damaged the building, there was no running water and it was desperately cold. Prowse had to perform complex surgery for skeletal damage, burns and severe abdominal wounds, and he recorded in his diary: 'Every corner held a stretcher. Orderlies kneeled over them giving pain relief or a drink. Medical officers gauged fitness for surgery or for travel. Padres comforted the fearful and murmured last rites. Noble sights, sad sights, horrifying sights, all there to be seen and so few to attend to so many.'[3]

Combat and Casualties

The military historian John Ellis wrote of the 1944 Cassino battle in Italy that a 'comparison with the charnel houses of the Western Front is in no way misplaced. The battle for Cassino should be borne in mind by anyone who might think that World War Two was any sort of soft option for the men at the sharp end.'[4] Overall army deaths in 1939–45 were less than a quarter of those of 1914–18, but 'during some battles losses approached or exceeded the worst experiences of the First World War.'[5] For Cassino could be substituted the fierce fighting round Caen in July 1944, the dour slogging matches in the mountains of Italy or the brutal hand-to-hand struggle across the Deputy Commissioner's tennis court at Kohima. The popular perception of the Second World War as a free-flowing war of movement in comparison to the attrition of the Western Front cannot be sustained, for attrition was the norm in Italy, the Normandy *bocage* and the jungles of Burma. The major difference between the two wars lies in the fact that the British Army was relieved for long periods from fighting the ceaseless intensive land battles which had characterised the First World War, relying instead on a combination of economic blockade, the Anglo-American bombing offensive and the Red Army to wear down the Germans.[6] The British Army as a regular force did not fight in Western Europe between June 1940 and June 1944, but during this period it fought intensive battles in North Africa, Burma and Italy. The daily casualty rate of Allied forces in Normandy exceeded that of the BEF at Passchendaele in 1917, the figures for Italy and North

Africa came close to those of Normandy, and Archie Elliott's battalion, 2 Scots Guards, suffered more casualties in the Second World War than in the First.[7] The fighting itself could often revive memories of the First World War. The war diary of a Canadian rifle regiment in the Scheldt estuary in late 1944 described the kind of bloody trench warfare familiar to any First World War veteran:

> The past few days have seen the fiercest fighting since D-Day. Lobbing grenades at an enemy ten yards away and continued attempts at infiltration have kept everyone on the jump. Ammunition has been used up in unbelievable quantities, men throwing as many as twenty-five grenades each a night and our own mortar platoon expended 1,064 rounds in three hours.[8]

The main casualties of such attritional warfare, as in the First World War, were the front-line infantry in closest contact with the enemy, particularly the junior officers, who in both wars came mostly from public schools. Eton's war dead in the First World War were 1,157, 20 per cent of those who served; in the Second the figure was 748, or 15 per cent. Among Eton's Second World War dead, 572 were in the Army, mostly junior officers. The casualty comparisons in public schools as between the two wars are surprising and striking, given popular perception of the 'slaughter on the Western Front' and the much lower army casualties of 1939–45 identified above. Analysis of the totals of ten leading boarding schools shows that war deaths in the Second World War were in some schools higher than in the First, and in most cases at least two-thirds of the latter.[9] These figures reflect the toll of lives in the RAF, while higher pupil numbers in some schools post-1918 are also relevant. In both wars public school war deaths, as a percentage of those who served, are considerably above the national average. In the First World War the average figure, from a sample of 185 schools, is 19 per cent, against the national figure of 11 per cent; in the Second, from a smaller sample of eighty schools, it is 13 per cent against a national figure of 7 per cent.[10]

It was again the youngest generation which bore the brunt of the casualties. H.K. Marsden's house at Eton saw about one hundred boys pass through in the 1930s. Twenty-nine were killed, all but six of them aged twenty-five or under and mostly junior officers in infantry or armoured regiments. Forty-six boys can be seen sitting with their housemaster in the 1937 house photograph; thirteen of them were killed, nearly 30 per cent. Henry Hely-Hutchinson was Captain of Marsden's house between the summer of 1943 and that of 1944, when eleven of them were killed, their deaths announced by Marsden at the midday meal, just as his predecessors had done in 1914–18. One was Michael Duberly, aged just twenty, killed by artillery fire in December 1943 in Italy and buried in the cemetery at Cassino, overlooked by the mountain and monastery which were the scene of some of the toughest fighting of the war. On every subsequent reunion of his old boys Marsden would remember their sacrifice in his first toast, *In Piam Memoriam.*[11]

Oxbridge networks were also decimated by the war in roughly the same proportions as public schools, unsurprising considering the overwhelming preponderance of places going to their alumni. It is estimated that 2,857 Oxford alumni were killed in 1914–18, and 1,719 in 1939–45, but 'the latter figure was clearly an underestimate, for one college alone had more than one hundred names to be added to the list.'[12] Maurice Bowra, Warden of Wadham College, found the casualty lists 'a permanent horror', just as headmasters did, while Hugh Trevor-Roper found, on a visit to wartime Oxford, an elderly Christ Church don in tears as he recounted the deaths of so many young men who had made up his reading parties in the years before the war. Eight of Trevor-Roper's own intimate circle of undergraduate friends at 1930s Christ Church were killed in the Army, including five Etonians and Colin Dillwyn (Marlborough), a history lecturer killed fighting in the Dunkirk rearguard. One of the Etonians was Lord Lyell, who had graduated in 1936 and won a posthumous VC in Tunisia in 1943.[13]

Stowe, only founded in 1923, had no comparisons to make with the First World War, but virtually all its alumni served in the forces and 270 Old Stoics died, a death rate of 15 per cent of those who served, more than double the national average. Over half were under the age of twenty-five, and the majority were in the Army, mostly serving as junior or company officers, for the school was not old enough to have many senior officers.[14] One such company officer was Major Jock Anderson, who won the DSO in Libya, and then the VC in the desperate battle of Longstop Hill in Tunisia on 23 April 1943. His citation could have been describing a First World War battle:

As leading company commander he led the assault on the battalion's first objective, in daylight, over a long expanse of open, sloping hillside and through intense enemy machine-gun and mortar fire. Very heavy casualties were sustained, including all other rifle company commanders, before even the first objective was reached … The commanding officer having been killed, he took command of the battalion and led the assault on the second objective, personally leading attacks on at least three enemy machine-gun positions … It is largely due to this officer's bravery and daring that Longstop Hill was captured, and it was the inspiration of his example which encouraged leaderless men to continue the advance.[15]

Anderson's study companion at Stowe was Leonard Cheshire, who won his own VC in 1944, while Cheshire's best friend at Oxford, John Randle (Marlborough), won a posthumous VC at Kohima in 1944.

Considerably fewer Victoria Crosses were awarded in the Second World War – 181 compared with 627 in the First World War. There does not seem to have been a conscious policy to restrict VCs, and the numbers probably reflect the fact that fewer servicemen were in constant active combat roles than in 1914–18. In the Second World War, sixty VCs went to British or Dominion public schools, 33 per cent of the total. This figure includes BRNC Dartmouth, which can claim seven VCs. Eton and Wellington both have five, Sedbergh and Marlborough, three each.[16] Two of Sedbergh's were awarded on the same day in Libya, in November 1941, to George Gunn and John Campbell. Thirty-seven public-school VCs, including all five of Eton's, were won in the Army, twelve in the Navy and eleven in the RAF. All were officers apart from John Harman, the son of the owner of Lundy Island, who went to Clifton and then Bedales. He preferred to serve in the ranks and won his posthumous VC singlehandedly charging a Japanese machine gun at Kohima in 1944.

Public Schools and the Army before 1939

Battlefield leadership has been an obligation for social elites throughout British history, and most officers in the Great War came from public schools because that reflected the hierarchy and preference of the 1914 Army. During the inter-war years the numbers and influence of the aristocracy declined, as politics and the armed forces became dominated more by the upper middle classes.[17] Many more Army officers in these years were being recruited from Wellington or Marlborough than from Eton, although the Brigade of Guards largely remained the preserve of the landed gentry. Attending public school met the Army's requirements in educational and social terms for potential officers, since 'neither Sandhurst nor Woolwich taught leadership as such. It was assumed that by the time a candidate reached either of these two institutions, he had already acquired the necessary social and moral qualities thought necessary for an officer and a gentleman.'[18] Character, for the Army, meant 'a combination of self-restraint, perseverance in the face of adversity and courage in the face of danger'.[19] Pre-1914 professional army officers in fact mostly came from those very few schools with an army class specialising in preparing boys for a military career. The army class at Marlborough, instituted in 1885, had in 1914 twenty-five pupils preparing for entry to Sandhurst or Woolwich. Half the Woolwich cadets in that year came from just five schools – Wellington, Marlborough, Clifton, Cheltenham and Winchester, with Wellington on its own providing about 10 per cent of the officer corps in France with the BEF in 1914.

Military leadership was first taught in public schools through the Officers Training Corps, set up by Lord Haldane's army reforms of 1907. Service in the OTC was virtually compulsory and, along with team sports, contributed to building character in pupils, a key element of the public-school ethos.[20] The OTC was under direct War Office control, specifically to provide a ready supply of officers in the event of war, and it fulfilled that purpose admirably. In the first seven months of the First World War nearly 25,000 officers were commissioned, almost all public schoolboys with OTC experience, and it remained the most important element in the selection of officers until the losses of 1916 forced a widening of the net.

By the 1930s the justification for the OTC was being increasingly questioned. Regard for militarism inevitably declined as hopes for the abolition of war took hold and organisations like the League of Nations Union spread their membership to many school branches. Successive governments became less generous in their funding and younger teachers were reluctant to become involved. The Oxford Union 'King and

Country' debate in 1933 highlighted this growing anti-war sentiment. John Masters, who left Wellington for Sandhurst in 1933, wrote that the Oxford Union motion reflected 'the intellectual climate which surrounded us at our schools and which we still encountered whenever we left the tightly closed circle of the regular army.'[21] Another future soldier, Tommy Macpherson, who became one of the most decorated officers in the war, had to join the OTC at Fettes, but 'I was so ambivalent about the whole exercise that I joined the pipe band in an effort to avoid the most militaristic aspects of the OTC.'[22] However, in April 1939, just before his last term at school, he joined a territorial battalion of the Queen's Own Cameron Highlanders, since he could see a war coming which he could not avoid and which would require him to do his duty. Macpherson went up to Oxford after the war with his three MCs and gained first class honours in PPE and an athletics blue. John Woodcock, cricket correspondent of *The Times*, came the same term straight from St Edward's School and remembered how much he was in awe of Macpherson and other returning war heroes, including one with the VC, Richard Wakeford (Westminster).[23]

Becoming an officer in the regular Army remained as much a public-school preserve in 1939 as it had been in 1914. Eighty-five per cent of entrants to Sandhurst and Woolwich between 1920 and 1939 came from public schools, the major boarding schools accounting for over 60 per cent of these in most years. The ten schools with a dominant grip on Sandhurst and Woolwich entry between 1890 and 1960 were Wellington, Cheltenham, Marlborough, Clifton, Charterhouse, Eton, Haileybury, Harrow, Winchester and Rugby, all of them boarding schools.[24] In 1939 itself, 587 public schoolboys entered Sandhurst, 83 per cent of the total, a reflection also of the number of free or subsidised places given at public schools to the sons of officers right through the inter-war years.[25] In 1900 just 4 per cent of public schools had special admissions procedures for sons of officers, but by 1936 it was 28 per cent.[26] Of 600 boys at Wellington in 1929, 401 were the sons of army officers, the college providing more cadets to Sandhurst than any other school.[27] The former rankers who had been commissioned in 1917–18 widened the social pool, but this trend did not last into the inter-war years, and by 1930 only about 5 per cent of the officer corps were ex-rankers.[28] Both the pre-1939 Army and public schools inhabited closed worlds, with traditions making them impenetrable to the rest of society, perhaps explaining the affinity they had for each other.

John Masters was among those who went from Wellington to Sandhurst in 1933 on a prize cadetship worth £37 per year, which paid most of the fees for the son of an impoverished officer. Those with more substantial means could pay up to £300. At Wellington, Masters had mixed largely with the sons of officers, but at Sandhurst he met a wider social group:

> Some were of the old land, and some of the new breweries and soap factories … Some were here on their way to spend a few years in the Guards or the cavalry, because it was traditional, or because it passed the time while they were waiting to inherit their estates, or because it was their only hope of introduction into decent society … At the other end of the scale there were young men from the lower-middle and working classes who had enlisted in the ranks and had then been selected as officer material.[29]

Sandhurst had many of the codes of behaviour, and the brutality, found in contemporary public schools; cadets had their own ways of settling 'crimes' such as lying, stealing or 'seeking the limelight', and pranks and fights were not uncommon. Masters passed out of Sandhurst as top cadet for the Indian Army, the destination of choice for many poorer cadets because of its higher pay and lower regimental costs, and sailed for India in 1934 to join the 4th Gurkhas, an experience evoked in his classic memoir, *Bugles and a Tiger*.

Public Schools and the Wartime Army

Conscription was introduced in April 1939 for the first time in peacetime, and in September 1939 all British men between the ages of eighteen and forty-one became liable for call-up. The volunteering spirit of 1914 gave way to a more ordered system in which public-school alumni with OTC experience could no longer go straight to a regiment with a commission but had to spend time in the ranks and at Officer Cadet Training Units (OCTUs). Men who volunteered before they were called up could opt for the service of their choice; throughout the war, more volunteered for the RAF and Royal Navy than these services required, leaving the Army to pick up the rest. Freddie Scott from Fettes described a typical cultural shock experienced while serving time in the ranks:

> Of the thirty-odd people in my platoon, only one other had been to public school and 'spoke proper'. He had, when I arrived, already been nick-named 'The Dook'. This meant that I got away without being ridiculed for being posh. The others were mainly from London and had been given the option by the court of joining the army or being sent to a young offenders' prison known as Borstal.[30]

The Army's preference for public-school alumni as officers did not alter much under the new regime. In the first two years of the war, the only selection procedure for OCTU candidates was a short interview with a senior officer, along with a report on their suitability for a commission. The interview and report focused more on family connections, sporting pursuits and character than on brains and application, so the Army restricted their intake of potential officers as far as possible to the same social and educational pool as before the war. It was soon clear, however, that the number of officer candidates from this source was not large enough. The spirit of the 'People's War' also meant that the Army was criticised for any 'Blimpish' attitudes. In January 1941 one OCTU commanding officer wrote to *The Times* complaining that too many commissions were being given to men from the lower classes: 'Man management is not a subject which can be taught; it is an attitude of mind, and with the old school tie men this was instinctive.'[31] He was swiftly removed from his post, but 'Colonel Blimp' was believed to have many allies in officers' messes, and there was criticism of the government, following early military setbacks, for allowing class privilege to count for more than merit in officer selection. Such attitudes are seen in correspondence relating to Major Warwick Thompson (Brighton), who was killed in Burma in July 1945. Thompson had a spell in the ranks in 1940 and was then commissioned. A note from a brigadier on his discharge papers from officer training displays the snobbery of the time: 'My dear Forester, a very nice boy I know wants to enlist in your regiment – was at Brighton College – has a lot of friends in the ranks. He is the son of a bookmaker but different class to the ordinary run.' The papers were marked 'suitable for India'.[32]

In April 1942, in response to this criticism, the War Office set up new officer selection boards, including, for the first time, psychologists and psychiatrists. The interviews lasted three days, with many psychological tests, and by the end of the war 60,000 officers had passed, of whom only 12 per cent were subsequently deemed wholly unsatisfactory. This instilled a new belief that the officer corps was not just a snobbish elite, while applications for commissions rose by a quarter over the 1939–41 level.[33] It also represented the abandonment of the Army's idea that leadership was socially inherited, or the preserve of a particular class, in favour of intelligence and psychological testing. Alex Bowlby (Radley) had been earmarked as a potential officer since his school was one of those from which the Rifle Brigade traditionally chose its officers. During his squad training in the ranks, his platoon sergeant became so infuriated with his ineptness that he rammed his face into Bowlby's with the words, 'If you ever get a commission, my prick's a bloater!'[34] His selection board interview with the psychiatrist did not go well, it was decided that he was not really officer material and he served in the ranks in Italy, his fellow riflemen cheerily suggesting that the money spent on his education had been badly wasted.

In the judgement of the historian Jeremy Crang, 'the People's War might have brought army and nation closer together but in many ways the Army remained a nation apart.'[35] That was certainly so in the Guards regiments, whose officers, virtually without exception, came from elite boarding schools. Nigel Nicolson, who joined the Grenadiers from Eton and Balliol in 1939, found himself subject to arcane codes of behaviour, including not being allowed to carry any bag, parcel or book, and being forbidden to discuss in the mess women, religion or politics.[36] In the Guards such traditions supposedly created pride and discipline, but they could get in the way of progressive thinking about warfare, while social barriers counted for little when officers had to prove their worth in action. Tradition and snobbery also existed in the smarter Yeomanry regiments like the Sherwood Rangers, where the peacetime officers in the 1930s came from the landed and hunting class, many of them Etonians, and the men were largely their estate workers.[37] The regiment was one of the last to give up its role as horsed cavalry, only making the reluctant conversion to armour in 1941.

A fascinating insight into the ethos of the Sherwood Rangers, and of the uneasy class relationships among officers, came from the waspish pen of Keith Douglas, the war poet. At Christ's Hospital Douglas was a scholar and rebel who enjoyed arguing the toss with the headmaster and was in trouble on many occasions. Surprisingly, he also enjoyed the OTC and, after a year at Oxford and then Sandhurst, was posted to the Middle East in February 1941 to join the Sherwood Rangers. It would have been difficult to find any regiment more unsuited to Douglas's personality, as 'he did not hunt, fish or shoot, he knew no one in Nottinghamshire, and the qualities of his school and background – intellectual excellence, literary depth and classlessness – meant little to these country gentlemen.'[38] Douglas regarded the regiment as a closed, outdated gentlemen's club and took every opportunity to make this point, while his fellow officers found him insufferably knowledgeable and recklessly outspoken. He could not resist provoking them and secretly gave each of them nicknames in his notebooks, including the commanding officer, 'Flash' Kellett (Cheltenham), a Conservative MP, whom he christened 'Piccadilly Jim'. Kellett was a man used to giving orders and expecting to have them obeyed without compunction, but Douglas insisted on bringing to his notice every regimental and tactical shortcoming he found, together with plenty of suggestions for their improvement. After a couple of months Kellett solved his problem by having Douglas posted away to a position on the staff as a camouflage specialist.

In October 1942 Douglas was still languishing in Cairo, while the Sherwood Rangers prepared for El Alamein. Unable to stand inaction any longer, he told his batman he was going forward to join the battle. The batman replied very succinctly: 'I like you, sir, you're shit or bust, you are.'[39] Douglas absented himself from his Cairo duties, drove west towards the sound of guns and reported to Kellett. The regiment had already suffered heavy casualties in men and tanks, and Douglas was forgiven and sent to command a troop of three Crusader tanks. In January 1943, near Tripoli, he was lucky to survive an armour-piercing shell which came through his tank's turret and set it on fire. He bravely rescued his driver, who was badly burned, and wrote later of the terrifying landscape populated by those who had lost their tanks and now hid in deserted German gun pits as the shells whizzed overhead. Others could be seen crawling towards cover, brutally wounded or burned beyond recognition.

'One artillery officer lay there', Douglas wrote later, 'his face strained and tired with pain. His left foot was smashed to pulp, mingled with the remainder of a boot. I spoke to him: "Have you got a tourniquet on you, Robin?" and he replied apologetically, "I'm afraid I haven't, Keith".'[40] This 'obsolescent breed of heroes' Douglas was later to celebrate in his poem *Aristocrats*.[41] While in hospital after being seriously wounded, Douglas read that Colonel Kellett had been killed: 'Piccadilly Jim was an institution: it seemed impossible that in a moment a metal splinter had destroyed him. He was killed as one might say, typically, while he was standing up in his tank, shaving under shellfire.'[42]

The true test of all young officers came in battle. The more refined methods of selection, and what was learned at OCTUs and GHQ Battle Schools, meant that young officers joined their regiments better trained than their predecessors, but still untried in battle. The leadership and stoicism expected of platoon and company officers differed little from that of the previous war, although the weaponry they faced was even more powerful, especially the potent German mortars and anti-personnel mines. In attack, the historian David French has written that 'the most important role of junior officers was, by their personal example, to give their men the momentum to go forwards and, a much more difficult task, to give them a renewed forward momentum if they had gone to ground before they had reached their objective.'[43] Effective battlefield leadership by junior officers was probably the single most important factor sustaining men in combat. Sydney Jary (Chigwell), joining 4th Somerset Light Infantry in Normandy as a platoon commander to replace heavy officer losses, was determined to lead from the front so that he could take immediate charge in the event of enemy contact. He believed that soldiers had to have faith in the professional ability of their officers and 'trust them as men'.[44]

In the most intensive battles, the casualties among junior officers were as heavy as on the Western Front in 1916. In the North-West Europe campaign, officers suffered 26.5 casualties per 1,000 men per month, compared to 19.6 for other ranks, and between June and November 1944 about one-third of rifle platoon commanders became casualties each month.[45] Dwin Bramall (Eton) landed on Juno Beach in Normandy on 7 June 1944, commanding a platoon of 2nd King's Royal Rifle Corps

(KRRC) for his first experience of combat, aged twenty. He had gone straight from Eton to nine months in the ranks, where his later military career benefited from irritation at being 'on the receiving end of bloody stupid orders'. His platoon were battle-hardened veterans from campaigns in North Africa and Italy, the platoon sergeant reassuring him: 'You'll be all right, sir. We'll look after you.' 'I knew,' Bramall said, 'that I had thirty pairs of eyes staring into the back of my head and that was all the encouragement needed to make sure I got it right.'[46] About Normandy he recalled later the occasion when he was wounded, a shell landing on top of the truck beneath which he was sheltering with another officer:

> I happened to be an Etonian and he was an Harrovian. I remember him saying to me: 'Do you think we have had it?' and at that moment there was a crash and the thing came right through the vehicle and burst underneath. When the dust had settled and I looked down, he was dead, completely black from head to foot as he had taken the full force of the blast.[47]

Bramall was wounded twice and won an immediate MC in Belgium, before going on to a glittering military career.

In armoured regiments casualties were generally lower than in the infantry, but still heavy in Normandy. In the Norman *bocage* tanks had to lead attacks down narrow lanes with no hope of avoiding the armour-piercing rounds of the infantry-controlled *Panzerfaust*. For Stuart Hills (Tonbridge), a twenty-year-old troop commander with the Sherwood Rangers, 'The sight of a burning tank was terrible to behold. Because the fire was contained within the armoured hull, flames and smoke were forced out of the turret with some strength and velocity. Then, if the shells stored inside were exploding, the smoke came out in puffs, assuming the form of symmetrical rings with a baleful beauty all their own.'[48] The Sherwood Rangers lost forty-four officers killed and wounded in Normandy, their full establishment being only thirty-six. The regimental padre, Leslie Skinner, had the awful task of clearing out destroyed tanks: 'Cleared what was left of Johnnie Mann's tank and two others brewed up yesterday. Fearful job searching ash. Remains broken and scattered in the tank. Two orderlies helping me had to give up.'[49]

The battlefield leadership of young officers could make the difference between success and failure in an attack. Charles Upham, from Christ's College in New Zealand, set an outstanding example to be followed by tens of thousands of others.[50] Upham, an agricultural student in peacetime, won the Victoria Cross in Crete as a platoon officer in May 1941. The citation highlighted what was required of junior officers – 'outstanding leadership, tactical skill and utter indifference to danger'. In one of several actions

> he commanded a forward platoon in the attack on Maleme and fought his way forward for over 3,000 yards unsupported by any other arms and against a defence strongly organised in depth. During this operation his platoon destroyed numerous enemy posts … in one, under heavy fire from a machine-gun nest, he advanced to close quarters with pistol and grenades, so demoralising the occupants that his section was able to mop up with ease.[51]

Upham became the only fighting soldier ever to be awarded a second Victoria Cross, for an action at Ruweisat Ridge in North Africa in July 1942, the VC citation recording that his 'personal bravery had become a byword in the whole of the NZEF'.[52] Taken captive, he became a difficult prisoner, ending up in Colditz, and only received the news of his second VC in September 1945 while sitting for a portrait commissioned by Christ's; characteristically, he put the telegram in his pocket without telling the artist. In his funeral eulogy to Upham in 1995, Field Marshal Lord Bramall identified the qualities needed by junior officers – 'the will to face danger and take risks, the will to decide under pressure, the will to win and, above all, in the execution of his perceived duty as a New Zealand officer, the will, if need be, to lay down his life'.[53]

Commanders

What of those who commanded this wartime army? Popular myth made the Western Front generals into the villains of the First World War, incompetent, uncaring and profligate with human lives, despite the famous victory they won in 1918. By contrast, the generals of the

Second World War have been treated less harshly, although from 1939 to 1942 they presided over a string of defeats. Whereas First World War commanders were criticised as 'cavalry generals', those of the Second almost all came from the infantry or artillery, reflecting their experience of the Western Front. Virtually all of them were from public schools, and a limited number of schools at that. None had been to university, but several were gifted linguists – Edmund Ironside (Tonbridge) and James Marshall-Cornwall (Rugby) both spoke seven languages, and many others were bilingual in either European or Indian languages. Archibald Wavell (Winchester) wrote and anthologised poetry and was hugely well read in the art of war, although he never hit it off with Churchill, who regarded him as 'a bookish Wykehamist of excessive caution and inclination to pessimism'.[54]

In 1913 59 per cent of lieutenant generals and upwards had been to public school, although some others had been 'educated privately' at crammers, but by 1939 the figure had increased to 82 per cent (with 73 per cent coming from major boarding schools).[55] The opportunities for high command were fewer in 1939–45, with only fourteen British divisions, three Canadian and one Polish in Normandy in 1944, as against sixty British and Dominion divisions deployed on the Western Front in 1918. Apart from Montgomery, few names of British Second World War generals resonate today with the general public. Arthur Percival (Rugby) achieved the greatest notoriety by surrendering Singapore, while Claude Auchinleck (Wellington) and Harold Alexander (Harrow) presided over the turning of the tide in North Africa, and Alexander went on to command all the Allied armies in Italy. In Burma William Slim (KES Birmingham) carved out a formidable reputation and seems to be the only public-school general of significance not to have attended one of the major boarding schools. The other odd man out is Alan Brooke, the wartime CIGS and Churchill's closest military adviser, whose home was in Ulster and who was privately educated at Pau in France, an agreeable area for climate and hunting, thus escaping the school conditioning which was the background of virtually all his contemporaries.

Bernard Montgomery, commanding Allied land forces on D-Day, took great delight in the fact that the headquarters for his 21st Army Group in the months before D-Day was in his old school buildings, St Paul's at

Hammersmith, he himself occupying the headmaster's office. The final invasion plan was presented to George VI, Churchill and Eisenhower in the school's lecture theatre on 15 May 1944, the school itself having been evacuated to Wellington. At Alamein in November 1942, and then in Normandy, Montgomery applied the doctrines of 1918 to win his battles, insisting on a master plan rigidly followed, and using artillery to batter his opponent and minimise casualties. This strategy derived from his experience on the Western Front as junior officer, but also from the realisation that the stock of manpower available to the British Army was limited and dwindling, especially in Normandy. If reliance on overwhelming firepower meant that the slow pace of advance was sometimes criticised, it ensured that the human cost was kept within acceptable bounds, which is probably the main reason why Montgomery's reputation, for all his personal faults, soars above that of Haig in the public mind. In contrast with the dour Haig, Montgomery also had a genius for public relations and promoting the image of himself and his army. Success ensured that the reputation of some of Montgomery's subordinates has also been high, such as Miles Dempsey (Shrewsbury), who commanded Second Army in Normandy, and Brian Horrocks (Harrow), badly wounded in North Africa, who was given the task of leading the spearhead XXX Corps in the last months.[56]

The general who arguably had most influence on the post-war world was Ronald Adam (Eton), the Adjutant-General, who believed that in a modern democracy soldiers had the right to know for what they were fighting. He set up in 1941 the Army Bureau of Current Affairs (ABCA) to provide compulsory weekly education for the troops. ABCA gave soldiers background political information and in the process strengthened their motivation to fight. Political discussion of this kind would have been anathema to First World War generals, who made sure that such issues were kept well away from the rank and file. When Labour won the 1945 election, the Conservatives concluded that ABCA must have been a left-wing plot, and it is sometimes quipped within the Army that the Army Education Corps, within which ABCA sat, has only one battle honour, the 1945 General Election.

Irregular Warfare

In the First World War irregular warfare had been limited to the exploits of Lawrence of Arabia and the Zeebrugge Raid of April 1918, but in the Second there were many more opportunities for individual enterprise in formations like the Commandos, Long Range Desert Group (LRDG), Special Air Service (SAS), Special Boat Service (SBS) and the Chindits. These units attracted an extraordinary mixture of volunteers, including many school rebels and free spirits looking for something more enterprising than traditional soldiering. The officers were both pre-war regulars and wartime conscripts, and to an even greater extent than in the Army as a whole, public-school alumni were dominant. In the aftermath of Dunkirk, Churchill looked for ways to maintain the offensive spirit by striking back at the enemy in daring raids: 'Enterprises must be prepared with specially trained troops of the hunter class. I look to the Chiefs of Staff to propose to me measures for a vigorous, enterprising and ceaseless offensive against the whole German occupied coastline.'[57]

The first force to emerge from Churchill's order was the Commandos. In June 1940 Lieutenant Colonel Dudley Clarke (Charterhouse), Military Assistant to the CIGS, looked to the example of the Boer Commandos in South Africa for his model of what the force should be. He raised ten Commandos in June and July 1940, each consisting of about 500 officers and men, bulldozing his way through a regular Army reluctant to give up any of its best men. Clarke's list of further war credits included providing the name for the SAS in the Middle East, thinking up the idea of having an actor 'double' for General Montgomery as part of the deception plans for D-Day, and being involved in Operation Mincemeat; no wonder General Alexander said that he had probably done more than any other single officer to win the war.[58]

Commando troop officers were all volunteers with a sense of initiative, mental toughness, tactical sense and, above all, adventurousness. They were predominantly ex-public school in the first years of the war, as in the rest of the Army, but came from a wide variety of military and non-military backgrounds. No. 8 Commando, led by Lieutenant Colonel Bob Laycock (Eton), had a particularly patrician complement, with an assortment of maverick volunteers. One of the troops was led by Captain

Mervyn Griffith-Jones (Eton), who was later to be a prosecuting counsel at Nuremburg and then moralist-in-chief at the Lady Chatterley trial of 1960. Others included those who were to form the basis of the later SAS like David Stirling (Ampleforth), Carol Mather (Harrow), George Jellicoe (Winchester) and Jock Lewes (King's Parramatta), but also less soldierly types in Randolph Churchill (Eton) and Evelyn Waugh (Lancing). For their training at Lochailort in Scotland, Stirling recruited rugged instructors including his cousin and fellow Amplefordian, Lord Lovat; Mike Calvert (Bradfield), a professional soldier and Army boxing champion who later found fame with the Chindits; and Freddie Spencer Chapman (Sedbergh), explorer and mountaineer who was to survive three years behind Japanese lines in Malaya. Waugh dedicated *Officers and Gentlemen*, the second volume of his *Sword of Honour* trilogy to 'Major-General Sir Robert Laycock, that every man in arms should wish to be'. Most of the officers in the trilogy are easily recognizable public-school types, from Tommy Blackhouse, loosely based on Laycock, to Brigadier Ben Ritchie-Hook, always trying to 'biff' the enemy, whose model was Major General Adrian Carton de Wiart (Oratory), who won the VC in the First World War and was wounded seven times.

Irregular warfare was not for the faint-hearted. Geoffrey Appleyard (Bootham), an international skier, volunteered for No. 7 Commando and wrote about the unit before he died in action: 'It is the greatest job in the Army that one could possibly get … no red tape, no paperwork, just pure operations, the success of which depends principally on oneself and the men one has picked oneself to do the job.'[59] As well as the wartime volunteers, there was also a strong leavening of hardened professional soldiers and pre-war Territorials. Corran Purdon, from Campbell College and Sandhurst, was commissioned as a regular into the Royal Ulster Rifles in 1939 before volunteering for the Commandos, and Donald Roy from Fettes had been a pre-war Territorial in the Liverpool Scottish.

Both took part in the most celebrated Commando exploit, the March 1942 raid on the French port of St Nazaire, which had the only dry dock capable of taking the battleship *Tirpitz*. Leading the Commandos on that night was Lieutenant Colonel Charles Newman, who came from Bancroft's, a school with deep roots in the local Essex community and little in the way of social pretensions. A civil engineer and pre-war Territorial in the Essex Regiment, his easy-going manner and soft voice concealed his fierce determination and popularity with his men in No. 2 Commando, when he formed it in 1940. One remembered a boxing match Newman attended between the Commandos, whose officer-man relations were less than formal, and a neighbouring artillery unit with strict protocol. When Newman entered, the whole Commando rose and belted out: 'Clap hands, here comes Charlie, good old Charlie, here's our Charlie now!' Newman grinned and turned with his hands clasped in the air like a prize-fighter, acknowledging the acclaim of his men, while the artillery officers looked on in disbelief.[60] The St Nazaire Raid was successful in destroying the gates of the dry dock used for major warships, but casualties were very high, 168 Commandos killed or captured out of 241 who took part. Newman was awarded the VC, along with the two most senior naval officers on the raid, both public-school Special Entry cadets to Dartmouth in Robert Ryder (Cheltenham) and Stephen Beattie (Rugby).

David Stirling proved to be an outstanding leader of irregular forces, 'one of those people who thrive in war, having failed at peace'.[61] He came from a wealthy landed family in Perthshire and was sent to Ampleforth, where he achieved no great distinction, followed by Cambridge, where he made little effort to do any work. After a year, the master of his college told him that he was being sent down and invited him to choose the three offences meriting expulsion (out of twenty-three) which 'would be least offensive to his mother'.[62] In the next few years he travelled the world trying various jobs before coming back to Britain in 1939 to join the Scots Guards. He found the training tedious and spent most of his time carousing at White's Club, where he heard for the first time about the Commandos and joined Laycock in No. 8. He went out to the Middle East with him, but again became frustrated at the difficulty of getting into action and began to develop the idea for the SAS.

His main collaborator was Jock Lewes, a high achiever at Australia's oldest school, King's Parramatta, and President of the Oxford University Boat Club. Lewes, who joined the Welsh Guards in 1939 and then No. 8 Commando, was very much the opposite of Stirling in character, workaholic and ruthlessly ambitious, but they shared a burning wish to get into action.[63] Together they tried a parachute jump, which nearly killed Stirling and left him with back pain for the rest of his life. While in hospital, they collaborated on a plan to infiltrate small groups of men behind German lines, from the desert side, to attack vulnerable lines of communication and airfields. They would use the adapted vehicles of the LRDG, a reconnaissance unit set up in 1940 by Ralph Bagnold (Malvern), a former professional soldier and pioneer between the wars of the exploration of the North African desert.

For Stirling to persuade the military authorities of the viability of his plan was a problem, as the Army elites did not look kindly on the irregular forces drawing away many of their best men, or on such forms of unorthodox warfare. He characteristically decided to bypass the usual channels and went straight to General Auchinleck (Wellington), the C-in-C Middle East, who happened to be an old friend of his father. At the end of their meeting Auchinleck authorised him to raise an initial force of six officers and sixty men, and it was Dudley Clarke who gave the unit the SAS name as part of his wider deception plans. The first raid, on five airfields, took place in November 1941, and by the end of the war the SAS had carried out operations all over German-occupied Europe.[64]

The amphibious equivalent of the SAS was the Special Boat Service, commanded by George Jellicoe (Winchester), the son of Admiral Lord Jellicoe who had commanded the British fleet at Jutland in 1916. Jellicoe had joined No. 8 Commando in White's Club and had also become frustrated at lack of action in North Africa, so moved to Stirling's SAS. In April 1943 he was given command of one of the four SAS squadrons, which was renamed the SBS, and he led it in attacks throughout the Aegean and finally in Greece. Jellicoe had much in common with Stirling in leadership skills and a vision of how irregular warfare could be conducted to support broader strategy. He later admitted to having had 'rather a good time during the war'. Raids on airfields and being dropped on enemy-held islands was 'rather exciting and one enjoyed above all the fellowship'.[65]

In the Burma campaign appeared the most influential and controversial leader of irregular forces, Orde Wingate. A boy at Charterhouse in the First World War under Frank Fletcher, Wingate endured unsuccessful and certainly unhappy schooldays; during free time, when most boys played cricket or football, he would go to the chapel and pray, an occupation regarded as unwholesome by staff. He spent much of the inter-war period as an artillery officer in the Middle East, where he became an ardent Zionist, organising 'Special Night Squads' of irregular Jewish fighters against the Arabs. Posted to the Far East in March 1942, he was tasked with creating a long-range jungle penetration unit to fight behind Japanese lines in Burma, and the first of two Chindit operations was launched in March 1943. Opinions of him were diametrically opposed; some thought him a dangerous, unstable maverick whose schemes consumed men at an appalling rate. Others, including Churchill, saw him as a brilliant if eccentric leader of unconventional operations. Wingate was the only leader of irregular forces 'who both planned and then carried out behind-the-lines special operations at the level of general officer' and who had also made and won his case to the Allied Combined Chiefs of Staff, and personally to both Churchill and Roosevelt.[66] John Masters, who took part in the Second Chindit operation in 1944, has left this portrait of him:

> His sense of mission and his rightness were genuine and deeply felt. He was a prophet of the Lord and those that stood against him were to be thrown down like the traitors they were. He had a driving will of tremendous force. His character was a blend of mysticism, anger, love, passion and dark hatred, of overpowering confidence and deepest depression. He could make all kinds of men believe in him and he could make all kinds of men distrust him.[67]

Within the various irregular forces there can be found examples of all those characteristics which give public-school alumni a bad name, including the power of old school tie networks, languid effortlessness and the attractions of belonging to elite institutions. Unlike their father's generation on the Western Front, there was also a fierce individualism and determination to make a difference, to break the normal rules of warfare and take the battle to the enemy in imaginative and daring ways. Many in these units who survived the war unsurprisingly struggled to find anything remotely as interesting in the peace which followed. David Stirling, who was captured in the desert in January 1943, made five escape attempts before being sent to Colditz. His post-war career was never likely to be particularly humdrum and included running a secretive security company, training men for African and Middle East rulers, and GB75, set up in the aftermath of the 1974 miners' strike as 'an organisation of apprehensive patriots' who would keep essential services running. The SAS he founded expanded into the most famous elite military regiment in the world, and Stirling was knighted in 1990 by an establishment which revered him as a wartime warrior.

Prisoners of War

The number of British PoWs taken in the Second World War was greatly in excess of 1914–18.[68] Between 1939 and 1945 the British Army had 259, 621 taken prisoner, more than were killed, and the RAF and Royal Navy added another 20,000 to that figure. Life at a boarding school has often been jokingly if inappropriately equated with captivity, Evelyn Waugh reflecting in *Decline and Fall* that 'anyone who has been to an English public school will always feel comparatively at home in prison'. In an episode of the television drama *Tenko* about imprisonment in the Far East, one male character spoke similarly about life in Changi prison in Singapore: 'In many ways Changi was like a public school, only a million times worse. We were all chaps, there was no privacy, even the way we behaved and the kind of jokes we cracked.' His woman friend, who had also been interned, agreed: 'There was choir practice and discussion groups, loss of privileges for letting the side down, a leader instead of prefects.'[69] Leonard Wilson, the Bishop of Singapore, compared his internment with his time at school, at St John's Leatherhead. He was subjected to weeks of torture in 1943 by the Kempeitai, the Japanese secret police, suspected of being implicated in operating a secret radio. He was badly beaten and left without food and water, before his torturers finally gave up when they saw they could not break him. He later wrote to his headmaster to say that Leatherhead had been a good preparation for a Japanese prison, whereupon the dry and unsympathetic reply came back on a postcard, 'I'm glad we had our uses.'[70]

Robert Kee, who left Stowe in 1937 and became a noted post-war broadcaster and journalist, was captured when his plane was shot down in 1942. For him the 400 square yards of the prison camp had features just like school. There were people to keep you in, libraries where you could read, classes for learning, chapel every day if you wished, and games on the sand outside, but also shortages of food, no women, remoteness from the outside world and ignorance of how long your imprisonment would last.[71] School rituals were reproduced, like the Old Uppinghamian dinner at Chungkai on the Burma railway in April 1944, while team games were just as important to prisoners as they had been at school. At Colditz 'stoolball' was invented, a cross between rugby and the Eton Wall Game and described by Pat Reid (Clongowes Wood) as the roughest game he ever played. In camps in the Far East 'Jim' Swanton (Cranleigh), doyen of cricket journalists, organised matches between England and Australia. One match at a camp in Thailand in 1945 was later recorded in *Wisden*, the winning England team helped by their fast bowler, Captain 'Fizzer' Pearson (Sedbergh), wearing a pair of boots, the only player with anything at all on his feet.[72]

At Colditz, a prison camp where public-school codes of behaviour were particularly dominant, about 500 British and Dominion officers were incarcerated, along with French, Polish and Dutch. Most of them were either prisoners with prominent backgrounds such as Lord Lascelles (Eton), nephew of King George VI, and Earl Haig (Stowe), son of the Field Marshal, or men who had escaped from other camps and were then sent to supposedly escape-proof Colditz. It was the ultimate challenge for those intent on escaping, and over thirty successful 'home runs' of great daring were made, along with many more unsuccessful schemes. Airey Neave (Eton) achieved the first successful home run by a British officer from Colditz..

Ellison Platt, a Methodist chaplain in Colditz, was a sharp observer of behaviour. He noted that 'the British community are of bolder spirit and larger initiative than their fellows in other camps.'[73] But he also disapproved of the way in which 'certain elite sets have segregated themselves'. The regular officers, who had almost all been to one of the major boarding schools, looked down on their Territorial counterparts, while 'the Eton set were another separatist coterie. They ate together; paced the exercise ground in twos, threes and fours; attended the same lectures; and went to the lavatory together. They were not offensively separatist, but sufficiently exclusive to be noticeable.'[74] Michael Burn, a left-wing Wykehamist captured at St Nazaire, recalled that the class structure in Colditz mirrored outside society – orderlies from the working class, middle class officers from public schools, and several lords of the realm. On arrival he was asked to join 'a very smart mess nicknamed the Bullingdon, after an exclusive club at Oxford. It was made up of the sons of landed gentry, and a few lords, but none of them knew that I had been blackballed from the real Bullingdon when I was at Oxford before the war.'[75] The humour of Colditz came straight from the prep school playbook, schoolboy pranks or 'goon-baiting', often brilliantly subversive mockery designed to undermine German authority.

Airey Neave complained at the imposition of the British military and class systems, with senior officers considering would-be escapers to be disturbers of the orderly life of the camp. For Neave the strongest motive to escape came from the 'animal desire to be free from any form of imprisonment'.[76] For others it was like a dangerous sport, 'where freedom, life and loved ones are the price of victory, and death the possible but not inevitable price of failure'.[77] In March 1942 three serial escapers arrived in Colditz. Michael Sinclair (Winchester), Ronnie Littledale (Eton) and Gris Davies-Scourfield (Winchester) had all been captured on the fall of Calais in May 1940. In 1941 they escaped together from a camp in Poland and remained on the run for several months before being captured and sent to Colditz. Littledale did eventually make it out of Colditz in October 1942 with Pat Reid (Clongowes Wood) and Billy Stephens (Shrewsbury), a naval officer captured at St Nazaire, and they reached Switzerland.[78] Sinclair was equally determined to get back to the war and made several attempts to escape from Colditz, including one in which he was lowered out of the window on 90ft of bedsheets. In January 1944 he heard that his Wykehamist younger brother John had been killed at Anzio, and Davies-Scourfield noticed how profound an effect this had on him, making him moody and introspective. He wrote to his former Winchester housemaster, Malcolm Robertson, in March 1944: 'It is a great blow about our John to us all. My mother and father are taking it all very bravely … Like so many others he did what he had to do – and did it nobly. It makes one feel even more useless here than usual.'[79] On 25 September 1944 Sinclair scaled the wire fence in the exercise field and was shot dead when he refused to stop.

The main organiser of the 'Great Escape' from Stalag Luft III in March 1944 was Roger Bushell (Wellington), a fighter pilot shot down over Dunkirk. Seventy-six officers escaped, and the Germans executed fifty as a reprisal, including Bushell, Anthony Hayter (Marlborough), Tom Kirby-Green (Dover), Denys Street and Cyril Swain (both from Mill Hill), James Catanach (Geelong GS), Ian Cross (Churchers) and Alistair Gunn (Fettes). Jimmy James (King's, Canterbury) survived but was sent to Sachsenhausen concentration camp. He tried to shut out the horror by focusing on memories of his school days at Canterbury and the 'vast and beautiful Cathedral which dominated our lives but taken for granted by most of us boys ... It now seemed to come back out of the past to cast a protective shroud over me in this satanic place.'[80] With James in Sachsenhausen were two other recaptured officers – Harry Day (Haileybury) and Sydney Dowse (Hurstpierpoint) – and together they managed to escape by tunnel from Sachsenhausen before being recaptured in Berlin and subjected to further torture. Dowse enjoyed an adventurously romantic life after the war, remarking that 'once one escapes from Sachsenhausen, life holds no difficulty'.[81]

The sharpest end of the prisoner war was in the Far East. Anthony Chenevix-Trench, classical scholar at Shrewsbury and Oxford, and later headmaster of Eton from 1963 to 1970, was badly scarred by what he endured on the Burma railway. Captured at Singapore while serving as an officer with an Indian artillery unit, he spent a year in Changi before being sent to work on the railway, where he contracted malaria, beri-beri and dysentery, as well as losing an eye and suffering kidney problems. He returned to teaching after the war at Shrewsbury and then as headmaster of Bradfield before going to Eton in 1963, and then Fettes in 1971. His headmasterships coincided with many battles in public schools between the forces of tradition and youthful rebellion, but the task for Chenevix-Trench was made all the harder by the demons of his wartime experience. His malaria came back and he turned to alcohol for relief. Further controversy arose over his readiness to use 'corporal punishment not as a last rcsort, but almost as the first resort in punishing boys'.[82] At Fettes he refused to give the school's Remembrance Sunday sermon, telling the chaplain, 'I can't do it because a colleague of mine was crucified.' His health finally gave out in 1979, when he died aged sixty, still in post at Fettes, but in his last years 'the past returned with a vengeance, its bitter memories an eerie curse upon the present'.[83] Such was the terrible reality of prison life in the Far East, its similarity to school confined only to those old jokes.

The Sharp End of War

The front-line soldier of the Second World War endured hardship and suffering in equal measure to his predecessors in the First. Unfortunately for historical balance, what he later wrote about these experiences is less well known than the more celebrated memoirs of the First World War trenches, although Raleigh Trevelyan's memoir of Anzio, *The Fortress*, deserves a wider readership. Historians like John Ellis have attempted to put this right, concluding that, in every respect except the totality of casualties, the two wars at the sharp end of battle were very similar. Fighting up the spine of Italy across rivers and mountain chains, against an enemy well dug in and determined to resist any advance, was particularly gruelling, especially in the terrible winter conditions of 1943–44. George Nangle (Sedbergh) won the DSO commanding 1/9 Gurkhas during their eight days' and nights' ordeal to secure Hangman's Hill, a shoulder of the mountain close to the Cassino monastery. They dug in on an exposed cliff-face in midwinter, largely unprotected against icy winds and driving rain, while constantly under German fire. When they finally withdrew, just eight officers and 177 other ranks were left from the 400 who had taken the position. Rifleman Alex Bowlby (Radley) missed through illness a battle in Italy in which many of his friends were killed and only one officer in the battalion was left unwounded. In a post-war visit to the battlefield he found the place where his section commander had stepped on a mine and been blown to bits, forcing Bowlby cathartically to revisit his wartime experiences and remember his dead comrades: 'You've been dodging the column, running away from the pain and guilt of being alive when the best are dead.'[84] Such sentiments echo memories of the earlier war.

For those taken prisoner, especially in the Far East, demons also had to be grappled with when peace returned. Peter Walker (Blundells) was tied to a stake as a punishment and forced to look at the sun for hour after hour. His post-war life was affected by permanently damaged eyesight, a digestive system wrecked after years of near starvation in prison camp and regular screaming nightmares as he relived his ordeal.[85] David Piper (Clifton), later a celebrated art historian and museum director, remembered the acuteness and urgency of hunger in Far East prison camps as 'the essential governor of survival; only when it faded could despair overwhelm fatally and the man would turn his face to the wall and simply surrender life and die.' Piper, like the gifted and lucky soldier writers of the First World War, knew the frivolity of fate at the sharp end of war: 'Often I am shaken with wonder at being alive. War taught me the fickle lightness of life, as prison camps taught me the frail tenacity of survival.'[86]

The First World War left its mark on a generation of politicians who came to prominence in the 1930s, and the Second World War was no different. Anthony Eden and Harold Macmillan lived with the knowledge that over a thousand of their fellow Etonians had been killed in 1914–18. Eden's biographer, Richard Thorpe, said of him that 'as a survivor of the lost generation, he felt it incumbent upon himself to work to create a better world. Idealism not cynicism was the legacy Eden drew from his experiences in war, and this unsentimental sense of responsibility for the welfare of others was always to condition his thinking.'[87]

Willie Whitelaw (Winchester) was the last political survivor of the post-1945 Conservative MPs who saw service in the Second World War. To have had a good war was an advantage to advancement in the Conservative Party after 1945, as it had been after 1918; others who benefited included Airey Neave (Eton), Enoch Powell (KES Birmingham) and Lord Peter Carrington (Eton). Whitelaw's own background personified the violence of war, his father and three uncles all killed in the First World War. He rose to the rank of major in the 6th Guards Tank Brigade, saw his second-in-command killed before his eyes when his tank was hit in Normandy and won the MC himself in an action in which one-third of the tanks in his squadron were destroyed. In 1955 he entered Parliament, rising to the Cabinet as Secretary of State for Northern Ireland during the Troubles. He had imbibed loyalty both at Winchester and in the Army and he refused to stand against Edward Heath in the first ballot of the leadership election in 1975, when he probably would have won. Thereafter, he was unswervingly loyal to the new leader, Margaret Thatcher, and particularly during the Falklands War gave her wise counsel and unflinching support, despite doubts, derived from his own experience, about sending men into another war.[88]

The war which Willie Whitelaw fought in Normandy was as violent and costly as the one in which his father died and Anthony Eden fought, but he represents a public-school generation for whom battlefield leadership was again an obligation to be shouldered uncomplainingly, bolstered by the values learned at school of courage and duty. Whitelaw, like Eden, used the experience of war to inform his political thinking and, as a survivor of his generation's war, to take responsibility for trying to create a better world.

Chapter 5

The Secret War

Within the Admiralty Citadel building on Horse Guards Parade lay the Operational Intelligence Centre (OIC), windowless and dank. From January 1941 Commander Rodger Winn RNVR ran the Submarine Tracking Room within OIC, perhaps the most important naval command centre in the war. Here on the walls were graphs of merchant ship and U-boat sinkings, the progress of new construction and details about every U-boat which put to sea. Winn sat for fourteen hours a day in front of a large table with a chart of the North Atlantic, assimilating information from Bletchley decrypts, agents' reports in the Atlantic submarine bases, calculations of the speed of convoys, the limits of Allied air cover and U-boat positions marked by coloured pins – red for a firm fix, white for a sighting. He drove himself to the point of physical collapse, using his legal training to fit together fragments of information about convoys and U-boats and exercising his judgement in deciding how to protect the vital convoys. A colleague wrote of Winn's 'uncanny flair for guessing a U-boat's behaviour' and described during running convoy battles 'the intense intellectual labour that went into this battle of tactics'.[1]

Rodger Winn was no crusty old salt. Afflicted with polio as a child, which left him with crippled legs and a permanent stoop, he went to school at Oundle. He left in 1922 to read law at Cambridge, was called to the Bar in 1928 and became a barrister of exceptional talent.[2] At the outbreak of war he volunteered for service to interrogate German prisoners but, still a civilian, was assigned to naval intelligence and to the Submarine Tracking Room. His intuitive understanding of U-boat tactics was so good that he was given the role of running the tracking room in January 1941 with temporary rank of Commander, an almost unprecedented promotion for someone with no formal naval training and within so traditional a service. The intelligence effort paid rich dividends:

between May 1942 and May 1943, 105 out of 174 convoys crossed the Atlantic without interference and, out of the 69 sighted, 53 escaped with little or no loss.[3]

The story of Winn and OIC demonstrates one of the most important British successes of 1939–45, the mobilisation of intellect to support the war effort in intelligence-based roles. This was in marked contrast to 1914–18, when men disappeared into the great mincing machine of the Western Front without much note being taken of where their talents might have been used to greater effect. Professor Harry Hinsley, Bletchley veteran and author of the official history of the British intelligence services in the war, was asked whether amateurs contributed more than intelligence service professionals and answered: 'Of course they did. You wouldn't want to suppose, would you, that in peacetime the best brains in our society wasted their lives in intelligence.'[4] Bringing together those 'best brains' depended on the existence of school and university networks, but these same institutions also produced public-school alumni who actively sought to undermine national security.

Intelligence is a subtle and fluid commodity, and although the intelligence war could not of itself ensure Allied victory, its contribution helped to affect outcomes in many theatres. The newcomers played roles as diverse as agents in the Special Operations Executive (SOE), creators of deception plans, and code-breakers at Bletchley Park. Britain's war effort was made up of many more component parts than in the Great War, when the Army could claim in 1918 to have been the backbone of the drive for victory. This time the British battlefield contribution was increasingly subordinate to that of the Russians and Americans, but in the secret war of intelligence they held their own and had some spectacular successes.

School and University Networks

Recruitment into intelligence roles, in many different forms, bore witness to the power of school and university networks. Networking contacts and skills are an important part of what public schools and Oxbridge give their pupils, and they are still used to access professional and social networks, based on a shared social code and experience. In wartime intelligence roles the 'old school tie' could be a force for good, for instance in bringing together an intellectual galaxy at Bletchley Park, but it could also go spectacularly wrong, as evidenced by the 'Cambridge spies'. The personnel of the Special Operations Executive contained a disproportionately high number of people educated at public schools. In the official history of SOE, the author M.R.D. Foot, himself a Wykehamist, published their schools against their names, defending this on the grounds that readers could make their own judgements on a man's competence and character by knowing to which school he had gone.

Oxbridge, another institutional network from which intelligence operatives were recruited in large numbers, was itself dominated by public schools. In the figures for Oxford undergraduate entry from 1909 to 1913, the average for public schools is 74 per cent, with another 13 per cent from direct grant schools, mostly within HMC.[5] The other 13 per cent came from a mixture of private crammers, overseas public schools and schools in some way maintained by the state. It is difficult to speak of 'state schools' before 1914 since virtually none were fully maintained by the state. The dial had shifted a little for undergraduate entry to Oxford by 1938. The figure for public schools dropped to 62 per cent, for direct grant schools it remained at 13 per cent, for 'maintained' schools it was 19 per cent, and 5 per cent came from 'other' schools, mostly Dominion public schools.[6] It is reasonable to conclude that the figures for Cambridge will have been very similar. Seventy-eight per cent of scholarships to Oxford in 1938 went to candidates from public schools, about one-third of these in classics and helped by the existence of closed scholarships, those tied by trust to a specific school, which favoured public schools by a ratio of sixteen to one.[7] The social composition of colleges could vary, but forty-six out of forty-eight freshmen at Trinity, Oxford, in 1934 came from public schools, with just two from grammar schools; Winchester accounted for seven of them, Eton for six, Dominion public schools for four, and virtually all the others came from prestigious boarding schools.[8] Entries to Brasenose, Oxford between 1909 and 1923 were mostly from the more prestigious boarding schools, led by Charterhouse with 32, Winchester 24, Eton and Malvern 23, Harrow 22, and Rugby 21.[9]

The Oxbridge college system further embedded the public-school ethos in its undergraduates, the two being virtually interchangeable.

According to the historian of Oxford University, Brian Harrison, public-school dominance was 'more than numerical: it was cultural, political, athletic and social', while Oxbridge 'reinforced the networks of those who came from the same school and further spread them to new friends from other public schools.'[10] College life was overwhelmingly male, and subject to the same innumerable quasi-monastic regulations as boarding schools. Rules were strictly enforced by university officers in the shape of 'proctors' and 'bulldogs', and by deans and porters in college – city pubs out of bounds to undergraduates, guests ushered out of college by twelve o'clock, women by ten o'clock, and misdemeanours punishable by 'gating'. The rules strengthened the closed society of the college, with undergraduates not allowed to sleep out during term. Inter-war bump suppers left a trail of destruction as public-school men 'asserted their authority in semi-tribal style', often targeting those with aesthetic, intellectual or left-wing tendencies.[11] Readers of *Decline and Fall* will recall 'the sound of English county families baying for broken glass' at the annual dinner in Oxford of the 'Bollinger Club'.[12] Each college had its own chapel and its own team sports, while school OTC training could be continued in the university OTC and air squadron. Tutorials prioritised moral values, with the institution of the moral tutor, akin to a public-school housemaster, lasting until the 1960s, when cultural change and anti-authority sentiment began to kill it off.

At Oxford, Christ Church, Magdalen and Trinity were particular bastions of patrician predominance. In 1920 one-fifth of the Christ Church entry and one-sixth of Magdalen's came from Eton alone.[13] New College had particularly strong links with Winchester, Christ Church with Eton and Westminster. Hugh Trevor-Roper found when he came to Christ Church from Charterhouse that he was surrounded by the 'effortless self-assurance of Etonians or the intellectual repertoire of boys from Stowe, who would casually drop the names of Marx or Freud, while I could only quote Sophocles or Seneca.'[14] Academic success was certainly not everyone's ambition, for it was more important to have been 'up' than to have been examined, and the 'pass degree' was perfectly acceptable socially. Louis MacNeice, who came to Oxford from Marlborough in 1926, wrote that 'we products of the English public schools came to Oxford either for sport and beer-drinking or for the aesthetic life and cocktails.'[15]

The public-school generation which went to Oxbridge in the inter-war years dominated wider cultural and academic circles during those years and beyond. At Oxford, the classicist Maurice Bowra, who had disliked his time at Cheltenham College, was described by Freddie Ayer as 'by far the most influential don in the university'.[16] He brought into his circle some of the most brilliant students of the inter-war years, almost all of whom had been to major public schools, including Noel Annan (Stowe), Evelyn Waugh (Lancing), Anthony Powell (Eton), Hugh Gaitskell (Winchester) and Isaiah Berlin (St Paul's). For most of his undergraduate acolytes 'Oxford was an interim stage between single-sex boarding schools and adult heterosexuality.'[17] Bowra preached freedom of thought to those who recoiled from the mores of the older generation, epitomised by headmasters' denial of individual liberty and repressive attitude to sex. Many of these young men, through their common background and connections, found their way into intelligence work in the war.

The struggle for national survival in the Second World War brought brilliant civilians into every branch of the intelligence services to join the professionals already there. They brought with them cerebral cunning, mathematical genius, linguistic gifts and sheer individual derring-do, to add to the intelligence skills of the pre-war professionals. The dominance of public schools in peacetime intelligence networks and at Oxbridge suggests that most of the key players came from them, and the role of school and university networks in recruitment was vital. One of the key figures using these networks to bring students into intelligence work was John Masterman (Dartmouth), history don at Christ Church, who went on to mastermind the Double Cross System within MI5, turning German spies into double agents for Britain. Masterman was 'like a character in a John Buchan novel, an easy-going bachelor don, well connected with those in power, and assiduous in helping pupils of whom he approved to find jobs'.[18] It was no coincidence that Christ Church students with the intellectual abilities of the historians Hugh Trevor Roper (Charterhouse) and Charles Stuart (Harrow), and the philosophers Gilbert Ryle (Brighton) and Stuart Hampshire (Repton), all found themselves by 1941 in the Radio Security Service within SIS. Nor was it coincidence that school and university networks also brought together the 'Cambridge Spies' from some of the most elite boarding schools – Kim Philby (Westminster), Guy Burgess (Eton), Donald Maclean (Gresham's) and Anthony Blunt (Marlborough) – who did such damage to Britain's interests.

Intelligence Networks

In 1909 Britain's historic intelligence-gathering operations were formalised by the Foreign Office in the creation of the Secret Service Bureau. From this emerged organisationally the 'foreign' section, specialising in the collection of intelligence from abroad on behalf of its parent department, the Foreign Office, and the armed services. It became known as the Secret Intelligence Service (SIS) or Military Intelligence 6 (MI6), and was led by Mansfield Smith-Cumming (Dartmouth). The 'home' section, dealing with counter-espionage in Britain, working with the Home Office and the Special Branch of the Metropolitan Police, was called the Security Service or MI5, and was led by an Army officer, Vernon Kell, educated at a military crammer. Smith-Cumming found recruitment to his fledgling organisation difficult in a war when young men wanted to do their bit in battle, but he used familiar networks to find men like the physicist Thomas Merton (Eton), who was rejected for military service on health grounds. Another with all the right connections was Colonel Freddie Browning, who had been at Wellington, won an Oxford blue at tennis, was a member of MCC and independently wealthy. He was a director of the Savoy Hotel and head of intelligence at the Trade Office, but now in effect became Smith-Cummings's deputy.

SIS emerged from the Great War with a reputation unmatched by any other secret service, but it mouldered in the inter-war years. Squeezed funding, with only moderately able men in charge, meant that it struggled to secure useful intelligence from Europe. Its leadership in these years came from pre-war Dartmouth. Smith-Cumming, who led SIS from 1909 to 1923, was succeeded by Admiral Sir Hugh Sinclair, the former Director of Naval Intelligence, who bought Bletchley Park with his own money in spring 1938 to become the home of the Government Code and Cypher School (GC&CS). Recruitment into SIS relied on familiar networks, with two Etonian army officers also playing an important leadership role in the form of Stewart Menzies and Desmond Morton, who became one of Churchill's main sources of intelligence about German rearmament. Menzies took over as head of SIS in 1939 and brought in two wartime deputies, long-serving intelligence officers who too often saw their task as protecting their SIS patch from rivals – Colonel Valentine Vivian, St Paul's-educated former Indian policeman, and Lieutenant Colonel Claude Dansey, professional soldier and intelligence officer from Wellington College. Menzies' chief achievement in the war was to recognise the importance of signals intelligence and what was going on at Bletchley, but he was regarded as a limited man.[19] The Duke of Buccleuch, who had been Menzies' fag at Eton, later told Hugh Trevor-Roper that none of his contemporaries could understand 'how so unbelievably stupid a man could have ended up in such a position'.[20] Trevor-Roper himself came to see SIS as 'a closed inward-looking society, recruiting by patronage', its members tending to be either rich men of limited intellect or unimaginative soldiers or policemen who 'could not begin to comprehend the new techniques of scientific intelligence made possible by the systematic study of radio intelligence'.

The recruitment into SIS in 1938 of Nicholas Elliott, son of the Eton headmaster, demonstrates how school networks could operate. Elliott left Eton in 1935 to go to Cambridge, but on leaving there in 1938 had no great idea of what he wanted to do. During an old boys' cricket match at Eton, a family friend and fellow Etonian, Sir Nevile Bland, approached Elliott and observed that the young man's father was concerned by his son's inability to get down to a solid job of work. Bland offered to take him to the Hague, where he had recently been appointed British Minister, as his honorary attaché. Elliott gratefully agreed and later wrote: 'There was no serious vetting procedure. Nevile simply told the Foreign Office that I was all right because he knew me and had been at Eton with my father.'[21] Within a year, Elliott had been moved into SIS after a meeting at Ascot races with Sir Robert Vansittart, another friend of his father and a diplomat with close links to SIS.

MI5 was less in thrall to public-school networks. The next two Directors after Vernon Kell, when he was sacked in 1940, had both been in the Indian Police, a service that had more in the way of 'heterogeneous backgrounds, thoughtful opinions and versatile minds', along the lines of Kipling's wily Lurgan Sahib in *Kim*.[22] They had some success in the

1930s in infiltrating and monitoring fascist networks, but the Home Office refused to issue warrants to intercept the communications of Sir Oswald Mosley (Winchester), leader of the British Union of Fascists, because they believed he was 'a sincere patriot who posed no threat to national security, despite the fact that he married his second wife at a private ceremony in Goebbels' drawing-room, attended by Hitler'.[23] Such was the influence of the 'old school tie'.

Public-school networks played an important role in recruitment to MI5 before and during the war. Two future Directors General, Dick White (Bishop's Stortford) and Roger Hollis (Clifton), were recruited as officers in the 1930s, the former in 1934 while teaching at Whitgift and helping to run a public-school tour to Australia with Malcolm Cumming (Eton), who had been recruited the previous year. Cumming wrote to Kell that, although White was likely to go to the top of the teaching profession, 'he often wishes that his work could bring him into closer touch with world affairs'. Once the war started it was reported that 'each officer tore around to rope in likely people. When they knew none themselves, they asked their acquaintances.' The result was a remarkable array of academic, legal and other talent, much of it from public schools via the traditional networks. They included Victor Rothschild (Harrow), one of Britain's most gifted polymaths, who founded MI5's first counter-sabotage department, and Martin Furnival-Jones (Highgate), who became Director General in 1965. The number of officers grew very rapidly by such methods, from 36 in July 1939 to 332 by 1943.[24]

In 1940, a man whose activities would damage severely the reputations of both security services joined SIS. Kim Philby (Westminster) had been recruited by the Soviet spy network at Cambridge in 1934. After Cambridge he worked as a foreign correspondent for *The Times* but in 1940 was recruited into SIS, the vetting procedure resting on the same networks which had helped Nicholas Elliott. MI5 conducted a routine background check and found nothing, and Valentine Vivian, deputy head of SIS, who had known Philby's father when they were both colonial officials in India, vouched for him in these terms: 'I was asked about him and I said I knew his people.' Philby joined Section V of SIS, the division devoted to counter-intelligence with a remit to liaise with MI5 to warn of espionage threats to Britain. He was made head of the Iberian section, particularly important in the espionage war with Germany. Vivian had another lunch with Philby's father before Kim took up his role, asking him again about his son's politics and suggesting he had been a bit of a communist at Cambridge. 'Oh, that was all schoolboy nonsense', St John Philby replied. 'He's a reformed character now.'[25]

Women were plentiful in MI5 and MI6, but mostly in subordinate clerical roles, and it was to be many years before attitudes within the intelligence community changed sufficiently to allow women like Stella Rimington (Nottingham HS) and Elizabeth Manningham-Buller (Benenden) to reach the top echelons.[26] The first woman recruited by MI5 was Jane Sissmore (Princess Helena College, Ealing), who joined as a clerk in 1916 but in 1929 was put in charge of investigating Soviet subversion. She had a formidable reputation as an interrogator, so much so that Kim Philby recognised her as 'perhaps the ablest intelligence officer ever employed by MI5'.[27] In 1940 she was sacked from MI5 after accusing the acting director of incompetence in not recognising the scale of Soviet activity. She was immediately re-employed in SIS in a section concerned with Soviet counter-intelligence, of which Philby became head, but he managed to sideline her into activities in which she could not uncover his treachery.

Some of the most effective intelligence operations involved deception strategies and were run by a mixture of intelligence professionals from SIS and MI5, and talented amateurs. The seeds were sown by Colonel Dudley Clarke (Charterhouse), who had founded the Commandos in 1940. He went out to the Middle East as an intelligence officer and became the main instigator of deception schemes there and in other theatres. It was said of him that 'a small acorn planted by Dudley Clarke in December 1940, in the shape of a few bogus units in the Western Desert, was to grow into a massive oak tree whose branches included the non-existent British Twelfth Army in Egypt and the First United States Army Group in England before D-Day.'[28]

The most elaborate operation was the Double Cross system devised by John Masterman and Lieutenant Colonel Thomas 'Tar' Robertson (Charterhouse), an MI5 inter-war professional described by Hugh Trevor-Roper as 'a real genius, with a knack of knowing how to spot a lie and how to tell one'.[29] This plot involved rounding up all known German spies in Britain, turning them into double agents and letting them send their German controllers a diet of misinformation which played an important part in wider deception plans for the invasion of Europe. Operation Mincemeat was another such operation, involving the planting of fake documents on a dead body to wash up on the southern shore of Spain in 1943 in order to convince the Germans that, following the capture of North Africa, the Allies would be launching an invasion of Greece rather than the real target, Sicily. The devisers were two 'amateurs', Ewen Montagu (Westminster), a barrister working in wartime naval intelligence, and Charles Cholmondeley (Canford), an RAF officer seconded to MI5. Montagu had been recruited by the Director of Naval Intelligence on the basis that 'only men with first class brains should be allowed to touch this stuff', and his colleagues in the department included men from the same background – 'two stockbrokers, a schoolmaster, a journalist, an Oxford classics don and a collector of books on original thought'.[30] The commander and first lieutenant of HMS *Seraph*, the submarine which transported the corpse of 'Major Martin, Royal Marines' and released it into the sea off Huelva, were Bill Jewell (Haileybury) and David Scott (Tonbridge). Montagu wrote his own version of the story, declaring that the dividends from the operation, especially in terms of lives saved, were 'far greater than we had imagined in even our most sanguine moments'.[31]

MI9, another small intelligence network set up in December 1939, facilitated the escape or evasion of prisoners from enemy territory and had a considerable impact in relation to its small size. Its head was Brigadier Norman Crockatt (Rugby), professional soldier in the Great War and then a stockbroker. Jimmy Langley (Uppingham), who lost an arm at Dunkirk, joined as his assistant, as did Airey Neave after his successful escape from Colditz. MI9 set up escape lines in Belgium and France, with the help of SOE, and produced aids for prisoners of war. One of those MI9 helped to escape was Etonian naval lieutenant David James who, supplied by MI9 with maps of German docks, escaped from a camp in full RNVR uniform and carrying a forged identity card in the name of 'Lt. I. Bagerov of the Royal Bulgarian Navy'. James described it as 'a name that will be remembered long after my own is forgotten'.[32] He hid in a Finnish ship at Danzig and made it to safety in Stockholm.

Meritocracy was not the criterion in recruiting for the intelligence services; secret organisations could not advertise openly for recruits, and it was only rarely questioned whether those from outside the magic networking circles might do a better job if selected. The two services were different in the networks they used, MI5 tending to recruit police officers and soldiers while SIS was more public-school and Oxbridge: 'SIS was White's Club, MI5 was the Rotary Club; MI5 was "below the salt", a little common, while SIS was gentlemanly, elitist and the old school tie; MI5 were hunters, SIS were gatherers.'[33] So much of what both services stood for reflected Britain's never-ending class skirmishes. Networks could be built from shared experiences at university, in regiments and certain elite professions like the Bar, but school networks were arguably the strongest, for they were built on loyalty to the codes and institutions which upper middle-class and aristocratic young men had experienced in their upbringing. When Nicholas Elliott reflected in later life on the treachery of Philby, who had been a close friend, 'one of us', he never ceased to wonder how 'someone who had been educated as he had, someone he had known extremely well over an extended period, could have chosen such a radically different path.'[34]

Special Operations Executive

SOE evolved out of Section D of SIS, which had been set up in April 1938 to organise sabotage, propaganda and subversion against Nazi Germany. In 1940 Section D's organisation and much of its personnel moved into SOE, set up on the express orders of Churchill in July 1940 'to set Europe ablaze' by assisting the people of occupied countries to resist. SOE was put under the control of the Ministry of Economic Warfare and its first political master was Hugh Dalton, wealthy Etonian Labour MP whom Churchill disliked but thought would be effective in running a 'dirty war', dubbing him the 'Minister for Ungentlemanly Warfare'.[35]

In common with other intelligence operations, recruitment was built around the familiar networks. The historian of SOE in the Far East, Charles Cruickshank, wrote that 'the early staff lists of SOE abound with names of graduates of the public schools and older universities did not reflect a conspiracy on the part of the old boy network, nor did it necessarily mean that those selected were not as well qualified as others. It was an inescapable fact of life.'[36] SOE's organisational leadership initially came from these networks. Frank Nelson (Bedford), a former MP who had also worked for SIS, was the first Director of SOE, to be succeeded in 1942 by Sir Charles Hambro, an Etonian businessman. Dalton was replaced as Minister of Economic Warfare in 1942 by the Earl of Selborne (Winchester), a former Conservative MP and minister who was a friend and fellow member of Churchill in the Other Club.

Such elderly office warriors from the pre-1914 generation lacked the drive and ruthlessness necessary to run guerrilla campaigns. That was provided by the main military man in the organisation, its Director of Operations, Major General Colin Gubbins, who had left Cheltenham to serve in the Royal Field Artillery in 1914–18. This army background belied his undoubted gifts, since he was fluent in French and German and had a working knowledge of Russian, having served there in 1919. He had seen further service in Ireland against Michael Collins and Sinn Fein, which had taught him much about irregular warfare. He joined military intelligence in the 1930s, and Section D of SIS in 1938, writing a definitive pamphlet on guerrilla warfare which was distributed through SOE in sixteen languages during the war. In 1940 Gubbins was put in charge of raising the 'Auxiliary Units', the British resistance to a possible German invasion.

When Hambro retired as Director of SOE in 1943, Gubbins succeeded him and became one of the heroes of the intelligence war. Gladwyn Jebb (Eton), SOE's former executive officer, wrote of him, 'I have seldom met a man more vigorous and a more inspiring soldier or incidentally possessing a more political sense. He is the lynch pin of the existing machine.'[37] The whole SOE operation under Gubbins exuded vigour and military precision. Its size by 1943 – about 13,000 personnel, of whom 5,000 were agents – made effective organisation from the top essential, and in general terms that was achieved, each occupied country having its own section and control. Powerful forces in Whitehall, including the Foreign Office and SIS, disapproved of SOE, which was often called 'the mob' or 'the racket', and there were certainly tragic mistakes in not spotting German infiltration of SOE operations in Holland and France, but Churchill liked unorthodox warfare and gave his strong support to SOE and Gubbins.

In looking for people to serve under him, Gubbins used his own school and military networks to find those who would know how to survive in tough environments. They included adventurers like Peter Fleming (Eton) who, as a travel writer with a first in English from Oxford, had explored the Amazon and crossed Central Asia, and Martin Lindsay (Wellington), a professional soldier who had led the Trans-Greenland expedition in 1934. Fleming's war was a series of exciting adventures in irregular warfare and military deception operations, his glamorous reputation enhanced by marriage to the actress Celia Johnson (St Paul's Girls'). Another recruit was Bill Hudson, a tough South African from St Andrew's, Grahamstown, who spoke six languages, had worked as a mining engineer in Yugoslavia before the war and was a sabotage expert sent back to Yugoslavia by SOE. Gubbins claimed to have picked up tips from Al Capone in what he called 'hitherto unthinkable methods of warfare'.[38] At the SOE training school in Scotland, he employed two ex-Shanghai policemen, Sykes and Fairbairn, to teach silent killing with a commando knife, a remit opposed by more fastidious people within the Whitehall establishment. When he first requested the RAF's help to put a party into France to kill some of the Luftwaffe's pilots, Air Chief Marshal Portal objected to the ethics of 'this entirely new scheme for dropping what one can only call assassins'.[39]

In SOE headquarters Gubbins broke with convention by using women as administrators to control the secret files of each country. One male officer visiting the Baker Street headquarters of SOE remembered the 'scores of refined, chatty, intelligent gentlewomen of impeccable pedigree who hailed from large mansions in the Home Counties'. One of these was Sue Ryder (Benenden), who worked in the Polish section and said that Gubbins' conviction that 'women were better at doing this work than men' won him few friends in the Whitehall establishment.[40] Joan Stafford-King-Harman, who had boarded at Abbot's Hill School in Hertfordshire, came out as a debutante in 1935 and at the outbreak of war was recruited into the naval section of MI6. She wrote later that 'people were always asking me if I knew of anyone else who would like to come and work for them, so one collected up friends and friends of friends.'[41]

SOE was no different from other secret organisations in not being able to recruit openly by advertising. In wartime, school and university networks still counted for something, but most recruits for dangerous roles, or jobs in SOE where foreign languages were needed, came from the other branches of the armed services, especially people already known to existing staff. This did have its disadvantages. Brigadier Terence Airey, serving on the staff in Cairo, was brought a cup of tea one day in 1941 by an NCO he recognised as the cleverest boy he had known at his school, Gresham's. He had him promoted to major and to a desk job with SOE serving the Balkans, but his school acquaintance was James Klugmann, secretary of the Cambridge University Communist Party in the 1930s, something which a routine security trawl did not pick up and which would certainly have debarred him from a role in intelligence.[42]

Collecting human intelligence on the ground in occupied countries required linguistic ability and political acumen, but also great courage. No intelligence agent had more of these qualities than Frank Thompson, who entered Winchester in 1933 where he became fluent in nine languages and a committed socialist determined to take a stand against fascism. Some of this derived from his family background; his father was an Oxford don specialising in Indian history and languages, while his brother was E.P. Thompson, the historian of English radical movements. Thompson spent a year at Oxford, where he joined the Communist Party, before joining up and serving in North Africa and Sicily. On the ship to Sicily Thompson attended a church service at which one of the hymns was *All People that on Earth do Dwell*. He wrote of this experience:

> It was a hymn with rich Wykehamical memories. I found Winchester
> a good thing to remember at this time. The teaching we had there
> gave us next to no idealism, but instead, and equally helpful, a
> strong intolerance of all folly, especially of folly which involves
> cruelty. Further, its long history gave us some sense of proportion,
> reminding one at every turn of one's own unimportance.[43]

Thompson's knowledge of Slavic languages led to his being recruited into SOE in Cairo in August 1943 by James Klugmann, by then in charge of the Yugoslav section. After parachute training, Thompson asked to be transferred to the Bulgarian section, a country under fascist rule since 1923, closely allied to Germany and which viciously suppressed Communist partisans. On the night of 25 January 1944, with a wireless operator and a large supply of weapons, he was parachuted into southern Yugoslavia to join the Bulgarian partisans. From the beginning the mission was beset with logistical difficulties of re-supply and the weakness of partisan forces. In mid-May Thompson and about a hundred poorly trained Bulgarians, calling themselves the Second Sofia Brigade of National Liberation, crossed the border into Bulgaria. They were ill-equipped and, as it turned out, could not rely on local support. On the night of 22 May locals betrayed them, and many in the party were killed in an ambush. Thompson managed to escape but nine days later he was taken prisoner. His admitted Communist sympathies and fluent Russian and Bulgarian did not go down well with his interrogators, who tortured him and refused to allow him prisoner-of-war status. He spoke out against fascism at his brief trial, was condemned to death and executed by firing squad on 10 June 1944. Five months later, over fifty thousand people attended a ceremony to re-bury him and the other partisans in a common grave, where a tombstone now reads 'Major Frank Thompson, Englishman'. In Bulgaria, where a village and streets are named after him, he has become an emblem of anti-fascist heroism.

SOE operatives often needed to cope with complex local politics, particularly in Yugoslavia. Here the opposition to the German occupiers had been made worse by a brutal civil war between the royalist Chetniks led by General Mihailovic and Tito's Communist partisans. Mihailovic wanted to maintain the Serb-dominated Yugoslav kingdom, Tito to overturn it through revolution. Those sent to liaise with Tito and Mihailovic had to be expert linguists and consummate politicians, and both liaison missions contained men of outstanding gifts as well as strong political connections. Jasper Rootham (Tonbridge), a double first in classics at Cambridge and one of Chamberlain's private secretaries, was dropped by parachute into Serbia with the British mission to Mihailovic. He was fluent in Russian and Serbo-Croat and spent a year helping the Chetniks with military operations against the Germans, pleading their case to SOE and through it to Churchill. Sent to liaise with Tito were two men with even closer links to Churchill – Bill Deakin (Westminster), Oxford history don who had helped Churchill research his *Life of Marlborough* before the war, and Fitzroy Maclean (Eton), a former diplomat, Conservative MP and officer in the SAS, who was told personally by Churchill that he was 'simply to find out who was killing the most Germans and suggest means by which we could help them to kill more'.[44] It was Tito who received the backing, so that Deakin and Maclean proved to be two of the most influential secret agents of the war, for persuading Churchill to throw the weight of British political influence and supplies behind a communist.

For SOE operations on Crete it was the public-school and Oxbridge classical networks which brought together many of the personnel. Paddy Leigh Fermor (King's, Canterbury) later wrote of himself and other public-school adventurers on Crete that 'it was the obsolete choice of Greek at school which had really deposited us here ... the army had realised that the ancient tongue, however imperfectly mastered, was a short-cut to the modern.'[45] Crete was captured by the Germans in May 1941 after a ferocious airborne assault. The island had strategic importance for operations in North Africa and the Balkans, and the Germans kept 70,000 troops there in 1943 which could have been deployed elsewhere. One of the reasons for the large number of troops was the effectiveness of the Cretan resistance, marshalled by only a dozen SOE operatives. They conducted sabotage operations before disappearing into the mountain range down the spine of Crete, and the Germans were never able to stop these attacks, however large their garrison. SOE operatives in Crete managed a successful campaign with nothing more than their creative wits, periodic re-supply of arms and the determination of the Cretan resistance, in the process forcing the Germans to squander time, money and manpower which could have been used elsewhere. It was a perfect demonstration of the value of unconventional warfare.

The first person to galvanise the Cretan resistance was John Pendlebury, who had been at Winchester in the 1920s and had a first with special distinction in archaeology at Cambridge. A Fellow of the Royal Society, his main archaeological work was in Crete, which he knew better than any other Englishman, not only from the dig at Knossos but from roaming the countryside and getting to know its people. He joined military intelligence in 1940 and transferred to SOE. When the Germans invaded Crete, Pendlebury was in Heraklion organising Cretan irregulars to help in its defence. He was a man of splendid contradictions

– an Oxford academic who relished the role of irregular soldier, leaving his glass eye on his desk to indicate that he was away conferring with local chieftains. He was described as 'a splendid figure, with a rifle slung like a Cretan mountaineer's, a cartridge belt round his middle and armed with a leather-covered swordstick … One could understand why everyone trusted, revered and loved him.'[46] He was wounded in an air attack and carried into a nearby house, where the Germans found him, an English soldier dressed in a bloodstained Greek shirt and with no identification, so they propped him up against a wall and shot him.

Pendlebury became the heroic figure of Cretan resistance against which all later activity was judged. Leigh Fermor wrote of him:

> At first his body was buried near the spot where he fell. Later, the Germans moved him to half a mile outside the Canea Gate beside the Rethymnon road. I remember bicycling past his grave the following year dressed as a cattle-dealer. To the SOE officers who were sent to Crete to help the Resistance, he was an inspiration. His memory turned all his old companions into immediate allies. [47]

The SOE officers who followed him mostly came from the same background, including Mike Stockbridge (The Perse), C.M. 'Monty' Woodhouse (Winchester), a double first in classics at Oxford and later a Conservative MP, then Tom Dunbabin (Sydney GS), Fellow of All Souls and one of the foremost classical scholars of his time.

Paddy Leigh Fermor, expelled from King's, Canterbury for serial misbehaviour in 1931, was more the romantic adventurer. After leaving King's, he decided to walk across Europe, and his charm ensured that everywhere barriers fell and arms were opened, especially female ones. He left Moldova in September 1939 to join the Irish Guards with a typically nonchalant view of his prospects: 'I had read somewhere that the average life of an infantry officer in the First World War was only eight weeks, and I had no reason to think the odds would be much better in the Second, so I thought I might as well die in a nice uniform.' The verdict of his commanding officer in 1940 was dismissive but also prescient: 'Quite useless as a regular officer, but in other capacities will serve the army well'.[48]

He survived evacuation from Greece and then from Crete, before being sent back to Crete as an SOE agent in June 1942. He stayed on the island until sent back for a rest to Cairo in October 1943, where he hatched an outrageous plot to kidnap the German General Müller, responsible for reprisal atrocities in Crete. He enlisted a housemate, Billy Moss (Charterhouse) from the Coldstream Guards, and they landed back in Crete in January 1944. Müller had been replaced by General Kreipe, but the ambush and abduction went ahead on 26 April, Moss driving the General's car through twenty German checkpoints to a safe house before they marched him across the island to a submarine rendezvous and back to Egypt. It was a remarkable feat of arms, one that boosted Cretan morale and entered SOE folklore, but higher command considered that some operations did more to fulfil the fantasies of its adventurous young officers in the field than to hasten Allied victory.

In representations of the secret war in popular culture, it is France which tends to take centre stage and female agents who have captured the popular imagination. SOE's French section was run by an Old Etonian in Maurice Buckmaster, but most of his female agents came from Anglo-French parentage and unconventional backgrounds. Odette Hallowes was born and brought up in France and only connected with England when she married an Englishman in 1931, moving to England at the start of the war and joining SOE in 1942. Her exploits, celebrated in book and film, have made her a more famous figure than the man she worked with and later married, Peter Churchill, whose background was of the more conventional kind – school at Malvern, modern languages at Cambridge and the Diplomatic Service. Female agents worked mostly as couriers or wireless operators, whereas their male counterparts offered military leadership and skills in irregular warfare. Francis Cammaerts (Mill Hill) and George Starr (Ardingly), a pre-war mining engineer in Belgium, led by mid-1944 military forces of several thousand French *maquisards* in their circuits on the left bank of the Rhone and in Gascony respectively. Cammaerts had been recruited to SOE through his friend and fellow schoolmaster in Beckenham, Harry Ree (Shrewsbury), who himself parachuted into France with SOE in 1943.[49]

In the Far East, SOE, known here as Force 136, was hampered by the difficulty for white Europeans of melting into the local population and by political opposition from those opposed to any moves that might result in the restoration of the British Empire in Malaya or Burma. One who overcame these problems was the 'Naga Queen', Ursula Graham Bower (Roedean), who had travelled out to the Naga Hills in the north-east of India in 1937 and fallen in love with the area and its people. In 1940 she returned to live in a Naga village to carry out anthropological studies, and in 1942, as the Japanese army advanced through Burma and threatened India, she was asked to form the Nagas into a band of scouts in an intelligence role, sending back information and laying ambushes of Japanese patrols, leading to the creation of what General Slim called 'Bower Force'.

Freddy Spencer Chapman, who survived three years in occupied Malaya, supported by Chinese communists, vividly described the embarrassment of relying for his survival on people who had lost all confidence in Britain. SOE attracted men and women who had a strongly individual streak, often previously revealed at school in battles with authority, and none more than Spencer Chapman, a school rebel who had loathed the monotonous bell-regulated routine of Sedbergh. After Cambridge he became a mountaineer and explorer in places as diverse as Greenland and Tibet, and taught at Gordonstoun, where headmaster Kurt Hahn said to him, 'If I am going to teach my boys to live dangerously, I might as well put them in the hands of someone who has made a practice of it all his life.'

During the Japanese invasion of Malaya he carried out sabotage raids behind enemy lines but found himself cut off in the jungle when Singapore fell, and then lived in Chinese communist jungle camps. Not until late 1943 did Force 136 re-establish contact with him and bring him to safety by submarine.

Bletchley Park

It was the galaxy of academic talent at Bletchley Park, the home of Government Code and Cypher School (GC&CS), which produced the most valuable contribution of the intelligence war. From here a stream of decrypts, known as Ultra, allowed the Allies to decode and read many of the communications between enemy commanders in the field and their higher commands. GC&CS had been set up in 1919 under the control of SIS, an amalgamation of army and navy code-breaking from the Great War, and not surprisingly school and Oxbridge networks played a large part in recruitment. Four of the leading Great War code-breakers in naval intelligence were Etonians – Dilly Knox, Frank Birch, William Clarke and Nigel de Grey – and they were all to play an important part in inter-war GC&CS and at wartime Bletchley. As chief cryptographer, Knox, along with Hugh Foss (Marlborough), a GC&CS veteran since 1924, took part in Anglo-French meetings with Polish cryptographers in 1939, building on Polish cryptanalysis of the German Enigma machine. Service networks also brought in key personnel. Both wartime Directors of GC&CS were Dartmouth naval officers, Alastair Denniston and Edward Travis. John Tiltman, who took over from Knox as Chief Cryptographer, was a regular Army officer from Charterhouse, fought through the Great War with an MC and three wounds and then joined military intelligence in 1919, switching to GC&CS in 1920. He became the first man on either side of the Atlantic to break JN25, the Japanese Navy's main code system.

Bletchley's critical wartime role in the gathering and use of intelligence rested entirely on the mobilisation of intellect. The academic disciplines needed were mathematics for the decrypting of messages, fluency in languages for translating them and the skills of historians and others in analysing them. To find at short notice, and in growing numbers, those with the right intellectual skills in these disciplines inevitably brought existing networks into play, for more open methods of recruitment were impractical. Code-breakers were only a small minority of the 10,000 people from a variety of backgrounds who eventually worked in Bletchley, but the academic elite were predominantly public-school and Oxbridge.

In 1939 began the trawl of universities, schools and other likely places for those with the necessary skills quickly to expand GC&CS from its pre-war complement of about thirty people. One school which provided many key personnel was Marlborough. The mathematician Derek Taunt wrote later that 'had he been at either Marlborough or Sidney Sussex College, Cambridge, instead of City of London School and Jesus, he might just have arrived at BP in the great pioneering days, rather than in August 1941.'[50] Marlborough had an outstanding maths department, led by Alan Robson, and between 1919 and 1939 Marlburians won seventy-eight Oxbridge maths scholarships, a quarter of their total haul. One of those Robson taught in the 1920s was Gordon Welchman, now a maths don at Sidney Sussex. He had been recruited to GC&CS in 1938 and went back to Marlborough and Robson for possible recruits. This produced former Robson pupils in Arthur Read, George Crawford, Bob Roseveare, Nigel Forward and John Manisty, who was by then teaching maths at Winchester and extended the network there.[51] Manisty worked with Welchman in Hut 6 on army and air force messages, combining the clues which might help with the identification of a message and the techniques of breaking the Enigma keys, while liaising with those in Hut 3 who transformed the mass of decrypted messages into coherent and insightful intelligence. He went back to Winchester after the war, where he is remembered for his encyclopaedic knowledge of railway timetables, but none of his pupils apparently had any idea about his wartime role.[52]

The most famous Bletchley name is Alan Turing, who was at Sherborne from 1926 to 1931. Sherborne was a middling academic school, but its maths department was outstanding under Edwin Davis. Turing's elder brother was at Marlborough but disliked it, so advised his parents to look elsewhere for Alan, who arrived, aged thirteen, by boat at Southampton for his first term at Sherborne, as his parents were living in France. Finding no trains because of the General Strike, he cycled the sixty miles to Sherborne, staying overnight at the best hotel in Blandford. The evidence suggests that Turing prospered at Sherborne, where he became a school prefect, and it was his friendship there with Christopher Morcom, who died of tuberculosis in 1930, which had the greatest effect on the rest of his life. They shared a passion for science and maths, and it was Morcom's early death which spurred Turing on to achieve in his life what had been denied to Morcom. When he left, his housemaster, Geoffrey O'Hanlon, wrote to him saying, 'I will guarantee that Turing will be a household name until the present generation has disappeared.' He underestimated the timespan of his pupil's fame. Turing won a maths scholarship to King's, Cambridge, became a Fellow in 1935 and joined Bletchley on 4 September 1939, where he led Hut 8 in decrypting German naval messages and was instrumental in developing electromechanical machines or 'bombes' to break codes on an industrial scale. Turing

Off to Camp

The Eton College OTC marches to Windsor station in July 1938 to entrain for annual camp at Tidworth, preceded by the pipes and drums of the Scots Guards. (*Reproduced by permission of the Provost and Fellows of Eton College*)

Stowe School

The statue on Prague station of Nicholas Winton, who helped bring over 600 Jewish children to England on the *Kindertransport*. (*Author's collection*)

Leonard Cheshire VC, decorated bomber pilot who was uniquely also awarded the Order of Merit in 1981 for his charitable work. (*Stowe archive*)

Edward, Prince of Wales plants a tree at Stowe on the school's tenth anniversary, 1933. Headmaster J.F. Roxburgh standing right. (*Author's collection*)

Public School Air Sections Camp

Cadets from the Air Sections of more than thirty public-school OTCs at RAF Hornchurch inspecting Spitfires and Hurricanes, August 1939. (*Bill Brown collection, Tonbridge archive*)

Evacuation

Scholars of King's School Canterbury process to the 'Cathedral' in a converted garage at the Carlyon Bay Hotel, Cornwall. (*King's Canterbury archive*)

Highgate School evacuees exercising in late 1939 on the beach at Westward Ho! (*Highgate archive*)

Headmasters

Claude Elliott, headmaster of Eton, inspecting ARP work. (*Reproduced by permission of the Provost and Fellows of Eton College*)

Robert Birley, headmaster of Charterhouse. (*Charterhouse archive*)

Edgar Castle, headmaster of Leighton Park School, who provided a haven and an education for many Jewish child refugees. (*Leighton Park archive*)

December 1940

Winston Churchill at Harrow for School Songs, 18 December 1940, with headmaster Paul Boissier. (*Harrow archive*)

HM King George VI visits Wellington College on 8 December 1940, accompanied by Queen Elizabeth, the Princesses Elizabeth and Margaret and the acting Master, Edwin Gould. (*Wellington archive*)

Battle of Britain

Pilots of 92 Squadron celebrate on a night out. Geoffrey Wellum (Forest), back right, Tony Bartley (Stowe), front row second left, Trevor Wade (Tonbridge), front right, Robert Holland (Malvern), behind Wade. (*IWM*)

Peter Townsend (Haileybury), commanding 85 Squadron.

Willie Rhodes-Moorhouse (Eton), 601 Squadron.

A Hampton Grammar School pupil at a summer agricultural camp. (*Hampton School archive*)

Early morning bayonet practice for boys of Sherborne School OTC and Home Guard under the watchful eye of RSM Brown, summer 1940. (*Sherborne archive*)

Air Raid Precautions

Wellington College boys head to the shelters, 1940. (*Wellington archive*)

Girls from Queen Anne's Caversham at fire and first aid practice, 1944. (*Queen Anne's archive*)

PoWs

The 'Laufen Six' at Colditz Castle, the first British officers imprisoned there in November 1940. (L to R) Harry Elliott, Rupert Barry (King's Canterbury), Pat Reid (Clongowes Wood), Dick Howe (Bedford Modern), Peter Allan (Tonbridge) and Kenneth Lockwood (Whitgift). (*Colditz Museum*)

Charles Upham VC and Bar (Christ's College, New Zealand), imprisoned in Colditz, 1944. (*Christ's archive*)

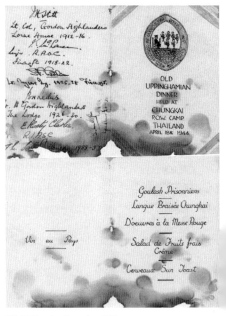

Old Uppinghamian Dinner menu, Chungkai Camp, Thailand, April 1944. (*Uppingham archive & William Christopher*)

Enduring Fame

The future Field Marshal Bramall (Eton) receiving his MC from Field Marshal Montgomery in May 1945. (*From* The Bramall Papers *by Field Marshal The Lord Bramall of Bushfield, Pen & Sword, 2017*)

Barnes Wallis visits his old school, Christ's Hospital, in 1953. (*Christ's Hospital archive*)

Celia Johnson (St Paul's Girls) starred in the wartime films *In Which We Serve* and *Brief Encounter*.

Alan Turing (centre) aged eighteen at Sherborne School. (*Sherborne archive*)

Public Schools and Jewish Refugees

Two unnamed Eton schoolboys lead in song Jewish refugee children from the *Kindertransport* at Dovercourt Bay camp, January 1939. (*Getty images*)

The Dam Busters

David Maltby (Marlborough), left, and Guy Gibson VC (St Edward's Oxford), right, meet King George VI after the raid. (*IWM*)

Michael Redgrave (Clifton) as Barnes Wallis and Richard Todd (Shrewsbury) as Guy Gibson in the final scene of *The Dam Busters*. (*Alamy*)

Intelligence Operations

HMS *Seraph*, the submarine involved in Operation Mincemeat. Commander Bill Jewell (Haileybury) second left, and Lieutenant David Scott (Tonbridge), third right. (*Richard Scott*)

Frank Thompson (Winchester), SOE agent executed in Bulgaria. (*Winchester archive*)

Major General Colin Gubbins (Cheltenham), Director of SOE. (*By kind permission of Michael Gubbins*)

Prime Ministers Visit Their Schools

Winston Churchill at Harrow for School Songs, 1950. (*Harrow archive*)

Clement Attlee at Haileybury, 1965. (*Haileybury archive*)

War Memorials

The CWGC cemetery and memorial at Monte Cassino, with the monastery in the background. The battle here was as fierce and costly as any in either war. (*Author's collection*)

The Cranleigh School War Memorial unveiled in 2016 to commemorate all Cranleighans who have died in war. (*Cranleigh archive*)

could lay claim, with Winston Churchill, to be the best-known public schoolboy of the war, his reputation, after his cruel conviction for gross indecency and his subsequent suicide in 1954, recently enhanced by becoming the face on the new £50 note. Turing returned to Sherborne often after he left, the last time being in 1953, between his conviction and his death, to deliver a paper to the science society. This visit, the naming of a science prize after him in 1956 and a science block in 1966, show the extent to which Sherborne, even in a less tolerant age, saw Turing as a victim of injustice and reciprocated the warm feelings he had towards the school, well before any public knowledge of Bletchley elevated him to the pantheon of Second World War heroes.[53]

The creative contribution of Gordon Welchman was second only to that of Turing. Together they persuaded the directing staff that 'bombes' would transform how Bletchley operated and devised them together. Welchman was also instrumental in the recruitment from university networks of other key Bletchley personnel, including the international chess players, Stuart Milner-Barry (Cheltenham) and Hugh Alexander (KES Birmingham), who had taught maths at Winchester; John Herivel, a mathematician from Methodist College, Belfast and Cambridge, who broke into the main Luftwaffe code; and Ann Williamson from Headington School and Lady Margaret Hall, who had been told by her headmistress that studying maths was unladylike.

Bletchley was not staffed just by mathematicians, for it needed linguists and others with sharp analytical brains. Gwen Hollington (Roedean), Cambridge languages scholar, translated messages from German and maintained a comprehensive database of enemy communications. Cicely Mayhew (Cheltenham Ladies') had a first in languages from Cambridge and translated decoded German naval signals. Eric Jones (King's Macclesfield), seconded to Bletchley in 1942 from RAF intelligence, interpreted, catalogued and prioritised the vast amounts of intercepted and decoded enemy intelligence which came into Bletchley, streamlining a system which fed information to front-line commanders in Normandy within three hours. Maurice Wiles (Tonbridge) was up at Cambridge taking the entrance exam in classics when he was recruited to Bletchley on the day of the Japanese attack on Pearl Harbor. The tutor at Christ's had already recruited Wiles's brother Christopher, adding Maurice's name as an afterthought. He was interviewed in London before leaving school earlier than planned to work on translating and interpreting Japanese messages.[54]

One day in 2011, a Bletchley guide was struggling to work one of the museum's code-breaking machines when a curly-haired octogenarian in his tour group offered to help. Rosemary Ince had not worked a 'bombe' for seventy years but she still knew exactly what to do. She went to Cheltenham Ladies' College, joined the WRNS in 1941 aged seventeen and was posted to Bletchley in late 1943. Here her job on eight-hour shifts was to wire up the eight 'bombes', each about twelve feet long and six feet high. When the 'bombe' produced a code-breaking result, she rushed it to Hut 6, where German Reichswehr and Luftwaffe messages were analysed. After the war she became a distinguished pathologist, but her wartime work remained secret until the Bletchley records were declassified in the 1970s.[55]

Bletchley did not win the war, but its contribution was significant. Just one example in 1942 will demonstrate its value. In August and September 1942 U-boats located twenty-one of the sixty-three convoys in the North Atlantic, sinking forty-three ships and nearly 500,000 tons of shipping. Only eight U-boats were sunk in those two months, and Rodger Winn in the Submarine Tracking Room had been deprived of the vital intelligence because of the newly installed Shark cypher being used between U-boats and their base. Turing and Alexander were working flat out on breaking Shark, but with little success until the code-books of U-559 were captured on 30 October 1942. These arrived at Bletchley on 24 November, and all efforts were intensified. Shaun Wylie, another Winchester and Oxford maths scholar, who had been teaching at Wellington until recruited to Bletchley in 1941, took over the code-breaking shift in Hut 8 at midnight on 12 December and worked through the night on weather reports which might fit U-boat weather messages. He found the link, tried it out on the 'bombes' and the crib came out. 'It was a great moment,' he wrote. 'The excitement was terrific, relief too.'[56] Within a few hours, messages began to arrive for Rodger Winn in the Submarine Tracking Room in an unending stream, providing critical guidance about the likely courses of U-boats. It was one of the most important moments in the intelligence war, a triumph of intellect and teamwork; U-boat sinkings soared, and Allied control of the Atlantic was never again lost.

Traitors

Intelligence was not just about code-breaking and sabotage; it also meant keeping track of Britain's internal enemies on the right and left, some of them from leading public schools. Anti-Semitism and Hitler's other policies found many supporters within the ruling elites of the 1930s. The British Union of Fascists (BUF) was founded in 1932 by Sir Oswald Mosley, who had gone to Winchester in 1909. After service in the First World War, he went into politics, first as a Conservative MP with progressive views, but then switching to Labour in 1924. When Labour won the 1929 election, Mosley was given junior ministerial office, but he resigned in 1931 over employment policy and founded his own New Party. By now he had become attracted to Mussolini's fascism, and the New Party evolved into the BUF. Mosley lacked the common touch, being described by the Labour MP Jennie Lee as possessing 'an overwhelming arrogance and an unshakable conviction that he was born to rule'.[57] Other members of his class and background took strong exception to his views. Julian Amery, an Eton schoolboy who attended one of Mosley's meetings, found that 'the anti-Semitism repelled and the black shirt and Roman salute seemed rather ridiculous in London.'[58] His attitude was shared by P.G. Wodehouse (Dulwich), whose character Roderick Spode, 7th Earl of Sidcup, leader of the 'Black Shorts', is presented as a pompous figure of fun. Fascism never made much headway in Britain, with MI5 estimating an active membership of not more than 10,000 at its peak in 1934, but it was a catalyst for violence.[59] Frank Pakenham, an Etonian don at Christ Church, attended in 1936 Mosley's packed meeting at the Carfax Assembly Rooms in Oxford and took strong exception to him. After being hit over the head by a Blackshirt with a steel chain, he was roused to berserk fury and was seen returning to his Christ Church rooms with blood pouring down his face and bruised kidneys.[60] Churchill in June 1940 did not underestimate the potential danger Mosley posed. In a telegram to Roosevelt he wrote that 'if Great Britain broke under invasion, a pro-German government might obtain far easier terms from Germany … this dastard deed would not be done by His Majesty's present advisers, but, if Mosley were Prime Minister, or some other Quisling.'[61]

MI5 was the body charged with home security, its task in the 1930s to counter the activities of communists and keep an eye on the British extreme right. It was too starved of resources to meet this twin threat, recruiting only two recent graduates in the 1930s. Christopher Andrew, the historian of the intelligence services, has described this as 'significantly fewer than the British graduate recruits of Soviet intelligence'.[62] MI5 interest in the BUF stemmed from evidence of foreign funding and growing concern about street fighting between its Blackshirts and Communist groups. When war broke out, MI5 was worried about collaboration between right-wing extremists and Germany, and secured the internment under Defence Regulation 1B of Mosley and many others who had shown sympathy for enemy powers. Those detained included other members of the upper classes such as Robert Gordon-Canning (Eton), who had been best man at Mosley's wedding, and a Conservative MP, Captain Archibald Ramsay (Eton), who had been a prominent supporter of General Franco and held virulent anti-Semitic views. In May 1939 Ramsay formed 'The Right Club' to unify all the right-wing groups in Britain, clear the Conservative Party of Jewish influence and come to terms with Hitler.

John Amery was another from the extreme right in the sights of MI5. The wayward son of the Secretary of State for India, Leo Amery, he had been a difficult child and had an inglorious career at Harrow, where his Old Harrovian father was a governor. Badly bullied and badly behaved, he resented the tight control of a school whose headmaster Norwood was 'obsessed by the danger from individualism'. He left Harrow for a year after being 'severely warned for shop stealing, moral breakdown and unsatisfactory work', then returned in 1928, but soon ran away again.[63] He drifted through many failed ventures before going to live in Paris in 1936, where he developed strongly anti-Semitic views, falling under the influence of the French fascist leader, Jacques Doriot. He stayed in France during the war, where he was interned for a time by the Vichy regime, but Doriot's influence secured his release. The Germans now became aware of the propaganda possibilities he offered and paid him a large sum of money to make a series of radio broadcasts in Berlin on the same 'Germany Calling' channel as William Joyce, 'Lord Haw-Haw'. He made his first broadcast in November 1942, full of anti-Semitic drivel, but also delivered an attack 'on the small clique who rule Britain', which included his father. He also visited a British internment camp outside

Paris on the hopeless mission of trying to raise volunteers for a 'Legion of St George' to fight Bolshevism. During all this period MI5 officers had been building the case against him from his broadcasts and from witness statements by those he had tried to recruit. Arrested in Italy, Amery went on trial at the Old Bailey in November 1945 on eight counts of high treason, to each of which he pleaded guilty. The trial lasted just eight minutes, he was sentenced to death and hanged at Wandsworth on 19 December 1945.

A more serious threat to the country came from communist spies, who passed on multiple secrets to their Russian paymasters during the war and were not unmasked until well after it. The revelation that young men from the most famous public schools had become Soviet agents turned into a long-running inquest into the culture, morality and patriotism of that whole generation and the schools which had nurtured them. Most attention has been fixed on the five 'Cambridge spies', four of whom went to elite boarding public schools – Kim Philby (Westminster), Guy Burgess (Eton), Donald Maclean (Gresham's) and Anthony Blunt (Marlborough). The fifth, John Cairncross, went to Hamilton Academy, a fee-paying Scottish school which ceased as an independent institution in 1972. The cluster of well-educated, upper-middle-class men and women who embraced Communism have not been easily understood. At best they are portrayed as 'blinkered and naïve, foolishly adopting positions they did not understand, children of the bourgeoisie suffering from acute class guilt'.[64] These are judgements made with the benefit of hindsight about the evils of the Stalinist system rather than with an understanding of the circumstances which led them to adopt the ideology to the point of betraying their country.

Those circumstances were rooted in the political and social conditions of the 1930s – the Great War and its human cost, the Depression and huge unemployment which resulted, and the failure of democracy and the League of Nations to prevent the rise of fascism. Denis Healey (Bradford GS), Oxford undergraduate in 1936–40 and future Labour Chancellor, explained the rationale thus:

I joined the Communist Party when I was an undergraduate at Oxford, and only for one reason, and that was that most of us could see the war coming … We saw the Russian communists as the only reliable anti-Hitler force, and being a member of the Labour Party did not seem enough because half the Labour Party were pacifists.[65]

Commenting in the mid-1930s, the Oxford student magazine *Isis* suggested that many of the university Communists had started their ideological journey at school:

It is in the interests of conservatism that the public schools be destroyed before they turn loose too many bitter young socialists and communists. If the latter wish to make the country a communist state, they really should insist that everyone is sent to a public school.[66]

Philby, Burgess, Maclean and Blunt did not become communists at school, but their political views were already moving that way. Maclean, the son of a former Cabinet minister, was described as the 'most dedicated communist of the five' and his formative influence at Gresham's was James Klugmann, a year older, who was keen to provoke the school authorities by calling himself a communist. [67] Maclean went on to Cambridge and the diplomatic service, and was protected from suspicion, in Philby's words, by the 'genuine mental block which stubbornly resisted the belief that respected members of the establishment could do such things'.[68] Neither Burgess nor Philby had reason to resent their schools, where they were academically successful. Burgess even visited Eton and his former history teacher, Robert Birley, now headmaster, on the day before he decamped to Moscow, and liked to wear his Old Etonian tie in Russia. Philby in 1963 reputedly wrapped himself against the cold in his Westminster scarf as the Russian ship taking him into exile pulled out of Beirut.[69]

It was at Cambridge in the 1930s that the five made the leap from left-wing sympathies to recruitment by the NKVD, the Soviet secret police and intelligence agency. They were all involved in radical politics at the university in the early 1930s, along with other public-school communists like John Cornford (Stowe), who was too open in his communist views to be as interesting to Soviet intelligence as those below the radar. Philby was the first to be recruited as a Soviet agent in 1934, passing to his handlers the names of seven other young Cambridge men who might also be susceptible. Top of the list was Maclean, who was recruited later that year, with Burgess following in 1935, and then Burgess drawing in Blunt in 1937 and both of them recruiting Cairncross. By this time all of them had embarked on careers which would take them into the heart of the British intelligence services. Burgess worked first for the BBC, finding speakers for current affairs talks, but his Soviet controllers asked him to cultivate relationships with MI6 officers, and Burgess was carrying out missions for them by 1938. Philby joined SIS in 1940, and Anthony Blunt MI5 the same year, while Maclean did most of his spying from within the Foreign Office.

A willingness existed within the political and intelligence establishment to accept that an individual's adherence to an ideology might only be temporary, Philby and Burgess both making efforts to suggest they had outgrown their dalliance with socialism by affecting new, more right-wing attitudes. It was a singular failure on the part of both MI5 and MI6 that they eluded discovery until the 1950s, but within the inner circles of Britain's ruling class and the Foreign Office, mutual trust was unquestioned. Philby's own memoir is a 'superbly cynical combination of truth, half-truth, falsehood and propaganda'. He insisted he had not betrayed anyone since 'to betray, you have to belong', but this, too, is deceit, for he and his Cambridge associates 'belonged firmly to the clubbable British upper class, which is why he got away with it for so long'.[70]

Intellect and Intelligence

No intelligence success could eliminate the difficulties of defeating the enemy on the battlefield, but the collective effort of men and women working in intelligence did make a vital contribution. The qualities needed of intellect, linguistic and mathematical skills, creativity, analytical sharpness and, in many roles, great courage, did not belong exclusively to the alumni of public schools and Oxbridge. It was a fact, however, that the pre-war intelligence leadership was dominated by people from that background, and when the great wartime expansion came, they turned to familiar networks. The public-school system was a key source of recruits, producing enough accomplished linguists, mathematicians and chess players turned cryptographers, as well as rugged adventurers and other oddballs, to cater for the diverse needs of the nation at war. There is an intriguing paradox in the individual stories related, that intelligence activity catered both for those who were intellectually stimulated by their schools and those who rebelled against the system, while the supposed nurseries of the establishment produced extremists on both left and right.

The products of those nurseries proved highly adept at using the networks which membership of the establishment brought them, networks which were useful in the wartime intelligence services, when rapid expansion was necessary, but more dubious in peacetime, when they covered up mediocrity and sometimes treachery. After the Cambridge spies were exposed, Sir Dick White (Bishop's Stortford), later head of both MI5 and SIS, wrote to a friend about the 'balance sheet': 'The cost was to have had Blunt in MI5, Philby in SIS, and Burgess and Maclean in the FO. On the other side of the equation, a massive intake of brain and abilities from the universities which set entirely new standards of intellectual achievement.'[71] White, perhaps trying to rationalise the damage done by the Cambridge spies, was also right to conclude that Britain's intelligence services benefited from the sheer diversity of people and talents working for them. Those intellectual talents were also to be seen in the important work done by scientists and inventors.

Chapter 6

Science and Innovation

Henry Moseley was a King's Scholar at Eton. He won a science scholarship to Trinity, Oxford in 1906 and went on to become one of the most brilliant physicists of his generation. Working first at Manchester with Ernest Rutherford, he returned to Oxford and established the atomic numbers of key elements. When war broke out in 1914 he was intent on joining up with his contemporaries, enlisted in the Royal Engineers and was killed by a Turkish sniper at Gallipoli on 10 August 1915, aged twenty-seven. It was a tragic waste of the intellectual talents of one who many believed would be a future Nobel Prize winner. Scientists of Moseley's eminence were not allowed to sacrifice their lives in mundane Second World War battlefield roles, but were used in the key scientific research facilities set up to underpin the work of the fighting services, as the policy of conscription and reserved occupations adopted a more ordered system than in 1914.

Science, technology and invention did not on their own win the Second World War for Britain and her allies, but it could not have been won without them. Britain's war strategy was built around keeping casualties low because of the experience of 1914–18 and a wider manpower shortage. In Normandy in 1944 Montgomery kept the numbers of troops in the immediate firing line at a minimum and compensated by using massive artillery and air power. This was a devastating war of machines, each of the three services having their own research and development facilities, bringing to the battlefield not just the heavy weaponry of aircraft and tanks but all the tools of electronic warfare, engineering invention, atomic research and medicine. The best minds in the country were employed in this research and development, including many temporarily drafted in from universities.

These scientific developments in warfare raise questions about the extent to which elite education in Britain, and the wider elites in government and civil service, valued and promoted science and technology before 1939. Correlli Barnett has been particularly critical of the historical anti-technocratic bias in Britain's elite education system.[1] However, although classics remained the dominant subject in most schools, a significantly high proportion of the war's top scientists came from public schools and made substantial contributions to the war of machines which Britain waged. It is arguable that there should have been more scientists in 1939 if public schools had put more money into providing better teachers and laboratories for the subjects, and steered more of the cleverer boys towards them, but wider elite culture had already embraced the importance of science. The historian David Edgerton gives as one of many examples the Oxford physiologist J.S. Haldane, brother of the lawyer and politician R.B. Haldane, both educated at Edinburgh Academy, and the father of the writer Naomi Mitchison (Dragon School and home-schooled) and the biologist J.B.S. Haldane (Eton).[2] Science may have been undervalued in elite schools, but it was everywhere in British public life, and all politicians by the twentieth century had to address themselves to scientific policy issues in medicine, agriculture, energy and armaments.

Science in Education

Correlli Barnett (Trinity School, Croydon) has argued that 'the powerful romantic bias in the education of the British ruling classes meant that any subject too closely connected with the contemporary world or with the business of making one's way in the world was shunned as insufficiently noble and uplifting.'[3] Barnett's has been a powerful voice in criticism of the English education system and the part it supposedly played in the country's industrial decline. His views have been supported by the American historian Martin Wiener, whose book, *English Culture and the Decline of the Industrial Spirit*, came out in 1981, blaming the anti-industrial ethos of the English elite for the country's economic malaise. The historian Colin Kidd has summarised their arguments as an 'influential narrative of self-inflicted economic decline, depicting a country whose leaders, entranced by rural nostalgia and ideals of gentility inculcated in public schools, failed to promote scientific education or to invest in industrial research and development.'[4]

Barnett asserts that Britain's governing class, their minds full of Christianity and classics, were supposedly ignorant of industry, science and technology, the public schools seeing their purpose as

> not in turning out technocrats to lead an industrial nation, but as forming Christian gentlemen ... to serve in public life, the church, the law or the civil service or to bring enlightened administration to the Empire ... The public schools and Oxbridge moreover taught the future governing elite and intelligentsia to despise 'trade' as beneath a gentleman, equally to despise any form of education that might be deemed vocational (such as technology) rather than liberal (like the classics).[5]

For Barnett the earliest villain of the piece was Thomas Arnold, head of Rugby from 1828 to 1841, whose regime was the major influence on the ethos of nineteenth century public schools and who gave 'late Victorian English education both its concern with moral conduct and its distinctive mark of romanticism.'[6] This educational bias, according to Barnett, survived the Great War:

> In the public schools, the classics continued to dominate the curriculum, especially for high-flyers, until after the Great War, and even though science and modern subjects such as modern languages, history and English literature had crept in from the 1860s onwards, for long they were regarded as refuges for the second rate.[7]

Oxbridge followed the schools in defending classics by offering a disproportionate number of scholarships in the subject, while these attitudes fed through into those joining the civil service, most of them public-school and Oxbridge, and through educational bureaucrats into the Board of Education and the state secondary sector, which looked to the public schools as models of liberal education.

What then is the evidence from schools themselves about this supposed neglect of science education? The picture is a mixed one. Science was introduced into the public-school curriculum in the second half of the nineteenth century, but grudgingly and subject to a strong rearguard action in defence of classics by headmasters who mostly came from that discipline themselves. Of the 114 headmasters in HMC schools at the outbreak of the Great War, 92 were classicists, and this did not change much by 1939 or even beyond.[8] The staunchest defenders of classics tended to be in the most traditional boarding schools with strong Oxbridge links, reinforced by Oxbridge's historic imbalance towards classics in scholarship awards.

At Rugby School, the birthplace under Thomas Arnold of liberal education in the 1830s, the first science labs were built in 1859 and science was introduced as a compulsory subject as early as 1864. By 1900 Rugby was in the forefront of science education, but science teachers had the difficult task of meeting the demand for natural science scholarships at Oxbridge, qualifying exams for various professions, including medicine, and the entrance exam for the military college of Woolwich, where potential artillery and engineer officers had to take papers in science and maths. Clifton was another major boarding school with strong military links which took science seriously and produced many fine scientists before 1914; the senior science masters between 1870 and 1908 were William Tilden and William Shenstone, who both became Fellows of the Royal Society. The problem at Rugby and Clifton, as in most schools, was that parents had other ambitions for their sons than a career in trade or industry; the science side was regarded as inferior to classics and it was generally the less able boys who were steered towards it.

Science came into the curriculum at Eton in the 1860s, with the first chemistry lab built in 1869, but not until 1919 were the salaries paid to non-classicist masters brought up to the same level as the classicists. Before 1914 several of the few boys who persevered with science proved to be exceptional, like Henry Moseley and the distinguished biologist Julian Huxley, who remembered the well-equipped science labs and the brilliant teaching of his biology master M.D. Hill, which led to Huxley winning a scholarship in zoology to Balliol in 1905. In that same decade Eton also educated Thomas Merton, J.B.S. Haldane and Alfred Egerton, who all went on to become Fellows of the Royal Society. Egerton, brother-in-law of Stafford Cripps, became Professor of Chemical Technology at Imperial in 1936 and was a member of the War Cabinet's Scientific Advisory Committee. Despite these illustrious examples, science was a poor relation at Eton because Etonian academic culture denied it time in the lower school and boys were not encouraged to take what housemasters regarded as not an 'Etonian' subject.[9] When Eton had its first Board of Education inspection in 1936, the school was criticised for not giving enough time to science, for not organising the course to make effective use of that time and for having too few good teachers of the subject. Yet the large numbers in the scientific and natural history societies showed that Etonians were interested in science, and the papers read to those societies reveal scope for boys to pursue wider intellectual interests outside the prescriptive curriculum.

In February 1916 a memorandum signed by leading scientists appeared in *The Times*. Responding to the increasingly technological demands of the war, it asked that science be given its proper place in education and pointed out that of thirty-five leading public schools, thirty-four had classicists as headmasters.[10] Not all thought this a bad thing; a counterblast followed in a letter to *The Times* in May 1916, signed by Lord Curzon and the Archbishop of Canterbury among others, arguing that mental training and scientific method, as opposed to mere scientific information, could best be acquired from the humanities.[11] But the scientists were determined to make their point, and in May 1916 a 'neglect of science' committee was formed by leading academics, asking that university scholarships should not unduly favour Latin and Greek, that natural science should be considered part of a liberal education, and that science should be an examined subject in admission to the home and Indian civil services.

Public school headmasters were stirred by this criticism to debate the place of science in the curriculum. Provision for the subject in terms of lesson time, properly equipped laboratories and the quality of teaching varied greatly between schools. Science, along with other modern subjects, had to fight in most schools for timetable slots which classics chose not to fill. Many heads opposed the utilitarianism of science, believing that clever boys could catch up later at university, but at HMC's annual meeting in December 1916 a resolution was agreed that a general science course should be compulsory for all boys up to the age of sixteen. The main spokesman to the resolution was John Talbot, head of RGS Newcastle who, unusually for an HMC head of the time, had a first-class degree in natural sciences. He argued that since scientists regarded classics as a mouldy anachronism, and classicists thought of science as a utilitarian upstart, the only solution to end this mutual contempt was for all boys to follow the same syllabus and then diverge according to their strengths and intended careers. The passing of this resolution might have been regarded as a landmark, but HMC resolutions carried little weight, and heads were under no obligation to implement those with which they had little sympathy, the usual arguments of timetable restrictions and the cost of new teachers and facilities militating against change.[12]

Progress in following up this resolution was inevitably slow. In 1919 the Prime Minister's Committee on the Teaching of Science reported that 'there has, in the public schools as a whole, been no general recognition of the principle that science should form an essential part of secondary education.'[13] Direct grant schools were praised as being less neglectful of science, winning a disproportionate share of Oxbridge science scholarships. In 1939 at Loughborough GS, twenty-five out of forty boys in the sixth form were specialising in science, and they had had significant success in Oxbridge awards throughout that decade.[14] In 1923 the HMC Annual Meeting once more debated science education, this time prompted by a report from the Science Masters' Association. It was again John Talbot, now head of Haileybury, who moved the resolution, focusing on establishing a minimum time to be given to science in prep schools; this could be achieved if public schools made science an option in scholarship and common entrance papers. The mood of the meeting was against imposing on prep schools, one headmaster declaring that he was 'all for nature study out of doors in prep schools, but I do not believe they have the men who can teach formal science, and I am sure in existing circumstances they have not the time.'[15]

Not until 1933 did HMC return to the topic of science education. While most contributors to the debate recognised that some progress had been made, the most telling contribution came from Hubert Wootton, head of The Perse and himself a scientist: 'It has been my lot for the past two years to examine in General Science, and I have been appalled by the dreadful nature of the answers and the complete lack of any scientific basis apparent in the teaching that must have gone on in those schools.'[16] Board of Education inspections in 1924 and 1934 revealed that Marlborough was typical of many inter-war public schools in teaching the subject well in the sixth form but giving it too little time in the lower school, so that the number of potential scientists was limited. Marlborough won 336 scholarships at Oxbridge between the wars, but 150 of those were in classics and only 45 in science, with mathematics, history and languages all more numerous than science, figures which reflected the balance of scholarship opportunities offered by Oxbridge.[17]

Much depended on the resources which governors were prepared to put in, the educational agendas of heads and the quality of science teachers they appointed. Oundle developed a formidable reputation for science and engineering education well before the Great War, proving what could be done. Frederick Sanderson, head from 1892 to 1922, restructured the curriculum to provide more time for science, bringing biochemistry and practical engineering projects into the workshops he built, together with new science labs, a botanical garden and an observatory. Oundle unsurprisingly produced many scientists and engineers like Alfred Owen, whose Rubery Owen company manufactured a vast range of wartime products from lifeboats to armour plate for tank hulls.[18] Richard Keynes left Oundle to work on radar as an experimental officer in a naval wartime research establishment and later became Professor of Physiology at Cambridge; his own family shows how science could be part of elite culture, his father Geoffrey a surgeon and literary executor of Rupert Brooke, his friend at Rugby, and his uncle the economist John Maynard Keynes. Gresham's was another in the vanguard of science education. At the HMC conference in 1933 its head, James Eccles, former science teacher at Clifton, declared that he led a school 'with a definitely scientific background in which every boy takes science up to sixteen years of age for nine periods out of thirty-six'. He favoured time given for intensive work on the subject rather than 'a cursory and superficial study'.[19] When the school was evacuated to Newquay in 1940, the pupils helped to build temporary labs and connect them to the town's gas supply. Dozens of Gresham's alumni went on to distinction in science and engineering at Oxbridge and elsewhere, many of whom, like Christopher Cockerell and Alan Hodgkin, made substantial contributions to the British war effort.[20]

At Wellington College, by contrast, a proposal in 1925 to build new laboratories was shelved for ten years, until governors decided they had become an educational necessity, although any Wellingtonian trying to get into RMC Woolwich already needed a grounding in science. Board of Education inspections could also turn a harsh spotlight on laggards. At King's, Canterbury the 1930 report was damning: 'The time allotted to science is not generous; indeed it is not adequate and the standard of work is not high.'[21] In public schools more generally, the classical culture still fostered by most heads acted as a brake on the emergence of scientists and engineers. Too many were of the same mind as Ralph Henderson, head of Alleyn's, who tried to persuade R.V. Jones to study classics for his university scholarship. Jones had won a London County scholarship to Alleyn's, and his hobby was building a radio receiver, so he held out against this pressure and won a scholarship in physics to Oxford in 1929. He became at Oxford a pupil of Professor Lindemann, Churchill's wartime scientific adviser, which brought him into the world of scientific intelligence before and during the war.

The more academic girls' schools took science seriously. One girl at St Paul's Girls' just after the Great War wrote that 'there were laboratories for biology, physics and chemistry, and teachers who were specialists in their sciences. I was not only permitted but encouraged to study science.'[22] Rosalind Franklin, who contributed much to the understanding of DNA before her untimely death in 1958, won a science scholarship from there to Cambridge in 1938. At North London Collegiate, science was also strongly encouraged, the evidence to be seen in minutes of science club meetings and schemes of study for all the sciences. NLCS's best known scientist is Marie Stopes, at school in the late 1890s before going on to study botany at UCL and become the first female academic at Manchester University. Girls' boarding schools like Cheltenham or Roedean were also noted for the quality of their science teaching, but there were many smaller schools where science barely existed or, if it did, was restricted to the botany or home economics varieties. Angela Mackenzie, evacuated from Queen Margaret's, York to Castle Howard, remembered the science curriculum as consisting of a wildflower test at the end of each summer term, with one hundred varieties of flowers from the park lined up in test-tubes.[23]

It is possible to find evidence from some schools supporting Barnett's assertions about the shortcomings of science education in Britain's pre-1939 public schools, but also evidence from others that it was valued and encouraged. HMC as a body may have wanted to move things forward but struggled to impose on individual heads with their own agendas. The state education system was no different. Barnett claims that the Board of Education code for secondary schools in 1902 'set its face against any technical or vocational bias and in general the effect of the new regulations was to broaden and liberalise the education in all schools under state supervision.'[24] In 1938 the Spens Report deplored 'the fact that the Board did little or nothing to foster the development of schools of quasi-vocational type to meet the needs of boys and girls who desired to enter industry and commerce at the age of sixteen.'[25] Yet many scientists emerged from state schools and contributed to the technological war in a variety of ways. Only the war itself, and the requirement for technical manpower during and after it, was able to deliver urgency to the need to iron out the scientific and technological deficiencies in the educational system and bring more schools up to the standard of the best.

The Scientific War: Research and Development

Barnett's purpose, in his attack on elite education and attitudes, was to identify one cause of Britain's protracted decline as an industrial country since the Second World War. He argued that the performance of the British economy in the war, impressive as it seemed at the time, 'manifested many of the characteristic failings of the British disease – poor management, restrictive practices, obsolescent plant and equipment, and critical shortages of labour and technically qualified personnel.'[26] He identified the irresponsibility of the governing elites who, in education and establishment attitudes from the nineteenth century onwards, failed to meet the need to modernise the British economy and render it able to compete in the markets of the world. In his post-1945 analysis he complained that the 'New Jerusalem' vision of Labour's welfare state diverted energies and investment away from a necessary modernisation of Britain's manufacturing capacity.

Barnett's 'declinist' interpretation of the British economy before and during the Second World War has been challenged by other historians. The most recent and compelling is David Edgerton, who has argued that the assumption of Britain's long-term industrial decline is a mirage and that there is no failure of manufacturing to explain before the 1970s. He makes clear that the way Britain waged war in 1939–45 was reliant on the most up-to-date mechanised armaments: 'Britain at war was a first class power, confident in its capacity to wage a devastating war of machines … Britain planned to fight, and largely did fight a war of machines, of warships, bombers and tanks, a war of science and invention.'[27] The role of scientists, engineers and doctors in public life, along with the impact of scientific ideas, has, according to Edgerton, been greatly downplayed: 'The elite of a rich and strong nation included figures with many trained in science, engineering and medicine and more receptive to and supportive of technocratic tendencies.'[28] The importance of the subjects was widely accepted by the political establishment. Edgerton cites Churchill's own interest in science and machines and the use he made of a scientist as his close personal adviser, Frederick Lindemann, schooled in Germany but Professor of Physics at Oxford. Churchill wanted a war of 'rockets, aeroplanes, radio and clever gadgets of all kinds, some of his own devising'.[29] Oliver Lyttelton (Eton), wartime Minister of Production, wrote that one of Churchill's great qualities as a war leader was 'his eager readiness to listen to new, sometimes fantastic ideas thrown up by scientists, engineers and academic figures'.[30] His interest in technology was at the level of gadgets rather than integrated systems, but he was a quick learner; when shown the prototype air defence system in June 1939, for example, he quickly understood it.[31] In early 1915, when First Lord of the Admiralty, he was a key figure in overseeing the development of what became the tank.

The tank was just one of the new war machines developed in the First World War by governments which recognised the importance of technology in war. From late 1915 scientists and engineers from universities were increasingly directed into research and development, the success of which could be seen in the new weapons which became available to the Army and Navy, and particularly in the major advances in aeronautics. William Bragg (St Peter's, Adelaide), a Cambridge physicist, developed with his father sound-ranging equipment to help the artillery establish the position of German guns, for which they were both awarded the Nobel Prize for Physics in 1915. Additional resources were given to Government military research institutes, including the Royal

Aircraft Factory at Farnborough, founded by Geoffrey de Havilland (St Edward's) in 1912 and renamed the Royal Aircraft Establishment (RAE) in 1918 to focus on research. Further underpinning came from armaments companies like Vickers, with its subsidiaries such as Vickers-Armstrong and Supermarine, and by aircraft and engine manufacturers like Rolls Royce and Bristol, whose main aircraft designer in 1918 was Frank Barnwell, educated at Fettes.

The First World War was therefore a catalyst for the mobilisation of scientists and engineers in the development of cutting-edge armaments, with the government's own agencies in the vanguard during and after the war. The research department at the Royal Arsenal, Woolwich, set up in 1907, employed 80,000 people during the war, the chemical warfare establishment at Porton Down was created in 1916, and the Admiralty Research Laboratory was built in 1921. The RAE at Farnborough employed over 500 personnel by 1939, part of a powerful military-scientific complex in the inter-war years, developing with the big armament manufacturers new weapons for future wars. Science and technology were to play a key role in the Allied victory in the Second World War by providing the firepower needed to win and the means to minimise human casualties. Britain deployed some of her best university brains into research and development of weapon systems, radar and other forms of electronic warfare, and into medical advances. Civil servants also developed a complex interface between themselves, scientists in research establishments and the military which brought organisation and efficiency into the prioritisation of projects. The personnel for this largely came from the most academically able elements of the education system.

One successful inter-war blueprint was the setting up in January 1935, within the Air Ministry, of the Committee for the Scientific Survey of Air Defence (CSSAD). This committee was chaired by Henry Tizard, who left Westminster School in 1903 and became one of the most influential scientists of his generation. Science at Westminster had been taught on a voluntary basis by occasional lecturers from outside the school, but Tizard was one of the first pupils to benefit from a new science block and inclusion of the subject within the curriculum. He read maths and chemistry at Oxford, to which he returned to teach, with his Great War spent in the RFC as both pilot and researcher into aeronautics. After the war he worked for the Department of Scientific and Industrial Research until in 1929 he became Rector of Imperial College, London. His links with aeronautical research continued, and the setting up of CSSAD in 1935 was a moment of great significance, with 'the recognition that scientifically trained research workers had a vital part to play not only in the weapons and gadgets of war but also in the actual study of operations'.[32] Tizard's greatest contribution with CSSAD was to encourage the development of radar, a revolution in the science of air defence, the work largely of Robert Watson-Watt (Brechin HS), superintendent of the radio research department of the National Physical Laboratory, of which William Bragg became director in 1937. Tizard himself played a practical role when, in a series of tests at Biggin Hill, he calculated the angle at which the faster fighters needed to be directed by controllers in order to intercept the slower bombers. This use of strict scientific principles became known as 'Tizzy's angle' and was used until computers took over the process in the 1960s.[33]

Government research institutions like Woolwich Arsenal and the Admiralty Research Laboratory were run between the wars by military and naval officers, specialist engineers and scientists, their personnel largely educated, like the rest of the officer corps, in public schools and Dartmouth. They included Alwyn Crow (Westminster), a Cambridge scientist wounded in action in 1916 who held a key post as director of ballistics research at Woolwich Arsenal between the wars and then moved to head projectile development at Fort Halstead. Another was Arthur Hall (Clifton), who became director of torpedo and mine production at the Admiralty in 1917, and then in 1929 chief superintendent at RAE Farnborough.

In refuting the anti-technocratic bias of Britain's elites, David Edgerton points out that scientists in the Second World War were prominent in every ministry that had a strong research and development component, that Britain's leaders were confident of winning a war of machines and that Barnes Wallis and others did not have to struggle against Whitehall indifference, but were given every opportunity to make their unique contributions to the war effort. Britain emerged from the war as 'an extremely powerful warfare state, brimming with new war machines, whose use was now mastered as never before'.[34] The impetus came from the top of government, where Churchill was not alone in appreciating the importance of science and technology. John Anderson (George Watson's), a brilliant student in maths, geology and chemistry, became a top civil servant in the inter-war years, then Home Secretary and later Chancellor of the Exchequer in Churchill's wartime government, as well as a central figure in the politics of the atom bomb. Lord Woolton (Manchester GS), Minister of Food and later of Reconstruction, had a science degree from Manchester University; Stafford Cripps (Winchester), Minister of Aircraft Production from 1942, studied chemistry at UCL and specialised in patent law when he became a barrister. The military also employed technocrats in senior appointments. Ronald Weeks (Charterhouse), pre-war chairman of the glass manufacturers Pilkingtons, became Director General of Army Equipment in 1941, responsible for equipment procurement and organisation, and in 1942 Deputy Chief of the Imperial General Staff.

Tizard was insistent, even in 1938, that in wartime pure research would become less important than the application of its findings: 'I am inclined to think that we have to get most of the research over before a war starts. When it starts, it will be too late, but there will be much to be done in hastening application.'[35] In September 1940, in an effort to secure American help in applying the fruits of research, he was sent by Churchill on a top-secret mission to the USA, taking with him examples of advanced defence technology, most of it highly secret, which he hoped would impress the Americans and lead to a shared approach to development. This included the cavity magnetron, developed at Birmingham University by John Randall (Ashton GS) and Harry Boot (KES Birmingham) and vital to the power and range of radar, details of Frank Whittle's jet engine, and a memorandum on the feasibility of the atomic bomb. Although the USA was still neutral, Tizard succeeded in persuading them of a shared interest in the research and development of key new technology, and a scientific office was opened in Washington to co-ordinate the exchange of ideas. Tizard was one of many scientific intellectuals advising the government on operational research. Another was J.D. Bernal (Bedford), Professor of Physics at UCL and adviser to Mountbatten as head of Combined Operations. It was Bernal who, as the only scientist present at the Quebec Conference of August 1943 between Churchill and Roosevelt, demonstrated the advantages of an artificial harbour for the Normandy landings, resulting in Mulberry. Bernal offered a post-war view that scientists were more fully employed in Britain, and with greater success, than in any combatant country.[36]

Other public-school educated Fellows of the Royal Society made key contributions to wartime research and development. Nevill Mott (Clifton), Professor of Theoretical Physics at Bristol University and later Nobel prize-winner, was scientific adviser to the head of Anti-Aircraft Command and then headed a theoretical research team at the Armaments Research Establishment at Fort Halstead, working on such projects as the mechanical properties of tank armour. Frank Ewart-Smith (Christ's Hospital), chief engineer at ICI Billingham in the 1930s, became Chief Engineer, Armament Design at Woolwich Arsenal. His scientific experience in reading intelligence reports led him to warn Churchill that the Germans were developing long-range rockets. David Pye (Tonbridge), with fellowships at both Oxford and Cambridge, joined in 1925 the Directorate of Scientific Research within the Air Ministry, located at Imperial College, and became its Director from 1937 to 1943, responsible for introducing new methods and equipment into the RAF. He was one of the first to appreciate the revolutionary importance of Frank Whittle's jet engine and is portrayed in *The Dam Busters* as the government scientist approving production of Barnes Wallis's bouncing bomb.

The private arms industry was another essential cog in weapons development. John Carden (Harrow), a self-taught engineer, became the main tank designer at Vickers before he was killed in an air crash in 1935. Vickers acquired Supermarine in 1928 and formed their own aviation division, presided over by Robert Maclean (Edinburgh Academy), who was responsible for the work of Barnes Wallis as an aircraft designer. Harold Yarrow (Bedford) and his son Eric (Marlborough), wartime officer in the Royal Engineers, presided over the Clydeside firm which built many of the Navy's most modern warships in both wars. Ronnie Harker (Shrewsbury) went from Fighter Command to become chief test pilot for Rolls Royce in 1942 and, while test-flying an American P51 Mustang fighter, noticed that its engine was not giving the necessary power or range at high altitude. He suggested that the latest Rolls-Royce Merlin engine should be tried, which completely transformed its performance, making it into a superb long-range fighter for the USAAF, escorting bombers on daylight raids into Germany.[37]

George Thomson (The Perse), Nobel prize-winner for physics in 1937, chaired the MAUD committee in 1940 to oversee the research required into the feasibility of the atomic bomb. When in 1941 Churchill decided to go ahead with building a British bomb, the secret project, known as Tube Alloys, was placed under the control of John Anderson, who appointed Wallace Akers (Aldenham), chief scientist at ICI, to run it under a consultative committee. Michael Perrin (Winchester), also an academic chemist at ICI, helped Akers run the key development teams for Tube Alloys and later worked with the Americans on the project. The Tizard mission to the USA in September 1940 had briefed their American counterparts on progress with the project and found that the Americans were working along parallel lines. The British doubted that they had the resources to take the project as far as an actual weapon, and it became by 1943 a wholly American development, known as the Manhattan Project.

Nowhere was more important to the scientific war effort than the Telecommunications Research Establishment (TRE), first on the Dorset coast and then at Malvern College, co-ordinating research into radio navigation and radar for both defensive and offensive operations. The 3,000 personnel who eventually worked at TRE came from a variety of backgrounds, but among them were two who would win Nobel prizes after the war – Alan Hodgkin (Gresham's), who worked on centimetric radar and the design of an airborne gun-laying system, and Martin Ryle (Bradfield), who worked on the design of antennas for airborne radar. Alan Blumlein (Highgate), an electronics engineer who had developed stereophonic sound for EMI between the wars, was the main developer of the H2S airborne radar system, the ground-scanning radar by which Bomber Command identified targets by day and night, but he was killed in 1942 in the crash of a Halifax bomber testing the equipment.

Military top brass, ministers and American notables flocked to Malvern to see its work, and in July 1944 the King visited TRE to put his seal of approval on the vital work being done there, a visit recorded by his private secretary, Tommy Lascelles:

We visited TRE, now housed in Malvern School ... we were shown many ocular demonstrations of the achievements of radar in its various manifestations. Without these astonishing inventions, we should certainly never have overcome the U-boats nor the German bombers ... In fact, had a few well-placed German bombs exterminated TRE, when it was precariously housed at Durnford, my old private school on the Purbeck coast, we should almost certainly have lost the war. This small and devoted band of scientists, originally led by Watson-Watt, has built up a truly wonderful organisation ... Stafford Cripps, as Minister of Aircraft Production, and his lady (looking very proletarian in a curious white beret) came with us.[38]

Lascelles was not the first layman to be astounded at the range and value of what was being done in scientific research and development to support the armed forces. On 21 June 1940 Churchill had summoned Tizard and Lindemann to discuss intelligence that the Germans were using electronic beams to guide their night-bombers to British targets. The meeting was also attended by R.V. Jones, then a twenty-eight-year-old scientific intelligence officer. It was clear that only Jones fully understood the issue, and he was asked by Churchill to explain. When he finished, Churchill ordered that Jones should be given every facility to investigate the German beams, which he succeeded in jamming. The episode showed Churchill at his best in providing the authority to scientists, even very young ones like Jones, to innovate with technology of which Churchill had only the most rudimentary understanding. Churchill used him after the war to write the relevant chapter in his official history about the 'wizard war', described by Churchill's research assistant as 'a brilliant short account'.[39] With Lindemann, Jones appears more often in Churchill's history than any other scientist.

Inventions

In the practical application of science to warfare, two twentieth century inventors have particularly caught the public imagination. The backgrounds of Frank Whittle and Barnes Wallis were similar, parents struggling financially to put them through school and engineering apprenticeships. Whittle's father was a practical engineer and mechanic who did not have enough money to keep him at Leamington College, the local endowed state grammar school, so Frank left at the age of fifteen to join the RAF Apprentice College at Halton. Three years later, he became one of the few Halton apprentices to be accepted into Cranwell, from where he was commissioned as a pilot in 1928. He was then sent to Cambridge to study engineering and started working on the concepts behind the design of the turbojet engine, but not until late 1940 was it ready to be put into production by Rolls-Royce. The first Gloster Meteor jet plane flew in 1943 and entered squadron service the next year, revolutionising aerial warfare.

Barnes Wallis was twenty years older than Whittle. His doctor father was stricken with polio and short of money, so Barnes owed his education to Colonel Newcombe, who submitted him for a place at Christ's Hospital, a unique public school in the opportunities it provided to those with little or no family money, where he shone at maths and science. Like Whittle, but two years older, he also left school to become an engineering apprentice, and moved to Vickers in 1913, aged twenty-five. Here he made his career and, when war broke out in 1939, he was assistant chief designer in the aviation section. He had already designed the Vickers Wellesley and Wellington bombers, then in service with the RAF, when he began his experiments in demolishing dams, which took effect with the bouncing bombs of the Dams Raid in May 1943. He produced other bombs, the Tallboy and the Grand Slam, designed to penetrate deep into the earth and used in several operations by 617 Squadron, and continued to generate new ideas until well after the war. The debt Wallis owed to Christ's Hospital was repaid by the considerable time and money he gave to the school in later life. He was so distressed at the heavy losses among crews in the Dams Raid, those he called 'my boys', that he donated in 1951 the whole sum of £10,000 awarded him by the government for his war work to a Christ's Hospital trust, to enable the children of RAF personnel killed or injured in action to attend the school.

Such inventiveness could also be found within the public-school dominated officer corps of the Army. Churchill's love of military gadgets led him to look with favour on Millis Jefferis (Tonbridge), a regular officer in the Royal Engineers. In 1940 the Prime Minister was looking for ways to strike back at the enemy and was impressed with Jefferis's fertile mind, sending him to work on sabotage devices for Military Intelligence Research, which merged with SOE. Jefferis reported directly to Churchill on designing and producing weapons to be used in both regular and irregular warfare and wrote a pamphlet, *How to Use High Explosives*, of which hundreds of thousands of copies were distributed all over enemy-occupied territory in sixteen different languages. Churchill recorded later that 'in order to secure quick action upon any bright idea or gadget, I decided to keep under my own hand as Minister of Defence, the experimental establishment formed by Major Jefferis ... In 1939 I had had useful contacts with this brilliant officer, whose ingenious, inventive mind proved fruitful during the whole war.'[40] The unit became known as 'Winston Churchill's toyshop' and among the weapons they devised were the PIAT mortar, the sticky bomb to be attached to the outside of tanks, and the magnetic limpet mine for the Admiralty. By May 1942 twenty-one devices had been invented, of which thirteen were in production, including booby traps, smaller clam mines and delay switches for use with explosives in demolition.[41] Stewart Blacker, another career soldier, from Cheltenham College, who retired from the Indian Army in 1932, worked with Jefferis, and his first weapon to go into production was the spigot mortar or 'Blacker Bombard'; demonstrated personally to Churchill in 1940, this resulted in an order for five thousand of them. It was used mostly as a weapon by the Home Guard but more importantly became the basis for both the Petard, fitted to tanks to throw plastic explosives at strong points, and the 'Hedgehog', a multi-headed anti-submarine grenade launcher which had many advantages over conventional depth charges and was used extensively by warships, destroying about fifty U-boats.[42]

The career of Percy Hobart also showed how soldiers with technological backgrounds could contribute to inventiveness in warfare. Hobart had gone from the army class at Clifton to Woolwich and then into the Royal Engineers in 1906, fighting in France and joining the fledgling Royal Tank Corps. In the 1930s he kept Churchill, with whom he felt a spiritual kinship, well informed in private meetings about deficiencies in the design and use of British tanks. The military hierarchy disapproved of his theories about the need for fast, powerful armoured columns, which the Germans were to put to good use in 1940, and he was forced into retirement. He joined the Home Guard as a lance corporal charged with the defence of Chipping Campden, but Churchill ensured that he was recalled in 1942 to raise and train 11th Armoured Division. He went into a meeting with Churchill dressed as a corporal in the Home Guard and left as an Army major general. In 1943 he commanded 79th Armoured Division, where he became a powerhouse of inventive energy, developing what became known as 'Hobart's Funnies', specialised armoured vehicles to lead ashore the amphibious assault in Normandy. Alanbrooke wrote in his diary on 27 January 1944:

> Eisenhower met me at the station and Hobart collected us at 9 o'clock and we went on to see various exhibits such as the Sherman tank for destroying tank mines, with chains on a drum driven by the engine, various methods of climbing walls with tanks, flame-throwing Churchill tanks, floating tanks etc. A most interesting day and one which Eisenhower seemed to enjoy thoroughly. Hobart has been doing wonders in his present job and I am delighted we put him into it.[43]

Thus were invented, and their crews trained, the DD swimming tanks, the AVREs to demolish pillboxes, the Crocodile flame-throwing tanks and the Crabs with a flail to detonate mines. Where this specialised armour was used on D-Day, complete success was achieved.[44]

Medicine

The global nature of the war and the use of higher-velocity weapons brought new challenges in the treatment of battlefield casualties, but significant medical advances were made. Among them were the treatment of burns in plastic surgery units organised by Harold Gillies (Wanganui CS), and the more common use of blood transfusions. The Army Blood Transfusion Service, the only one existing in 1939, was headed by Lionel Whitby (Bromsgrove), a leading haematologist who had taken up medicine after service with the Machine Gun Corps in the First World War, in which he won the MC and had one of his legs amputated near the hip.[45] The ready availability of blood was one of the most important factors in the successful treatment of casualties. Whitby trained initially as a doctor at Cambridge, but many others came via public schools to their first degrees at the London medical schools. They were second in popularity only to Oxbridge for those moving from the best known boarding schools to university, medicine having a social respectability and perceived earning power that other branches of science lacked. Life for students at the medical schools, not least in sporting rivalry, resembled that of boarding schools and Oxbridge colleges. Glyn Hughes, from Epsom College, originally founded as the Royal Medical Benevolent College, was one who trained in London, at University College Hospital. His medical training was accompanied by serious rugby, like many other medical students, and he later became President of the Barbarians. He distinguished himself in both wars, winning two DSOs as a front-line medical officer in 1914–18 and then, as a Brigadier, Chief Medical Officer in the North-West Europe campaign, taking control of the liberated Belsen concentration camp.

Psychiatrists were more likely in this war to be positioned near the front line to deal with cases now defined as 'battle exhaustion' rather than 'shellshock', a reflection of the better understanding of battlefield trauma. In 1942 the dedicated Directorate of Psychiatry was set up in the War Office, led by the inter-war medical director of the Tavistock Clinic, John Rawlings Rees (Bradford GS), and by 1944 over two hundred psychiatrists were working for the Army on officer selection as well as battlefield issues.[46] The work of Wilfred Bion (Bishop's Stortford) and John Rickman (Leighton Park) is less well known than that of William Rivers (Tonbridge), the pioneering psychiatrist of the First World War in his treatment of Siegfried Sassoon and Wilfred Owen, but, working at Northfield Hospital in Birmingham, they achieved 'some of the greatest successes in military psychiatry in the Second World War'.[47]

Major advances were also made in nutrition. In 1941 Hugh Sinclair (Winchester) was asked by the Ministry of Health to head the Oxford Nutrition Survey, its purpose to establish the health of the British population and ensure nutritional adequacy was maintained, even with food rationing. Sinclair collected data on the diet of different groups in society to try to establish links between diet and disease. In 1944 the Dutch government-in-exile recognised his pioneering work by commissioning him to investigate the nutritional status of the Dutch population badly affected by famine in the last months of the war. Another important figure in this field was Jack Drummond (KCS Wimbledon), Professor of Biochemistry at UCL, who was appointed chief scientific adviser to the Ministry of Food in 1940. Drummond produced for Lord Woolton (Manchester GS), the Minister, a plan for rationing which included more protein and vitamins. Studies after the war showed that, despite rationing and the hardships of war, the general health of the population improved.

The most significant medical advance in the war was the use of penicillin. Alexander Fleming, from humble farming roots and Kilmarnock Academy in Scotland, was a bacteriologist who saw service as a doctor on the Western Front, where he saw too many soldiers dying of infected wounds. In 1928, while working at St Mary's Hospital, he came by accident across a new substance which killed disease-causing bacteria, and he gave it the name of penicillin when he wrote up his findings in a medical journal. Over the next twelve years Fleming was unsuccessful in making a stable form of penicillin for mass production, but in the late 1930s Howard Florey, Professor of Pathology at Oxford, brought together a team of biochemists to undertake clinical trials and try to produce penicillin in large quantities.

Florey was an Australian, son of an English immigrant. He was sent to St Peter's College, Adelaide, one of Australia's oldest private schools, and after a first degree at Adelaide University went as a Rhodes Scholar to Oxford in 1921. The other leaders of the team Florey put together at Oxford included Ernst Chain, who had arrived from Berlin in April 1933 as a German Jewish refugee and took a job at Oxford as a lecturer in pathology, Edward Abraham (King Edward's, Southampton), whose role was to determine the chemical structure of penicillin, and Norman Heatley (Tonbridge), with a doctorate in biochemistry from Cambridge. In May 1940 Heatley tested the antibiotic power of penicillin on eight mice, all of which were injected with virulent bacteria. Four were then injected with a dose of penicillin, and in the morning he reported to Florey that the four injected had survived, while the four untreated were dead.[48] In early 1941 the first human patients were treated and the results published in *The Lancet*, after which Florey and Heatley flew to the USA to organise mass production of the drug, because no company in Britain was able to take it on.

Penicillin was first used in large quantities in Sicily in 1943, and then much more generally in the Italian and North-West Europe campaigns. In particular, 21st Army Group had a fully organised penicillin programme, with special officers to supervise its administration, so that the wounded had their first injection within hours. By 1945 the US Army was using two million ampoules per month, and penicillin is estimated to have saved 15 per cent of the cases which would otherwise have been fatal.[49] Stuart Mawson (Canford), parachuted into Arnhem in September 1944 as a doctor with the RAMC, later recounted an incident when a soldier with gas gangrene in his badly wounded leg was brought into the casualty clearing post. The senior surgeon doubted whether the leg could be saved but said, 'It will be a good opportunity to test all they have claimed for this penicillin stuff.' Mawson consulted his treatment book, prepared and administered the penicillin intravenously and intramuscularly, and hoped for the best. The penicillin did its work.[50]

Public School Science and the War

Provision for science between the wars at public schools was undoubtedly patchy between and within schools, as science fought for space with other subjects and historical prejudices had to be overturned. Until the 1920s the focus for science in most schools was essentially in the sixth form and army class, where specialisation was allowed, numbers were much smaller and outstanding science teachers like M.D. Hill at Eton or Ashley Lowndes at King's, Canterbury and Marlborough could work their magic.[51] There would certainly have been more scientists in 1939 if the cleverer pupils in public schools had had more exposure to it at a young age, but this was a wider educational problem, and academic priorities in the grammar school system were little different.

Despite this, David Edgerton has written that 'most of the important Second World War scientists had been to public school.'[52] Even as classically diehard a school as Westminster produced a significant cohort of top scientists, including Henry Tizard, Edgar Adrian, Richard Doll and Andrew Huxley. The contribution of scientists was critical to a war effort relying increasingly on the power of machines, and academic merit rather than old school networks brought the best scientific brains to the work. Among the youngest was Francis Crick, one of Britain's greatest twentieth century scientists, who won a scholarship to Mill Hill in 1930 and shone in maths, physics and chemistry, inspired, as he later said, by the quality of the science teaching. He failed Cambridge entrance, ironically in Latin, but took his first degree in physics at UCL, where his PhD was interrupted by the outbreak of war. He worked through the war in the Admiralty Research Laboratory on the design of magnetic and acoustic mines, and after it turned to the life sciences and became a molecular biologist, sharing the 1962 Nobel Prize for Physiology for the investigation of the double helix structure of the DNA molecule.

The importance of army classes at public schools should not be underestimated. They were looked down on by the Oxbridge stream in schools but played a crucial role in producing army engineers and gunners, as well as airmen. Ninety per cent of cadets entering RMC Woolwich before and after the First World War were public-school alumni, for whom admission to Woolwich was by competitive exam, and they passed out from there to join the two most technological corps in the army, the Royal Artillery and the Royal Engineers. Candidates in the entrance exam were ranked in order of merit according to marks received in a variety of subjects, but particularly science and maths, and there was a high failure rate. Army classes at schools like Wellington, Clifton, Cheltenham and Marlborough have produced soldiers and airmen of great distinction, Wellington more than a hundred of general or air marshal rank, including Geoffrey Baker, who won the Sword of Honour at Woolwich in 1930 before going on to war service with the Royal Artillery and field marshal rank in 1968. A higher proportion of gunners and sappers reached the top command posts in the Second World War than in the First, and the armed forces' own research departments were stocked with specialist officers from this science and engineering background.

In peacetime the scientific elite in universities was reluctant to encourage its best students to enter government service, but the demands of war changed that. The evidence suggests that Britain in the Second World War succeeded in becoming 'a technological, industrial and liberal nation', that success in the war was based on machines and firepower, and that the public-school educated wartime elites saw warfare in economic and industrial terms. Politicians and the administrative class of the civil service, the majority from public schools, recognised the importance of science and technology to the British economy and way of warfare, with Churchill himself in the vanguard. The controversial policy of strategic bombing resulted from a strong British faith in technology and was 'a way of warfare which owed little to liberal values or romantic chivalry'.[53] Freeman Dyson (Winchester), one of the outstanding physicists of the twentieth century, was called up in 1943 and, despite strong pacifist leanings, became an analyst for Bomber Command, calculating ways to improve mission efficiency. As his analyses led to the obliteration of whole cities, he felt guilty at allowing himself to become involved 'in this crazy game of murder'.[54] Michael Howard (Wellington), the eminent military historian, remembered as a boy the sombre school remembrance services every November, with their message that he and his generation must be prepared to follow the example of their predecessors and make their own sacrifice. When he joined his OCTU in 1942, the senior officer welcomed the new cadets by making clear that they should forget any ideas of laying down their lives for their country: 'It's not your job to get yourself killed; it's to kill the other chap and you are here to learn how to do it.'[55] In 1939–45 the romantic approach to war was once and for all buried, as science and technology took the leading role.

Part III

Shaping the Peace

The war won, the nation's attention turned to the shaping of the peace and the country that Britain would be after the war. The seeds of this had been sown in 1940 as the 'People's War' brought greater social cohesion, while the 1942 Beveridge Report laid the basis for welfare policies followed by Labour after 1945. Education came to the front of the queue, with the 1944 Act reshaping state secondary education and the Fleming Committee's proposals in the same year recommending that a quarter of places at boarding schools should be made available to pupils paid for by the state. Both presented challenges and opportunities to the public schools.

Chapter 7

The Post-War Settlement

Between 1919 and 1945 British public schools found themselves on a transformative journey in their relationships with the state and public opinion. In the 1920s independent education was booming and there were few reasons for the sector to engage with the state or with its critics, but the public-school image was still Victorian, absorbed in looking back to the models and traditions of the past. As criticism of the schools' social exclusiveness began to sharpen, there were men within the sector who professed to want to build bridges. Cyril Norwood wrote in 1926 that 'one of the chief dangers for the future of our country arises from the segregation of its social classes, and in particular from the utter separation of the children of the well-to-do during the whole course of their education from all other children.'[1] He did little about this, however, when head of Marlborough and then Harrow. In the more adverse economic conditions of the late 1930s, as numbers fell, self-preservation took over and HMC held tentative discussions with officials at the Board of Education to find ways to help the sector out of its financial problems.

In the first two years of the war the finances of many schools deteriorated, as requisitioning and evacuation affected some and fee income fell more generally. Several were identified by the Board as being in danger of closure, including some well-known names. The Board itself took a close interest in the situation, not least because its top civil servants all came from that educational background. There was pressure, too, on public schools from those proponents of the 'People's War' who wanted a more meritocratic education system, to reflect the demand for greater social equality and an end to privilege. Education moved to the top of the domestic political agenda as the Education Act, reforming state secondary education, was passed in 1944.

Paul Addison in his influential book *The Road to 1945*, published in 1975, argues that 1940 was not only the nation's 'finest hour' but also the moment 'when the foundations of political power shifted decisively leftward for a decade'.[2] This change took place almost unnoticed in the shadow of great events, but it was hastened by the need for Churchill to bring the Labour Party and the forces of organised labour into coalition government, and to respond to the pressure of public opinion. More recently, David Edgerton in *The Rise and Fall of the British Nation* (2018) has challenged what he terms 'the myth of the People's War', arguing that there was continuity after 1945 with pre-war governments, that Labour projected itself as a national party determined to maintain great power status, more than one aiming for social equality, and that spending on preparations for warfare was always higher than spending on social welfare. Edgerton's thesis does not detract from the enduring validity of Paul Addison's, and at the heart of the 'New Jerusalem' vision underpinning Labour's programme for government after 1945 were two pre-1914 public schoolboys, William Beveridge and John Maynard Keynes.

A combination of financial troubles, criticism of privilege, the burgeoning state education agenda and the initiative of R.A. Butler (Marlborough), the new President of the Board of Education in 1941, brought the issue of public schools into the open. The result was the setting up by Butler of the Fleming Committee in 1942 to inquire whether the association between the public schools and the state could become closer. The committee reported in 1944, just before the Education Act became law, and its impact was diminished by such a fundamental piece of educational legislation. Its recommendations did, however, open the door of opportunity to a major change in the social composition of boarding schools. By 1945 the journey which public schools had taken since 1919 ended with them engaging with the state and having to balance their wish for independence against their financial needs and the pressures of public opinion.

Increasing Pressures on Public Schools 1939–41

In December 1939, as the financial plight of the public-school sector worsened with the coming of war, HMC passed a resolution empowering a small committee to draft a report, with the Board, on the future of public schools.[3] This so-called 'committee of three' comprised Spencer Leeson (chairman of HMC and headmaster of Winchester), Geoffrey Williams (Westminster and previously assistant master at Wellington and Lancing), in charge of secondary education at the Board of Education, and Alfred Emden (King's, Canterbury), Principal of St Edmund Hall, Oxford. Williams was an indefatigable supporter of public schools who went beyond his job remit to help them. The information they gathered showed that many boarding schools were surviving only from term to term as numbers and fee income dropped. The committee's report was published in March 1940, raising once again the possibility of setting up a royal commission on the relationship with the state system, as well as putting in a contentious request for the government to consider income tax relief on school fees. When news of the latter broke, the headmasters of Rugby and three others issued a statement to the press denying that the public schools were facing a crisis.[4] It took Dunkirk and the fall of France for the HMC committee to accept that any consideration of special favours for public schools was patently absurd in the immediate crisis engulfing the nation, while governing bodies registered strong opposition to any scheme which would limit their independence. It was now up to public schools in the crisis of 1940 to show that they could embrace the new national consensus, their future existence in any case being bound up with that of the nation.

In the summer of 1941 Bill Deedes (Harrow), future Conservative MP and editor of the *Daily Telegraph*, was stationed at Duncombe Park, near Helmsley, with his battalion of the King's Royal Rifle Corps. The headquarters was in nearby Ampleforth College, where Father Paul, the headmaster, arranged discussions on current events between the senior boys and the battalion sergeants, something which would never have been contemplated in the more deferential age of 1914-18. Discussion invariably ended with the sergeants declaring that they were fighting the war so that places like Ampleforth could survive, while the boys, aware and critical of Ampleforth's exclusiveness, thought it was about making it possible for the sons of the sergeants to enter the school.[5]

As the danger of German invasion diminished and thoughts began to turn to the future, such discussions about plans for the reformation of post-war British society were becoming commonplace. In 1940 fear of defeat had sowed the seeds of change. Yet the disasters continued with the fall of Singapore in February 1942, bringing into question one of the main justifications for public schools, their role in producing leaders capable of defending and governing Britain and her empire. Criticism continued to come from the left-wing intelligentsia, who saw public schools as part of a world which should be consigned to history. Terence Worsley, Marlborough boy and Wellington master before becoming a writer, returned to the attack in 1941: 'If public schools are national assets because of their leadership and training qualities, what are we to think of those qualities when we survey the mess into which their leadership has brought us.'[6]

George Orwell (Eton) wrote a foreword to Worsley's book demanding that the issue of education be dealt with as soon as the war was over, and then himself published an essay in February 1941 going even further in his prescription for reform. Orwell believed that the outdated British class system was hampering the war effort and that socialist revolution was needed to defeat Nazi Germany – but a democratic English socialism, in contrast to the totalitarian Stalinist version which he had seen at first hand in Spain. Liberation from Empire and from the decadent ruling classes should be the aim of this revolution. He wrote that 'we could start by abolishing the autonomy of public schools and the older universities and flooding them with state-aided pupils chosen simply on grounds of ability.'[7]

In April 1941 the writer E.C. Mack forecast the future:

> Provided that complete ruin does not overwhelm England, the public schools may yet be saved, despite the hatred of their enemies, their seeming decadence and the disastrous state of their finances. Though engaged in a death struggle with Hitler, England is at this very moment literally seething with plans for reform of the public schools …The most likely solution would be one in which the public schools would take state money and accept state interference in order to bring into their ranks the best elements of the working-class, would reform in the direction of liberal working class aims, and yet would remain at least semi-independent boarding schools, emphasising training for leadership.[8]

Even an insider like Cyril Norwood, former head of Bristol GS, Marlborough and Harrow, doubted the viability of the sector in the face of wartime egalitarianism. Norwood had long favoured merging the grammar and public-school traditions into one elite national system and now saw the possibility of making this happen.[9] He wrote to Williams in December 1939: 'I do not see how as a system the public schools are to survive this war. They have had their hundred years and rendered great service with certain limitations. But the order of society to which they belong is at an end, or near it, however much we may regret the fact.'[10]

By the end of 1941 the question of education had assumed great importance in the drive for a more meritocratic post-war nation. That drive would focus on equality of opportunity, reorganisation of secondary education, including the abolition of fees in maintained schools, and a rise in the school leaving age to fifteen.[11] If England was going to be a better place after the war, then improvements in state education were vital. The evacuation programme had opened the eyes of the social elites to the serious shortcomings in the education of the poorest children, and to invidious comparisons with their own. In 1938 the proportion of children admitted to state secondary schools was just 14 per cent, and only a very small proportion of working-class children made their way to grammar schools and top universities. This also shone the spotlight on public schools. In a debate on education in the Commons in 1940, the veteran Liberal MP, Sir Percy Harris (Harrow), declared on behalf of his Bethnal Green constituency: 'The public school is a symbol of the feeling that there is a class character in our education, and that a privileged few have opportunities which are denied to the masses.'[12] Even within the public-school system, there was disquiet. In January 1941, Hugh Lyon, head of Rugby, wrote in the *Spectator* that heads had 'uneasy consciences' and were disturbed by the criticism that 'they thrive upon, and tend to perpetuate, a class system which is undemocratic and unjust'.[13]

In the summer of 1941, R.A. ('Rab') Butler was appointed President of the Board of Education. It was a ministerial role in which the average tenure in the 1930s had been eighteen months, and all but one of the previous incumbents had been Etonians. Butler had been educated at Marlborough, although his biographer said of him that 'he was never a worshipper at the public school shrine and quite enough of a rationalist to see the advantages of ending the great divide in British education'.[14] Butler himself bluntly revealed his own sense of detachment, and perhaps his memories of Marlborough, in a letter to his son's housemaster at

Eton in April 1943; 'I do not personally think that the whole of the public school system is necessarily the best form of education, particularly when there is too much worship of games and the herd spirit.'[15] He had seen his reputation damaged by his strong association with the appeasers in the Foreign Office, so welcomed the opportunity to redeem it with a popular reformist agenda in bringing in a major piece of social legislation for the post-war period. That was to bear fruit in the 1944 Education Act, reorganising state secondary education. He saw more clearly than most Conservatives what the domestic political consequences of the war would be. In Attlee he had a strong supporter in the War Cabinet for a major measure of educational reform, and he acknowledged the importance of Labour support when he wrote in October 1941 to Alec Dunglass (Eton), Chamberlain's former Parliamentary Private Secretary: 'I find in education that much of the drive towards a vaguely progressive future comes from Labour.'[16] However, progress in public-school reform faced major roadblocks in the form of Churchill and the Conservative majority in the Commons.

HMC and the Board held discussions throughout 1940 and 1941 about the serious existential problems facing many schools. One consequence of the manoeuvring of Spencer Leeson towards a royal commission on the public schools had been to show school governors the need for a properly constituted representative body of their own. Sir Ernest Pooley, Clerk of the Drapers Company, responsible for Bancroft's School, complained to Maurice Holmes, on behalf of several livery companies with responsibility for schools, that 'we are all up in arms. Leeson is an arch-wangler and his so-called joint committee has never been properly constituted. We will not be run away with by a handful of headmasters, and we do not want a royal commission at this juncture.'[17] The result was the Governing Bodies Association (GBA), set up in July 1941 under the chairmanship of Geoffrey Fisher, Bishop of London, former headmaster of Repton and now chairman of its governors.

Geoffrey Williams, secondary schools' spokesman at the Board, continued to go beyond the call of duty in pursuing the interests of public schools. In a 'private and unofficial' letter to Butler in September 1941 he set out his belief that 'the public school traditions as handed down by Thomas Arnold and Samuel Butler are worth preserving', but he also suggested that the benefits of boarding education should be diffused more widely. He also kept Butler and the Board informed of the parlous state of many schools. In October 1941 he had drawn up a paper classifying individual schools according to their financial prospects and identifying those at most risk. The most vulnerable group comprised schools 'in danger of extinction', named as Dover, Imperial Services College, Rossall, Canford and Brighton, but the next group 'whose future was doubtful' contained many prestigious names, including Harrow, Haileybury, Malvern, Cheltenham, Tonbridge and Repton.[18] Repton's numbers were down from 353 in 1939 to 273 by 1943, it had debts of £50,000 and was being charged interest of £2,000 per year.[19] Williams feared that 'more and more schools are finding it necessary to close houses and reduce staffs; overdrafts and loans are increasing in volume; and in general the majority of schools are just holding their own in the expectation of a revival after the war or some form of state assistance.'[20]

Butler was sympathetic but conscious of the political difficulties. He invited Fisher to a meeting in October 1941 but insisted on it being private and unofficial, because 'there is such a big avalanche which will be let loose on the subject of the public schools'.[21] He was part of a wartime coalition, and James Chuter Ede, Labour MP and Parliamentary Secretary to the Board, effectively Butler's deputy, made it clear that public schools raised issues likely to be disruptive of wartime political unity and cautioned Butler against pursuing schemes which he could not recommend to the Parliamentary Labour Party. Chuter Ede told Butler that, although Eton's endowments made it safe, some public schools would have to go, and that if they wanted public help, then they must render public service.[22] Butler's main focus was anyway on plans for state education, to be packaged in the 1944 Education Act, on which he needed consensus with Labour ministers in the Coalition.

Williams and Leeson, however, were intent on furthering the cause of public schools. In autumn 1941 Williams' own sense of urgency was displayed in a paper he sent to Maurice Holmes, Permanent Secretary to the Board, claiming that financial disaster was about to overtake many schools. He encouraged GBA and HMC to approach the Board about the possibility of government and local authority funding for boys to attend boarding public schools. Leeson's main concern was also with the boarding schools, favouring state boarding scholarships so that schools would be both helped financially and brought within reach of a wider section of the population by means of state assistance.[23] In this way some of the financial problems would be solved, while the most socially exclusive schools would be given a means of becoming more inclusive, as long as their independence from state control was preserved. The balance between financial necessity and altruism in Leeson's thinking is open to interpretation.

Churchill's attitude was critical. In August 1941 he remarked to Lord Halifax that it was the secondary schoolboys who had saved this country and 'they have the right to rule it'.[24] He presumably meant boys at grammar schools, given the very few other secondary schools in 1941. Later that year, he wrote to Butler with a warning: 'It would be a great mistake to stir up the public schools' question at this time. No one can possibly tell what the financial and economic state of the country will be when the war is over. Your main task at present is to get the schools working as well as possible under all the difficulties of air attack, evacuation etc.'[25] By February 1942 his views had surprisingly softened, as recorded by Chuter Ede:

> The PM was glad to know the public schools were receiving our attention. He wanted 60–70 per cent of places to be filled by bursaries – not by examination alone but on the recommendation of the counties and the great cities. We must reinforce the ruling class. We must not choose by the mere accident of birth and wealth but by the accident of ability. The great cities would be proud to search for able youths to send to Haileybury, Harrow and Eton.

This was not perhaps how a Labour veteran, a former elementary schoolteacher, would have viewed the issue, but it was a remarkable utterance from the leader of the Conservative Party, and it opened the way for Butler to make progress.

Appointment and Deliberations of the Fleming Committee

Butler wanted the public schools to make the first move and suggested to Geoffrey Fisher that he should write him a letter saying that 'the public schools were ready to provide boarding accommodation to state-funded pupils'. After some dithering, Fisher sent the letter in May 1942, confirming the agreement of HMC and GBA to this and asking Butler for a committee to explore a scheme for state bursaries to boarding schools. As chairman of governors at Repton, Fisher was aware that Repton, along with Trent and Abbotsholme, had in fact already opened discussions with Derbyshire's education committee to 'formulate a publicly-funded bursary scheme for local residents'.[26] The claim that the Fleming Committee was set up at the behest of the GBA and HMC is therefore not the whole story, Butler himself remarking about 'leading a horse to water'.[27] The process reflected the close-knit and influential nature of the old-school-tie network. Butler and Fisher had both been at Marlborough, where Cyril Norwood had been Butler's headmaster, and it was Norwood who proposed the Scottish judge Lord Fleming (Glasgow HS) as chairman.

As a result of Fisher's approach, Butler agreed in July 1942 to set up a committee, under Lord Fleming, 'to consider means whereby the association between the Public Schools (by which term is meant schools in membership of GBA or HMC) and the general education system of the country could be developed and extended; also to consider how far any measures recommended in the case of boys' public schools could be applied to comparable schools for girls'.[28] Chuter Ede's interventions meant that membership of the committee was widened beyond HMC, GBA and the Board to include representatives of universities, the National Union of Teachers, the Labour Party and LEAs. Girls' schools were represented by the headmistress of Roedean, Dame Emmeline Tanner, and HMC by the headmaster of Nottingham HS, Cedric Reynolds, and Robert Birley, headmaster of Charterhouse, who played a significant role in drafting the final report.

The definition of public schools used in the committee's terms of reference was representation in HMC or GBA, which excluded some independent boarding schools. The most notable omission was any reference to associations representing girls' schools. The attitude of the Board was clear in a note sent by Maurice Holmes to the Fleming Committee in 1942:

> I am not convinced that it is necessary in the national interest that
> the Girls' Public Boarding Schools should be made available to a
> wider clientele ... women do not in fact attain to high positions
> in public life to anything approaching the extent which might on
> purely numerical considerations be expected.[29]

Three distinct political views existed on the future of public schools. The
left wanted to abolish them or force them to merge with the state system.
The centre favoured leaving them independent but sponsoring some
of their places. In 1940 the Labour MP Hastings Lees-Smith, former
President of the Board of Education, argued that 'public schools would
have to accept a large proportion of children from elementary schools, a
proportion which will have to increase stage by stage until it reaches a very
substantial number in a comparatively limited space of time.'[30] On the
right, any association between public schools and the state was regarded
as an unacceptable encroachment on freedom. These positions were not
held in a disinterested political vacuum. The future of public schools
attracted a great deal of attention in the war, with one detailed study of
wartime education policy stating that public opinion was more interested
in the public-school question than other areas of schooling. Certainly
the interest was out of all proportion to the very small percentage of the
nation's children attending public schools.[31]

Butler's decision to appoint the Fleming Committee meant that,
for the next two years, public schools were effectively and deliberately
removed from wider discussions surrounding educational reform and
what became the 1944 Education Act. Butler would occasionally speak
of the public-school question, but only in vague terms. Maisky, the
Soviet ambassador, recorded him saying in June 1943 that 'the education
system should be democratised, i.e. almost all public schools should be
abolished (though Butler would like to keep two or three of them)'.[32]
Some of the press became excited at the setting up of Fleming, with the
Evening Standard optimistically proclaiming in a headline, 'Public and
Secondary Schools to be Merged'.[33] Butler's own comments to the press
were non-committal, reflecting a broad aspiration to bring public schools
and national system closer, but playing for time in waiting for Fleming
to report. Spencer Leeson wrote to his own Winchester governors in
August 1943 of his hopes for the outcome:

Much of the feeling against the public schools is founded upon a mixture of resentment at the protection given in them to social and financial privilege in education, regret in the hearts of their opponents that they did not themselves have the chance of being educated there, and a great desire that the benefits which those schools offer may in future be made available over a wider area.[34]

The deliberations of the Fleming Committee lasted two years and were overshadowed by progress towards the 1944 Education Act. Butler was in no hurry, later writing that the appointment of the committee defused an issue on which 'some Labour members breathed a certain amount of ritual fire and fury about social exclusiveness and privilege', also commenting that 'in a railway metaphor, the first-class carriage had been shunted on to an immense siding'.[35] Evidence was taken from 54 statutory bodies and 170 individuals. The views ranged from demands to abolish public schools to suggestions that they just be left alone to survive or die according to public demand. Some questioned the social wisdom of boys from poorer homes going to schools where other parents paid large fees, an argument refuted by the head of Christ's Hospital, who argued that boys from prep schools and boys from state elementary schools mixed in his school without serious problems. HMC and GBA wanted public schools to be made accessible to all boys with the character and ability to profit from them, but stated that the schools should retain their independence in order to preserve their special character. At the other end of the argument, the London County Council maintained that the future educational structure should be based on the state system and declared it did not wish to be associated with any scheme of collaboration. The most influential witness was Maurice Holmes, who wanted public-school facilities extended to a wider clientele and hoped that the direct grant system would continue, since he valued the freedom from local authority control which such schools enjoyed.

While Fleming was sitting, and before any plans for state-funded bursaries materialised, there was a significant change in the circumstances of public schools. From 1942 pupil numbers began to increase in many of those schools whose parlous financial position had so concerned Williams. At Tonbridge, which only had 75 entries in 1940 against an average figure for the 1930s of just over 100, admissions increased to 121 in 1943 and

127 in 1944. Harrow, down to 292 boys at the start of 1943, was back up to 400 by 1945. One reason for the improvement in school numbers was the increase in wartime economic activity after 1940 which, even with high levels of taxation, brought prosperity to many in the professional and business classes. Changes in the social composition of state grammar schools, with a rising number of free places awarded, also drove middle-class parents to seek the more socially acceptable alternative of public schools, a trend intensified after 1944 when fees were abolished in state secondary schools and parents faced the prospect of their children failing the eleven plus and going to a secondary modern. Butler himself wrote six weeks after the Fleming Report was published that 'the view of the big public schools is that they are so full that they are not in a hurry to implement [the recommendations].'[36] The change in circumstances was also reported by the Board in September 1944: 'In 1939 the public schools as a whole were suffering from a decline in the number of pupils – in a few cases very seriously. Today the position is reversed and the schools are experiencing an almost unprecedented wave of prosperity.'[37]

The 1944 Education Act

The background to the deliberations of the Fleming Committee was the 1944 Education Act, which did not directly address the public-school question but had a bearing on its possible solution. Butler's goal was to persuade the Coalition to embrace a major piece of educational legislation on which civil servants, and the Norwood Committee established by Butler in 1941 to report on the secondary school curriculum, had already been working. This fundamental reform of secondary education was something hoped for by educational progressives since 1918 but regularly postponed in the inter-war years. It proposed a tripartite system, which became the basis of the 1944 Act, establishing three types of state secondary school – grammar schools for the cleverest, technical schools for those skilled with their hands, and secondary modern schools for the rest. In July 1943 Butler published his legislative proposals in a Green Paper which passed through Parliament and became law in August 1944.

The 1944 Act had to be agreed by both the main parties in the Coalition based on a House of Commons with an overwhelming pre-war

Conservative majority (432 MPs to Labour's 154). Churchill was minded to delay education reform until after the war, but the Conservatives had suffered by-election reverses, which made him readier to accept the 1942 Beveridge Report on social welfare, and now a major piece of social legislation, under pressure from the progressive element in his own party. Attlee had to threaten to resign to persuade an increasingly fractious Labour Party to back it, a battle he won, meaning that it was therefore owned as much by Labour ministers as Conservatives and became the cornerstone of education policy once Labour came to power in 1945.[38]

By the time the Fleming recommendations were published in July 1944, the Education Act had already passed most of its parliamentary hurdles. As well as introducing free secondary education with three main streams of schools, it raised the school leaving age to fifteen with a promise to extend it to sixteen, and abolished fees in state secondary schools. The creation of non-fee-paying grammar schools was especially popular. The demand from the left of the Labour Party for a system of comprehensive schools was defeated, and there was no mention of public schools. The Labour MP John Parker, educated at Marlborough, raised the issue in the debate on the Bill in January 1944: 'We believe that unless the position of these schools is dealt with in this Bill, it will not be dealt with for many years to come ... This Bill will still keep a particular form of education available to a section of the people because of their ability to find money to pay for it. That is what we object to.'[39] He was given bland assurances that the recommendations of the Fleming Committee were being awaited, but Butler was intent on not provoking Conservative backbenchers. In the event, both types of HMC school, those fully independent and those receiving government subsidy, were omitted from the scope of the Education Act, which abolished fees in all other state maintained schools.

Butler had played his hand skilfully in defusing politically controversial elements. The legislation was acclaimed as historic, with Harold Dent, editor of the *Times Educational Supplement*, declaring it the 'greatest and grandest educational advance since 1870' and claiming that it embraced equality of opportunity.[40] Labour ministers within the Wartime Coalition supported it as providing for the first time a clear ladder of opportunity for working-class children to reach university, although critics within the party objected to enshrining the pecking order of the tripartite system as orthodoxy. Its more negative significance was not much appreciated at the time, notably the refusal to define specifically the structure of secondary schools or provide an argument in favour of selection. The pushing into the background of the comprehensive alternative favoured by the left, the strengthening of the grammar schools and the failure to bring the public schools within the remit of the Act ensured that the 1944 Act could not bring in a truly national system of education in tune with the wider post-war vision for 'New Jerusalem' and ensured these issues would create persistent political controversy in the future.

The Fleming Report and its Reception

The Fleming Report was published in July 1944, the month before the Education Act became law. It conceded that to leave public schools unchanged would make it impossible 'to close in the world of schools a social breach that aggravates, if it does not actually cause, the much more serious divisions in society at large'.[41] To remedy this, it proposed two schemes of association between public schools and the general education system. Scheme A was to replace the direct grant system, with LEAs allowed to take up places at these schools, after negotiation with governors and payment of the cost. LEAs would also have the right to nominate at least a third of governors at schools to which they sent pupils. This was later modified, as direct grant schools were vehement in their opposition, dreading the encroachment of local authority control and what they saw as an inevitable decline in standards. Geoffrey Williams was again helpful in resolving this issue with modified proposals, known as Scheme D and agreed by all parties, which continued the operation of the direct grant system on customary lines, schools retaining their independence and keeping the grants which made them distinctive.

Virtually all subsequent scrutiny of the Fleming Report focused on the proposal known as Scheme B, which applied only to independent boarding schools. including the most socially prestigious. It proposed that they should allocate at least 25 per cent of their places to means-tested bursaries, funded by the government, for children from state primary schools. The plan would be regularly reviewed 'with a view to progressive application of the principle that schools should be equally accessible to all pupils and that no child otherwise qualified shall be excluded solely owing to lack of means'.[42] The Fleming Report proposed that these places would be funded centrally by the Board of Education, but local authorities would also be able to reserve means-tested places within or above the 25 per cent minimum. The report envisaged such LEA bursaries only as a bolt-on element to a national scheme. Competitive exams were rejected as the entrance criterion in favour of broader considerations of the potential benefit of boarding education to each applicant.

The reception given to the report was mixed. *The Times* claimed that it gave public schools 'an unparalleled opportunity of cementing unity in a society which is as never before disposed for it'. Individual unions passed motions attacking Fleming, with the National Union of Women Teachers declaring that 'it was reactionary and opposed to the best interests of education'. The TUC protested at the continuing existence of a system which transferred educational privilege from one group in the community to another. Butler wrote, in response to the TUC opposition: 'They are of course too late. The public schools are saved and must be made to do their bit. All this is whining.'[43] Most local authorities were unenthusiastic, since it was an expensive way of educating a small number of children.

Designed to bring new cohesion to the secondary education system, Fleming went less far than some had hoped. Norwood's own vision of reconciling grammar and public-school strands in one system was not fulfilled, and having just a quarter of places at some independent schools was a long way from a single system of secondary education. Butler recognised the reviving fortunes of public schools, writing in September 1944 that there had been 'no class prejudice in Parliament and very little adverse comment … but on detail the scheme is thought to be vague. The view of the big public schools is that they are so full that they are not in a hurry to implement the scheme, but they are in favour of its general lines.'[44] Given the time needed for interested parties to consult and deliver their considered responses to Fleming, and the great events between D-Day and VE Day, any progress on implementing the proposals was postponed to the end of the war. Only in March 1945 did any formal negotiations start between the schools' associations and the Board, by which time they were soon to be disrupted by the change of government.

Public School Contribution to the Post-War Settlement

During the years of the wartime Coalition a common approach to the long-term future emerged among the different parties, heralding an era of political consensus which extended into the 1960s. The intellectual underpinning of the post-war settlement, particularly the shift towards economic planning, had been done in the 1930s. Kenneth Morgan, historian of the Labour Party, contends that it was 'the younger educated intelligentsia who dominated political ideas from around 1931, a great turning-point in Labour's ideas'. He believes that 'the whole notion of post-war planning was very congenial to public-school intellectuals', citing the particular influence of Hugh Dalton (Eton), economics lecturer at LSE, who gathered round him in the 1930s a circle of younger economists like Douglas Jay (Winchester), Hugh Gaitskell (Winchester) and Evan Durbin (Taunton).[45] Think tanks like Political and Economic Planning (PEP) also made important contributions. PEP had been set up in 1931 as a non-governmental planning organisation. Its founding members included Gerald Barry (Marlborough), editor of *Weekend Review*, Max Nicholson (Sedbergh), a pioneering environmentalist, Basil Blackett (Marlborough), an international financier and Israel Sieff (Manchester GS), the vice-chairman of Marks and Spencer. PEP produced reports in the 1930s on several industries, as well as on housing, social services and health, helping to pave the way for the Beveridge Report and the policy initiatives of the 1940s.

Other key members of this left intelligentsia included Kingsley Martin (Mill Hill), editor of the *New Statesman* for thirty years; G. D. H. Cole (St Paul's), leading light in the Fabian Society and Oxford don who taught both Harold Wilson and Hugh Gaitskell; and Harold Laski (Manchester GS), spokesman for socialism in the war years, who became chairman of the Labour Party in 1945–6. Most revered was the economic historian R. H. Tawney, whose education at Rugby and Oxford, and his pre-1914 work at Toynbee Hall with William Beveridge (Charterhouse), later his brother-in-law, convinced him that major economic and political change was needed to deliver better life chances to the poor. Tawney had identified in 1931 the monopoly of elite positions by public school alumni. Education was for him an engine of change in society which should be organised so that 'all its members may be equally enabled to make the best of such powers as they possess'.[46]

Tawney's best friend at Rugby was William Temple, who shared his abiding concern for the socially and intellectually deprived. Temple's father, Frederick, had been headmaster of Rugby and later Archbishop of Canterbury. William followed him into the church and was ordained in 1908, the same year in which he took on the presidency of the newly formed Workers' Educational Association. In 1910, at the age of just twenty-nine, he was appointed headmaster of Repton but, inspiring though he was to colleagues and boys, he had too many interests in the wider world to settle to the administrative details of school life and left after four years. He returned to parish work, ascended rapidly the hierarchy of the church and by 1939 was Archbishop of York, a distinguished theologian but also a man renowned for his commitment to Christian Socialism and social support for the unemployed. In 1942 Temple became Archbishop of Canterbury and published a best-selling book, *Christianity and Social Order*, which sold 139,000 copies, setting out practical proposals for greater equality and social care, including family allowances, a higher school-leaving age and better housing. It popularised the idea of the welfare state, and he led public meetings on the issue, flanked by Cyril Garbett (Portsmouth GS), the new Archbishop of York, and Stafford Cripps (Winchester), the Lord Privy Seal, to argue the Christian basis for social reconstruction. When he died suddenly in 1944 he was mourned as a great leader, a true friend of the poor and inarticulate everywhere and as 'someone above politics who symbolised the social aspirations of the People's War, the vision of a decent society'.[47]

William Beveridge, whose 1942 Report became the blueprint for the welfare state, was at Charterhouse in the 1890s, his political views and social conscience shaped there by one of his teachers, Leonard Huxley. Working with Tawney at Toynbee Hall before the First World War, he became fired by the need to deal with social problems in deprived areas. He moved into the pre-war civil service, leaving it in 1919 to become Director of LSE, where he built a reputation as the leading social scientist of his day, and then in 1937 Master of University College, Oxford, from where he accepted opportunities to chair commissions relating to social issues and unemployment. In 1941 he became chairman of a committee looking into social insurance schemes and he used this platform to write a report on 'Social Insurance and Allied Services', better known as the Beveridge Report. Published in December 1942, it sold 635,000 copies and recommended that the government should pursue reconstruction by fighting the evils of want, disease, ignorance, squalor and idleness. This should be achieved through a plan to eliminate poverty by maintaining full employment in order to underpin social security for all from the cradle to the grave.

The public reaction to the report was universally enthusiastic in a country beginning to look with hope to the future, so politicians of both parties broadly accepted its recommendations as the basis for post-war reconstruction. Correlli Barnett later derided Beveridge as the personification of the high-minded, public-school-educated liberal establishment, describing him in his skill at manipulating the press to support his plan as 'the Field Marshal Montgomery of social welfare'.[48] Barnett, however, underestimated the deep reserves of social consensus into which plans for a better world tapped, and the support for the war effort from all sections of the population, which Beveridge consolidated. His greatest legacy was arguably to convert the Conservative Party to the ideas of the welfare state and progressive capitalism. Traditionally a party worried about the cost of social services and the encroachment of the state on individual freedom, its philosophy was changed by pressure from younger Tories, notably three Etonians in Harold Macmillan, Lord Hinchingbrooke and Quintin Hogg, who saw it 'as an opportunity to re-establish a social conscience in the Tory Party'.[49] In March 1943 Churchill himself made a speech which did not refer to Beveridge by name but declared that he and his colleagues were 'strong partisans of national compulsory insurance for all classes for all purposes from the cradle to the grave'.[50]

The welfare state could only be successfully created with the help of John Maynard Keynes, the founding father of the managed economy and described as 'easily the most important academic intellectual in the state machine during the war'.[51] An Eton scholar in 1897, he went on to King's, Cambridge and an academic career, taking on the editorship of the *Economic Journal* in 1911. He worked for the Treasury during the First World War, after which he published the best-selling *Economic*

Consequences of the Peace, in which he criticised the scale of the reparations demanded of Germany, predicting the damaging consequences of the Versailles treaty. Between the wars he worked towards his greatest achievement, the reform of western capitalism through the evolution of economic doctrine, publishing in 1936 his revolutionary economic theory in *General Theory of Employment, Interest and Money*. Traditional doctrine held that the laws of supply and demand tended to create full employment, and that unemployment was caused by high wage demands. Keynes demonstrated that 'by stimulating consumption and investment, the government could increase demand to the level at which full employment was created'.[52]

By early in the Second World War, Keynes had persuaded the Treasury 'to accept at least a substantial measure of demand management as the principal way of regulating the economy in order to keep the level of unemployment down'.[53] He advised the British government to finance the war effort by raising taxes rather than borrowing. In 1944 his views inspired the government's White Paper on Employment Policy, which contained a commitment to maintain a high and stable level of employment in the future. This was endorsed by all the political parties in 1945 and became the basis of the post-war consensus. He also played a key role in the 1944 Bretton Woods Agreement, which dominated international monetary policy in the post-war years and led to the setting up of the International Monetary Fund, while Keynesian economics continued to dominate the world economy until the 1970s. The influence of Beveridge and Keynes on post-war Britain was immense, along with those like William Temple who saw the war as the chance to build a better society. For thirty years or more after 1945 'the instruments of the state were in the hands of those in both the big political parties who believed in the full employment/welfare state nostrums of Keynes and Beveridge and of those who carried with them the intense shared experience of the Second World War, whether lived on the battlefronts or the home front.'[54]

Between Fleming and May 1945: Response from Public Schools

The response from the public-school sector to Fleming was tortuous. The GBA and HMC committees voted in October 1944 to form a subcommittee to discuss details with the Minister, but it only met for the first time in March 1945. From this came a new negotiating committee under the chairmanship of Maurice Holmes and including representatives from HMC, GBA and other independent school bodies. Although this committee gave unqualified approval to the principles of Scheme B, it came too late to be submitted to the wartime Coalition and was sent to Ellen Wilkinson, the new Labour Minister, in August 1945, a full year after publication of the report. The conclusions were self-serving in places, including the suggestion of only gradual implementation of Scheme B over a seven-year period and opposing any proposal for the Ministry to nominate governors at participating schools. Labour's response was also predictably slow, for the government was busy with many other issues, including the greater educational priority of implementing the 1944 Act.

Not until January 1946 did the HMC Annual Meeting get a chance to consider Scheme B, when it was accepted in principle. In the interim the sector gave the Fleming Report a guarded welcome, with discussions revolving around three practical issues. The figure of 25 per cent of places was controversial – too large for some in that it might destroy the very traditions they sought to preserve, too small for others who saw the bursary pupils being assimilated into the system and lost to their way of life. The whole issue of pupil selection was also a very important practical difficulty – who was to decide and on what criteria, boarding need or academic need. Another practical difficulty was how to fill the two–year gap between leaving primary school at eleven and entering at thirteen, as in most boarding schools.

Heads of individual schools reacted to the Fleming Report cautiously, reflecting the wide diversity in the sector and the improving numbers and finances of most schools. Sevenoaks already allocated up to a quarter of its places to children from primary schools, maintained with public funds, the head declaring in 1942 that he saw nothing to apologise for in the form the public school system had already taken there.[55] Bristol GS, which applied to the Ministry for permission to remain on the list of direct grant schools, saw the proportion of maintained pupils rise from 10 to 25 per cent, with the remaining 50 per cent paying fees on a graduated scale related to parental income.[56] Charterhouse responded positively at first. In September 1944 the first four boys were sent to the school by Surrey County Council for £50 per year, less than a quarter of the normal fees. In 1945 the governors said they could no longer afford to accept boys at such a low fee, and Surrey agreed to pay the full fee that year and for some time afterwards. Charterhouse also came up against the problem of boys transferring from primary school at age eleven. Birley tried to persuade the governors to set up a junior house from eleven to thirteen to overcome this, but it did not find favour, on the grounds of financial viability and the traditions of the school. Birley was personally very committed to the Fleming proposals. He believed that the public schools 'had to come to terms with the state while they were in a strong enough position to safeguard what seemed to them the essential features of their independence'.[57] He also wanted to look at the issue from the standpoint of what schools like Charterhouse could contribute to the good of the nation. Such altruism was more difficult to sustain across the sector as prosperity gathered pace and the need for state help lessened.

Rab Butler's biographer believed that his handling of the public-school question 'represented the one real failure in his general strategy for educational reconstruction. The time was ripe, the public mood was propitious, the opportunity was there.'[58] He appeared to lack enthusiasm for the task, and not because he was himself a public school man who sent his three sons to Eton and sat as a governor of Felsted in his constituency. Butler was a meritocrat, but he was reluctant to fight on too many fronts. His main focus was on the 1944 Education Act, to secure which he had to overcome significant opposition from the churches; and there were enough warning shots from the public school lobby, which was very strong on the Conservative benches and also overlapped in many ways with the Anglican establishment, to suggest that he might endanger the gains he was making if he pushed the public-school issue. His setting up of the Fleming Committee would appear to have been a deliberate tactic. For all his liberal credentials as far as public schools were concerned, there are great doubts as to whether he really wanted Fleming to produce any significant results, preferring to focus on the much bigger prize of the wholesale reform of the state education system, without getting caught in the political mire of trying to do something about public schools. By the time Fleming's proposals had been digested and considered by various parties, Butler was out of office, and any decisions about implementation were in the hands of the Labour government.

By the beginning of 1945 prospects for public schools had clearly improved compared to 1939. They had aligned themselves with the national war effort in the 'People's War', emerged from political isolation and acknowledged that the problem of their educational and social exclusiveness needed to be addressed. Their financial situation had been ameliorated by rising numbers of pupils, but at the same time they had engaged with the possibility of state-funded entries to their schools and enjoyed a cosy relationship with the Board and its public-school-educated senior officials. If these improved circumstances produced a tendency to complacency as the war entered its final stages, then public schools were about to receive a nasty shock in mid-1945 when Labour won a landslide victory in the General Election. This put future education policy and the implementation of Fleming into the hands of a party historically hostile to the system, although it was led by a prime minister in Clement Attlee who had been educated within it.

Chapter 8

Reaching Out

Reaching out beyond their privileged comfort zone was not something which came easily to public schools in the first half of the twentieth century, but they showed their humanity in the help they gave to Jewish refugees from Nazi-dominated Europe. More than one hundred boys' and girls' public schools took in Jewish refugees, not only providing educational opportunities, but also saving many children who would otherwise have found themselves trapped in Nazi-occupied Europe and suffering the terrible fate of so many of their families. It is a little-known aspect of public-school history, and many of those children went on to make distinguished contributions to British public life. The heroes of this story included heads and governors of schools, as well as pupils, but also alumni who were prepared to go abroad to rescue as many Jews as possible in a desperate race against time. The numbers involved were no more than a drop in the ocean of suffering humanity, and it is always arguable that schools and individuals could have done more, but the compassion and courage shown reflect well on a public-school system which had plenty of other issues preoccupying it in the late 1930s.

One example will suffice for this introduction, for it demonstrates not just the opportunity given, but the lasting effect public-school generosity had on British life. Two refugees who came to Rydal School in North Wales from Tubingen in Germany were Ludwig and Gottfried Ehrenberg. Their mother wrote a pleading letter to the chaplain of Rydal, asking for a place after she and her husband, Victor, Professor of Classics at the German University in Prague, had fled to Britain in 1938. The chaplain persuaded the headmaster to offer a full-fees scholarship to both brothers, who arrived on 20 February 1939 with scarcely a word of English between them, Gottfried aged seventeen and Ludwig fifteen. By March 1939 they were reading Milton's *Paradise Lost*, and in June both passed Higher

School Certificate in all subjects, Gottfried winning the school English essay prize. Of his arrival in England, Gottfried wrote many years later: 'Within a few months it dawned upon me that I had arrived in the country in which I ought to have been born.' Gottfried Ehrenberg changed his name to Geoffrey Elton and later became Professor of Modern History at Cambridge and the pre-eminent Tudor historian of his day. Ludwig, who changed his name to Lewis Elton, became Professor of Education at University College, London (UCL) and is the father of the comedian and author, Ben Elton. Ben later recalled that Geoffrey Elton had written him a furious letter when *Blackadder Goes Forth* came out on television, saying that he had ruined a good series by being so disrespectful to the British Army to which Lewis Elton owed his life.[1]

Pressure to do something to help European Jewry came from the realisation that lives were at stake, but a sense of social responsibility for those closer to home was harder to find in public schools in the inter-war years. Only more recently have public schools had to develop policies and practices in this respect, both to respond to pressure from staff and pupils, and to justify their charitable status. The most shining example of peacetime altruism towards other communities lay in the charitable missions which schools set up in cities during the late 1800s and which continued to give important service to deprived communities through to the end of the next century. Such examples of reaching out were important not just for the good that they did in the communities they served, but for the inspiration it gave to many pupils and alumni who worked in them. Clement Attlee was one of them, his experience in the Haileybury Club having a lasting effect on the course of his life and therefore on Britain's history in the twentieth century.[2]

The end of the war also revived discussions about commemoration of the dead. In the aftermath of the First World War most school memorials possessed strong symbolic and emotional force, invoking the example of the dead to inspire the living and offering constant reiteration to later generations. These war memorials encouraged reverence for the traditions of the past, a belief that victory confirmed the superiority of the pre-war way of educating the country's elites. In 1945 the emotional engagement was palpably less, utilitarian solutions generally triumphing in the form of new buildings or other practical memorials to benefit future generations. Rather than hark back to the past, the new mood in schools was to put the war firmly behind them and reach out to the future.

British Jews and the Public Schools before 1939

Wealthy and ambitious Jewish families were a lucrative potential market for public schools, and many took Jewish children as pupils. British Jews in 1914 numbered about 300,000, one per cent of the population. Virulent ideological anti-Semitism never took hold in Britain, as it did in Europe, but 'casual anti-Semitism' was to be found in the inter-war years at all levels of English life. It could be found 'in popular novels, in the recruiting habits of the civil service, in the ubiquity of Jewish jokes, and in public schools'.[3] Traditional British establishment institutions could operate social exclusion through discriminatory but hidden criteria for admission and promotion. The higher civil service was thought to have only one Jewish official, while anti-Semitism was also prevalent in the Army. The most revealing incident was the sacking of Leslie Hore-Belisha (Clifton) as Minister of War in January 1940 after disputes with the Army high command in which anti-Semitism was believed to have played a part. Henry Pownall (Rugby), chief of staff to the BEF, commented in his diary on the relationship between the Minister and General Gort: 'The ultimate fact is that they could never get on. You couldn't expect two such utterly different people to do so – a great gentleman and an obscure shallow-brained charlatan, political Jewboy.'[4]

The greatest number of Jewish pupils in the public schools were in city day schools like Manchester GS or the City of London School, where Kingsley Amis recalled in the late 1930s that 'about fifteen per cent of the boys were Jewish'.[5] Isaiah Berlin, the philosopher and son of a wealthy Latvian Jewish family who fled Russia in 1921, came to St Paul's in 1922. When one of his tutors suggested he change his name to 'Jim' at school, he refused, but it made him aware that visible marks of Jewishness might hinder his efforts to enter Britain's elite circles. The fact that his two closest friends at St Paul's were Jewish suggests that 'integration was not smooth and unproblematic for him'.[6]

Jewish children could also be found in most of the big boarding schools, although discrimination could exist in the form of undeclared quotas and other means of deterring Jewish applicants. Cheltenham and Clifton Colleges both established separate houses for Jewish boys in the nineteenth century, and The Perse in Cambridge followed in 1904. Eton absorbed Jewish boys into existing houses. The philosopher Alfred Ayer, at Eton in the 1920s, was once passed a note by another boy telling him that 'his tabernacle was in St John's Wood' but excused such anti-Semitic remarks by blaming himself for his 'cleverness and sarcastic tongue'. He also found himself excluded from the Collegers' debating club until every other boy from his year and the one below had been elected, which hurt him deeply.[7] At Rugby School, George Strauss, from a family of prosperous Jewish metal merchants, was grateful for the high-quality teaching, but 'a scar was left at the rough treatment meted out to Jewish boys at school. From that time on Strauss cared vehemently about issues of race.'[8] He went on to become a Labour MP, a strong crusader against fascism in the 1930s and a minister in the post-war Labour government.

Harrow opened a separate Jewish house in 1881 but found that Jewish parents wanted their boys to integrate in existing houses, and it closed in 1903; it was then agreed that Jews could enter any boarding house, but only two per house. This itself reflected an implicit anti-Semitism, for housemasters were able to refuse to take any Jews, so that in effect Harrow operated a quota, with the prejudices of housemasters, as much as school policy, providing the determinant factor. Schools like Harrow appeared to operate a contradictory approach: they needed Jewish pupils but still found ways to discriminate against them. The smaller percentage of Jewish pupils at boarding schools was more likely to promote the prejudice which came from difference, and among the boys at Harrow (and more discreetly among the masters) there was 'much unthinking, traditional upper-class, overt anti-Semitism'. The school admitted boys from a wide variety of faiths and countries, including the future Prime Minister of India, Jawaharwal Nehru, but as an institution it remained 'culturally monochrome, with racism and anti-Semitism endemic'.[9] In November 1939 a major row broke out at Harrow when the chaplain wrote to a Jewish school monitor about his reading the New Testament lesson in Chapel: 'In my view it should be as impossible for you to wish to do it as for anybody to allow it.' The boy's father was furious, and the headmaster, Paul Vellacott, was scarcely less so, not least because he was trying to persuade Old Harrovians, including two Rothschilds, to bail the school out of potential financial ruin.[10]

At Repton anti-Semitism affected Harold Abrahams, the *Chariots of Fire* sprinter, a pupil during the Great War. His father was a Lithuanian Jew who had arrived in Britain as a penniless teenager in the 1870s, but his success as a financier meant that he was able to send three sons to Bedford Modern School and Harold to Repton. Here Harold was more isolated and certainly hurt by discrimination: 'I was good at athletics at Repton. There was quite a deal of anti-Semitism at schools in those days and I had to find something where I could score off people. And by running you can win, and I was determined to do so.' He excelled in athletics and became a school prefect, but did not get on with the headmaster, Geoffrey Fisher, later Archbishop of Canterbury. Harold's nephew recalled: 'Harold disliked the headmaster, Fisher ... Although head of house, he was not allowed to read the prayers or the lesson in assembly.'[11] The 1981 Oscar-winning film *Chariots of Fire* makes much of the anti-Semitism Abrahams endured at Cambridge as the spur to his athletics ambition, although he claimed it was worse at Repton. David Puttnam, producer of the film, remembered when filming at Caius, Cambridge that the college was hypersensitive about anti-Semitism:

> One of the reasons I had problems filming at Caius was that anti-Semitism had been rife in Harold's time and Caius got very neurotic about us filming there because they thought we would go further in our portrayal of the anti-Semitism. I remember a phrase was, 'We don't want all that being dragged up again.'[12]

A more tolerant environment could be found at The Perse School. The first advertisement to attract Jewish boys to Hillel House was placed in the *Jewish Chronicle* in 1904, at a time when the school was in some financial difficulties. The headmaster had taught at Cheltenham and had seen there how a Jewish house could thrive. From 1929 the housemaster was Harry Dagut, a significant figure in the national Jewish community, and during the difficult economic circumstances of the 1930s Hillel was oversubscribed, the boys in it representing about 10 per cent of the school. Dagut was a committed Zionist and took a central role in providing help to Jewish refugees in Cambridge. All the evidence from the time suggests that anti-Semitism was simply not present in the school. One Hillel pupil wrote later that 'anti-Semitic incidents were so rare that one was actually logged', while a non-Jewish boy in another house wrote that they were 'subconsciously educated to perceive the evils of intolerance and tyranny from the start, and to behave properly to our fellow boarders whatever their colour or creed'.[13]

Help for Jewish Refugees 1933–8

The crisis which engulfed European Jewry began with Hitler's accession to power in January 1933. Between then and the start of the war about 500,000 Jews in Germany, and then about 200,000 in Austria and 360,000 in Czechoslovakia, came under his control. In Germany, Nazi policy moved from boycotts of Jewish shops in 1933, accompanied by random violence towards Jews, to the Nuremberg Laws of 1935 denying Jews German citizenship and forbidding marriage or sexual relations between Jews and 'Aryan' Germans. In early 1938 more drastic restrictions followed, beginning with the 'Aryanisation' of the economy and a ban on Jewish professionals offering their services to Germans, while Jewish children were excluded from German schools. The *Anschluss* with Austria in March 1938 unleashed anti-Jewish pogroms there, followed on 9/10 November by *Kristallnacht*, when synagogues and Jewish shops were burnt down all over Germany and in Vienna, and Jews subjected to savage violence by Nazi thugs.

In April 1933 Jews were forbidden to work in any part of the civil service, including schools and universities, which prompted the first efforts in Britain to help those affected. The Academic Assistance Council (AAC) helped dismissed scholars in German universities to find university positions in Britain. By 1939, 128 refugee academics had been found posts in British universities, twenty-seven of them at Oxford.[14] The richness of the haul for British universities was enormous – four Nobel prize-winners, sixteen who would go on to win Nobel prizes and seventy-four who would become Fellows of the Royal Society. William Beveridge, Director of LSE, was instrumental in setting up the AAC along with Archibald Hill (Blundell's), professor at UCL and Nobel prize-winner in physiology. The academic world was much more patrician and elitist in 1933, most of its members having attended the same public schools and universities, so the AAC was adept in using their networks to place German academics and to raise funds.[15]

One spin-off from the arrival of many distinguished German Jews in Britain after 1933 was the entry of their children to British public schools, most of them at this stage being able to pay at least a portion of their own fees. The head of King's, Taunton gave places to fifteen boys, including Kurt Abrahamsohn from a middle-class German Jewish family in Stettin who, while still at school in 1938, managed to secure visas for his parents and sister to come to England. He joined the RAF during the war, changing his name to Kenneth Ambrose, in case he fell into German hands bearing an obviously Jewish name. In 1936 Ernst Sondheimer joined University College School and his brother Max joined Highgate, after their father left Stuttgart to re-establish his business in London. Ernst remembered that 'UCS was a release and a revelation; in its liberal atmosphere there was no trace of prejudice against me as a German and a Jew.' [16] He later went on to become Professor of Mathematics at Westfield College, London. Rolf Griessmann, son of a Bavarian industrialist, joined Highgate in 1936 after his father emigrated to start a new factory in Walthamstow. Rolf later anglicised his name to become Ronald Grierson, banker and government adviser. Highgate took in over twenty German Jewish refugees through the influence of Professor Hill, one of its governors.

Jewish children who came to Britain from Germany before the second half of 1938 mostly arrived with their families, their fathers having anticipated political events and being able to find professional work or set up businesses. At this stage it was possible to take assets out of Germany, so they were able to afford at least some of the school fees. Claus Moser's father was a banker and his mother a talented pianist, whose elegant home played host to intellectuals and musicians during the years of the Weimar Republic. Claus remembered vividly the torchlight procession of SA and SS men the night Hitler came to power, as well as the bullying he and another Jewish boy endured at school. The family came to England in 1936 and Claus, aged fourteen, went to Frensham Heights, regarded by some in the public-school establishment as dangerously progressive, where he 'found four years of total happiness' and where his intellectual and musical talents were recognised, before he went on to the LSE in 1940.[17] He later became Director of the Office for National Statistics, Warden of Wadham College, Oxford and Chairman of the Royal Opera House. Sir David Attenborough, a close friend, wrote that 'Claus felt an overwhelming debt to this country. British society saved him. His life has been about paying it back.'[18]

The Eberstadts, a banking family from Hamburg, also came to England in 1936. Walter Eberstadt was sent to Tonbridge, where his astute observations on English boarding school life focused on the arcane dress code, the hierarchy of fagging and the obsession with sport. He left to go to Oxford in 1939, and in later life reflected:

> I wanted very much to be accepted in the ways of an English public school. It was part of the process of becoming English ... Few of the boys were Jewish. The wealthy Jewish families often went to Harrow, though on the whole Jewish families did not like to send their children to boarding school ... If they lived in London, they were day boys at Mill Hill or Highgate, which are close to Hampstead, Golders Green and St John's Wood.

Anti-Semitism existed at Tonbridge but 'it was a different anti-Semitism from German, let alone the Nazi German. Many simply did not like aliens but notwithstanding the ingrained prejudice, which is part and parcel of human nature, England was a tolerant nation which prided itself on having taken throughout its history the persecuted and on benefiting from their talents.'[19]

Two years later, in January 1938, Otto Fisher came to Charterhouse, aged fifteen. His father, a Viennese diamond merchant, sent his wife to England with Otto to find a school to take him, and it was Robert Birley who gave him a place, taking him into his own house and family. When the *Anschluss* happened two months later, Otto's father was one of the first to be arrested, and Birley, realising that the British Consul-General was a Carthusian, wrote immediately to him: 'You cannot let the parents of a Carthusian smart in Hitler's prison.' His release, and visas for the whole family to come to England, were forthcoming. When in June 1940

Otto's father wanted to take the family to the USA, Otto refused to go as his loyalties were now with Britain. Birley arranged for father and son to meet him on Woking station, and he mediated between them, advising the father that Otto was determined to stay. Otto later wrote of Birley:

> The men of Munich and you were poles apart. When you went out of your way to meet my father in the black days of the war at Woking station to discuss my future with him, that schoolboy had no hesitation that he wanted to stay in England to fight for King and Country.[20]

Kristallnacht and *Kindertransport*

The signing of the Munich Agreement at the end of September 1938 dramatically increased the number of Jews to be rescued from Nazi control in Austria and Czechoslovakia. The prospect of a huge number of Jews fleeing persecution presented the British government with difficult political questions in respect of public opinion at home and the immigration quota into Palestine, which Britain then controlled. The official line was that none would be admitted to Britain unless the already overstretched voluntary organisations could take responsibility for their maintenance.

One British volunteer was determined to do something. Doreen Warriner had intended to fly to the USA on 13 October 1938 to take up her Rockefeller Fellowship, but she was so ashamed by Chamberlain's betrayal of the Czechs that she flew instead to Prague. 'I had no idea at all what to do', she wrote, 'only a desperate wish to do something.' A pupil at Malvern Girls' College, she had gained a first in PPE at Oxford in 1926 and was then appointed in 1933 to a lectureship in political economy at UCL. Once in Czechoslovakia, she helped refugees in makeshift camps around Prague, Jewish families as well as political refugees from Germany and Austria, all now in danger of arrest. She worked long hours collating lists of names, applying for visas, administering relief funds and organising transport, often crossing the line between humanitarian relief effort and political resistance. Even after the Germans occupied Prague in March 1939, Warriner was still there helping people and herself experiencing police intimidation at the station as they hunted out and seized 'communist and Jewish garbage'. She had to leave in a hurry in April 1939 after she was warned that her arrest was imminent.

Only five weeks after Munich came *Kristallnacht* on 9/10 November 1938. That night of violence across all German-speaking areas resulted in the mass incarceration of Jews, wholesale destruction of Jewish property and terrible violence against individuals, as well as the confiscation of most Jewish wealth in a penal fine. *Kristallnacht* was widely reported in the British press and stirred public opinion in Britain more than any other single event. Pressure was put on the government to act by two Foreign Office officials at the Berlin embassy, both from Roman Catholic public schools – Sir George Ogilvie-Forbes (Beaumont), counsellor since 1937, and Frank Foley (Stonyhurst), passport control officer as cover for his MI6 intelligence work. In a letter to Foreign Secretary Lord Halifax on 16 November 1938, less than a week after *Kristallnacht*, Ogilvie-Forbes described how he and his staff had witnessed the violence and the looting of Jewish property: 'It has let loose the forces of medieval barbarism … I can find no words strong enough in condemnation of the disgusting treatment of innocent people.' Foley used his influence to expedite the emigration of Jews to Palestine by obtaining visas for them, telegraphing Jerusalem to be sent extra Palestine certificates, including 1,000 for young Jews unaccompanied by parents. He even went to concentration camps with Palestine certificates to secure the release of prisoners.[21]

Kristallnacht proved a turning point not just in public perception of the Nazi regime, but also in government policy. Four days later, Neville Chamberlain met leaders of the Jewish community to discuss the government's response, correctly judging that vulnerable children would attract public support more than any other group. The result was the start of what became known as the *Kindertransport*. Unaccompanied children, without a limit on numbers, would be allowed into Britain to stay temporarily, provided each had financial backing in the form of a £50 guarantee. The government did not organise the *Kindertransport* nor did it accept financial responsibility, handing these jobs over to the voluntary organisations under their own umbrella group, the Refugee Children's Movement (RCM), an inter-faith grouping of Christian and Jewish aid organisations, including in particular the Quakers. The RCM put in place the systems for choosing, organising and transporting the children, and built up a complex network of volunteers to implement the plans. They set up a temporary transit camp at Dovercourt Bay near Harwich, along with sponsorship, fostering and education. The first party of 200 German children arrived on 2 December 1938, and in the following nine months about 10,000 children came. Dovercourt was staffed by volunteers, including Oxbridge undergraduates, and in the Christmas holidays of 1938 by six Eton boys. When another camp at Lowestoft was closed by flooding in December 1938, the staff of St Felix School gave up their Christmas holidays to look after 250 newly arrived children.

One of the beneficiaries of the *Kindertransport* was Otto Hutter, who had just turned fourteen when German troops marched into Austria. His jurist father explained to him that the clock of history had been turned back by the new Nazi decrees and that Jews in Austria had been left without the protection of the state. On *Kristallnacht* the power of the mob was witnessed by Otto's aunt, who saw Jews being thrown from the church spire, as synagogues burned and Jewish shops were ransacked. Otto's father, a decorated officer of the old Austro-Hungarian army, was rounded up and imprisoned along with thousands of other Jewish men. He was later released because of his wartime service, after signing an undertaking that he would leave the country with his family, although the doors of the world seemed closed.

On 4 December 1938 Otto met a friend who told him that he was soon leaving for England and directed Otto towards the Hotel Metropole, where the registration of children for emigration was under way. Otto ran there to become the 359th of 360 children registered that day and, interviewed, photographed and medically examined, he raced home to tell his parents, for whom there now came the agonising ordeal of parting with him. In the next few days Otto was fitted out with stout boots, a new winter coat and other essential clothing, each item lovingly embroidered with his name by his heartbroken mother. With all his belongings packed into a small case, and a manila card bearing the number 359 tied around his neck, he went with his parents to the station late on the evening of Saturday, 10 December 1938 to join the first *Kindertransport* train to leave Vienna. He still recalls how he rushed to join the other children on the train, thinking of it more as an adventure than a sorrowful parting. His father, filled with premonition, held him back to bestow the traditional Hebrew blessing, comforting himself with the thought that when Otto later blessed his own children, the chain of generations would remain unbroken. The train took twenty hours to reach the border with Holland, and later that evening they crossed to Harwich and then travelled to Dovercourt Bay. Otto had reached the school leaving age in England of fourteen, and refugee children of that age were encouraged to take up a trade, but postal communications were still open with Austria via Red Cross messages, and his father urged him to continue his education.

The *Kindertransport* stirred the consciences of many public schools, and the Old Stortfordian Society, consisting of the alumni of Bishop's Stortford College, was one organisation determined to help. The president wrote, on 22 February 1939, to all Old Stortfordians, asking them to make 'a worthy and lasting contribution towards the solution of an urgent and difficult problem ... Among the refugees in this country are many boys who have lost their homes and are now exiles in a strange land. Their parents, even if they have escaped imprisonment or death, can no longer provide for them. What then can Stortford do?'[22] Over £1,000 was subscribed, enough to pay the fees of two boys, and in March 1939 one member of the society's committee, Alec Blaxill, chose Otto to look after and took him to his Colchester home. In April 1939 Otto started at Bishop's Stortford, complete with blazer, scarf and tuck-box, to enjoy the last peacetime term. The Blaxills looked after him in the school holidays, treating him as one of the family, and when he left school in 1942, found him a job as a laboratory assistant at the Wellcome Foundation in Beckenham, testing early batches of penicillin. After the war his academic career flourished, culminating in his being appointed Professor of Physiology at Glasgow University. The opportunities given him by the Old Stortfordians' magnanimous gesture Otto still regards as 'a wonderful example of true human compassion, reflecting so praiseworthily on the values the College stood for'.[23]

The *Kindertransport* was a monumental task of organisation, relying on effective systems and fund-raising, but also on brave and committed individuals like Doreen Warriner. On 20 December 1938 she was joined in Prague by a friend, Martin Blake, a master at Westminster School who gave up his Christmas holidays to come out to help. Blake had another friend, Nicholas Winton, who had been due to go on a Christmas skiing holiday but now also flew to Prague. One of Roxburgh's first pupils at Stowe, Winton had left without much in the way of academic qualifications and became a stockbroker, but Roxburgh had imbued him with a proper respect for humanitarian values. When he arrived in Prague he toured the refugee camps with Warriner and Blake, and they were joined by another schoolmaster, Trevor Chadwick. Winton could only stay briefly in Prague, as he had to get back to his job, but he agreed to organise things in London for what became called the British Committee for Refugees from Czechoslovakia, Children's Section. Every evening after work, he would write to people who might provide money or homes for the children. A slow trickle of agreements to help came in, so their names, along with money Winton raised, were sent to Trevor Chadwick in Prague to match with children and get the exit permits and transport arranged. Winton met every *Kindertransport* train at Liverpool Street station, along with the people who had agreed to take the children. The last transport from Prague, with 250 children, would have been the biggest of all, but was stopped by the outbreak of war.[24]

The part played by Trevor Chadwick in Prague is less well known. Chadwick had been a boy at Sedbergh and taught at Forres, the Dorset prep school founded by his father. He wrote later: 'I was teaching at our family prep school. Rumours of the many distressed children in Central Europe reached us and it was decided to adopt two. Another master at the school and I set off to Prague to select our pair.' He decided to stay there to help, often negotiating with puzzled German officials who did not understand why England wanted Jewish children. Sometimes, when essential papers did not come through, Chadwick improvised by creating his own, and he exploited the corruption endemic in Nazi officialdom. Between them Winton and Chadwick arranged six transports from Prague with 669 children, many of whom found their way to public schools, including Ellesmere and Woodhouse Grove.

Behind the volunteers like Winton, Blake, Chadwick and Warriner lay a vast network of fund-raising activities. In December 1938 the Earl Baldwin Fund was launched by the Harrovian former Prime Minister in a radio appeal which raised over £500,000 by July 1939 with the support of City of London institutions, money which was allocated to those voluntary organisations bringing in refugees. In February 1939 the HMC Committee publicised the Earl Baldwin Fund and called for help from schools: 'It is thought that the schools of this country would feel a special interest in both the child refugee and the professional adult refugee … although much has been accomplished, it is insignificant in comparison with the dimensions of the problem.'[25]

Winchester was one of the first schools to respond to the Baldwin appeal. In February 1939 the headmaster, Spencer Leeson, was authorised by his governors to offer five free places to the sons of persons expelled from their homes in Central Europe, provided that they were intellectually suitable for the school and had someone prepared to offer them a home. These places were advertised by the Earl Baldwin Fund, and one selected in 1939 was Edgar Feuchtwanger, son of an academic publisher from Munich imprisoned in Dachau after *Kristallnacht*. Edgar's love of history was nurtured and sustained at Winchester, where he stayed until 1943, looked after in the holidays by his housemaster, Harry Altham, and his family, and describing the school as 'liberal, tolerant but also very conscious of itself as an elite both social and intellectual'.[26] Leeson had to tell his governors about a protest he had received from some Old Wykehamists 'against the admission of Jewish boys to a Christian school'.[27]

Foremost among the schools offering help was the Quaker foundation, Leighton Park School, near Reading. Some German families had already sent their sons to the school for a year or two in the mid-1930s to distance them from the increasing influence of Nazi policy and indoctrination; these included Fritz Luce, whose anti-Nazi father simply wanted to keep him away from the Hitler Youth. Luce never settled at Leighton Park, returned home in 1939 to join the German Army and was killed in action, his name now appearing in the Leighton Park Memorial Book alongside many of his classmates. Between 1935 and 1940 Leighton Park took in forty refugee boys, not all Jewish. Although the governors had imposed, in November 1938, a limit of twelve refugee boys at any one time within the school, Edgar Castle, the headmaster, was deeply committed to finding places for all who wanted to come, although he insisted they must meet the school's academic and behavioural expectations. In the school files there is evidence of vigorous correspondence with individuals and agencies seeking assistance with school fees or family accommodation in the school holidays. Castle took several into his own home.

Pavel Reisz was one who came to Leighton Park in 1936, the son of Jewish Czech parents who could afford the fees. He was happy there and, in the spring of 1939, his mother wrote asking if he could help get his brother Karel into an English school. Pavel later wrote:

> I immediately approached the headmaster, Edgar Castle, and he told me to leave the matter in his hands. In June 1939 he called me to his office (generally implying an imminent punishment for some misdeed), gave me one pound and told me to take the train from Reading to London and be at Liverpool Street station at 11 a.m. where my brother would arrive.

Karel arrived on a train from Prague organised by Chadwick and Winton. Castle had engaged in lengthy correspondence to secure his visa and bought him a bicycle to help him fit in with other boys. The Reisz parents could no longer afford the fees for either boy, but these were covered by the school and a local Quaker family. Karel Reisz ended up as head boy, before joining the RAF, and later became a highly regarded film director. He never forgot the debt he owed to Edgar Castle and wrote to him in 1944: 'There seems to be little I can say now to repay the debt which I owe you personally; for your part in my getting over to England at all; for the care you took to buy a bicycle for me even before I got here (the impact this little deed made on my mind was deep).'

This story should not obscure the many problems Castle faced in implementing his generous policy. In his letters about boys he frequently refers to 'refugee troubles', characterised as disturbed behaviour and difficulty in adjusting. Boys were accepted into Leighton Park on a somewhat ad hoc basis, sometimes with unreliable sources of funds, and it was often Castle himself who had to find the money from existing bursaries, requests to benefactors or his own pocket. In a letter Castle wrote to another leading Quaker in 1940 he asked whether 'there are any funds, Friends or otherwise, available for the education of refugee children ... I am already providing the keep and paying part of the fees for one refugee boy I have living with me and I feel I cannot do it for this other one, whose father has been interned and has no income to pay the fees.'[28]

The list of the many other public schools which offered places is long, numbering at least a hundred across Britain. The Girls' Public Day School Trust, consisting of twenty-three schools, gave sixty scholarships to Jewish refugee girls. Bootham School gave a place to Harry Baum, who arrived on a train from Vienna in December 1938 aged eleven, with his older sister. They were fostered by the Hughes family, Quakers from near York, who recognised that Harry could win a scholarship to Bootham. His daughter said of her father that, although he suffered from dementia in later life, he could still remember what he had packed in his suitcase at Vienna.[29] Hulme GS for Boys in Oldham gave places to four boys, and Hulme GS for Girls admitted nine girls between 1936 and 1941, some sponsored by local Jewish families but two paid for by spontaneous collections among pupils and their parents. The school magazine records in 1939 that the school charity fund would be used to keep a German refugee, 'but so generous were the promises of parents, staff and girls that two girls were adopted by the school, Kitti and Lilli Spitz, who arrived in summer term 1939.'[30] Forest School in Essex took twenty refugee boys and employed Jewish teachers, including Heinz Spitz, who came from Vienna on a *Kindertransport* in 1939 aged seventeen and started teaching science at Forest in 1942, the year his parents were murdered in Sobibor extermination camp.

Three refugee boys were admitted to Sherborne, with the school taking financial responsibility for them. One was Lothar Markiewicz, who arrived from Berlin in April 1939 with his sister, and started that summer at Sherborne, his sister at Sherborne Girls' School. In July 1940, aged sixteen, Lothar was arrested as an enemy alien and deported to Australia on HMT *Dunera*, which arrived in Sydney in September, the dreadful conditions on the ship condemned by the Australian authorities. He was transferred to an internment camp, the second youngest person there, but through vigorous representations by the Sherborne headmaster, his case was raised in Parliament and his release authorised. He finally arrived back in England in November 1941 and returned to Sherborne, where he passed his Higher School Certificate in summer 1942.[31]

Another arrival in 1939 was Peter Briess, aged eight, from a prosperous Jewish family who had a business trading in grain, seeds and pulses in Olomouc, Moravia, part of Czechoslovakia. His parents built a new Bauhaus-style villa, where his grandparents also lived, and it had been an idyllic life for a small boy until Peter saw the Germans marching into the town past his house, parking their tanks and burning down the only synagogue. His father and grandfather were imprisoned for a week with other leading Jewish citizens, and their businesses were confiscated. A few weeks later, the local Gestapo chief demanded to live in their family villa, and his father had the presence of mind to ask that in return he and his family should be allowed to leave the country. They left on 30 June 1939 and arrived at Harwich with very little, his father having also lost all his business assets. They settled in Harpenden, just opposite a small prep school called Hardenwick, and his father walked across the road to ask the headmaster if he would take Peter, on the basis that the fees would be paid when he could afford them. To his credit, the headmaster agreed, and Peter stayed there until 1944, when he went first to Bedford and then to Mill Hill. He acknowledges 'the great kindness and understanding of so many British people who helped them, including the head of Hardenwick, who was paid back all the outstanding fees.'[32]

Also striking is the number of individuals within schools who were prepared personally to support child refugees. At North London Collegiate School many staff acted as financial guarantors, and Winnie Myers, an old girl, helped to place refugees in London Jewish families. Shulamith Englander came from Prague in 1939 to NLCS, the only school to accept her out of several approached. Her mother saw her off at Prague station and she never saw her again. The head, Isabella Drummond, paid her fees as she did for several girls.[33] The generosity of the head was also apparent at Wycombe Abbey, where Lisa Fuchs arrived in 1939. Her uncle was supposed to provide for her, but defaulted, and it was the head, Miss Crosthwaite, who took responsibility until the school had to close in 1942, when Lisa went for a time to Headington School and then joined the WAAF. Miss Crosthwaite was also instrumental in helping Eva Guttman from Munich, who arrived at Wycombe Abbey in 1937. When Eva was interned in May 1940, Miss Crosthwaite's personal intervention helped to secure her release and her return to Wycombe, where she stayed until 1941.

One of the last children to arrive in Britain was Hans Rahmer, who arrived from Berlin on a *Kindertransport* train on 11 August 1939. His father was arrested after *Kristallnacht* and on his release seven weeks later stood on the family doorstep like a skeleton. He was determined to get his children, Hans and Erica, out of Germany, but almost left it too late. Hans described his arrival in Britain thus: 'The sun was shining and if ever freedom was a tangible thing, it was so that morning in Harwich.'[34] He lived with the Stannard family in Durham and went to Durham School, where he excelled academically and at sport. Attending services in chapel, he was troubled as a Jew by certain of the words he was obliged to recite, until the Revd Stannard advised him that, whatever else he did, he could join with the utmost conviction in the opening words of the Creed, 'I believe in God'.[35] After war service in the Durham Light Infantry and anglicising his name to John Rayner, he won a Cambridge scholarship and became a distinguished rabbi in the tradition of liberal Judaism. He last heard from his parents in early 1943 in a short note via the Red Cross, sending their love and asking him to pray to God. They were arrested in December 1943 and deported to Auschwitz the next day.[36]

Wartime and Post-War

The arrest in the summer of 1940 of German nationals like Lothar Markiewicz was a response to the threat of invasion. Deciding who might help the invaders induced an unedifying hysteria among the authorities and the public. There were theoretically 80,000 enemy aliens in Britain, including German Jewish refugees who had no reason to love the Nazis. Nobody in authority bothered to think too hard about this, and German Jews over sixteen were treated with a breathtaking lack of sympathy and understanding. They were held in often wretched camps in the Isle of Man and elsewhere while their cases were considered by tribunals, and many were deported to Canada or Australia. Headmasters spent much time pleading cases before tribunals in efforts to help their pupils. Claus Moser, his father and brother were arrested in late May 1940 and held in a camp at Huyton, near Liverpool, where they founded their own 'university', giving concerts and classes. Moser never quite forgave the British authorities for this and could be moved to tears by the memory of the petty humiliations heaped on his father.[37]

Walter Eberstadt was another who castigated insensitive British officialdom. Arrested in June 1940 and interned at Huyton, he remembered the barbed wire and the fear of being deported. He wrote later that 'during the year at Oxford I had become Anglicised, and I could not believe what was being done. Since internment I have felt different about the English. I had foolishly fancied that a few years at public school and a year at Oxford had made me part of them.'[38] He was later wounded serving in the Army in Normandy. Another Tonbridge Jewish refugee, Hans Hoffman, was put on a ship to Canada with other enemy aliens and prisoners of war, including U-boat crewmen. The ship's captain, clearly believing all the internees were confirmed Nazis, paraded them on deck to show them where another liner had been torpedoed and 'our German friends' had murdered women and children.[39] Hoffman later returned to England to join the Army, volunteering in 1943 for the 21st Independent Parachute Company, an elite force acting as pathfinders for larger airborne landings in Italy and south-east France. As the force operated behind enemy lines, with obvious dangers if captured, Hoffman changed his name to Compton, as he had enjoyed cricket at Tonbridge and Denis was his hero.

When the end of the war in Europe came in May 1945, those who had made it to safety in England wanted to find out what had happened to families in occupied Europe. Otto Hutter knew that his parents had managed to escape from Vienna into Russian-occupied Poland just before the outbreak of war, but all contact between them and Otto had then ceased. After the war he spent many hours helping to compile lists of survivors of the camps, but no trace of his parents was ever found, and when and where they perished is still unknown. Pavel and Karel Reisz also found out that their parents had died in one of the camps. The parents of Peter Briess tried to find out what had happened to his grandparents and the rest of the family, and found they were all dead. Peter now reflects on 'the wanton destruction of a wonderful long-established culture which has left a great gap in Central Europe which will never be restored.'[40]

Josef Behrmann, a Latvian Jew who came to Hillel House at The Perse in 1938, also disappeared into the camp system. He had returned home to Riga in the 1939 summer holidays, and his mother decided not to send him back to England that September, thinking he would be safer in neutral Latvia. When the Germans overran Latvia in June 1941 during their invasion of the Soviet Union, all Latvian Jews were forced into a ghetto. Behrmann, now aged fifteen, saw his mother shot dead, and between 1941 and 1945 he passed through fourteen camps. He was liberated from Buchenwald in April 1945 weighing only four stone and scarred for life by his experiences. In July 1954 he returned to the school and recalled how, in the death camps, his mind had often gone back to the playing fields of The Perse and the training in skills and endurance they had given him.

Walter Eberstadt, who had left Hamburg for Tonbridge in 1936, returned there a week after VE Day to help run the radio station. Already he had visited Belsen to witness what members of his family had endured, finding that his mother's parents had been deported there from Holland in 1943 and had died from disease and starvation. Now a captain in the British Army, his sensitivities were a constant challenge as he played his part in re-educating the German population. He was careful not to abuse his authority, whatever his personal feelings. 'Victory', he mused, 'goes to the head, defeat to the heart.' One special day he went to a performance of Mendelssohn's *Violin Concerto* given by Yehudi Menuhin for a German audience in the cause of re-education. As Menuhin finished, the tears were pouring down his face as the German orchestra stood up and applauded this symbolic moment: a formerly banned Jewish work being performed by a Jewish soloist, a moment of atonement for the past and hope for the future.[41]

Also working on German re-education was Robert Birley. In 1947 he resigned the headmastership of Charterhouse to become Educational Adviser to the Deputy Military Governor of the British zone in Germany, General Sir Brian Robertson, who also happened to be a Carthusian. Birley's remit was the reconstruction of the school and university system, and the development of cultural links between Britain and Germany. He helped build the educational structures necessary to deliver German democracy, rewrote history textbooks to remove their racist and ultra-nationalist influences and encouraged German universities to develop intellectual independence. Birley was described by one of his friends as 'the headmaster of Germany', but his skill lay in not trying to do everything himself. He wanted 'to give heart and hope to those Germans to whom it did fall to rebuild the schools, the youth organisations and the universities – a crusade of reconciliation'.[42] When he left Germany in 1949 to become headmaster of Eton, he continued to find ways to bring Germans and Britons together, including founding the Königswinter Conference, now in its sixty-eighth year, for the discussion of political and social issues of mutual interest at the highest levels of government.[43]

Charitable Missions

The welcome given to Jewish refugees built on an earlier example of public-school altruism. Many schools established charitable missions in deprived areas of cities in the late Victorian age, and these continued to be well supported through to the end of the twentieth century and beyond. The motivation for these missions was overtly Christian at a time in the Victorian age when the Anglican Church 'felt that it should give as much attention to shepherding the heathen of England's vast working-class suburbs as it gave to converting Africans and Indians.'[44] Winchester, Clifton, Eton, Marlborough and many other schools had established missions in 1870s and 1880s Rugby set up its first mission in India in 1848 and then a home mission in 1884 in Notting Dale, a notoriously deprived enclave of London near the wealthy Notting Hill. Clubs were established for boys, girls and mothers, so that throughout the twentieth century the Rugby Clubs in Notting Dale acted as a community centre. The Old Rugbeian rugby international, Ronald Poulton Palmer, worked regularly in these clubs before being killed in 1915. The premises were destroyed by a bomb in 1940 but rebuilt in the 1950s, and the Rugby Clubs have continued to play an important role in the local community through to the twenty-first century, as well as offering many opportunities for Rugbeians to engage in community service.

Charitable clubs could often inspire pupils and alumni to improve the lives of others. The Rugby tradition in this field fired William Temple, future Archbishop of Canterbury, and R.H. Tawney, the most influential theorist and exponent of socialism in the inter-war years. In a later generation it inspired Alec Dickson, who founded Voluntary Service Overseas in the 1950s for young people to work abroad for a year on community development, and then Community Service Volunteers in

1962 to give the same opportunities in Britain. Henry Brooke, classmate of Rab Butler at Marlborough and future Home Secretary, was always grateful for the chance to help as a schoolboy in Swindon camps, which replaced Marlborough's Tottenham Mission in the 1920s. After leaving Oxford he also worked for a year in 1928 in a Quaker settlement for the unemployed in the Rhondda Valley, before going into politics.

The most notable convert to charitable work of this kind was Clement Attlee, future Labour Prime Minister. In 1905 Attlee, now a barrister after leaving Haileybury and Oxford, visited the Haileybury Club in Stepney, founded by his old school, where working class boys met under the supervision of Haileyburians. He initially made the journey out of a sense of loyalty to his school, an emotion he continued to feel in later life, but he was impressed by what he found and became a regular volunteer at the club, struck particularly by the boys' lack of time and opportunity for the kind of education he had enjoyed. He taught the boys a Haileyburian version of self-discipline through drilling and sport, but he also enjoyed the sense of fellowship and solidarity he came across in working-class families. In 1907 he became the resident manager at the club and moved to Stepney to live on the premises. In this role he found his sense of mission in life, no sudden conversion but a maturing into socialism.[45] Attlee joined the Independent Labour Party in 1908 and, after serving in the First World War, he came to realise that only through political action could the lives of the most deprived be improved.

War Memorials

In the aftermath of the First World War, war memorials represented duty, sacrifice and pride, and a conscious effort to reach out to future generations with the ideals and traditions of the past. The process produced many beautiful works of art, like Christopher Whall's 'Mother's Window' at Denstone, along with the involvement of architects like Edwin Lutyens, Herbert Baker and Ernest Gimson, whose Arts and Crafts Memorial Library at Bedales is now Grade 1 listed.[46] The memorials also used traditional imagery and iconography 'to express a complex raft of emotions designed to console the bereaved and honour the dead by providing the certitude that their deaths had been meaningful'.[47] They used the Crucifixion as an image of self-sacrifice and St George as the Christian knight who triumphed over evil, as well as Latin inscriptions and, at Eastbourne College, the words of John Bunyan's *Pilgrim's Progress* and Mr Valiant-for-Truth: 'My marks and scars I carry with me, to be a witness to me that I have fought His battles who will now be my rewarder.' Future generations, lacking an understanding of such imagery and far removed from the grief which underpinned these memorials, sometimes regarded them as romanticising war.

At Winchester, Herbert Baker was commissioned to design their war memorial, having had a design for a memorial cloister turned down at his old school, Tonbridge. He had built a reputation as the leading imperial architect and had been employed with Lutyens by the Imperial War Graves Commission to design cemeteries and memorials on the Western Front. War Cloister at Winchester is now regarded by Historic England as 'arguably the most distinguished of all memorials at public schools' and was upgraded to Grade 1 listing in 2017. The strongest supporter of the project was Winchester's head, Montague Rendall, who wanted the memorial to be a building of dignity and beauty, somewhere that would 'stand amid the highways of school life, and yet retain its character as a place of memories and inspirations'.[48] Critics argued that Rendall and his generation wanted to idealise the dead in terms necessary to their own comfort and faith.

When Winchester came to consider their Second World War memorial, there was no new icon and little debate. Spencer Leeson, the head, argued that 'the two wars are essentially one and that the memorial to the fallen should also be one.'[49] War Cloister was re-dedicated in 1948 at a ceremony led by the most famous Wykehamist soldier, Earl Wavell, while Winchester also compiled a War Service Record, introduced by a poem written by Frank Thompson, SOE agent executed in Bulgaria. To those who commemorate his generation he bids:

> Write on the stone no words of sadness –
> Only the gladness due,
> That we, who asked the most of living,
> Knew how to give it too.[50]

As at Winchester, an exhausted country in 1945 stopped well short of re-creating the many iconic symbols of remembrance which had followed the First World War. In 1918 they had expressed the idea that war on such a scale should never be allowed to happen again, but it had happened, and this time there was not the same emotional engagement. As national symbols, the Cenotaph and the Unknown Warrior would continue to suffice, and a utilitarian solution triumphed in most schools. Survivors of the war were hostile to the building of further stone monuments, largely wanted to put their war experience behind them and opted for practical or useful memorials which would help the next generation. Most schools added names to their First World War memorials and then used the funds raised to commemorate the war dead in buildings or other schemes to enhance school facilities.

That remained the situation until Cranleigh in 2016 used the Great War's centenary to reach out across generations and reconsider attitudes to war. They commissioned Nicholas Dimbleby, an Old Cranleighan figurative sculptor from a talented family, to create the centrepiece for a new memorial designed to commemorate all former members of the school who had died in war since the school's foundation in 1865. The memorial is in a prominent position outside the south door of the chapel in a semi-circle of glass engraved with 384 names and includes the sculpture of a boy entitled 'Leaving'. On it are the words of W.H. Auden, taken from his poem 'September 1, 1939': 'We must love one another or die.' Dimbleby wrote of his creation:

> Through conversations with pupils, it became apparent that the desire for peace greatly outweighs the nobility of death in battle, and that therefore this should not be just a generic memorial, simply a listing of the fallen. This age is more sceptical. Alongside leaving and service to the outside world, the sculptural element of this memorial is intended to convey vulnerability and the devastation of war.[51]

Thus in a hundred years had schools moved on from the emotions of 1918, consciously appealing to future generations' hopes and ambitions for the world rather than looking back to the past.

Social Responsibility

The war brought new scrutiny to public schools and greater accountability. Demonstrating a sense of service and commitment to the wider community was in tune with the ethos of both the 'People's War' and the 'New Jerusalem' vision which underpinned post-war reconstruction. That sense of social responsibility in public schools has gathered pace since 1945, building on the mission work they undertook in deprived communities and the help they gave to Jewish refugees. Many schools in recent years have given bursaries to refugees from Syria and other war-torn areas or to children from deprived communities in Britain.

It has been possible to identify, from school archives and other sources, about 450 Jewish children from German-occupied Europe who came to at least one hundred British public schools between 1936 and 1939. There were probably many more, for stories have drifted unknown into the mists of time, unrecorded in school registers and only coming to light when told to children or grandchildren. Some of those schools were HMC members or well-known girls' schools, others were smaller schools which have long since closed. Some offered places free of charge, some heads paid out of their own pockets and sometimes benefactors were found who paid at least a portion of the fees. Education played an important part in helping these children to rebuild their lives. Public schools should be proud of what they achieved in providing safe havens for those suffering emotional extremes of displacement from place and family, giving them a chance to contribute to public life in their adopted country.

Most of these children who came to British public schools before the war had witnessed unspeakable acts of cruelty and humiliation. Those who came with their families were often in financial difficulties as parents struggled to rebuild lives and careers in a new country not uniformly welcoming to refugees. Others, many of them very young, who had left their parents on train stations in Prague, Berlin or Vienna in a last bid for freedom and safety, must have been deeply traumatised by that moment's experience. They experienced not only the difficulty of settling into new schools and homes, but the nagging fear of permanent loss, often cruelly revealed to be true when the full horrors became known after the war. Ann Kirk, aged ten, said goodbye to her parents on Berlin station in April

1939 and never saw them again. Looked after by a family in Finchley, she was given a place at South Hampstead High School, where she prospered. In December 1942, now thirteen, Ann received a Red Cross message from her father: 'Sorry bad news. Mummy emigrated 14th December. Am terrified myself but confident of family reunion after the war.' In January came one further message, and then silence.[52]

It is also legitimate to ask of public schools not why they did so much, but why they did so comparatively little in the face of such a huge tide of suffering humanity, a question which could also be asked more widely of British government and society. There were many public schools which do not appear to have taken in any Jewish refugees, and those which took just one or two could have accepted more. The problems associated with taking them in could be considerable: refugees with little or no English, doubts about their ability to cope with rigorous academic study, unreliable provision for payment of fees and often behavioural problems brought on by the severe emotional upheaval all had endured. But doors were opened, problems were overcome and the many stories of young refugees making the most of their new opportunities reflect well on the schools which helped them. This story has been little recognised in the years since 1945, but it deserves to be known.

Chapter 9

How the War was Portrayed

The cultural legacy of the Second World War is very different from the First in giving a more sympathetic view of the officer class and, by implication, the public schools which educated them. Popular perception in Britain is of a war fought for a clear moral purpose, while the political and military elites are seen to have performed their roles valiantly in leading Britain to victory against the odds. The dominant cultural medium is film, especially the war feature films of the 1950s, in which the officer class is consistently presented in a heroic light. The historian Peter Hennessy, one of the baby-boomer generation born as the Second World War ended, wrote that 'we spent the fifties in the cinema absorbing an endless diet of war films in which Richard Todd and Kenneth More convinced us that there is a singular mixture of insouciance, bravery and flair that we British could bring to the conduct of international affairs.'[1] That message was replayed many times in other films of the 1950s – by Kenneth More (Victoria, Jersey) playing Douglas Bader (St Edward's, Oxford) in *Reach for the Sky*, Anthony Quayle (Rugby) as Commodore Henry Harwood (Dartmouth) in *The Battle of the River Plate*, and Trevor Howard (Clifton) as Captain Peter Churchill (Malvern) in *Odette*. Particularly for that generation who first saw these films in the cinema, it was 'the golden age of British individualism, witnessed in brilliant improvisation, casually laconic dialogue, and the cool bravado of confident men'.[2] Very little has emerged since, in the cinema or wider popular culture, to undermine that message.

By contrast, the cultural legacy of the First World War, reshaped in the 1960s by drama productions like *Oh! What a Lovely War* and reawakened interest in war poets like Wilfred Owen, testified to a war without a clear aim marked by futile slaughter on the Western Front. Public-school alumni like Siegfried Sassoon and Robert Graves contributed to this interpretation of the war, while their schools suffered collateral damage for nurturing and brainwashing the elites of 1914–18 in pursuit of the supposedly outdated concepts of imperial glory and patriotic sacrifice. Later renewed interest in the First World War coincided with the youth revolt of the 1960s, which had in its sights any figure of authority, from politicians to generals to headmasters. In that decade the First World War was reassessed in a negative way, not historically but in literary and cultural terms, in tune with the anti-war sentiment of the time. The television series *Blackadder Goes Forth* confirmed that reassessment when it was broadcast to popular acclaim in the 1990s. The recent centenary in 2014 has succeeded in recognising the heroism, leadership and disproportionate sacrifice of the junior officers from public schools, but the wider cultural perceptions have remained largely untouched.

The cultural portrayal of the Second World War has benefited public schools. The permanent truth established during and immediately after the war itself, and then reinforced in the 1950s during a long period of Conservative political dominance, was of a heroic national effort. It was nostalgically comforting in an era when Britain's world role declined and confidence in her future became more uncertain. Public-school alumni contributed to this interpretation through art, photographs, novels and histories. The message of the war poets of 1939–45 evokes the varied experience of a global struggle in a justified war, not futility and anger. Television has emphasised the comparison, the negative vibes of *Blackadder* contrasting with the imaginative escape schemes of public-school officers in the BBC television series *Colditz* or the comfortable humour of *Dad's Army*. While the duplicitous and callous officers of *Blackadder Goes Forth* remain the popular image of the public schoolboy at war in 1914–18, it is Guy Gibson, Alan Turing and Winston Churchill himself who are the role models of 1939–45.

R.C. Sherriff and his Portrayal of Two Wars

Barnes Wallis: 'Fifty-six men lost. If I'd known it was going to be like this, I'd never have started it.'

Guy Gibson: 'You mustn't think that way. If all those fellows had known from the beginning that they wouldn't be coming back, they'd have gone for it just the same. I knew them all and I know that's true.'

(Closing sequence from the film *The Dam Busters*, 1954)

One cultural bridge between the two wars is the writer R.C. Sherriff (Kingston GS), author of the play *Journey's End* and writer of the screenplay for *The Dam Busters*. The character similarities in these works are more obvious than their differences. *Journey's End* is Sherriff's semi-autobiographical and much acclaimed account of his service as an officer in the trenches. First produced on the stage in 1928, it is the only play by a veteran to enjoy any longevity and is still being staged in new productions today, including a 2017 film. It is forthright, powerful, emotional and authentic, but presents an interpretation of the war at odds with its generally accepted negative image. Sherriff wrote later that his characters were 'simple unquestioning men who fought the war because it seemed the only right and proper thing to do … It was a play in which not a word was spoken against the war.'[3] It was also focused on public-school life. Raleigh, the fresh young subaltern, hero-worshipped Stanhope, the company commander, since he had been a junior under him at school, while Osborne, the housemaster, had once played rugger for England. Joan Littlewood loathed *Journey's End* because it was all about public-school officers, and others have disliked it for its analogy of trench and school life: 'There is the same idolising, the same adolescent emotionalism, the same team spirit and self-sacrifice … that model of behaviour, so English, so male and so anachronistic was killed on the Western Front. In Sherriff's play it was resurrected and sentimentalised.'[4] Sherriff did not invent the public-school spirit he found in France, but he described it accurately, and the sentimentality certainly existed as young men tried to put aside their fears by recalling past certainties. Osborne, Stanhope and Raleigh in *Journey's End* are the authentic public-school officers of the First World War, even if Blackadder is the model more widely recognised.

The most popular war film of the 1950s, *The Dam Busters*, was first screened in cinemas in 1954 and is still regularly shown on British television. The officer class Sherriff portrayed in it is remembered for a consummate act of skill, bravery and sacrifice. The suppression of emotion by these men, the understatement of their achievement and their acceptance of sacrifice all come out of the character playbook established in public schools and portrayed in *Journey's End*. The heroes of the film were mostly young public-school-educated RAF officers, with Richard Todd (Shrewsbury) playing Guy Gibson (St Edward's) and Richard Leech (Haileybury) as 'Dinghy' Young (Westminster), along with Michael Redgrave (Clifton) playing Barnes Wallis (Christ's Hospital). All personify British skill, ingenuity and superiority, with the social message of the film focusing on the 'inspiring leadership of the social elites, the essential priority of character over caution, and hard work in fighting life's battles'.[5]

Sherriff had felt in the trenches the responsibility for the lives of his men that he articulated in the characters of Stanhope in *Journey's End* and Guy Gibson in *The Dam Busters*. Just as Stanhope felt personal responsibility for Raleigh, as a school senior did towards a junior, so many of those who died on the Dams Raid were Gibson's friends. The younger John Hopgood, 'Hoppy', whose violent death he witnessed over the Moehne Dam, was his protégé from earlier service in 106 Squadron, the Raleigh to Gibson's Stanhope. Gibson was described as representing 'the apogee of the pre-war public schoolboy, the perpetual team captain, of unshakeable courage and devotion to duty, impatient of those who could not meet his standards', but this could also have been Stanhope.[6] It is not surprising that Sherriff was eager to write the screenplay for *The Dam Busters*, for Gibson is 'like Stanhope without the drink'.[7]

The playwright of the Second World War who came closest to Sherriff's skill in portraying the officer class was Terence Rattigan (Harrow), who wrote two plays with a wartime theme, *Flare Path* in 1942 and *The Deep Blue Sea* in 1952, both made into films.[8] He served as a rear gunner in the RAF, and *Flare Path* is based on the life and loves of an RAF bomber station. At its heart is the stoicism of the main characters, the pilots who undertake dangerous missions over Germany and the wives left behind fearfully to await their return. Rattigan's dialogue displays his genius for portraying suppressed emotion, the stiff upper lip which British public-school alumni supposedly learned, but the varied characters in *Flare Path* also make clear that, unlike in *Journey's End*, this is a war which embraces on an equal footing all classes and nationalities, and in which women are in the front line. *Flare Path* became the successful 1945 film *The Way to the Stars*, with screenplay by Rattigan and direction by Anthony Asquith (Winchester). *The Deep Blue Sea* is set in post-war Britain, but one of the three central characters is Freddie Page, fighter pilot and war hero, who struggles to find a place in the modern world and is too shallow to understand the emotional morass in which he has found himself, carrying on an affair with an older married woman. There were many Freddie Pages in the respectable middle classes of post-war Britain, unable to find roles which matched their successes on school playing fields or their wartime glories, emotionally illiterate, unhappy and frustrated behind apparently untroubled facades.

Visual Images

The Second World War also recognised the importance to propaganda and the wider war effort of visual images, something which military authorities in the First World War had been slow to grasp, for not until 1916 were official war photographers allowed in France. Instead, the authorities encouraged the work of war artists, but this rebounded on them when the images became increasingly dominated by the horrors of war. The canvases of artists like Paul Nash (St Paul's) reinforced the cultural message of the war poets. Paintings like *The Menin Road* or the ironic *We Are Making a New World* illustrate the horror and futility of Nash's own experience. He wrote in a letter from Ypres to his wife: 'I am no longer an artist, interested and curious. I am a messenger who will bring back word from the men who are fighting to those that want the war to go on forever. Feeble, inarticulate will be my message, but it will have a bitter truth and may it burn their lousy souls.'[9]

War artists were commissioned again in 1939 by the War Artists Advisory Committee, chaired by Kenneth Clark (Winchester). Thirty-six men and one woman were given full-time employment by the committee, including other First World War artists like Eric Kennington (St Paul's) and John Nash (Wellington), but also younger men like Graham Sutherland and John Piper (both Epsom) and Edward Ardizzone (Clayesmore). The primary purpose of the committee was propaganda, organising exhibitions at home and abroad to raise morale and promote Britain's image. This time Paul Nash was an impassioned supporter of the war. His most iconic painting was the epic image of the Battle of Britain, portraying the nation's heroic battle for survival. His own description of the painting stressed that it was 'an attempt to give the sense of an aerial battle in operation over a wide area and thus summarises England's great aerial victory over Germany.'[10] Nash's attitude was shaped by his revulsion for Nazi Germany and its culture, the painting showing the RAF rising up out of the English landscape to combat the regimented ranks of the Luftwaffe.

The artist who best captured the dauntless spirit at large in the war was Rex Whistler (Haileybury), whose inter-war career embraced all aspects of art from theatre design to book illustration, portraits to murals, including the café at the Tate Gallery and the *trompe l'oeil* at Plas Newydd. His *Self-Portrait in Uniform*, painted in 1940, captures a moment of sombre reflection as the artist puts aside his brushes to go to war. Whistler painted portraits of many with whom he served, until he was killed in Normandy in July 1944 while serving with the Guards Armoured Division. His pre-war portraits had made him the darling of high society, and his popularity was such that when his death was reported, *The Times* obituarist received more correspondence about him than any other person killed in the war.

Photography played a greater role than paintings in boosting wartime morale and shaping the understanding of the war for later generations. Photojournalistic magazines like *Picture Post*, established in 1938 by Sir Edward Hulton (Harrow), was by 1943 selling nearly two million copies per week. The wartime editor, Tom Hopkinson (St Edward's, Oxford), laid out a vision for the future in 1941 with the 'Plan for Britain', to include a national health service and an overhaul of the education system. It stimulated much discussion about the post-war future a year before the Beveridge Report. Cecil Beaton (Harrow), the favourite photographer of the Royal Family in the late 1930s and beyond, produced stunning pictures of Britain at war. His 1940 portrait photo of Churchill in the Cabinet Room exactly captures the image conveyed through his defiant speeches, while his haunting image of a three-year-old victim of the Blitz, with her teddy bear, influenced public opinion both in Britain and America.

War Poets

The poets of the Second World War have never had the same impact as their First World War predecessors, who became the voice of that war, easily recognised by a wider public and important in establishing the war's cultural message and legacy. It was in 1930 that Frederick Brereton published an anthology of war poems, mostly by officers critical of the war, which established this enduring message. The preface was by Edmund Blunden, who had published his own war memoir two years before, describing his journey from Christ's Hospital schoolboy to war service.[11] He entitled his preface 'The Soldier Poets of 1914–18', with five junior officers specifically named in his essay in chronological order – Rupert Brooke (Rugby), Charles Sorley (Marlborough), Robert Graves (Charterhouse), Siegfried Sassoon (Marlborough) and finally Wilfred Owen (Birkenhead Institute and Shrewsbury Technical School), whose first edition of collected poems Blunden edited in 1931. For Blunden the task of war poetry was to make 'effectual and eager complaints against the survival of that false gross idol, War', and the best men to speak were those who had fought and could bear witness to the horrors of that war.[12] Later anthologies, especially from the 1960s onwards, 'sanctified Blunden's canon of Great War poetry – the verse of junior officers steeped in Romantic literature who moved from patriotic innocence to horrified candour and eventually a recognition in Owen's clichéd words of the pity of war rather than its glory.'[13]

It was anticipated by the general public that the Second World War would produce the same response, but in 1940 the *Times Literary Supplement* asked the question, 'Where are our war poets?' The Second World War produced just as many poets as the First, but the general view even now is that they wrote little verse of merit and nothing to compare with the icons of 1914–18. Second World War poetry had a less clear message. It was not 'anti-war' in the way Blunden had described, for most of the poets believed strongly in the war against Nazism, so there was no motive for the moralising of a poem such as Owen's *Dulce et Decorum Est*. Keith Douglas, war poet and also from Christ's Hospital, answered in an essay the question posed by the *TLS* in May 1943, while convalescing from wounds received in the Western Desert. He explained why 'in the fourth year of this war we have not a single poet who seems likely to be an impressive commentator on it', and made it clear that the poets of the Second World War could not hope to duplicate the success of their predecessors:

Hell cannot be let loose twice: it was let loose in the Great War and it is the same hell now. The hardships, pain and boredom; the behaviour of the living and the appearance of the dead, were so accurately described by the poets of the Great War that every day on the battlefields of the Western Desert, their poems are illustrated. Almost all that a modern poet on active service is inspired to write would be tautological.[14]

Douglas was a fighting soldier with plenty of experience of modern battle, faster moving than in 1916 and even more brutal in the impact of lethal modern weaponry. Whereas Owen wanted to tell his readers what he felt about war, Douglas wanted them to know what he saw. In a conscious parody of Owen's preface to his poems, Douglas wrote in a letter to a friend in August 1943: 'My object (and I don't give a damn about my duty as a poet) is to write true things.' True things could only be learned by the experience of battle, and Douglas went on: 'I never tried to write about war until I had experienced it. Now I will write of it.'[15] The quality of his poems is matched by his prose memoir, *Alamein to Zem Zem*, a vivid account of the tank war in the desert which ranks with the classics of the Great War. Unlike Blunden's *Undertones of War*, which was published ten years after the war, Douglas's book was written as a day-by-day journal on and off the battlefield.[16] In his poems he is different to Owen in not questioning the moral implications of fighting a war or killing fellow human beings. The poem *How to Kill* reminds us that the soldier is constantly faced with such decisions and opportunities. Death is the penalty for error or misjudgement in battle, and Douglas himself perished for such a reason in Normandy three days after D-Day. Douglas was that unusual combination of poet and man of action; for him 'the battlefield is the simple central stage of the war: it is there that the interesting things happen.'[17]

Douglas came from a generation which had been taught to question the values of their fathers. They possessed none of the jaunty innocence of the 1914 volunteers and they knew that the war against Hitler was 'a just war which had to be fought to the end at whatever personal and national cost'.[18] They were not disillusioned, because they possessed no illusions in the first place, knowing what war had been like in 1914–18 and would inevitably be again. If the 1939–45 poet was to adapt his work to this new spirit of the age, then he would not be writing the same kind of poems as Rupert Brooke wrote in 1914, or even those of Sassoon and Owen. W.B. Yeats famously refused to include any poems by Owen in his 1935 anthology, *The Oxford Book of Modern Verse*, as he thought them too emotional and called it 'all blood, dirt and sucked sugar-stick'.[19] In 1939 poetry had to be ironic and complex, and the models were modernists like W.H. Auden (Gresham's), who experienced war in the 1930s in Spain and China and wrote poems engaging with the political issues of his generation. The war poems of Sidney Keyes (Tonbridge), who was killed in Tunisia in 1943, had modernist leanings: 'Readers of Douglas are able to trace a course, the particular theatre of war evoked or described in navigable ways. With Keyes this is not the case, his work often garnished with obliquities, deeply embroiled allusions, and his poems from the African front were lost with him, so we have no direct poems of combat.'[20]

The position of the poet in the Second World War must be seen against a background of the triumph of modernism among intellectuals, along with the rise of fascism and Stalinist communism, the Spanish Civil War and the politicisation of literature. Any study of the influential intellectuals of the inter-war years 'will see how many of the household names went to the same few schools'.[21] Most of them turned against the public-school ethos, although Auden taught in prep schools for five years. He, together with other left-wing public-school literati like Christopher Isherwood (Repton), Louis MacNeice (Marlborough), Cecil Day-Lewis (Sherborne) and Stephen Spender (Gresham's), exerted considerable intellectual influence in the 1930s, but their faith in communism, and the respect in which they were held by others, were undermined by Stalin's purges and the Nazi-Soviet pact. Auden damaged his cause further by emigrating to the USA when war broke out, together with Isherwood, an escape jeered at by the right-wing British press and even regarded by their admirers as abandonment of their right to be heard. Virginia Woolf, in a lecture to the Workers' Educational Association in 1940, declared that Auden had tried to hold to the privileges and sense of superiority given by a superior education to press for dramatic social and political change in the 1930s, but had failed to resolve the contradictions in his position with the coming of war.[22] George Orwell was concerned about the detachment of left-wing intellectuals from the common culture on which the future of the country depended in the crisis of 1940, declaring that 'many intellectuals of the Left were flabbily pacifist up to 1935, shrieked for war against Germany in 1935–9 and then promptly cooled off when the war started.'[23] Some of those intellectuals became reconciled to the state by taking wartime jobs in intelligence, the civil service or research, although the mood remained one of 'hanging about with our friends'.[24]

In Westminster Abbey a memorial stone records the names of sixteen British poets of the Great War, eleven of whom were public-school junior officers. If a similar stone was to record the best known British poets of the Second World War, it would be hard to agree on names beyond Douglas; however, the most extensive bibliography of poetry from both world wars identifies 2,225 British poets from 1914–18 and 2,679 from 1939–45, so in terms of output the Second World War was just as 'poetic' as the First.[25] In his critical survey of Second World War poets, Vernon Scannell considers fourteen, including Douglas. Of the other thirteen, eight went to British public schools, and two to public schools in Australia and South Africa, so the class background is similar to 1914–18.[26] Any such list is subjective, but the names will be unfamiliar to most readers and, unlike their First World War predecessors, have mostly been lost in the mists of time. One condescendingly dismissed by Scannell for 'shallow sentimentality' was John Pudney, contemporary of Auden at Gresham's, whose poem *For Johnny*, later used in the film, *The Way to the Stars* (1945), evoked the wartime heroism of pilots and those they left behind and has lasted better than most in public memory.

Comparisons between the poets of the two wars were highlighted in 1962 when the *War Requiem* by Benjamin Britten (Gresham's) was first performed to mark the consecration of the new Coventry Cathedral, built after the original was destroyed in the Blitz. Britten had originally conceived the piece after Hiroshima, and might have looked to poets from the Second World War, but the music is woven around Owen's *Anthem for Doomed Youth* and *Strange Meeting* which 'fitted the 1960s attitude to war better than poetry which focused on the moral ambiguities of fighting and killing'.[27] Yet Keith Douglas believed that in his incessant observation of death and suffering through his various battlefield experiences his poetry would attain 'a vision not just different from, but surpassing even the achievement of his Great War predecessors'.[28]

Memoirs and Novels

Second World War memoirs lack the sharp focus and recognisable identity given by the Western Front but share many of the same emotions. One of the finest of the First World War is Guy Chapman's *A Passionate Prodigality*, combining shock at the horrific conditions in which the war was fought with a celebration of the joy of comradeship and shared experience. Educated at Westminster and Oxford, Chapman had just entered the publishing business when war broke out. He was commissioned into the Royal Fusiliers and served on the Western Front from 1915 to 1918, but delayed writing until the early 1930s, because war had been such an overwhelming emotional experience that he admitted to being unable to escape its thrall: 'Once you have lain in her arms, you can admit no other mistress. You may loathe, you may execrate, but you cannot deny her.'[29]

The fascination of war, the impact of battle and the joy of comradeship also infuse memoirs from the Second World War. It is again the same 'temporary gentlemen' like Chapman who dominate the Second World War genre, products of inter-war public schools for whom the reality of war came as a terrible shock, even if they had read or heard of what their fathers had gone through. The books are more diverse in the battlefields they describe, but the experience of war was just as brutal. Raleigh Trevelyan (Winchester) wrote a harrowing account of the Anzio battlefield, where the Allies lost 7,000 killed, 36,000 wounded and another 44,000 sick or injured. It is also painfully honest about how he responded to the terror of coming under heavy fire, an experience which left him unable to return to Anzio until 1968, when he wrote a piece for the *Observer* on how his war experience had scarred him psychologically. He remembered how his father, a 1914–18 veteran, had told him that the worst part of battle was wondering beforehand how you would behave in front of other people. His own emotions were tested to the limit when his platoon corporal, just behind him on a fighting patrol, stepped on a mine and lost the whole bottom half of his body.[30] First World War memoirs by men serving in the ranks are few, but it was more common for public-school alumni to serve in the ranks in 1939–45, and two of the most highly praised memoirs came from this source, the strength of comradeship in adversity again their strongest theme. *The Recollections of Rifleman Bowlby* by Alex Bowlby (Radley) is about his war in Italy, which haunted his sleep ever afterwards, and *Quartered Safe Out Here*, about the jungle war in Burma, is by George MacDonald Fraser (Glasgow Academy).[31] As the reviver of one of the most infamous characters in public-school fiction, the fag-roasting Harry Flashman of Rugby School, Fraser has performed a double service to the cultural legacy of public schools.

Guy Gibson's *Enemy Coast Ahead*, written in 1944 and published in 1946 after his death, is regarded by the historian Max Hastings as one of the greatest warrior stories from any war or service. Gibson was a professional airman, but the book 'reveals a sensitivity that few of his men recognised in him, together with a consciousness of his own mortality'.[32] Gibson had few rivals as a writer among bomber crews, not least because so few survived to tell the tale, but the Battle of Britain has elicited more memoirs, mostly by wartime volunteers. *The Last Enemy* by Richard Hillary and *First Light* by Geoffrey Wellum are worthy to be compared with the earlier war's *Sagittarius Rising* by Cecil Lewis (Oundle) as compelling stories of young men's reaction to the confusion and brutality of aerial battle.

Young public-school officers also dominate the host of prisoner-of-war memoirs which came out after the Second World War. PoW escape was portrayed as a particularly British form of heroism, and an upper-class one at that, and many comparisons are drawn between the camps and boarding school life. Colditz has spawned a cultural legacy all of its own in books, film and television, depicting it as a school boarding house for unruly young officers seeking freedom; this began in the 1950s with *The Colditz Story* by Pat Reid (Clongowes Wood) and *They Have Their Exits* by Airey Neave (Eton). Pat Reid even referred to the camps from which officers escaped as 'prep schools', with the 'Common Entrance' qualification for transfer to Colditz being at least one escape. Such was the popularity of the subject that the television series *Colditz* ran for twenty-eight episodes on BBC between 1972 and 1974, featuring public-school actors like Edward Hardwicke (Stowe), David McCallum (UCS) and, rather improbably, Willie Rushton (Shrewsbury) as a Scottish commando.

Vera Brittain's *Testament of Youth* is one of the best memoirs of 1914–18 but is the only one by a woman to achieve a lasting reputation. By contrast, the Second World War examples reflect the more varied parts played by women. Wartime nursing formed the theme of *One Pair of Feet* by Monica Dickens (St Paul's Girls' – expelled after throwing her school uniform over Hammersmith Bridge), but *Spreading My Wings* by Diana Barnato Walker (Queen's College, London) was about her wartime life as a pilot in the Air Transport Auxiliary, and *The Past is Myself* by Christabel Bielenberg (St Margaret's, Bushey) was about an Englishwoman living in Germany during the war. A best-selling addition to this genre was *To War with Whitaker* by Hermione Ranfurly (Southover Manor) about her determination to follow her aristocratic soldier husband to the Middle East in 1940, against express military orders, and her subsequent adventures working for SOE in Cairo and as personal assistant to General 'Jumbo' Wilson, Supreme Allied Commander in the Mediterranean. In her *Daily Telegraph* obituary she was described as 'the kind of woman for whom the words pluck and spirit might have been invented'.[33] Her story also shows how the right kind of connections helped members of the social elites of both sexes to have an interesting war.

The war serves as the background to some of the most highly regarded novels of the twentieth century. They include *The Heat of the Day* by Elizabeth Bowen (Downe House), evoking passionate love affairs in wartime London, the war volumes of *A Dance to the Music of Time* by Anthony Powell (Eton), and the broadly autobiographical *Sword of Honour* trilogy by Evelyn Waugh (Lancing). In the 1970s came *The Singapore Grip* by J.G. Farrell (Rossall), the third in his Empire trilogy, less well known than *The Siege of Krishnapur* but a wonderfully entertaining story of class issues and the fall of Singapore as deserved retribution for years of colonial greed. More recently, *The English Patient* by Michael Ondaatje (Dulwich), set in North Africa and Italy, was voted in 2018 the best winner in the fifty-year history of the Booker Prize.

More accessible to a reading public avid for good war stories was the well-populated tranche of more 'middlebrow' fiction, and indeed non-fiction, which was unique to this war. The historian John Ramsden was a champion of this genre and the films they spawned: 'With the canon to the left of them but the cannons to the right, historians may feel that someone has blundered; the writing of Anthony Powell is certainly *magnifique, mais ce n'est pas La Guerre Mondiale* for most British readers.'[34] What Ramsden and readers did like were those books produced for the mass markets of the 1950s by such publishing houses as Pan and Fontana, reflecting the public taste for heroic exploits told in a largely restrained and understated way as became young public-school officers. The best known included true stories like *The Dam Busters* and *Reach for the Sky*, both by the Australian author Paul Brickhill (North Sydney BHS), the former having sold over a million copies. In the introduction to *They Have Their Exits* young officers are described in phrases recognised as archetypes by the public – 'high-spirited', 'unconquerable', 'the high resolve of courageous men to break their bonds'.[35] Middlebrow fiction is led by *The Cruel Sea* written in 1951 by Nicholas Monsarrat (Winchester) and brilliantly conveying the human stories involved in the gruelling conditions of the Battle of the Atlantic; it has sold over eleven million copies.[36] Nevil Shute (Shrewsbury) was the most prolific of these writers, publishing between 1940 and 1955 eight novels about the war, of which *A Town Like Alice* and *Requiem for a Wren* are the best known. He had few literary pretensions, but his exciting and well-constructed stories of wartime derring-do and sacrifice attracted a vast readership eager for good stories and comfortable with the battlefield leadership of the officer class.

War Reporters and Historians

Sir John Reith (Gresham's), first Director-General of the BBC, laid down in the inter-war years that all announcers on the radio should use a standard and proper accent, known as 'upper received pronunciation', or 'posh' in colloquial terms. This generally meant that most such announcers, and later war reporters, came from a public-school background. Two of those who became familiar voices before and during the war were Alvar Lidell (KCS Wimbledon), who broadcast the announcement of Edward VIII's abdication and then became the main newsreader during the war, and John Snagge (Winchester), who commentated on the coronation of George VI and presented a magazine programme *War Report* during the war, featuring reports from correspondents who mostly spoke with the same posh accents. Few were not in that mould, but Wynford Vaughan

Thomas was one, from Bishop Gore GS in Swansea, and Godfrey Talbot (Leeds GS) was another, who 'learned to modify his Yorkshire accent to the more genteel tones essential to employment by the pre-war BBC'.[37]

The most memorable and moving report of the war was delivered from Belsen by Richard Dimbleby (Mill Hill). Son of a journalist, Dimbleby joined the BBC as a radio news reporter in 1936 and became its first war correspondent, reporting from many battlefields, including North Africa and Normandy. It is his report from Belsen in April 1945 that marks his quality as a correspondent. Dimbleby's dignified tones, sense of gravitas and ability to find the right words to describe the horrors he saw there have become the model against which all accounts of atrocities have since been measured, although he had to threaten to resign when the BBC initially refused to broadcast it because of its candour. Fittingly, both Dimbleby and Godfrey Talbot gave their last public performances as commentators at the funeral of Winston Churchill in 1965.

Two Australians from rival Melbourne schools managed to make the leap from war correspondent to historian. Alan Moorehead (Scotch College) covered battlefields across North Africa and Italy for the *Daily Express*, his copy avidly read in Britain. In the immediate aftermath of the war he wrote *African Trilogy*, a popular compendium of three journals covering the war in North Africa. Chester Wilmot (Melbourne GS) covered the war for the Australian Broadcasting Corporation and then the BBC, including flying in by glider on D-Day with the 6th Airborne Division. He became the first historian to try to encapsulate the war into a single volume, and his book *The Struggle for Europe*, published in 1952, opened the eyes of John Keegan (King's, Taunton) 'to a way of writing the history of the Second World War which was not just an essay in triumphalism … and never, never without remembrance that the drama of war is a tragedy for those touched by its fatal consequences.'[38] Keegan's own *Six Armies in Normandy* (1982) set new standards in the depiction of the experience of battle by soldiers on the ground.

The foremost military historian of the post-1945 era knew exactly what battle meant. Michael Howard left Wellington in 1941 to join the Coldstream Guards and won the MC in 1943 for leading his platoon in a successful night attack on a German hill-top position near Salerno. The memories of the war stayed with him for the rest of his life. He returned to academia in Oxford and London before founding the Department of War Studies at King's College, London. Ground-breaking books followed on all aspects of war, including the volume on *Grand Strategy* in the *Official History of the Second World War*. He founded the Institute of Strategic Studies and became Regius Professor of Modern History at Oxford. No historian of the post-war period combined his distinguished military service with profound thinking on all aspects of war and current events, and he inspired Max Hastings (Charterhouse) 'to try harder and better for him than anybody else outside my family'.[39] Hastings and Anthony Beevor (Winchester) have written many scholarly yet highly readable books on the Second World War, mastering the art of the tiny anecdote which reveals a big truth.

The greatest influence on writing the history of the Second World War was Winston Churchill, who wrote his war memoirs between 1948 and 1954 in six volumes, entitling it *The Second World War*. He enjoyed the priceless advantage, through an arrangement with the Cabinet Office, of consulting and quoting, often selectively to his advantage, from wartime official documents which remained closed to other historians for several decades. The autobiographical aspect was deliberately stressed, and even now the titles Churchill gave to each volume, such as 'The Gathering Storm' and 'Their Finest Hour', have set the tone and the narrative structure by which history judges the period. There was no statesman of the twentieth century 'whose retrospective accounts of the great events in which he has taken part have so dominated subsequent historical thinking'.[40] He saw his personal biography and role as war leader as 'unfolding history, and was determined to write his own version of it to increase the chances that posterity would see him as he saw himself.'[41] The appeasers of the 1930s were nailed into a literary coffin, Britain's part in the victory highlighted at a time when the Americans were making all the political and historical running, and Churchill's own centrally important historical role in the iconic events of 1940 firmly celebrated for posterity.

War Films

The British public bought thirty million cinema tickets per week during the war and into the late 1940s.[42] Even in 1959 there were still fifteen million seats sold every week in British cinemas, matching the circulation figures of all the national daily newspapers, until the counter-attraction of television brought a change of social habits and a sharp decline in the 1960s.[43] Not surprisingly, therefore, film, whether feature, documentary or newsreel, shaped the cultural legacy of the war more than any other medium. Many of those feature films still have strong followings when shown on television, those made during the war focusing on national unity and class cohesion, and those of the post-war era featuring epic stories and war heroes, mostly of the officer class.

Three of the most successful directors of wartime feature films all went to King's, Canterbury between 1916 and 1928 – Michael Powell, Carol Reed and Charles Frend. There is no obvious explanation for this, not least because King's was regarded at the time as 'a poor school, going through a bad period' by the writer and journalist Alaric Jacob. The head, Algernon Latter, was out of touch with the contemporary world, and Jacob felt it must have been a simple case of 'human nature rebelling, that some of Latter's more recalcitrant subjects managed to become actors, film directors, and even young men of gentlemanly anonymity married to rich wives'. The beauty of Canterbury itself had some effect on sensitive boys, most obviously in Powell's 1944 film *A Canterbury Tale*, which culminates in the pilgrimage of the central characters to the city and its cathedral, an attempt to create a modern equivalent of Chaucer's morality tales and to explain the values for which Britain was fighting. Powell himself had lived outside Canterbury as a dayboy, making his own pilgrimage into the city every day, and the closing scenes of the film in the war-damaged city made him recall later 'the semi-mystical feeling that you get … anyone who has lived near Canterbury's old stones must have this feeling'.[44]

Films with strong 'people's war' messages of national unity and class cohesion dominated the wartime cinema. Charles Frend's *The Foreman Went to France* (1942) is the story of a factory foreman who goes to France on his own initiative in 1940 to rescue machinery used to make guns for Spitfires. It is unusual in having as its central character a British working man who is a serious not a comic character, and it dwells on the class divisions which frustrate what he is trying to achieve, the foreman complaining that 'the people at the top think they're fighting the last war all over again'.[45] In Michael Powell's *The Life and Death of Colonel Blimp* (1943), the main theme is the clash between the older generation of career officers and the new young men who have risen through the ranks on merit. It is also unusual in covering and comparing the two world wars, with explicit criticism of the regular officer corps in 1914–18. The film does not condemn 'Blimp' for his old-fashioned gentlemanly views but suggests they are inappropriate to fighting a total war against a ruthless enemy. The film was popular, but government and the military disliked its depiction of 'Blimpish' officers and commissioned *The Way Ahead* in 1944 to offer a different view of the Army. This was directed by Carol Reed, with the central character, played by David Niven (Stowe), rising through the ranks to win his commission on merit, then welding together his platoon into a strong body of fighting men. The natural leadership of the elites was illustrated most effectively in *Henry V*, directed by and starring Laurence Olivier (St Edward's, Oxford). It was released in the autumn of 1944, its stirring account of Henry V crossing the Channel to Agincourt offering obvious parallels with D-Day, together with the young king's exhortations to comradeship and courage in battle. Olivier, a Hollywood star before the war, was released from service in the Fleet Air Arm to make the film.

The most influential maker of documentaries was Humphrey Jennings, whose wartime films captured the authentic experiences of ordinary people and pointed the way to hopes of a better post-war world. Jennings went to The Perse in Cambridge, from where he won a scholarship in English to Cambridge in 1926. Joining the GPO Film Unit in 1934, he started the Mass Observation project in 1937, and this anthropological study of popular behaviour informed his wartime documentaries, of which the most celebrated are *Listen to Britain* in 1942, *Fires were Started* in 1943 and *A Diary for Timothy* in 1945, looking forward to post-war Beveridge-inspired Britain. *Fires Were Started* is the record of a fire station in the London Blitz and is now widely regarded as 'the finest film testament to the people's war'.[46] It was about the way ordinary people went about getting things done during the Blitz, with a lack of overt heroics by the firemen and a focus on the camaraderie rather than the dangers. *Diary for Timothy*, directed by Jennings and produced by Basil Wright (Sherborne) for the Crown Film Unit, with commentary penned by E.M. Forster (Tonbridge) and narrated by Michael Redgrave, is a collection of images of Britain's future presented to a baby born on the fifth anniversary of the outbreak of war. It portrays 'the ruins of the present reveal[ing] the possibility of a new more equitable and democratic society in the post-war world'.[47]

Post-war films carried a different social message, and Michael Powell adapted to it in *The Battle of the River Plate* and *Ill Met by Moonlight*. The war films of the 1950s were more about nostalgia than national consensus, reminding cinemagoers that Britain had won the war with heroism and ingenuity. Their popularity was phenomenal in the last great age of mass cinema audiences, as Suez and the loss of empire provided a more sombre real-life backdrop. War films were the highest or second highest grossing British films in every year from 1955 to 1960. They focused on the heroism and natural leadership of the officer class, with other ranks reduced to 'the matey, tea-swilling lower deck cockney types'. The films were simple in their proudly patriotic message, with hints of subversion only emerging in the 1960s, and the rousing march music at their finales celebrated the rightness of the cause and offered faith in the future. The more the public loved these films, the more lukewarm were the critics, who condemned them for social conservatism and encouraging irresponsible attitudes to warfare. Michael Powell's *Battle of the River Plate* was described as 'a very British film, with such a stiff upper lip that it is almost expressionless', while of *Reach for the Sky* it was hoped that 'the cinema, having shown us how the last war was won, will now give us a little enlightenment on how to prevent the next'.[48]

Most of the actors playing the officer heroes had been educated at public schools and had wartime military experience themselves. Anthony Quayle (Rugby), star of *Ice Cold in Alex* and *The Guns of Navarone*, served with SOE in Albania. Leo Genn (City of London) was a colonel in the Royal Artillery when he was given leave to play the Constable of France in *Henry V*, and most of the cast of *The Dam Busters* served in the war, including Richard Todd, a paratrooper subaltern on D-Day. Kenneth More saw active service as a lieutenant in the Royal Navy, while Michael Hordern (Brighton) served as a naval officer on board the aircraft carrier *HMS Illustrious* and later claimed that in his films he had 'worn the insignia of every rank and rating in the British Navy except midshipman, ending up as Commander-in-Chief in *Sink the Bismarck* in 1960'. Questioned about the motivation of war films, he said that 'the war was a tremendous slice of most men's lives, men of my age, and there were many good stories to be told and morals to be drawn.'[49]

Most 1950s war films were unvaryingly positive in tone; they did not question the validity of the war and they 'conveyed a largely heroic narrative centred on white British masculinity, reinforcing the 1940 narrative of Britain Alone and having a lasting impact on national identity.'[50] David Lean's 1957 film *The Bridge on the River Kwai* was, however, more ambivalent, with Alec Guinness's spellbindingly stiff-upper-lip portrayal of Colonel Nicolson collaborating with his Japanese captors to build the bridge and prove the superiority of British engineering skill. Veterans thought it a cruel and false parody of Colonel Philip Toosey (Gresham's), the real officer involved, but the film asked serious questions about what made an effective officer and about the madness of war, and presaged a different approach. *Ice Cold in Alex*, made in 1958, starred John Mills (Norwich HS) as an officer struggling with battle fatigue and alcoholism, and gave a more sympathetic treatment of the enemy.

The genre started to be mocked in the 1960s, when radical changes in the social and political climate made it impossible to make films with a message of uncomplicated patriotism and an elevated view of the military caste system. The send-up by Peter Cook (Radley), in a sketch in *Beyond the Fringe*, of the stereotypical RAF officer of war films, only worked because it was parodying something with which the audience was very familiar. This particular sketch caused offence for mocking those who had lost their lives in the war, and at one performance a military gentleman stood up shaking his fist and shouting, 'You young bounders don't know anything about it!'[51] The 1960s were instrumental in revising views of the First World War and rendering those political and military elites toxic in public opinion, but despite the mockery in *Beyond the Fringe*, the esteem in which the elites of 1939–45 were held could not be completely shifted. New war films have kept coming in subsequent decades for modern audiences, with updated social messages but little undermining of the cultural legacy. They include *The Imitation Game* in 2014, celebrating British intellect at Bletchley Park, questioning attitudes to homosexuality in public schools and wider society and creating a new type of hero in Alan Turing, played by Benedict Cumberbatch (Harrow).

This positive narrative of the war was so well accepted by the 1960s that even 1940 and the Home Guard were impervious to the mockery that came with the comedy series *Dad's Army*, which ran for an astonishing eighty episodes in nine series on the BBC between 1968 and 1977. The writers were Jimmy Perry (St Paul's) and David Croft (Rugby), while three of the stars were Clive Dunn (Sevenoaks), Bill Pertwee (Frensham Heights) and John Le Mesurier (Sherborne). Some of the most delicious interplay lies in the class conflict between Le Mesurier playing Sergeant Wilson and Arthur Lowe playing Captain Mainwaring. Wilson is 'the Honourable Arthur Wilson', who went to a public school named Meadow Bridge, having failed the entrance exam to Harrow. He fought as an officer in the Great War but ended up as chief clerk at the bank in Walmington-on-Sea since, with his easy-going nature, he has few career ambitions. Mainwaring is the bank manager, who considers himself middle-class because he went to the local grammar school, although his origins are working-class. He had no combat experience in the war but served in the 1919 army of occupation – 'Someone had to clear up the mess', he says. Issues of class, together with Mainwaring's social and military pretensions, are at the heart of the comic relationship between him and Wilson. Mainwaring believes that Wilson's public-school experience made him 'wet', and often rants that the class system has prevented his own promotion to the higher echelons of the bank. The gently mocking humour of *Dad's Army* is in sharp contrast to the biting satire of *Blackadder Goes Forth*, reflecting the much greater sense of comfort we feel about issues of class and war in the Second World War.

Cultural Legacy

One historian has written of British perceptions that 'the First World War was not really about anything, or not about anything important; the Second World War was about national survival at home and defeat of a vile tyranny abroad.'[52] The image of the First World War as the 'bad' war was largely established in the 1960s, reflecting the more general anti-establishment attitude of that decade, when any voice of authority was challenged. Historians like John Terraine (Stamford) have tried to place the war more squarely in the context of political and military history, arguing that it was fought to protect British strategic interests, and that the sacrifices of the Somme and Passchendaele opened the way to the stunning victory largely achieved by the British Army in 1918. It was the war poets, however, who prevailed, and it is still 'a literary war, detached from its moorings in historical events ... the history has been distilled into the poetry'.[53]

Perceptions of the Second World War in Britain have also become shrouded in myth, but this time the myths, and indeed the literature and wider culture, are of a positive, reassuring, even triumphalist kind. We had won a war vital to our survival, with 'the concepts of the Dunkirk spirit and the Finest Hour achieving mythic status and stretched retrospectively to cover the whole conflict'.[54] The exaggerated view of Britain's contribution to victory has been clearly established in the public mind and has made a significant contribution to political debate since 1945. The war had been manifestly just, cost fewer lives than its predecessor, shown the imagination of the British in intelligence-led operations such as Bletchley Park, and was clearly a moral crusade against evil. There had been military failures in 1940–1942, worse than anything in the First World War, but they had later been redeemed, with some help from the Russians and Americans, and none of the generals or politicians qualified for the *Blackadder* treatment. Academic historians have argued about the myths of the Blitz or strategic bombing, but these debates have rarely reached the wider public.

That cultural legacy of the Second World War has been of great benefit to public schools in the post-1945 era. The portrait of the officer class in books and film highlights insouciance and effortless courage. The memory of the People's War is one of a united country, where Britons pulled together, whatever their class or background, in a spirit of shared effort and sacrifice and a sense of common purpose in a moral crusade against an evil enemy. In *Dad's Army* it is the debonair public-school Sergeant Wilson whose paternalistic concern for the men is greater than that of the more class-conscious Captain Mainwaring from the local grammar school, but both speak to a nostalgic vision of England. Little criticism emerged in the post-war decades of the ruling elites in government, which had anyway taken the form of an all-party coalition; the cost in human lives around the world was far bigger than in 1914–18, but not in Britain; and this time, the sacrifice was recognised as clearly worth it. Britain had won by being 'the comically amateurish and yet the quietly heroic country of the conservative vision'.[55] Schools themselves had a 'good war' in reality and perception, and after surviving the initial threat posed by a Labour government, flourished in the post-war world. In a history of the public schools written in 1957 it was suggested that 'the climate of opinion is kindly disposed to traditional institutions and it is arguable that the class structure of England is accepted with more equanimity than for many a long day.'[56] For that generous verdict on public schools, the images of Kenneth More as Douglas Bader, climbing into his Hurricane in August 1940, and Richard Todd as Guy Gibson, leading his squadron to German dams, provide an appropriate justification.

Part IV

The Opportunity Closes

The 1945 General Election brought a Labour landslide and hopes of a more integrated relationship between public schools and state secondary education, along the lines of the Fleming recommendations. These hopes were to be dashed by a government unwilling to commit resources on a national scale to an issue not seen as a priority, and by the public-school sector, its numbers and finances recovering from the war, unable and increasingly unwilling to press forward on its own. There was never to be a better opportunity of meaningful reform than in 1945.

Chapter 10

The Failure to Reform Public Schools

In 1945 hope existed that a unique opportunity had arrived to end the social exclusiveness of public schools. By the time Labour left power in 1951, those hopes had been dashed and were not to be raised again with anything resembling the same chance of success. The catalyst was the Fleming Report of 1944 which, compromise though it was, offered concrete steps towards opening places in the most exclusive boarding schools to children from different classes through state bursaries. Within a year of its publication, a reformist Labour government had come to power in a landslide victory and with a party behind it which had long identified public schools as the single most important source of political, social and economic privilege.

The Fleming Report proposed that a quarter of the places at HMC boarding schools should be offered to pupils paid for by the state. The public schools accepted its recommendations, and initiatives were set in train at a local level, but a lack of will and money on both sides prevented Fleming from becoming a successful national scheme on which later expansion could be based. It was a brief window of opportunity, for, as David Edgerton argues, Labour in government proved that it merely wished to 'reform an existing education system rather than create a new one'.[1]

In the 1950s public schools rode a wave of prosperity. Numbers increased, partly because of the concern of parents that their children might be consigned to secondary modern schools if they did not pass the eleven-plus. In 1964 the return of a Labour government created a more hostile political environment, in which integration of public schools with the state sector returned to the agenda. The 1968 Public Schools Commission proposed that some schools should assign at least half their places to state pupils with boarding needs, their fees to be publicly subsidised. This found little support, for many of the same reasons which had caused Fleming to founder. The public-school sector was also made more distinctive and popular by the introduction of comprehensive schools by both Labour and Conservative governments in the 1960s and 1970s, and especially by Labour's abolition of direct grant schools in 1975. The majority of these chose to become fully independent, strengthening the public-school sector in terms of numbers and academic quality. Although Margaret Thatcher's Assisted Places Scheme in 1980 tried to replicate the benefits of the direct grant system, and included boarding schools, Tony Blair abolished it in 1997, and the vision of bringing the two sectors closer together receded even further into the distance.[2]

The 1945 General Election

VE Day came on 8 May 1945. On the streets of London the celebrations matched those of November 1918, but there was to be nothing so predictable in the political events which followed. On 18 May Churchill wrote to the leaders of the other parties, inviting them to remain in the Coalition until Japan was defeated. Labour rejected the proposal, and the country went to the polls on 5 July. Although there had been straws in the wind in previous by-elections, the size of Labour's victory in the General Election of July 1945 came as a surprise. Labour won 393 seats (47.8 per cent of the total vote) against 213 Conservatives (39.8 per cent), with five members of Churchill's Cabinet and thirty-two members of his administration losing their seats. The Labour campaign had been optimistically forward-looking, its manifesto *Let us Face the Future* chiming with popular attitudes. Labour promised full employment, a National Health Service and implementation of social security schemes along the lines of the 1942 Beveridge Report, and its victory was the culmination of the positive spirit about post-war reconstruction which had begun in 1940. The rich felt that their world had come to an end. Peregrine Worsthorne (Stowe), a young officer with the Army in Holland, remembered when the news reached his mess 'the panic which hit some of my rich fellow officers – Astors and Barings. They thought the game was up and blocked 21st Army Group's headquarters communications system telephoning anguished instructions to sell to their stockbrokers.'[3]

Labour's broader appeal, which took it to victory in middle-class areas for the first time, was reflected in the composition of the new Parliamentary Labour Party. Trade unionists, always previously in a majority, were outnumbered for the first time by members of the professions.[4] Ninety Labour MPs, nearly a quarter of the party, had been educated at public schools, mostly in the inter-war years. Seven Etonians sat on the Labour benches, along with four from Winchester, four from Haileybury and three each from Rugby and Westminster, and most of the major schools had members on both sides of the House of Commons. Among those elected for the first time as Labour MPs were Michael Foot (Leighton Park), Hugh Gaitskell (Winchester), Aidan Crawley (Harrow), Barbara Castle (Bradford Girls GS), Frank Soskice (St Paul's) and John Freeman (Westminster), who made his first speech in the uniform of a major in the Rifle Brigade, indicating the change in the character of the party. The speech was so moving that, when Attlee later introduced him to Churchill, the great man supposedly wept, exclaiming: 'Now all the best men are on the other side.'[5] The Conservative benches remained dominated by public-school alumni, 160 out of the party's 197 MPs, including fifty-two Etonians and eight Harrovians. On the extreme left sat the Independent Labour MP, Denis Pritt (Winchester), who had been expelled from the Labour Party in 1940 for his close ties with Soviet communism.

One of the Labour newcomers in 1945 was Dick Crossman. The son of a judge, Crossman had a stellar career at Winchester, where he rose to be head boy, claiming later that even as a cabinet minister he never again wielded the same power. Intellectually he was head and shoulders above most of his contemporaries, but he later reflected that, although the school had over-developed him intellectually, he was correspondingly under-developed in facing the problems of life: 'Here I was reading Dostoevsky at fourteen – and going to Oxford feeling everything was over ... but gauche, naïve, boring, not used to handling myself with women.'[6] In 1924 at Winchester he had stood as the Labour candidate in a mock election, but at Oxford he did not become involved in student politics. As a Fellow of New College, he became a Labour city councillor in Oxford before joining the Political Warfare Executive in 1939, producing anti-Nazi propaganda broadcasts. He was adopted as Labour candidate for Coventry and won the seat in 1945 with 60 per cent of the votes. In that Labour intake were many like Crossman who had come to left-wing politics at public school and Oxbridge in the inter-war years, and who had a driving ambition to improve social and economic conditions for the whole nation. They included Francis Noel-Baker (Westminster), Geoffrey de Freitas (Haileybury) and Geoffrey Bing (Tonbridge), who had been a journalist with the International Brigades in Spain and was active on the socialist left.

The Labour Cabinets between 1945 and 1951 had an even higher percentage of public-school alumni than the parliamentary party. Of thirty-five ministers in the Cabinet between 1945 and 1951, thirteen came from public schools, including four Etonians – Hugh Dalton, and Lords Pethick-Lawrence, Listowel and Pakenham. Apart from Attlee and Dalton, who became Chancellor of the Exchequer, the most significant public-school alumni were Stafford Cripps (Winchester), who became Chancellor of the Exchequer in 1947, followed by Hugh Gaitskell (Winchester), Hartley Shawcross (Dulwich) who became Attorney-General and William Jowitt (Marlborough), the Lord Chancellor. By contrast, Ernest Bevin, the Foreign Secretary, and Herbert Morrison, the Deputy Prime Minister, had both left school by the time they were fourteen, exceptional products of a pre-1914 education system which had failed so many of their class. The new Minister for Education was Ellen Wilkinson, MP for Jarrow, who had helped organise the 1936 unemployment march and was the first Education Minister not to have gone to public school. She had only been able to continue her education beyond the age of fifteen in Manchester by winning a bursary to train as a teacher for half the week, spending the other half teaching in an elementary school and eventually winning a scholarship to Manchester University. This was the government which now held the future of the public schools in its hands.

Public Schools and the Labour Government

The public schools had potentially much to worry them. For well over a decade they had benefited from the political protection of a predominantly Conservative government and the great majority of MPs who were alumni of leading public schools. Butler had diverted criticism of public schools into what he called the 'railway siding', and any progress on the Fleming recommendations was effectively postponed until after the war; but now the massive Labour majority posed a significant threat, for the Labour Party during the war had been hostile to the very existence of public schools. In association with its affiliated organisations like the WEA, it had proposed and backed in 1942 a radical programme of educational change. This envisaged a comprehensive system of secondary education, abolition of all fees in maintained secondary schools, including direct grant grammar schools, and the 'abolition or at least effective assimilation of the public schools as a step towards the creation of a single, national system of education'.[7] A polemical pamphlet written in October 1942 by the respected editor of the *Times Educational Supplement*, Harold Dent, accused the public schools of breeding 'an exclusive social caste which has seized and holds fast the keys to political, diplomatic, religious, social and economic power'.[8] Labour's National Executive in 1943 demanded 'acceptance of the broad democratic principle that all children of school age shall be required to attend schools provided by the State'.[9]

The sector was still vulnerable because of the severe financial straits in which some schools found themselves at the end of the war. Numbers generally had begun to rise from 1942, but recovery remained slow, especially for schools which had been evacuated. One school in difficulty was Westminster, which had 370 boys in 1939 but 130 when it returned to London from Wales in 1945. The school's annual deficit had risen from £5,000 in the late 1930s to £67,000 in 1945, and bomb damage to school buildings at Westminster contributed to a total loss by the end of the war of £400,000 (over £17 million today), with little government compensation forthcoming. Key college buildings, including the historic Busby Library, had been destroyed in air raids, there were no classrooms, a brick air raid shelter stood in the middle of Little Dean's Yard, and Vincent Square, the main playing field, was unusable until 1948, its field scarred by trenches and littered with American Army trucks and barrage balloon anchorages. It was just as well the school had shrunk in numbers, since there was no room for more in the shattered buildings. All cricket fixtures were cancelled in 1946 as the school could not afford them.[10]

Wycombe Abbey, requisitioned by the US Air Force in 1942, had been forced to close completely, its girls and staff dispersed around other schools, and it did not re-open until May 1946. Rent had been paid for use of the premises, but there was no compensation for loss of fee income, and the school's financial situation was dire. War damage to property portfolios depressed income elsewhere. The Harpur Trust, which endowed Bedford School, suffered such serious damage to its property in Holborn that rent income in 1943 reverted to the levels of 1825.[11] Dulwich had been one of the few schools to stay in London but by 1941 was close to insolvency, with numbers down to 450 compared to 800 in 1939, one boarding house a bombed ruin and the college running at an annual loss of £5,500. By the end of the war numbers had picked up again to 700, but the head spoke of the 'dead weight of war damage like a millstone round the College's neck' as endowment income fell.[12]

If the Labour government had been as hostile to public schools as the left of the party, then any concerted pressure on the sector could have seen many schools unable to continue. Hopes of radical action in left-wing intellectual and educational circles were not, however, in tune with the more socially conservative attitudes of Labour ministers and many Labour MPs. The wartime parliamentary Labour Party and the union movement were controlled by 'men who were essentially moderate social patriots'.[13] Its foreign policy hardly differed from what the Conservatives would have done and in expenditure, as David Edgerton points out, it had 'a higher warfare-to welfare ratio than in the inter-war state'. This was not a government likely to want to bring in controversial changes in elite education.[14]

Labour ministers in the Coalition had worked with Churchill to represent national unity, while individual Labour MPs had been happy to visit public schools in wartime. Ernest Bevin came to speak at Eton and 'as he was escorted back to the Headmaster's house, he stopped, waved his arms at the boys and the buildings around him, saying, "We must never change any of this".'[15] Later, the King's private secretary, Tommy Lascelles, recorded Bevin speaking at a dinner party about his admiration for Eton and Harrow: 'Various ministers started a round of old-school-tie chaff. Ernie fetched a gargantuan sigh and said in my ear, "I always wish I'd been at one of them places".'[16]

The mood in the Labour government was for a measured and uncontroversial approach to public schools, partly because the administration had too many other pressing priorities. With another leader than the deeply middle-class Attlee it might have been different, but Labour under him was preoccupied with establishing a managed economy and the expanded welfare state envisaged by Beveridge, while also coping with post-war austerity and many difficult foreign policy challenges. According to Attlee's biographer, John Bew, none of his Cabinet, except Aneurin Bevan, saw 'the public schools as a cultural issue which needed radical treatment, as happened with health and industry, while civil servants shared the same pragmatic assumptions'.[17] The emphasis in education was on carrying through the provisions of the 1944 Education Act and making state education as good as possible, while Labour and Attlee had been part of the government which had agreed the setting up of Fleming, whose recommendations had to be at least considered. Attlee recognised that Butler had taken the steam out of the public-school issue with the Fleming Committee, and had said to Butler in 1941 that 'like most of our institutions the public schools should not be killed but adapted'.[18] Another historian, Ross McKibbin, suggests a different angle:

> Labour in practice left untouched those institutions which were strongly defended. No one was ready to go to the stake for privately owned coal mines ... but they were for cavalry regiments, the public schools or even grammar schools. Once a decision had been made to exclude those areas of society which would be strongly defended, at the only moment when their defences might have been overcome with popular support, the Labour Party let slip an opportunity which was unlikely ever to recur.[19]

It has been insinuated that Attlee prevented any moves against public schools because of his nostalgic devotion to Haileybury.[20] That devotion was certainly real, and demonstrated many times. John Bew confirms that Attlee was 'very fond of his school and was delighted to encounter Old Haileyburians throughout the rest of his life'.[21] He kept in touch with his contemporaries, writing to his brother in 1958 on the death of a fellow member of his house: 'I last saw him at an O.H. dinner at Rawalpindi in

1928.'[22] Jock Colville was asked by Attlee in August 1945 for his views on Geoffrey de Freitas, who Attlee wanted to appoint as his Parliamentary Private Secretary. Colville remarked that he was charming and highly intelligent, to which Attlee replied, 'Yes, and what is more he was at Haileybury, my old school.'[23] Kenneth Morgan, historian of the Labour Party, agrees that Attlee's attachment to Haileybury was 'not a trivial matter' in deciding his attitude to the public-school issue, describing how he drew up a list showing that there were more Haileyburians than Etonians or Wykehamists in his government.[24] When he spoke as guest of honour at the Haileybury Speech Day in June 1946 he made clear his views on the future of public schools: 'This country changes, but it is in our way to change things gradually, and I see no reason for thinking that the public schools will disappear. I think the great tradition of public schools will be extended.'[25] Such words would have been beyond belief if they had come from any later Labour Prime Minister, or even a Conservative one.

It was not, however, just sentimental attachment to Haileybury which explains Attlee's attitude. He had no time for the class jealousy which could be found in others on the left, and none, according to John Bew, in his Cabinet 'were gunning to do anything about public schools'.[26] Patriotism underpinned his socialism, his own distinguished service in the First World War helping him to 'understand the strength of the ties that bind men to the land of their birth'.[27] Traditions meant much to a man who never 'questioned the institutions which formed him – Haileybury, Oxford, the Army, the Labour Party – "Old England" if you like.'[28] Westminster head John Rae was unconvinced that Labour's lack of action towards public schools was mainly due to Attlee's love of Haileybury, arguing that his government simply had more important things to do: 'In education its priority was to extend and improve the maintained system. The question of public schools was not forgotten. It was postponed.'[29] Attlee's attachment to Haileybury continued into his retirement, and he visited the school regularly to watch cricket. The headmaster 'organised a rota of housemasters to sit with him and do their best to make conversation'.[30]

Ellen Wilkinson, the new Minister for Education, who died in 1947, and her successor, George Tomlinson, both Attlee loyalists, saw their main task as ensuring that the provisions of the 1944 Act were implemented.

Wilkinson's priority was to raise the school leaving age from fourteen to fifteen, which she successfully achieved just before her death. Kenneth Morgan makes it clear that outright abolition of public schools was never considered within the government, for it was enough of a task to build up the state sector, and the huge costs incurred in replacing public schools were unaffordable, in both political and financial terms. The establishment of the tripartite system in secondary education was supported by both Wilkinson and Tomlinson, who came from a strand in the Labour Party which was hostile to any system which discriminated against working-class children. They 'saw admission to grammar school as a reward for striving. Comprehensive schools eliminated the need to strive and thus depreciated the quality of working-class culture.'[31] Their focus was to make grammar schools, and the kind of knowledge and self-confidence they imparted, accessible to the working-classes to enable them to join the political elites, not to stir the pot further.

George Tomlinson went out of his way to reassure independent schools that they were safe under Labour. Kenneth Morgan describes him as 'a very inadequate, though gentle figure whose own slim education left him with feelings of inferiority. He once said that, if he had gone to Eton, he could have won the Battle of Waterloo himself.'[32] In 1950 he was given rousing applause by the preparatory schools' annual conference when he told them: 'There is no suggestion that your schools, or, I might add, the independent public schools, should be compulsorily absorbed into the state system or anything of that kind ... And personally I do not see the sense of getting rid of something that is doing a useful job of work, or making everything conform to a common pattern. I am all for variety, especially in the field of education.'[33] He visited Eton to deliver the same message. Labour's generally benevolent attitude to the public schools was shown further in 1948, when the Treasury agreed that public-school teachers' pensions would be funded via general taxation, thus making it easier for teachers to move in mid-career between the private and maintained systems.

If abolition of public schools was never a serious possibility under the 1945 Labour government, what about the Fleming scheme? One historian has suggested that Wilkinson, her hands full with other educational priorities, in effect killed off Fleming, Brian Simon writing that 'no decision of any kind about the original Fleming proposals was announced or apparently made by Ellen Wilkinson'.[34] These claims are misleading because, although no national scheme was forthcoming, Wilkinson between 1945 and 1947 encouraged, through official circulars from the Ministry, engagement between LEAs and individual public schools. One from March 1946 stated: 'Some LEAs are already making arrangements with independent boarding schools to enable pupils in suitable cases to receive the benefit of education at such schools. The Minister is generally of the opinion that such arrangements are to be encouraged.'[35]

Public schools remained committed to honouring the recommendations of Fleming. At the HMC conference in January 1946 Robert Birley argued that HMC had to show it was in earnest in wanting change. The HMC Committee in May 1946 concluded that schools should 'build on the existing foundations of local arrangements in the hope that, as these schemes multiply, they could be built into a national scheme'.[36] Spencer Leeson recognised Winchester's responsibilities when he reported to his governors in August 1946: 'Those who value the work of the independent schools and desire it to continue, but insist that they shall be made more generally accessible, are I believe slowly growing in numbers.' Winchester had already entered into an agreement with Hampshire LEA for five places, but Leeson raised doubts about whether going up to the Fleming limit of 25 per cent of places, even if feasible financially, might alter the essential character of the school, including 'the right of housemasters to select their own boys, a right they prize'.[37] This touched on the question of how far some public schools were prepared to accommodate Fleming. Not very far.

At the end of 1946, in his chairman's address to that December's HMC conference, John Wolfenden summarised how things had developed towards Fleming. He warned that, although no national policy had emerged from the government, there was political danger in backing away from the recommendations, even though public-school numbers were now on the increase. He feared that local arrangements would impede rather than foster a national system of boarding education, but ended on a rousing note by declaring:

> Any delay in carrying out proposals for closer relations between the independent schools and the national system of education is not to be laid at our door … If we maintain that the Fleming report arose

from our own initiative, we cannot evade the responsibility of co-operation in bringing about a far closer relation between our own schools and the national system than has ever been present in the past. I hope I am right in taking it that this Conference welcomes that responsibility and is determined to fulfil it.

Conference passed, without dissent, a resolution welcoming such a national scheme and expressed hopes that heads and governing bodies would work with the Ministry and local authorities to implement it.[38]

One victory for lobbying by HMC concerned the direct grant schools, which saw the threat of radical action lifted from them. Ellen Wilkinson had wanted to follow through on Fleming's first interim report and abolish all fees in direct grant schools, but this never happened. The number of schools on the direct grant list was reduced from 232 to 164, some going independent and others passing to local authority control, but they survived as an outpost of the public-school system until Labour abolished the direct grant list in 1975, when most went fully independent.[39] Dulwich, regarded by most people as a bastion of the independent sector, was one direct grant school thrown a lifeline by its LEA. By 1947 90 per cent of the boys at Dulwich were being paid for, without means tests, by London County Council and other local authorities, with just eighteen places a year kept open for fee-payers. This was regarded by headmaster Christopher Gilkes as 'a strategy of survival' for the school, its estate and endowments having been badly damaged by the war.[40]

Following that HMC conference in December 1946 there was no further collective discussion of the Fleming boarding recommendations, since no initiatives emerged from the Ministry for a national scheme with which HMC could engage. George Tomlinson confirmed in a written parliamentary answer about Fleming in 1950 that 'it has not been possible to carry out the Committee's specific recommendations regarding independent boarding schools'.[41] It highlights the fact that Labour was simply not interested in implementing the Fleming recommendations on any national level, because of other spending priorities, opposition within the Party and, not least, because legislation did not exist to cover a national system of centrally funded bursaries, which under existing laws had to flow through LEAs.

Schools did take advantage of opportunities at local level, which were more productive than is sometimes assumed, but these were the result of direct arrangements between LEAs and individual schools. The 1952 *Yearbook of Education* found that 123 out of 146 LEAs were partially or fully assisting 4,741 boarders, of whom 2,096 were at independent schools. This only equated to 5 per cent of the 39,500 places at boarding schools within Fleming's terms of reference, rather than 25 per cent. Hertfordshire LEA was particularly enthusiastic, initially sponsoring twelve boarding places at local independent schools like Haileybury, but then also at Eton, Shrewsbury, Winchester, Rugby and four girls' schools, including Westonbirt and Wycombe Abbey.[42] If all LEAs and schools had moved in this way, the scheme might have flourished, but the experience of Winchester after Leeson's retirement shows the difficulties. In September 1946 it had only three applicants for Fleming places, and subsequently there was no more than a trickle of county scholars because 'most LEAs could not justify the spending of three times as much on the few as on the many'.[43] Participating schools also enjoyed all the balance of advantage, with 'no minimum percentage of bursary places, no rules on their fee-setting and no public representation on their governing bodies. They also retained control over who to admit, giving them access to public funds without strings attached.'[44]

The example of Harrow also shows both the potential and the difficulties inherent in Fleming. Harrow was the beneficiary of enthusiasm from Middlesex LEA, admitting five Middlesex scholars per year for twenty-five years from 1947, selected from local schools, the proportion of fees paid by the LEA determined by parental means test. But the numbers were proportionately tiny in relation to the size of the school, some housemasters had to be cajoled into accepting them and some of the scholars suffered from the scorn of snobbish adolescents. The principle was, however, important for the future. As the Harrow historian Christopher Tyerman has pointed out, 'The significance of the Fleming Report lay in its identification of a social conscience in public schools which persisted, at least in public, even after the financial imperatives that had first encouraged its discovery had disappeared.'[45]

Labour lost power in 1951, but well before this the Fleming scheme for state-sponsored boarding places was withering on the vine. The expense of the scheme meant that central government, with so many other priorities, tried to push responsibility on to local authorities, who themselves lacked the financial resources to support it and were reluctant to cream off their best pupils. Grant-aided secondary schools cost £30 per year per pupil, whereas the Fleming Committee found that the cost of boarding places was anything from £80 to £245, rising to £500 by 1960.[46] Outside, and even within, the public-school sector, scepticism existed as to whether the value derived from boarding education was sufficient to justify the cost. The schools themselves lost interest in what remained a purely local scheme as rising prosperity made it easier to fill places, and the problems over selection of pupils became more difficult, particularly the tension between boarding need as identified by LEAs and the selective entrance criteria on which schools insisted, often including a requirement for Latin. This is not to deny the continuing desire of some school heads to draw pupils into their schools from a wider social background, but 'once it was no longer essential to do this in order to save the schools themselves, the very considerable practical and political difficulties involved proved to be effective obstacles.'[47]

Idealists within public schools saw Fleming as the best chance to break out of a narrow class base. In the vanguard was John Dancy, who came back after war service to his old school, Winchester, to teach classics for five years, before moving to headmasterships at Lancing and Marlborough. He was a progressive who claimed that 'all my friends at Winchester shared my left-wing views'.[48] This may be disputed, but many headmasters, even more members of staff and not an inconsiderable number of pupils in the post-war years were politically left of centre. Long before most of his fellow heads, 'Dancy saw that the pre-war pattern of public-school life had become inappropriate to the modern world and he did more than any of them to change it.'[49] In his 1963 book, *The Public Schools and the Future*, he celebrated the shared social faith and unified national spirit which swept through the country during the war, with hopes of equal opportunity to follow. He believed that this faith was held within the public schools no less than outside them, and that their motives in pushing for the Fleming Committee were high-minded rather than based on economic stringency. He wanted real integration with the state system and in the mid-1960s offered twenty boarding places at

Marlborough to boys from Wiltshire state schools, paid for jointly by the college and a Ministry research project on boarding led by Royston Lambert. The experiment produced mixed results, with some boys benefiting but others becoming disorientated by the unfamiliar setting. When Dancy explained the scheme to Labour MPs, they repudiated it on the grounds that it had merely produced a group of 'pseudo-middle-class sophisticates'.[50] Dancy himself came round to the view that, if such a scheme was to work, then the pupil proportions would have to be more even, which would bring much deeper changes to school culture and tradition.

Both Spencer Leeson and John Wolfenden claimed that public schools were ready to implement the boarding proposals laid out by Fleming, but they anticipated it would take time to approach the 25 per cent figure. Wolfenden later chaired the 1957 Committee whose report recommended the decriminalisation of homosexuality. Robert Birley laid most of the blame at the government's door, reflecting later that 'if the Conservatives had won the election in 1945, something on the lines of the Fleming Scheme would have been started. If so, I think by now it would be regarded as quite commonplace.' Labour, Birley believed, was not against the scheme in principle but 'were not prepared to have a scheme run under the Ministry and the Treasury: the whole thing was to be run by LEAs. As soon as I heard of this decision, I realised the scheme was doomed.'[51]

The hopes which animated the 1944 Act and the Fleming Report, for a more national, democratic system of education, were none of them achieved. The system, according to historian Ross McKibbin, was 'not national because too much lay outside it', and it was not democratic because 'it could never guarantee equality of opportunity (or anything approaching it) and because it frustrated any commonality of experience'.[52] Public schools were one of the impediments to the growth of a national system, but they had powerful defenders and faced weak opposition. Public attitudes to the schools were benign or neutral, and elements within Labour, though believing them socially exclusive, also thought them educationally excellent. Ernest Bevin, the Labour Foreign Secretary, said to Robert Birley in 1949 when he left his role in Germany to take over the headmastership of Eton: 'Birley, keep on sending us your boys: we can't get along without them.'[53] Bevin was less enamoured of the Foreign Office official, with a public-school classics background, who used the term *mutatis mutandis* on a briefing paper. He scribbled the tetchy reply, 'Please do not write in Greek.'[54]

The social mobility which Fleming and more progressive elements within HMC tried to promote, albeit a small step at a time, never materialised by the time Labour left office, while the new state system, based on selection at eleven, established a hierarchy in education, with the elite public boarding schools and revivified grammar schools still at the top, and secondary moderns in the most deprived areas at the bottom.

Public Schools and Conservative Governments 1951–64

The Conservative governments from 1951 to 1964 did not encourage any change to the status quo. The *TES* noted in 1952 that the number of LEAs applying the principles of the Fleming Report 'can be numbered on the fingers of one hand'.[55] In 1957 the Conservative-aligned Bow Group proposed that between one-third and one-half of entries at leading public schools should be grant-aided pupils, but the Treasury was sceptical of the cost, and the Education Minister, Lord Hailsham (Eton), saw little educational advantage when 'only a tiny minority of public schools were superior to the top-performing grammar schools'.[56] In 1958 HMC tried unsuccessfully again, when the full Conference reaffirmed the Fleming principle and 'regretted that no Minister of Education as yet felt able to accept the co-operation offered by the public schools in carrying out such a scheme'.[57] It was a Wykehamist Conservative Minister of Education, David Eccles, who in 1961 finally killed the Fleming scheme because 'he could see no reason to use public money to subsidise the transfer of boys from one system to another'.[58] John Rae later recalled that 'there was a fairly widespread view among headmasters that the Tories had missed an opportunity in the 1950s of working out an acceptable form of integration'.[59]

The 1950s were years of economic security; with little fear of recession if parents over-committed themselves financially, the public-school market was buoyant. Admissions had risen by 20 per cent under the Attlee governments, boosted by middle-class families whose children had failed the eleven-plus and 'who were determined not to confine their offspring to a secondary modern'.[60] Demographics also played a part, with the post-war baby-boomer generation coming through the system. Under both Labour and Conservative governments, middle-class parents abandoned the state sector if they could afford to, as part of a process of social distancing. Although by 1955 numbers within the public-school system had reached nearly 7 per cent of the total school population, there was no new wave of public-schools foundations, as represented by Stowe, Canford and Benenden in the 1920s. Numbers entering state secondary schools always grew faster than those attending public schools, and the majority of the middle classes continued to use the free state system, where they suffered less competition from the working class, in entry to grammar schools, than they had expected.[61] The political battleground in education shifted away from focus on public schools to issues of selection within the state sector, as Labour pressed for its elimination and a move towards comprehensive secondary schools, while the Conservatives, mindful of their natural middle-class constituency, became more committed to maintaining selection.

The monopoly of top jobs by the public-school educated was as marked as ever. In 1955 over half of Eden's first Cabinet and another fifth of all Conservative backbenchers had been to Eton. More than a third of the entries in the 1961 edition of *Who's Who* were Etonians.[62] The same figures for public schools generally could be found across large swathes of public life – over 80 per cent of judges and QCs, over 60 per cent of physicians and surgeons at London teaching hospitals. At Oxbridge, in 1961 54 per cent of the entry came from public schools and another 16 per cent from direct grant grammar schools. In a pioneering survey in 1954, the sociologist David Glass wrote that 'though the 1944 Education Act will no doubt greatly increase the amount of social mobility in Britain, there is an upper limit to that increase which the Act itself imposes by leaving the public school system substantially intact.' This was, he added, a fundamental inequality of educational opportunity 'blocking ascent to, and limiting descent from, the upper reaches of social status'.[63] The Conservative politician Angus Maude voiced an increasingly common riposte by arguing that the 1944 Act gave clever children of poor parents a free place in a school which would develop their aptitudes to the full, so that 'the parent who is prepared to make sacrifices to provide his child with better-than-average schooling has as much right to spend his money on that as on a better television set.'[64]

The office of Prime Minister saw meritocracy triumph, if only temporarily, as those educated in public schools before and during the First World War – Churchill, Attlee, Eden, Macmillan and Douglas-Home, three of them Etonians – passed on. Historian Peter Clarke recorded that Harold Wilson (Royds Hall GS and Wirral GS) in the 1960s became 'the first major leader to represent the new ruling class – an upwardly mobile Oxbridge meritocracy recruited through provincial grammar schools'.[65] He was followed by Edward Heath (Chatham House GS), James Callaghan (Portsmouth Northern GS), Margaret Thatcher (Kesteven and Grantham Girls GS) and John Major (Rutlish School), before the office reverted to the public-school-educated Tony Blair (Fettes) and the two Etonians David Cameron and Boris Johnson – with brief interludes from Gordon Brown (Kirkcaldy HS) and Theresa May (Wheatley Park School).

Public schools continued largely to follow in the 1950s the ethos and culture of the 1930s. Conditions remained spartan, with corporal punishment by prefects, cold showers and compulsory CCF persisting into at least the 1960s. The ethos continued to value hierarchy, duty and tradition, but there was a growing emphasis on improving academic standards, as public schools faced competition from selective state grammar schools. Spending on state secondary education rose by 80 per cent in real terms between 1944 and 1955, with another surge in the late 1960s.[66] One of the consequences of the 1944 Education Act was to intensify competition for places at the top universities between public school and grammar school pupils, a trend noted in the 1960s by the Oxford don, Maurice Bowra, who saw it as creating there a welcome rise in academic standards.[67]

A new qualification designed to mark pupils as fit for a university place, the A level, was born in 1951. In the 1950s public schools were complacent about this new qualification, and Etonians did not sit A Levels at all until 1958, but parents began to become more worried about their sons' futures in a more competitive world and started to complain about low academic ambition and poor teaching. A telling survey in

The Times in 1964 looked at the principle of value for money in public schools, concluding that Eton, Harrow and Charterhouse all fell into the 'high fees, low A levels category'.[68] Good A level grades became essential not just for high-flyers but for the average pupil, whose aspirations for university were blocked by too much focus on the likely Oxbridge entrants. John Rae later wrote of what he found when he took up the headship of Westminster in 1970: 'The future of the majority of boys was sacrificed to the pursuit of Oxbridge scholarships for the chosen few. Boys who could easily have got good A levels ended up having to go to a crammer to take them again. I am amazed parents did not complain.'[69]

Cultural change also came to public schools in the 1960s. In the era of *Beyond the Fringe* and *That Was the Week That Was*, no figure or institution of authority was beyond attack. The justification for fagging, that 'those who hope to rule must first learn to obey', articulated by a Harrow master in 1928, no longer cut much ice in a post-imperial world. The growing influence of pop music idols who challenged accepted norms encouraged the young to kick against petty regulations of dress and hair, and those elements of public school life which represented tradition and hierarchy, such as the CCF and compulsory chapel, while both fagging and corporal punishment gradually fell into disuse. The film *if....*came out in 1968, written by David Sherwin and John Howlett (both at Tonbridge), and directed by Lindsay Anderson (Cheltenham), delivering a withering attack on the public-school ethos, perfectly catching the zeitgeist. In 1968 Marlborough under John Dancy became the first of the major boys' boarding schools to admit girls, just fifteen to begin with into the sixth form. It is difficult to appreciate now just how bold a step this was and the opposition it aroused, but it proved to be the start of a revolution which by the mid-1980s saw two-thirds of boys' public schools become co-educational. In part a survival tactic, it nevertheless marks the moment schools started looking forward.

But how much sooner would long-overdue change have come if the proportion of state-sponsored pupils under the Fleming scheme had reached higher levels?

The 1968 Public Schools Commission

Labour returned to power in 1964 for the first time in thirteen years. Over the next six years of the government's course the public schools had once again to confront political hostility as well as adverse economic conditions. From January 1965, education policy was in the hands of Anthony Crosland (Highgate) as Secretary of State, a prominent intellectual on the left. Crosland wanted to have another stab at integration, and the idea of a new Fleming-style commission 'to advise on the best way of integrating the public schools into the state system' was promised in the 1964 Labour manifesto. When Crosland took over the education brief in 1965 from Michael Stewart (Christ's Hospital), he wanted to implement this manifesto commitment as soon as possible, but the shift towards comprehensive schools and the expansion of universities was a higher priority. Public schools were never seen as a priority by the Prime Minister, Harold Wilson, who had sent his son to University College School in the late 1950s and who could not see any political gain with the wider public in taking on public schools and the aspiration they encouraged. Even left-wing Labour MPs followed such a course, Kenneth Morgan remembering that his contemporaries at University College School included the sons of Sydney Silverman and George Strauss, while Hartley Shawcross (Dulwich) claimed in 1956 that he 'did not know a single member of the Labour Party who can afford to do so, who does not send his children to a public school'. His own son went to Eton.[70]

The Public Schools Commission was eventually announced in December 1965. John Newsom, former Chief Education Officer for Hertfordshire and deeply imbued with public schools, having been to Imperial Service College and a governor of Haileybury, was indicatively selected as chair. The two public school heads among the fifteen members were John Dancy of Marlborough and Tom Howarth of St Paul's, who had taught together at post-war Winchester. Crosland ruled out a small-scale Fleming solution in its terms of reference, preferring a national plan for integrating the schools that would 'consider how the public schools could contribute to the comprehensive (non-selective) approach that was being pushed within the state financed system'.[71] In April 1968, over two years later, the Commission presented its recommendations, above all for a cadre of boarding schools which would assign a minimum of half their places within seven years to pupils from maintained schools with a social or academic need for boarding. This would have seen a figure way above the 36,000 pupils receiving some form of state assistance to board in 1966 and was widely seen as impractical.[72] More than half the members of the Commission expressed dissent from this main recommendation, and even the first page of the report warned that 'whatever plan we devise will please neither the independent schools nor their sternest critics, neither the local authorities nor the teachers in the maintained schools with which we are told the independent schools must be integrated.'[73]

Such equivocation was unlikely to sell the plan to any of the stakeholders. Wilson refused to allow a detailed discussion in Cabinet and the press was hugely critical, the *Guardian* pounced on this, calling it 'impractical, expensive and harmful to children'. The National Union of Teachers described as 'disastrous' the idea of spending public money on public school places, given other educational priorities. HMC wanted to co-operate, not least because the independent sector had been suffering from a renewed downturn in demand, with a drop of 11 per cent in the number of pupils at public schools between 1962 and 1967.[74] An injection of public money would therefore have been welcome, while integration was better than abolition, which some still feared at the hands of Labour. The biggest obstacle was again money, but also the wish to use boarding public schools to meet a social need. The *Guardian* commenting that 'the Commission is proposing to use these mainly backward, deprived or maladjusted children to cure the public schools of their social divisiveness. This would not be fair on the children.' The Commission's findings were effectively rejected by the government, and no reform of any substance occurred. Change was also opposed by much of the electorate, two-thirds of those consulted in a 1968 opinion poll telling the government to leave public schools alone.[75] Wilson's instincts had proved correct.

The failures of both Fleming and the Public Schools Commission to establish anything transformative have common reasons. One was their cost in the face of competing educational priorities: one child in an independent boarding school cost five times the average per pupil outlay. Clear selection processes were also difficult to achieve, whether these should be based on social need or academic ability. The public schools themselves were keen to engage when their future looked bleak, as in the 1940s or in the mid-1960s, but life had improved by 1950 and again after 1970. Abolition was never seriously considered by those in power, while integration posed all kinds of problems of marrying different educational traditions.

Public schools benefited in the 1960s and 1970s from the consequences of two other Labour policies. Anthony Crosland's Circular 10/65, from the Department of Education in 1965, which requested local authorities to convert their secondary schools to comprehensives, created doubts in the public mind over the quality of state education. Even greater benefit came from Labour's decision in the 1970s to target the direct grant schools, with their mixture of fee-paying and state-maintained pupils. In 1975 there were 174 such schools, some with boarding places and most with high academic standards, including schools like Manchester Grammar School and Bradford Grammar School, where Labour ministers Harold Lever and Denis Healey respectively had been pupils, and which were described in the press as 'pinnacles of academic excellence and well-trodden avenues for the progress of working-class children'.[76] When Labour returned to power in 1974, direct grant schools were forced to choose between joining the state system and becoming fully independent. Sixty schools, only a third of the total and most of them Roman Catholic grammars, chose to become comprehensives, and the rest became fully independent, their governors believing that only in this way could their ethos be preserved. The head of Queen Elizabeth's Hospital School in Bristol, which now went independent, called it 'insane' that 'an historic bluecoat school with nearly 400 years of service to the less well-off of Bristol is being forced by a central socialist government to go independent, raise its fees in consequence and thus move beyond the reach of the very people the socialists have traditionally wanted to help.'[77] The public-school sector was greatly strengthened by the addition of these large and high-performing schools, expanding its share of the secondary school population from 4.4 per cent in 1977 to 6.2 per cent in 1981.[78] Manchester GS alone sent three-quarters of its sixth-formers to university, a quarter to Oxbridge.[79] It was a sad irony that this Labour government managed to create more private schools than any administration since the reign of Edward VI.[80]

Labour's attempts in the 1960s and 1970s to integrate public schools with the state sector all failed. Public schools became more selective as the state sector became less so. Crosland's attack on grammar schools meant that public schools became even more appealing to those who could afford them, helped by the disquiet felt by many in the middle class at standards in comprehensive schools and what seemed an overly progressive culture in education. Public schools now re-branded themselves as 'independent schools' to suit the prevailing political mood in Thatcherite Britain and to acknowledge that, despite a rise in the percentage of pupils educated privately in the 1980s, 'numbers at boarding schools were declining and many independent schools (i.e. former direct grant schools) had never conformed to the stereotype of the traditional public school.'[81]

From the 1980s public schools, despite being no longer under pressure to agree a closer alignment with the state, began to reform themselves. They jettisoned outdated traditions and began spending millions improving often spartan facilities, under pressure to make themselves more attractive to parents who demanded ever increasing quality. A facilities arms race was thus unleashed. The schools continued to raise academic standards in response to intensifying competition for places at top universities, encouraged the arts and the cultural side of school life alongside continuing excellence in sport, and rapidly increased diversity within schools through co-education, the recruitment of international students, bursaries raised from appeals to alumni, and growing numbers from Britain's own ethnic minorities. The Children Act of 1989 brought a sea-change, particularly in boarding schools, by introducing far-reaching and overdue safeguards for pupils. This increased, albeit gradually, the importance of the concept of pastoral care and ushered in a period of investment in infrastructure which transformed boarding accommodation and every other aspect of school life.[82]

The Fading Vision

The argument of this book is that the Second World War provided public schools, and the political system, with a unique opportunity to reshape the schools' relationship with state education and the wider nation. The opportunity was squandered. The way was eventually opened for public schools to transform themselves from the austere, narrow institutions which they had been from Victorian times through the two world wars to 1945 and beyond, but the wider, grander vision was lost.

Financial circumstances had forced public schools in 1939 to look for ways in which the state could help them, reluctantly accepting that this might carry the price of losing a measure of independence. The experience of the war, shared on the Home Front with the rest of the nation, converted financial necessity into something more resembling altruism, as they came to understand the new spirit of democracy and equality sweeping the country from 1940 onwards. They accepted in their words and actions, if not necessarily in all their hearts, in the words of David Cannadine that 'the Second World War was not a battle to defend the old established order but a crusade to build a new, a better, a very different world, a welfare society in which privilege was neither wanted not admired.'[83] They engaged with the 'Dunkirk spirit' and with the 'People's War', adapted to their often very difficult circumstances as best they could and were on an equal footing with the rest of the Home Front in suffering the dangers of bombing, including the V-weapon attacks of 1944, and the discomforts of rationing. They lent support in practical ways to the national war effort, including involvement in the Home Guard, deployment of boys to agricultural camps in the holidays and the use of school premises for war-related research and other activities.

This spirit we argue could have been followed by the public schools becoming part of the 'New Jerusalem' vision after the war, and there is a sense of frustration that the moment could not be grasped. The Second World War acted as a catalyst for so much other progressive change, including the Beveridge Report, Keynesian full employment, the National Health Service, even the 1944 Education Act – 'pessimism breakers', as Peter Hennessy called them, contrasting the post-war period with the endless depression of the 1930s.[84] It is a continuing national loss that the public schools could not be part of this wave of change. By engaging with Fleming, even after the financial imperative had disappeared, public schools showed a new awareness of criticism of their privilege, and a desire to share the benefits of their system of education more widely with those barred from it by poverty or class. Robert Birley, before the Fleming Committee had even met, had suggested a target of 50 per cent state-aided pupils in public schools.[85] The fault, and it must be called that, lay more with a Labour government which did not see public schools as a priority and had so much else to do. Without any move from Attlee's government to negotiate with public schools about the Fleming recommendations, it was not surprising that little came of them as public schools recovered from the war at a gathering pace and on their own terms.

At no point in the next seventy-five years did the vision come as close to being realised as it did in 1945. Progressive voices in the public schools continued to look for ways to implement Fleming's and similar proposals until well after the war, even as far as Margaret Thatcher's Assisted Places Scheme in the 1980s, but the pupil numbers were never that significant, and hope foundered on successive governments' unwillingness to meet or even share the costs, and on schools' reluctance to take further initiatives themselves. Sceptical members of HMC suspected from early on in the Fleming process that if local LEA initiatives were proving controversial when it came to selection procedures, there was little likelihood of Labour pressing for a national scheme against the wishes of many of its affiliated groups, even if the money could be found. Labour was reluctant to coerce public schools, for there were few votes to be had in such an approach from a public which broadly agreed with the freedom of parents to pay for education and favoured the aspiration which high-performing schools encouraged.

Traditionalists within the public-school sector, concerned about encroachment on their independence and their traditional way of education, were content to see the issue kicked into the long grass. The best that could be said in the post-1945 period is that a model for future thinking was established. The issue was revisited in the 1960s, and rather more wholeheartedly in the twenty-first century, but as William Richardson, former General Secretary of HMC, wrote, 'selflessness does not come all that naturally to independent schools who have sustainable finances to worry about and sometimes need incentives and regulation, like the 1989 Children Act, in order to keep them in touch with wider society.'[86] The focus in independent schools since 2000 on broadening access, sponsoring state academies and openly acknowledging social responsibilities has come sixty years later than it might have done, although continuing issues with admission criteria 'make it increasingly difficult to envisage a form of integration of state and independent schools that would be widely accepted as holistic and progressive.'[87]

The quality of education independent schools now provide is beyond recognition to what was on offer in the 1930s or even 1970s, although their academic pre-eminence is under increasing challenge from the best state schools. In the bursaries they provide, and in partnership with state schools and sponsorship of state academies, they are also addressing their insularity and social exclusiveness, albeit insufficiently for those for whom abolition alone will suffice. In all this, public schools now brand themselves as distinctively modern, innovative and international, an ironic reversal of the backward-looking ethos of the sector in 1939 and those nostalgic glances back to Victorian times. Public schools have repeatedly been blamed for low social mobility, but sociologist John Goldthorpe, who has written on social mobility for fifty years, argues in the *Guardian* on 17 March 2020 that differences in family and home environment are the main obstacles to equality of opportunity, and that the education system in general and public schools in particular should not be 'an instrument to achieve social mobility in Britain'. Public schools now brand themselves as distinctively modern, innovative and international, an ironic reversal of the backward-looking ethos of the sector in 1939 and those nostalgic glances back to Victorian times.

The public schools had, in public perception, a much better war in 1939–45 than in 1914–18. This process started in the late 1930s with the generous help which many gave to Jewish refugees from Nazi-occupied Europe, to the wider benefit of Britain. Public schools benefited from a war with a strong moral cause, a heroic narrative and a victorious ending, to all of which they and their alumni contributed in many significant ways. Their heroism and sacrifice were equal to those of their predecessors in 1914–18, with public school losses, as a proportion of those who served, again double the national figure. The popular myths of 1940 have stood the test of time, and the political and military leaders of the era have never faced the cultural opprobrium suffered by their 1914–18 predecessors.

The public schools produced many war heroes, often in more adventurous and enterprising roles than their predecessors in the slogging match on the Western Front, with character, developed at schools, again putting duty before self-interest. The officer class was derided in the post-1960s revisiting of the First World War, but nothing similar has ever happened to challenge the standing of their Second World War equivalents. In 1944 Air Chief Marshal Sir Arthur Harris wrote the foreword to Guy Gibson's account of his war in *Enemy Coast Ahead*: 'If there is a Valhalla, Guy Gibson and his band of brothers will be found there at all the parties, seated far above the salt.' It is a verdict which still stands.

The two figures in this book who had the greatest influence on the future of public schools are Winston Churchill and Clement Attlee, the one securing their survival in 1940, the other shaping their post-war course. 'If', as the historian Leo McKinstry says in a recent book, 'Churchill was the giant of the war, Attlee was the hero of the peace.'[88] Paradoxically, it was his public school which set Attlee on his road to socialism through his involvement with Haileybury House, the boys' club in Stepney founded by the school; and although he was an avowed reformer, his devotion to Britain's traditional hierarchies, including the public schools, was clear. On hearing that Attlee had chosen the Old Haileyburian Geoffrey de Freitas as his new Parliamentary Private Secretary, John Colville noted in his diary: 'Churchill, though he sometimes said nice things about me, never included in his recommendations that we were both Old Harrovians. I concluded that the old school tie counted even more in Labour than Conservative circles.'[89]

The support of Attlee helped Churchill to supplant Chamberlain as Prime Minister in May 1940, and as Deputy Prime Minister through five years of war, Attlee was often more loyal to Churchill than many of his Conservative colleagues. They shared a mutual respect and esteem which lasted until the end of their lives. Churchill would never allow others to speak disrespectfully of Attlee in his presence. 'Mr. Attlee', he would say, 'is a great patriot. Don't you dare call him "silly old Attlee" at Chartwell or you won't be invited again.'[90] Churchill asked that Attlee be one of the pallbearers at his state funeral in 1965, and Attlee insisted on performing the honour despite his ill-health, viewers watching his frail figure stumble as the coffin was carried up the steps of St Paul's. Both Churchill and Attlee retained a strong emotional attachment to their old schools which saw them make regular visits as they grew older, a loyalty which no modern politician of either main party would now dare to show.

On 18 December 1940 Winston Churchill visited Harrow to hear School Songs, an annual ceremony dating back to 1864. Accompanied by his wife Clementine and six Old Harrovians, including Leo Amery, Secretary of State for India, and Colville, he was 'ecstatically received at an emotionally impressionable period of his life'.[91] He wept copiously through the singing of *Forty Years On* and other songs, the boys cheered him in a way that seemed to go on for ever, and at the end he spoke;

> Hitler, in one of his recent discourses, declared that the fight was between those who have been through the Adolf Hitler Schools and those who have been at Eton. Hitler has forgotten Harrow, and he has also overlooked the vast majority of the youth of this country who have never had the advantage of attending such schools, but who are standing staunchly together in the nation's cause. When the war is won by this nation, as it surely will be, it must be one of our aims to work to establish a state of society where the advantage and privilege which hitherto have only been enjoyed only by the few shall be far more widely shared by the many and the youth of the nation as a whole.

In December 1944 he visited Harrow again to reiterate that vision, telling the assembled school that it was 'by broadening the intake, by the schools becoming more and more based upon aspiring youth in every class in the nation, and coming from every part of the island – it is by that that you will preserve the great Public Schools, and make them possession of all our fellow countrymen, and of lads from every part of the island.'[92] Churchill continued to return each year to Harrow to hear the songs, but the vision which had inspired him in 1940 and 1944, of a school thrown open to all classes, was not mentioned again and was not to be realised when he returned to power in 1951. Public schools survived the war, when the odds were stacked against them, and standing behind Churchill, they contributed leadership, steadfastness, decisiveness, imagination and enterprise. But his vision was squandered, to the untold loss of the nation and all its citizens. 'The Generation Lost' was the sub-title to our first book on the Great War; we might have made the sub-title to this book 'The Opportunity Lost'.

Notes

Acknowledgements
1. S. Wearne, To Our Brothers, 2018.

Introduction
1. David Edgerton, email to author, 9 November 2019.
2. A. Seldon and D. Walsh, Public Schools and the Great War, 2013, p.xii.
3. W. Churchill, War Speeches, 1951, p.233.
4. M. Gilbert, Winston Churchill, Vol 6, Finest Hour, 1983, p.420.
5. M. Hastings, Chastise, 2019, p.37.
6. B. Harrison, 'College Life' in The History of the University of Oxford, Vol 8, p.94.
7. M. Foot, SOE, 1984, p.66.
8. Dominic Sandbrook, conversation with author, 15 November 2019.
9. B. Macintyre, A Spy Among Friends, 2014, p.20.
10. C. Andrew, The Defence of the Realm, 2009, p.226.
11. A. Sampson, Anatomy of Britain, 1962, p.634.

Chapter 1
1. F. Green and D. Kynaston, Engines of Privilege, 2019, p.73.
2. R. Barker, Education and Politics, 1972, p.98.
3. A. Waugh, The Loom of Youth, 1917.
4. T. Macpherson, Behind Enemy Lines, 2010, p.39. Macpherson's war brought him three Military Crosses in the Commandos and SOE.
5. Frank Fletcher's scrapbook, Charterhouse Archives.
6. C. Douie, The Weary Road, 1929, p.145.
7. P. Henderson, King's School Canterbury and the Great War, 2018, p.115.
8. I. Weinberg, English Public Schools, 1967, p.108.
9. C. Tyerman, Harrow School, 2000, p.445. The War Memorial Building held a roll of honour, shrine to the dead and portraits of distinguished officers.
10. D. McDowell, Carrying On, p.291.
11. D. du Croz (ed), Marlborough College and the Great War in 100 Stories, 2018, p.163.
12. P. Francis, Old Yet Ever Young, 2020.
13. A. Quick, Charterhouse, 1990, p.116.
14. H. Cecil, The Flower of Battle, 1996, p.257.

15. R. Gurner, Pass Guard at Ypres, 1930, p.vii.
16. The nine were Eton, Harrow, Rugby, Westminster, Shrewsbury, Charterhouse, Winchester, St Paul's and Merchant Taylors'. Since the last two were day schools, to those whose conception of a public school meant boarding it was only the first seven which counted. Many other nineteenth century foundations like Marlborough, Wellington and Clifton were thought generally to be the equal of the Clarendon nine.
17. Other schools invited to play at Lord's were Marlborough v Rugby, Tonbridge v Clifton and Cheltenham v Haileybury; there was also the Roman Catholic test match, Beaumont v Oratory.
18. B. Simon, The Politics of Educational Reform 1920-40, 1974, p.272. Some schools within HMC had received grants from the 1890s from central and/ or local government. In 1926 their situation was formalised when they had to choose a single source of grant, either a direct grant from the Board of Education or to be grant-maintained by the local authority. In the 1930s there were 240 schools in receipt of direct grant and 1,138 schools aided by local authorities. In 1939, 40 of the 240 centrally funded schools were members of HMC, the Board funding up to a quarter of pupils. Schools with pupils funded by local authorities also included some in HMC membership. In 1945, following the Education Act and Fleming Report of the previous year, the direct grant scheme was formalised with schools on the 'direct grant list' required to offer a quarter of their places free of charge to children from primary schools and at least another quarter for places paid for by the local authority. In 1975 Labour abolished the direct grant, forcing schools either to become fully independent or join the state sector.
19. D. Allport and N. Friskney, Short History of Wilson's School, 1987, p.128.
20. Y. Maxtone Graham, Terms and Conditions, 2016, p.28.
21. C. Harington, Plumer of Messines, 1935, p.295.
22. A. Sisman, Hugh Trevor-Roper, 2010, p.17.
23. R. Morris, Guy Gibson, 1994, p.14.
24. E. Pearce, The Golden Talking-Shop, 2016, p.369.
25. J. Field, The King's Nurseries, 1987, p.83.
26. Report of HMC Annual Meeting 1922, p.35.
27. E. Mack, The Public Schools and British Opinion, 1941, p.367.
28. A. Sisman, Hugh Trevor-Roper, 2010, pp.21–2.
29. D. Walsh, A Duty to Serve, p.93. Keyes was killed in Tunisia in 1943.
30. J. Blackie, Bradfield 1850–1975, 1976, p.151.
31. L. Kennedy, On My Way to the Club, 1989, p.55.
32. Report of HMC Annual Meeting, 1934, p.76.
33. J. Field, The King's Nurseries, 1987, p.86–7.
34. H. Purcell, A Very Private Celebrity, 2015, p.5.
35. Ibid., p.6.
36. T. Card, Eton Renewed, 1994, p.167.

37. C. Tyerman, Harrow School, 2000, p.446.
38. Report of HMC Annual Meeting 1930, p.30.
39. C. Tyerman, Harrow School, p.447.
40. G. Turner, paper in Marlborough archives, 1933.
41. P. Francis, Old Yet Ever Young.
42. R. Barker, One Man's War, 1975, p.48.
43. T. Hinde, Paths of Progress, 1992, p.136.
44. B. White and C. Wood (eds), History of Rendcomb College, 2012, p.2.
45. Author conversation with Anthony Wallersteiner, headmaster of Stowe, June 2018.
46. N. Annan, Roxburgh of Stowe, 1965, p.58.
47. B. Rees, Stowe, 2008, pp.101–2.
48. N. Annan, Our Age, 1990, p.185.
49. D. Taylor, book review of Gilded Youth by J. Brooke-Smith, published in the Guardian, 6 April 2019.
50. S. Faulks, The Fatal Englishman, 1997, p.115. Hillary fought in the Battle of Britain and was badly burned when shot down. He wrote a best-selling book, The Last Enemy, and was killed in a training accident in 1943.
51. A. Cooper, Patrick Leigh Fermor, 2012, p.27.
52. J. Elmes, M-Mother, 2015, p.66.
53. T. Card, Eton Renewed, 1994, p.184.
54. Report of HMC Annual Meeting 1915, p.91.
55. Report of HMC Annual Meeting 1919, p.59.
56. H. Dent, History of Education, 1968, p.354.
57. R. McKibbin, Classes and Cultures, 1998, pp.207–8.
58. H. Dent, History of Education, 1968, p.407.
59. F. Fletcher, After Many Days, 1937.
60. Quoted in B. Simon, Education and the Social Order, 1991, p.282.
61. B. Inglis, John Bull's Schooldays, 1961, p.108.
62. Author conversation with Dominic Sandbrook, 15 November 2019.
63. G. Greene (ed), The Old School, 1934, p.11.
64. R.Tawney, Equality, 1931, p.96.
65. T. Card, Eton Renewed, 1994, p.217.
66. S. Faulks, The Fatal Englishman, 1997, p.214.
67. T. Card, Eton Renewed, 1994, p.227.
68. C. Tyerman, Harrow School, pp.505, 512.
69. C. Tyerman, Harrow School, 2000, p.410.
70. S. Leeson, The Public Schools Question and Other Essays, 1947, p.15.
71. P. Gosden, Education in the Second World War, 1976, p.329.
72. Ibid., p.330. Williams had taught at Wellington and Lancing before joining the Board.
73. B. Simon, Education and the Social Order, 1991, p.275.
74. Report of HMC Annual Meeting, 1938.

75. R. Verkaik, Posh Boys, 2018, p.70.
76. HMC membership lists, 1919–39.
77. The two West Indian schools were Harrison College, Barbados and Munro College, Jamaica. The biggest contingent was the fifteen Australian schools.
78. P. Gosden, Education in the Second World War, 1976, p.329.
79. Ibid., p.331.
80. City of London livery companies comprise ancient and modern trade associations and guilds. Over several centuries they had built up substantial wealth and used it for charitable purposes, including education. They had founded and now governed several public schools like St Paul's Boys and Girls', run by the Mercers' Company and Oundle by the Grocers' Company. Their governing bodies invariably comprised just the Master and Court of those companies.
81. B. Scragg, Sevenoaks School, 1993, p.138.
82. A. Hearnden, Red Robert, 1984, p.92.
83. N. Watson, The Family Album, 2008, p.57.
84. R. Davenport-Hines, Enemies Within, 2018, p.173.
85. J. Dancy, Walter Oakeshott, 1995, p.69.
86. A. Roberts, Holy Fox, p.96.
87. The Elizabethan, December 1938.
88. The Marlburian, July 1939.
89. A. Hearnden, Red Robert, 1984, pp.93–4. Cartland, whose father had been killed in 1918, was killed at Dunkirk in May 1940.
90. J. Dancy, Walter Oakeshott, 1995, p.95.
91. The Provost is in effect the chairman of governors (known as Fellows), but he also lives on the school site.
92. T. Card, Eton Renewed, 1994, p.200.
93. H. Bailes, Once a Paulina, 2000, p.86.
94. P. Hobbs (ed), Memories of NLCS in Wartime, 1995, p.8.
95. G. Wellum, First Light, 2002, p.19.

Chapter 2
1. N. Nicolson (ed), The Harold Nicolson Diaries, 2004, p.192.
2. P. Addison, The Road to 1945, 1975, p.131.
3. Roll and Record for Old Wykehamists, 1943.
4. C. Tyerman, Harrow School, 2000, p.411.
5. P. Gosden, Education in the Second World War, 1976, p.330.
6. The Central Foundation School was voluntary-aided through a trust set up by wealthy financiers from the City of London. It was also supported by the Dulwich Estate, which provided the endowments for Dulwich College and Alleyn's School.
7. M. Gilbert, Winston Churchill, Vol 6, 1983, p.290.
8. D. Faber, Speaking for England, 2005, p.18.

9. N. Shakespeare, Six Minutes in May, 2017, pp.306, 316.
10. N. Nicolson (ed), The Harold Nicolson Diaries, 2004, p.208.
11. J.B.Priestley, Postscripts, July 1940, pp.2, 12, 13. Priestley had been to a Yorkshire grammar school, Belle Vue, and after 1914–18 war service went to Cambridge, later establishing himself as novelist, playwright and broadcaster.
12. W. Churchill, speech, 14 July 1940.
13. T. Worsley, Barbarians and Philistines, 1940, p.274.
14. The Shirburnian, March 1940.
15. The Carthusian, June 1940.
16. Bewerley Street School was maintained by the local education board in Leeds. Yorkshire College became Leeds University.
17. P. Hennessy, Never Again, 1992, p.8.
18. Wikipedia, list of Churchill's wartime government.
19. P. Addison, The Road to 1945, 1975, p.113.
20. Wilson called his school 'Kurnella School' although its full name was 'Kurnella Board School'. From such a background it was a significant achievement for him to go to LSE and into the Civil Service.
21. P. Hennessy, Whitehall, 1989, p.88.
22. P. Addison, 'Oxford in the Second World War', Chapter 7 of History of Oxford University, Vol 6, p.183.
23. Ibid., p.182.
24. P. Hennessy, Whitehall, p.107.
25. A. Seldon, The Cabinet Office 1916–2016, 2016, p.xviii.
26. J. Colville, Footprints in Time, 1976, p.92.
27. Ibid., p.78.
28. Those present at the War Cabinet were Churchill, Attlee, Halifax, Chamberlain, Greenwood, with Sinclair co-opted. Cadogan and Bridges also attended.
29. H. Dalton, The Fateful Years, 1957, p.335.
30. K. Rice (ed), Garside's Wars, 1993, p.55.
31. M. Partridge, Eastbourne College in the Second World War, 2010.
32. Dame Emmeline Tanner, report, July 1940, Roedean archives.
33. Y. Maxtone Graham, Terms and Conditions, 2016, p.116.
34. D. Walsh, A Duty to Serve, 2011, p.19.
35. A. Hearnden, Red Robert, pp.100–1.
36. Papers in Merchant Taylors' archives, including an article in The Taylorian, July 1947 by Birley.
37. H. Bailes, Once a Paulina, 2000, p.86.
38. E. Hossain, Grace and Integrity, 2011, p.125.
39. Report of HMC Annual Meeting, December 1940.
40. Old Cliftonian website.
41. M. Beckett, Wycombe Abbey Re-Visited, 2016.

42. Charterhouse Miscellany, p.202.

43. T. Hinde, Paths of Progress, 1992, p.175.

44. N. Longmate, How We Lived Then, 1971, p.71.

45. N. Scarfe, unpublished memoir in KSC archive.

46. J. Dalrymple, unpublished memoir in KSC archive.

47. J. Field, The King's Nurseries, 1987, pp.88–92.

48. V. Collenette, Elizabeth in Exile, 1996.

49. P. Gosden, Education in the Second World War, 1976, p.37.

50. D. Allport and N. Friskney, Wilson's School, 1987, pp.143–5.

51. W. Churchill, War Speeches, 1951, p.233.

52. P. King, Hurstpierpoint College 1849–1995, 1996, pp.191–203.

53. The Stoic, December 1940.

54. H. Flecker, Reflections on the War, Christ's Hospital archives.

55. B. Rees, Stowe, 2008, p.112.

56. P. Mileham, Wellington College, 2008, p.97.

57. The OTC became in 1941 the Junior Training Corps, to dispel assumptions of expected privilege.

58. J. Christie, A Great Teacher, 1984, p.55.

59. R. Lewis, History of Brentwood School, 1981, pp.255–6.

60. J. Pigott, Dulwich College, 2008, p.264.

61. W. Pasmore, The Night the School was Bombed, unpublished memoir in SPGS archive.

62. P. Burden, The Lion and the Stars, 1990, p.152.

63. Christopher Wright, letter to author, September 2018.

64. Wellington College digital archive.

65. D. Walsh, A Duty to Serve, 2011, p.22.

66. The Harrovian, October 1940.

67. J. Blackie, Bradfield 1850–1975, 1976, p.164.

68. J. Ramsden, Man of the Century, 2003, p.64. The new verse was added to the song 'Stet Fortuna Domus': 'No less we praise in sterner days the leader of our nation/And Churchill's name will win acclaim from each new generation/For you have power in danger's hour our freedom to defend, Sir/Though long the fight we know the right will triumph in the end, Sir.'

Chapter 3

1. Until Osborne closed in 1921, naval cadets went there for two years at the age of thirteen before transferring to Dartmouth. In 1921 all training was concentrated at Dartmouth from the age of thirteen.

2. Thirty per cent of Dartmouth's pre-war entry came from existing service families.

3. C. Moore, Daily Telegraph, 14 April 2007.

4. C. Lewis, Sagittarius Rising, 1935, p.10.

5. R. Mahoney, 'Trenchard's Doctrine', British Journal of Military History, 2018.

6. M. Hastings, Chastise, 2019, p.94.
7. P. Bishop, Air Force Blue, 2017, p.38.
8. Sixty-two Cranwell cadets were killed in accidents between the wars.
9. P. Townsend, Time and Chance, 1978, p.61.
10. Ibid., pp.66, 75.
11. Report of HMC Annual Meeting, December 1936, p.22.
12. P. Bishop, Fighter Boys, 2003, p.45.
13. P. Bishop, Air Force Blue, 2017, p.67.
14. R. Hillary, The Last Enemy, 1943, p.16.
15. S. Faulks, The Fatal Englishman, 1997, p.121.
16. A. Boyle, Trenchard, 1962, p.519.
17. L. Deighton, Fighter, 1977, p.44.
18. P. Bishop, Air Force Blue, 2017, p.85.
19. For this information on naval education we are indebted to a PhD thesis published online by Exeter University: E. Romans, 'Selection and Early Career Education of Executive Officers in the Royal Navy 1902–39', March 2012.
20. Young won the DSO, DSC and Bar and wrote One of Our Submarines in 1952.
21. A. Hichens, Gunboat Command, 2014.
22. Bruce Fraser was in the navy class at Bradfield, his brother Cecil in the army class.
23. King's School Canterbury WW2 website.
24. J. Colville, The Fringes of Power, 1985, p.327.
25. K. Wynn, Men of the Battle of Britain, 1999, p.2.
26. P. Bishop, Fighter Boys, 2003, p.72.
27. The numbers reflect those whose school can be positively identified.
28. After Eton, the other schools' numbers were: Sherborne, Wellington 6; ISC, Marlborough 5; Charterhouse, Shrewsbury, Stowe, Tonbridge 4. Despite these figures, Eton had proportionally fewer alumni serving in the RAF than most schools, 512 out of 4,958, just 10 per cent.
29. Rhodes-Moorhouse had married Amalia Demetriadi in 1936. After he was killed, the RAF refused to recover the body as it was too deeply buried, and his wealthy father-in-law, Sir Stephen Demetriadi, paid for civilian contractors to do it. His own son Stephen had been shot down into the Channel a month before Rhodes-Moorhouse. The father gave land at Ditchling Beacon to the National Trust in his memory.
30. P. Bishop, Fighter Boys, 2003, p.145.
31. G. Wellum, First Light, 2002, p.173.
32. Geoffrey Wellum obituary, The Times, 21 July 2018.
33. G. Wellum, First Light, 2002, p.152.
34. S. Bungay, The Most Dangerous Enemy, 2001, p.246.
35. M. Parker, The Battle of Britain, 2000, p.263.

36. G. Mayfield, Life and Death in the Battle of Britain, 2018, p.70. The pilot, Peter Watson (Harrogate GS), was shot down into the Channel and killed on 26 May 1940.
37. H. Dundas, Flying Start, 1988, p.5.
38. Ibid., p.6.
39. T. Molson, The Millionaire's Squadron, 2014, p.57.
40. H. Dundas, Flying Start, 1988, p.3.
41. The only awards which can be made posthumously are the VC and Mention in Dispatches.
42. T. Molson, The Millionaire's Squadron, 2014, p.99.
43. Dame Felicity Peake obituary, the Guardian, November 2002.
44. D. Allport and N. Friskney, Short History of Wilson's School, p.259.
45. J. Terraine, The Right of the Line, 1985, pp.464–8.
46. P. Bishop, Bomber Boys, 2007, p.35.
47. Ibid., p.53.
48. M. Hastings, Bomber Command, 1979, p.167.
49. Ibid., p.263.
50. R. Morris, Guy Gibson, 1994, p.131.
51. M. Hastings, Bomber Command, 1979, p.256.
52. R. Morris, Guy Gibson, 1994, p.320.
53. A. Sisman, Hugh Trevor-Roper, 2010, p.3. Richard Trevor-Roper was killed in 1944 serving with another crew.
54. R. Morris, Guy Gibson, 1994, p.181, and Derek Henderson, conversation with author, September 2018.
55. G. Gibson, Enemy Coast Ahead, 1946, p.297.
56. Others not mentioned in the text are David Maltby (Marlborough), Bill Astell (Bradfield), Bill Townsend (Monmouth), Cyril Anderson (QEGS Wakefield). Geoff Rice (Hinckley GS) was the odd man out. The other nine pilots came from Australia, Canada, New Zealand and the USA.
57. J. Elmes, M-Mother, 2015, p.218.
58. Ibid., p.230.
59. M. Hastings, Chastise, 2019, p.101.
60. R. Morris, Cheshire, 2000, p.20.
61. Ibid., p.28.
62. W. Bartlett, The Dam Busters, 2011, p.216.
63. D. Walsh, A Duty to Serve, 2011, p.103.
64. Lancing College online War Memorial.

Chapter 4

1. W. Elliott, Esprit de Corps, 1996, p.95.
2. B. Bond, Britain's Two World Wars Against Germany, 2014, p.86.
3. D. Walsh, A Duty to Serve, 2011, p.133.
4. J. Ellis, Cassino, 1984, p.14.

5. The British Army suffered 705,000 deaths and 1,165,000 wounded in the First World War. In the Second the figures were 144,000 deaths and 425,000 wounded, missing or taken prisoner (D. French, Raising Churchill's Army, 2000, p.147).

6. D. French, Raising Churchill's Army, 2000, p.284.

7. B. Bond, Britain's Two World Wars against Germany, 2014, p.72.

8. J.L. Moulton, The Battle for Antwerp, 1978, p.90.

9. The schools analysed are Wellington with 707 in WW1 and 501 in WW2, Marlborough 749 and 415, Oundle 221 and 254, Charterhouse 687 and 350, Harrow 644 and 340, Bradfield 279 and 198, Eastbourne 164 and 164, Sherborne 221 and 242, Bishop's in Cape Town 112 and 146, Christ's NZ 132 and 150.

10. The highest identified figures in schools for the Second World War are: Imperial Service College 18% of those who served, Wellington, Gresham's and Woodbridge, 17%. In the First World War over one quarter of schools had a casualty rate of 20 per cent or more. Interestingly, more than a few schools have better records of service and casualties in the First World War than in the Second.

11. H. Hely-Hutchinson (ed), H.K. Marsden's War Dead, 2009.

12. P. Addison, 'Oxford in the Second World War' in History of Oxford University, Vol 8, 1994, p.181.

13. H. Trevor-Roper, The Wartime Journals, 2012, p.207.

14. Of Stowe's 270 war deaths, 161 were in the Army, 124 of them junior officers (2/Lt, Lt and Captain) and seven serving in the ranks. The others mostly held the rank of Major.

15. Stowe Book of Remembrance. Anderson was killed in Italy in October 1943.

16. Etonians had won thirteen VCs in 1914–18. The number of MCs awarded to Etonians in the two wars also reflects the fewer battlefield opportunities: 389 MCs in the Second World War compared with 744 in the First. MCs were awarded to junior officers for gallantry in combat.

17. R. McKibbin, Classes and Cultures, 1998, p.35.

18. K. Simpson, in I. Beckett and K. Simpson (eds), A Nation in Arms, 1985, p.65.

19. D. French, Raising Churchill's Army, 2000, p.50.

20. There were also OTCs in state grammar and direct grant schools.

21. J. Masters, Bugles and a Tiger, 1956, p.40.

22. T. Macpherson, Behind Enemy Lines, 2010, p.37.

23. John Woodcock, conversation with author, September 2018.

24. C. Otley, 'Public School and Army', New Society, November 1966, p.755.

25. C. Otley, 'The Educational Background of British Army Officers', in Sociology, Vol 7, 1973, p.755.

26. R. McKibbin, Classes and Cultures, 1998, p.245.

27. P. Mileham, Wellington College, 2008, p.85.

28. D. French, Raising Churchill's Army, 2000, p.51.
29. J. Masters, Bugles and a Tiger, 1956, pp.49–50.
30. D. McDowell, Carrying On, p.424.
31. A. Calder, People's War, 1969, p.247.
32. D. Turner, Be Grateful, 2019, p.164.
33. J. Ellis, The Sharp End, 1980, p.227.
34. A. Bowlby, Recollections of Rifleman Bowlby, 1969, p.83.
35. J. Crang, The British Army and the People's War, 2000, p.142.
36. J. Holland, Together We Stand, 2006, p.29.
37. Yeomanry regiments were the horsed cavalry (and later armoured) component of the Territorial Army. The pre-war commanding officer of the Sherwood Rangers was the Earl of Yarborough, and the regiment mustered for war in 1939 at his family seat, Welbeck Abbey.
38. D. Graham, Keith Douglas 1920–44, 2009, p.136.
39. K. Douglas, Alamein to Zem Zem, 1946, p.17.
40. Ibid., p.131.
41. K. Douglas, Collected Poems, 1951.
42. K. Douglas, Alamein to Zem Zem, 1946, p.147.
43. D. French, Raising Churchill's Army, 2000, p.76.
44. S. Jary, 18 Platoon, 1987, p.8.
45. D. French, Raising Churchill's Army, 2000, p.77.
46. Field Marshal Lord Bramall, interview in the Daily Telegraph, 2 June 2019.
47. Lord Bramall, interview in the Sunday Times, 28 July 2019.
48. S. Hills, By Tank into Normandy, 2002, p.167.
49. L. Skinner, The Man Who Worked on Sundays, 1996, p.58. Padre Skinner's first sermon in Normandy had the text 'there are no atheists in a slit trench'.
50. His headmaster was the former Marlborough chaplain, Ernest Crosse, who first established the Devonshire cemetery at Mametz on the Somme.
51. K. Sandford, Mark of the Lion, 1962, p.115.
52. The other two double VCs were both medical officers – Arthur Martin-Leake (Westminster) and Noel Chavasse (Magdalen CS and Liverpool College).
53. R. Brodhurst (ed), The Bramall Papers, 2017, p.350.
54. J. Keegan, Churchill's Generals, 1991, p.12.
55. C. Otley, 'The Educational Background of British Army Officers', in Sociology, Vol 7, 1973, p.756.
56. After the war Montgomery took a keen interest in education as a governor of St Paul's, St John's Leatherhead and King's, Canterbury, where it was said that 'he met more than his match in the redoubtable Canon Shirley whom he tried unavailingly for a long time to unseat as headmaster'. (T. Howarth, 'Education and Leadership' in Monty at Close Quarters, 1985, p.61).
57. C. Messenger, The Commandos, 1985, p.26.
58. N. Rankin, letter in The Times, 14 August 2018.

59. H. Saunders, The Green Beret, 1949, p.29.
60. R. Lyman, Into the Jaws of Death, 2014, p2.3.
61. B. Macintyre, SAS Rogue Heroes, 2016, p.7.
62. Ibid., p.8.
63. Ibid., p.17.
64. Jock Lewes was killed on a raid in November 1941.
65. J. Holland, Heroes, 2006, pp.137–51.
66. J. Gordon, 'Wingate' in J. Keegan (ed), Churchill's Generals, 1991, p.279.
67. J. Masters, The Road Past Mandalay, 1961, p.160. Wingate was killed in an air crash in March 1944, but the Second Chindit operation continued, involving 20,000 troops.
68. There were about 180,000 British PoWs in the Great War, but two-thirds of these were only imprisoned for a few months as they were captured in the German Spring offensive of 1918. The majority of PoWs in the Second War were captured in its first half.
69. Tenko, BBC drama first shown in 1981.
70. R. McKay, John Leonard Wilson Confessor of the Faith, 1973, p.54.
71. R. Kee, A Crowd is not Company, 1947, p.9.
72. B. Macarthur, Surviving the Sword, 2005, p.275.
73. M. Duggan (ed), Padre in Colditz, 1978, p.70.
74. Ibid., p.70.
75. H. Chancellor, Colditz, 2001, p.247.
76. A. Neave, Saturday at MI9, 1969, p.53.
77. P. Reid, The Colditz Story, 1952, p.17.
78. After his escape, Littledale was given command of 2 KRRC, in which the future Lord Bramall was a platoon commander, and was killed in 1944 in Holland.
79. M. Sinclair to M. Robertson, 31 March 1944, Winchester College archives.
80. B. James, Moonless Night, 1983, p.151.
81. Sydney Dowse, obituary in the Daily Telegraph, April 2008.
82. T. Card, Eton Renewed, 1994, p.246.
83. M. Peel, The Land of Lost Content, 1996, p.61.
84. A. Bowlby, Recollections of Rifleman Bowlby, 1969, p.227.
85. A. Venning, To War with the Walkers, 2019.
86. D. Piper, I Am Well, Who Are You?, 1998, p.22.
87. D.R. Thorpe, Eden, 2003, p.42.
88. Willie Whitelaw, obituary in the Independent, July 1999.

Chapter 5
1. M. Hastings, The Secret War, 2015, pp.216–7.
2. Winn became a Lord Justice of Appeal in 1965.
3. R. Overy, Why the Allies Won, 2006, p.59.
4. M. Hastings, The Secret War, 2015, p.xxiv.

5. 'Public schools' by this definition are the fully independent and mostly boarding schools.
6. B. Harrison, 'College Life 1918–39' in B. Harrison (ed), The History of Oxford University, Vol 8, 1994, p.94.
7. R. Mckibbin, Classes and Cultures, 1998, p.249.
8. Trinity College archive. Seven of these Trinity freshmen were killed in the war including 'Dinghy' Young on the Dam Busters raid.
9. The Brazen Nose, 1923.
10. Sir Brian Harrison, phone call with author, 12 December 2019. One example was Henry Yorke (Henry Green), who had been at Eton and became friends at Oxford with Evelyn Waugh (Lancing). They were both part of an intellectual circle including the writer Harold Acton (Eton) and the economist Roy Harrod (St Paul's and Westminster).
11. B. Harrison, 'College Life 1918–39' in B. Harrison (ed), The History of Oxford University, Vol 8, 1994, p.96. Bump suppers were held if the college rowing eight was successful in races on the Thames.
12. E. Waugh, Decline and Fall, 1928, Prelude.
13. B. Harrison, 'College Life 1918–39' in B. Harrison (ed), The History of Oxford University, Vol 8, 1994, p.95.
14. A. Sisman, Hugh Trevor-Roper, 2010, p.28.
15. L. MacNeice, The Strings are False, 1965, p.102.
16. A. Sisman, Hugh Trevor-Roper, 2010, p.37.
17. Ibid., p.38.
18. Ibid., p.37.
19. M. Hastings, The Secret War, 2015, p.395.
20. A. Sisman, Hugh Trevor-Roper, 2010, p.92.
21. B. Macintyre, A Spy among Friends, 2014, p.7.
22. R. Davenport Hines, Enemies Within, 2018, p.255.
23. C. Andrew, MI5 in the Inter-War Years, www.mi5.gov.uk.
24. C. Andrew, The Defence of the Realm, 2009, pp.135, 219.
25. B. Macintyre, A Spy among Friends, 2014, pp.20, 26.
26. Rimington was Director General of MI5 from 1992 to 1996, and Manningham-Buller in 2002–7, the only two women to have held the post.
27. B. Macintyre, The Times, 18 May 2019.
28 M. Howard, British Intelligence in the Second World War, Vol 5, 1990, p.xi.
29. B. Macintyre, Double Cross, 2012, p.36.
30. B. Macintyre, Operation Mincemeat, 2010, p.26. The Director of Naval Intelligence in 1939 was Vice-Admiral John Godfrey (Bradfield). His personal assistant was Ian Fleming (Eton), creator of James Bond.
31. E. Montagu, The Man Who Never Was, 1953, p.114.
32. M. Foot and J. Langley, MI9: Escape and Evasion, 1979, p.250. James later became a Conservative MP who helped Airey Neave with Margaret Thatcher's campaign for the party leadership.

33. B. Macintyre, A Spy among Friends, p.159.
34. Ibid., p.283.
35. A. Roberts, Churchill, 2018, p.580.
36. C. Cruickshank, SOE in the Far East, 1983, p.11.
37. G. Milton, Ministry of Ungentlemanly Warfare, 2016, p.171.
38. Ibid., p.63.
39. M. Foot, SOE in France, 1966, p.131.
40. G. Milton, Ministry of Ungentlemanly Warfare, 2016, p.94.
41. Lady Dunn obituary, Daily Telegraph, August 2018.
42. M. Foot SOE in France, 1966, p.65.
43. Winchester College at War, College website.
44. F. Maclean, Eastern Approaches, 1951, p.287.
45. A. Beevor, Crete: The Battle and the Resistance, 1991, p.23.
46. Patrick Leigh Fermor, quoted in Winchester at War website from a speech delivered on the sixtieth anniversary of the Battle of Crete.
47. Ibid.
48. A. Cooper, Patrick Leigh Fermor, 2012, p.124.
49. Cammaerts was the uncle of the author Michael Morpurgo. He returned to teaching after the war, becoming head of Alleyne's GS in Stevenage and later principal of Rolle College, a teacher-training establishment. Harry Ree became head of Watford GS and Professor of Education at York University.
50. A. Briggs, Secret Days, 2011, p.36.
51. Winchester's head of maths was Clement Durell, author of maths books remembered by those of a certain age.
52. 'The Trusty Servant', Winchester College archives.
53. R. Hassall, Alan Turing, Sherborne School archives.
54. Maurice Wiles later became Professor of Divinity at Oxford.
55. Rosemary Ince, obituary in The Times, May 2018.
56. M. Smith, Secrets of Station X, 2011, p.181.
57. J. Lee, My Life with Nye, 1980, p.75.
58. D. Faber, Speaking for England, 2005, p.308.
59. C. Andrew, Defence of the Realm, 2009, p.91.
60. A. Sisman, Hugh Trevor-Roper, 2010, p.34. Pakenham became a Labour peer and minister in Attlee's government, later inheriting the title Lord Longford.
61. Telegram, 9 June 1940. Churchill papers 20/14. Vidkun Quisling had collaborated with the Germans in their invasion of Norway.
62. C. Andrew, Defence of the Realm, 2009, p.844.
63. D. Faber, Speaking for England, 2005, pp.188–90.
64. N. Deakin, Radiant Illusion, 2015, p.15.
65. Ibid., p.157.
66. Ibid., pp.27–8.
67. N. Annan, Our Age, 1990, p.225.
68. B. Macintyre, A Spy among Friends, 2014, p.141.

69. Ibid., p.266.
70. B. Macintyre, review in The Times of Kim Philby, My Silent War, 22 June 2019.
71. M. Hastings, The Secret War, 2015, p.367.

Chapter 6

1. Correlli Barnett's The Audit of War came out in 1986, preceded by The Collapse of British Power (1972) and followed by The Lost Victory (1995).
2. D. Edgerton, The Rise and Fall of the British Nation, p.170.
3. C. Barnett, The Collapse of British Power, 1972, p.28.
4. C. Kidd, 'Britain's Twentieth Century Industrial Revolution', New Statesman, 11 July 2018.
5. C. Barnett, The Lost Victory, 1995, p.15.
6. C. Barnett, The Collapse of British Power, p.24.
7. C. Barnett, The Audit of War, 1986, p.217. The political impact of Barnett's books has been considerable. Audit of War was reputedly read by every member of Mrs Thatcher's Cabinet, at the instigation of Keith Joseph.
8. T. May, The Victorian Public School, 2009, p.31.
9. T. Card, Eton Renewed, p.128.
10. D. Cardwell, 'Science and World War 1', Proceedings of the Royal Society, Vol 342, No 1631, 1975.
11. The Times, 5 May 1916.
12. Report of HMC Annual Meeting, December 1916.
13. F. Green and D. Kynaston, Engines of Privilege, 2019, p.76.
14. Email from John Weitzel, Loughborough GS archivist, 10 August 2018.
15. Report of HMC Annual Meeting 1923.
16. Report of HMC Annual Meeting 1933. General Science was part of School Certificate, the equivalent of GCSE. Higher School Certificate corresponded with A-levels.
17. Marlborough College Register 1843–1952.
18. M. Downes, Notable Old Oundelians, 2006.
19. Report of HMC Annual Meeting 1933.
20. James Dyson, one of the foremost inventors of the current age, was also at Gresham's.
21. B of E Inspection Report, KSC 1930.
22. C. Payne-Gaposchkin, An Autobiography, 1996, p.108.
23. Y. Maxtone Graham, Terms and Conditions, 2016, p.175. The 'swimming pool' for the girls at Castle Howard was the vast Atlas fountain in front of the house, slimy with frogs and with four tritons pouring water out of their trumpets as the girls swam round.
24. C. Barnett, Audit of War, p.225.
25. Ibid., p.226.
26. J. Stevenson, review of Audit of War, Historical Journal, Vol 30, 1987.

27. D. Edgerton, Britain's War Machine, 2011, p.2.
28. D. Edgerton, The Rise and Fall of the British Nation, 2018, p.168.
29. D. Edgerton, Britain's War Machine, 2011, p.3.
30. O. Lyttelton, Memoirs of Lord Chandos, 1962, p.180.
31. D. Reynolds, In Command of History, 2004, p.98.
32. J. Terraine, The Right of the Line, 1985, p.21.
33. T. Downing, Churchill's War Lab, 2010, p.158.
34. D. Edgerton, Britain's War Machine, 2011, p.5.
35. Sir Henry Tizard to A.V. Hill, 15 February 1939, Hill papers in Churchill Archives Centre.
36. D. Edgerton, Britain's War Machine, 2011, p.291.
37. Ronnie Harker, obituary in The Times, June 1999.
38. D. Hart-Davis (ed), King's Counsellor, 2006, p.246.
39. D. Reynolds, In Command of History, 2004, p.188.
40. W. Churchill, The Second World War, Vol 2, 1949, pp.148–9.
41. D. Edgerton, Britain's War Machine, 2011, p.259.
42. Ibid., p.261.
43. A. Danchev and D. Todman (eds), War Diaries, 2001, p.516.
44. K. Macksey, 'Percy Hobart' in J. Keegan (ed), Churchill's Generals, 1991, p.243.
45. Whitby later became Vice-Chancellor of Cambridge University.
46. R. Bailey, 'Shellshock to Psychiatry', Gresham College lecture 2014.
47. Ibid.
48. Norman Heatley, Daily Telegraph obituary, January 2004.
49. J. Ellis, The Sharp End, 1980, p.170.
50. S. Mawson, Arnhem Doctor, 1981, p.115.
51. Ashley Lowndes taught biology at Marlborough from 1921 to 1938, his biological expeditions and quality of research enthusing two of Marlborough's greatest scientists, J. Z. Young and Peter Medawar, Nobel Prize winner for Physiology in 1960.
52. David Edgerton, email to author, 9 November 2019.
53. D. Edgerton, 'Barnett's Audit of War: an Audit', Contemporary British History, November 1990.
54. Freeman Dyson, obituary in The Times, 10 March 2020. Dyson was the son of Sir George Dyson, Director of Music at Marlborough, Rugby, Wellington and Winchester, whose evening canticles sung in school chapels were familiar to generations of public schoolboys.
55. A. Seldon and D. Walsh, Public Schools and the Great War, 2013, p.xiii.

Chapter 7
1. C. Norwood, 'Public Schools and Social Service', Spectator, November 1926.
2. P. Addison, The Road to 1945, 1975, p.17.
3. Report of HMC Annual Meeting, December 1939.

4. The Times, 14 March 1940.
5. W. Deedes, Dear Bill, 2005, p.70.
6. T. Worsley, quoted in D. Verkaik, Posh Boys, 2018.
7. G. Orwell, The Lion and the Unicorn, 1941.
8. E. C. Mack, The Public Schools and British Opinion, Vol 2, 1941, p.459.
9. G. McCulloch, Cyril Norwood and the Ideal of Secondary Education, 2007. Norwood was now President of St John's College, Oxford, and Chairman of the Secondary Schools Examination Council. His Norwood Report in 1943 on the secondary school curriculum influenced the 1944 Education Act.
10. N. Hillman, 'Public Schools and the Fleming Report', Journal of the History of Education, Sept 2011, p.239.
11. A. Calder, People's War, 1969, p.541.
12. Hansard, 5 March 1940.
13. Spectator, 24 January 1941.
14. A. Howard, RAB, 1987, p.119.
15. Ibid., p.120.
16. Ibid., p.117. Alec Dunglass later became Prime Minister in 1963 as Alec Douglas-Home, the last PM to come from a public school until Tony Blair in 1997.
17. See note 79 in Ch 1 explaining the relationship between livery companies and public schools.
18. P. Gosden, Education in the Second World War, 1976, pp.333 and 494 (note).
19. N. Hillman, 'Repton and HMC in the Second World War', Conference and Common Room, 2012.
20. P. Gosden, Education in the Second World War, 1976, p.333.
21. Ibid., p.336.
22. N. Hillman, 'The parallels between admissions to independent boarding schools and admissions to selective universities', Higher Education Review, Vol 46, 2013.
23. Winchester College, Headmaster's report to the Warden and Fellows, 10 August 1941.
24. John Colville, quoted in P. Hennessy, Never Again, 1992, p.156.
25. R. Butler, The Art of the Possible, 1973, p.95.
26. N. Hillman, 'Repton and HMC in the Second World War', Conference and Common Room, 2012.
27. Author conversation with Nick Hillman, 13 January 2020.
28. Winchester College, Headmaster's Report to Warden and Fellows, 10 August 1942.
29. N. Hillman, 'Public Schools and the Fleming Report', History of Education, Vol 41, No 2, p.244.
30. Hansard, 5 March 1940.
31. P. Gosden, Education in the Second World War, 1976, p.332.

32. G. Gorodetsky (ed), The Maisky Diaries, 2015, p.523.
33. P. Gosden, Education in the Second World War, 1976, p.341.
34. Winchester College, Headmaster's Report to Warden and Fellows, 10 August 1943.
35. P. Gosden, Education in the Second World War, 1976, p.342.
36. Ibid., p.352.
37. Ibid., p.497 note 94.
38. J. Bew, Citizen Clem, 2016, p.312.
39. Hansard, 19 January 1944.
40. D. Kynaston, Austerity Britain, 2007, p.28.
41. Fleming Report, pp. 3–4, 30.
42. Fleming Report, p.66.
43. N. Hillman, 'Public Schools and the Fleming Report', History of Education, Vol 41, No 2.
44. Butler to G.M. Young, September 1944, Education Department 12/518 (National Archives)
45. Kenneth Morgan, correspondence with author, 10 February 2020
46. R. Tawney, *Equality*, 1931, p.46
47. A. Calder, *The People's War*, 1969, p.486.
48. C. Barnett, The Lost Victory, 1995, p.129.
49. A. Calder, The People's War, 1969, p.530.
50. P. Addison, The Road to 1945, 1975, p.227.
51. D. Edgerton, Britain's War Machine, 2011, p.232.
52. P. Addison, The Road to 1945, 1975, p.37.
53. D. Kynaston, Austerity Britain, 2007, p.23.
54. P. Hennessy, Winds of Change, 2019, p.496.
55. B. Scragg, Sevenoaks School, 1993, p.143.
56. C. Hill, History of Bristol GS, 1951, p.216.
57. A. Hearnden, Red Robert, 1984, p106.
58. A. Howard, RAB, 1987, p.122.

Chapter 8
1. J. Seabrook, The Refuge and the Fortress, 2008, p.39.
2. Many boarding schools had their own missions, including Bradfield, Cheltenham, Clifton, Eton, Haileybury, Marlborough and Rugby.
3. R. McKibbin, Classes and Cultures, 1998, p.56.
4. A. Trythall, 'The Downfall of Leslie Hore-Belisha', Journal of Contemporary History, 1981, p.400.
5. K. Amis, Memoirs, 1991, p.34.
6. A. Dubnov, Isaiah Berlin, 2012, p.40.
7. A. Ayer, Part of My Life, 1977, p.57.
8. T. Dalyell, obituary of George Strauss, Independent, June 1993.
9. C. Tyerman, Harrow School, 2000, p.463.

10. Ibid., p.464.
11. M. Ryan, Running with Fire, 2012, p.19.
12. Ibid., p.27.
13. Author's correspondence with D. Jones, The Perse School archivist, December 2018.
14. P. Addison, 'Oxford in the Second World War' in History of Oxford University, Vol 8, p.173.
15. J. Seabrook, The Refuge and the Fortress, 2008, p.29.
16. M. Gilbert, Kristallnacht, 2006, p.122.
17. Lord Moser, Daily Telegraph obituary, September 2015.
18. Lord Moser, Guardian obituary, 6 Sept 2015.
19. W. Eberstadt, Whence We Came, Where We Went, 2002, pp.136–47.
20. Address and other papers from Otto Fisher's memorial service, April 2016, Charterhouse archives.
21. M. Gilbert, Kristallnacht, 2006, p.175.
22. Letter from President, Old Stortfordian Club, 22 February 1939. Bishop's Stortford College archives.
23. Otto Hutter revealed his story to the author in October 2018 through letters and documents.
24. Winton's story was revealed by Esther Rantzen on television in an episode of That's Life in 1988. He was subsequently knighted, and died in 2015, aged 106.
25. HMC Committee Report, February 1939.
26. P. Alter (ed), Out of the Third Reich: Refugee Historians in Post-War Britain, 1998, p.43. Feuchtwanger became an academic historian and wrote several books about Victorian Britain.
27. Headmaster's report to Warden and Fellows, 10 August 1939, Winchester College archives.
28. Information about Leighton Park from school archives and from a Sussex University DPhil thesis by Rosie Holmes, 'A Moral Business: British Quaker Work with Refugees from Fascism 1933–45', December 2013, pp.168-72, found online at http://sro.sussex.ac.uk.
29. BBC North website, January 2009.
30. Records of the Old Girls Association, Hulme GS for Girls, 1938/9.
31. 'Sherborne's Kindertransport children', Sherborne School archives.
32. Email to author from Peter Briess, 12 October 2018.
33. Correspondence in North London Collegiate archives.
34. B. Leverton (ed), I Came Alone, 1990, p.247.
35. John Sidgwick, personal recollection in Durham School archives.
36. Rabbi John Rayner, information from archives of Durham School.
37. Lord Moser, Daily Telegraph obituary, September 2015.
38. W. Eberstadt, Whence We Came, Where We Went, 2002, pp.159–63.
39. D. Walsh, A Duty to Serve, 2011, p.148.

40. Email to author from Peter Briess, 12 October 2018.
41. W. Eberstadt, Whence We Came, Where We Went, 2002, p.339.
42. N. Annan, Changing Enemies, 1995, p.161.
43. A. Hearnden, Red Robert, 1984, p.252.
44. T. Hinde, Paths of Progress, 1992, p.141.
45. J. Bew, Citizen Clem, 2016, pp.50–3.
46. The window at Denstone was conceived by the head's wife to honour the mothers whose sons were fighting and dying.
47. S. Wearne, To Our Brothers, 2018, p.10.
48. Ibid., p.205.
49. Headmaster's Report to Warden and Fellows, August 1945 and August 1946.
50. Quoted in J. Firth, Winchester College, 1949, p.241.
51. N. Dimbleby, quoted on Cranleigh School website.
52. 'Remembering the Kindertransport', exhibition at Jewish Museum, Camden, January 2019.

Chapter 9
1. P. Hennessy, Modern History in the Making, quoted in J. Ramsden, The Dam Busters, 2003, p.122.
2. R. Morris, Guy Gibson, 1994, p.315.
3. Quoted in B. Bond, The Unquiet Western Front, 2002, p.35.
4. S. Hynes, A War Imagined, 1990, p.442.
5. J. Ramsden, The Dam Busters, 2003, p.121.
6. M. Hastings, Bomber Command, 1979, p.256.
7. R. Gore Langton, Journey's End Explored, 2013, p.45. Stanhope drank whisky to blot out the memory of the horrors he had seen.
8. The Deep Blue Sea was made into a film in 2011, all three main characters played by boarding school alumni – Tom Hiddleston (Eton), Simon Russell Beale (Clifton) and Rachel Weisz (Benenden and St Paul's).
9. P. Nash, Outline, 1949, p.211.
10. Imperial War Museum website.
11. E. Blunden, Undertones of War, 1928.
12. E. Blunden, 'The Soldier Poets of 1914–18', in F. Brereton (ed), An Anthology of War Poems, 1930, pp.13–24.
13. D. Reynolds, The Long Shadow, 2013, p.347.
14. D. Graham, Keith Douglas, 2009, p.192.
15. Ibid., p.218.
16. Blunden was Douglas's tutor at Merton College, Oxford just before the war.
17. K. Douglas, Alamein to Zem Zem, 1946, p.15.
18. V. Scannell, Not Without Glory, 1976, p.19.
19. M. Stephen, The English Public School, 2018, p.165.
20. P. Carpenter, Talking to History, in D. Walsh, A Duty to Serve, 2011, p.99.
21. N. Annan, Our Age, 1990, p.8.

22. V. Woolf, 'The Leaning Tower', in R. Bowlby (ed), A Woman's Essays, 1992, p.167.

23. G. Orwell, The Lion and the Unicorn, 1941.

24. N. Annan, Our Age, 1990, p.206. These words were attributed by Evelyn Waugh (Lancing) to Peter Pastmaster in his novel Put Out More Flags (1942). Waugh himself served in the Commandos.

25. D. Reynolds, The Long Shadow, 2013, p.342. Also note Catherine Reilly, English Poetry of the Second World War: a Bibliography, 1986.

26. V. Scannell, Not Without Glory, 1976. The eleven are: Douglas, Alan Ross (Haileybury), Roy Fuller (St Paul's), Hamish Henderson (Dulwich), Bruce Gutteridge (Cranleigh), Gavin Ewart (Wellington), Drummond Allison (Bishop's Stortford), R.N. Currey (Kingswood), F.T. Prince (CBC Kimberley SA), John Manifold (Geelong GS), Sidney Keyes (Tonbridge). The three others are Alun Lewis (Cowbridge GS), Charles Causley (Launceston) and Henry Reed (KES Aston).

27. D. Reynolds, The Long Shadow, 2013, p.347.

28. T. Kendall, Modern English War Poetry, 2006, p.166.

29. G. Chapman, A Passionate Prodigality, 1933, p.226.

30. R. Trevelyan, The Fortress, 1956, p.106.

31. G. MacDonald Fraser, Quartered Safe Out Here, 1993.

32. M. Hastings, Chastise, 2019, p.xxix. Hastings examines doubts raised about whether Enemy Coast Ahead was Gibson's own work but concludes that, with a few editorial changes, it was.

33. Hermione, Countess of Ranfurly, obituary in the Daily Telegraph, November. To War with Whitaker was published in 1994.

34. J. Ramsden, 'Refocusing the People's War: British War Films of the 1950s', in Journal of Contemporary History, January 1998.

35. Lord Birkett in They Have Their Exits, 1953, p.19.

36. Monsarrat served as a naval officer on convoy escorts.

37. Godfrey Talbot, Daily Telegraph obituary, 2000.

38. J. Keegan, The Battle for History, 1995, p.34.

39. M. Hastings, obituary of Sir Michael Howard, The Times, 2 Dec 2019. Most of the significant contributors to the Official History were historians educated at public schools, including Noble Frankland (Sedbergh), James Butler (Harrow), Stanley Woodburn Kirby (Charterhouse), Basil Collier (King's, Canterbury) and Ian Playfair (Cheltenham).

40. D. Reynolds, In Command of History, 2004, p.526.

41. P. Hennessy, Distilling the Frenzy, 2013, p.198.

42. A. Calder, The People's War, 1969, p.367.

43. D. Reynolds, The Long Shadow, 2013, p.313.

44. Information from Peter Henderson, KSC archivist.

45. J. Chapman, The British at War, 1998, p.173.

46. Ibid., p.176.

47. G. Eley, 'Finding the People's War' in American Historical Review, June 2001.
48. J. Ramsden, 'Refocusing the People's War: British War Films of the 1950s', in Journal of Contemporary History, January 1998.
49. Ibid. Other public–school–educated actors in war films include Dirk Bogarde (UCS), Alec Guinness (Fettes), Celia Johnson (St Paul's Girls') and Vivien Leigh (Woldingham).
50. D. Reynolds The Long Shadow, 2013, p.312.
51. D. Kynaston, Modernity Britain, 2013, p.625. Cook's actual words were: 'I want you to lay down your life, Perkins. We need a futile gesture at this stage. It will raise the whole tone of the war. Get up in a crate, Perkins, pop over to Bremen, take a shufti, don't come back. Goodbye, Perkins. God, I wish I was going too.' Beyond the Fringe, 1960.
52. J. Bourne, 'A Personal Reflection on Two World Wars' in Liddle, Bourne and Whitehead (eds), The Great War 1914–45, Vol 1, p.17. The point could be made that other participants have different perceptions of the contrast between the two wars.
53. D. Reynolds, The Long Shadow, 2013, p.xv.
54. B. Bond, Britain's Two World Wars, 2014, p.17.
55. N. Ascherson, 'Into the Storm', feature in the Observer, 1 September 2019.
56. V. Ogilvie, The English Public School, 1957, p.216

Chapter 10
1. D. Edgerton, *The Rise and Fall of the British Nation*, 2018, p.218.
2. Between 1981 and 1997, 80,000 children participated in the scheme at 355 schools.
3. P. Hennessy, Never Again, 1992, p.88.
4. P. Addison, The Road to 1945, 1975, p.268.
5. H. Purcell, A Very Private Celebrity, 2015, p.62.
6. A. Howard, Crossman: The Pursuit of Power, 1990, p.23.
7. B. Simon, Education and the Social Order, 1991, p.53.
8. H. Dent, History of Education, 1968, p.31.
9. D. Verkaik, Posh Boys, 2018, p.78.
10. J. Field, The King's Nurseries, 1987, p.97.
11. M. De-La-Noy, Bedford School, 1999, p.143.
12. J. Piggott, Dulwich College, 2008, p.273.
13. P. Addison, The Road to 1945, 1975, p.276
14. D. Edgerton, *The Rise and Fall of the British Nation*, 2018, p.245.
15. Claude Elliott file, Eton archives.
16. P. Weiler, Ernest Bevin, 1993, p.192.
17. Author conversation with John Bew, 21 January 2020.
18. J. Bew, Citizen Clem, 2016, p.268.
19. R. McKibbin, Classes and Cultures, 1998, p.535.

20. R. Verkaik, Posh Boys, 2018, p.89.
21. J. Bew, Citizen Clem, 2016, p.51.
22. Clement Attlee, Oxford DNB entry.
23. D. Kynaston, Austerity Britain, 2007, p.153.
24. Kenneth Morgan, correspondence with author, 10 February 2020.
25. M. Francis, Ideas and Policies under Labour 1945–51, 1997, p.163.
26. Author conversation with John Bew, 21 January 2020.
27. J. Bew, Citizen Clem, 2016, pp.24, 90.
28. P. Hennessy, Never Again, 1992, p.436.
29. J. Rae, The Public School Revolution, 1981, p.34.
30. Author conversation with Joe Davies, recent head of Haileybury, 12 January 2020.
31. R. McKibbin, Classes and Cultures, 1998, p.233.
32. Kenneth Morgan, correspondence with author, 12 February 2020.
33. F. Green and D. Kynaston, Engines of Privilege, 2019, p.37.
34. B. Simon, Education and the Social Order, 1974, p.137.
35. Ministry of Education Circular 90, 8 March 1946.
36. Report of HMC Annual Meeting January 1946 and HMC Committee May 1946.
37. Headmaster's Report to Warden and Fellows of Winchester College, 10 August 1946.
38. Report of HMC Annual Meeting December 1946.
39. B. Simon, Education and the Social Order, 1974, p.139.
40. J. Piggott, Dulwich College, 2009, p.273.
41. Parliamentary Debate, June 13, 1950.
42. N. Hillman, 'Public Schools and the Fleming Report', Journal of the History of Education, 2011.
43. J. Dancy, Walter Oakeshott, 1995, p.147.
44. N. Hillman, 'Parallels between admissions to independent schools and selective universities', Higher Education Review, 2014.
45. C. Tyerman, History of Harrow School, 2000, p.413.
46. N. Hillman, 'Public Schools and the Fleming Report', Journal of the History of Education, 2011.
47. P. Gosden, *Education in the Second World War*, 1976, p.362.
48. Author conversation with John Dancy, 4 September 2018.
49. John Dancy, obituary in The Times, 16 February 2020.
50. T. Hinde, Paths of Progress, 1992, p.203.
51. J. Rae, The Public School Revolution, 1981, p.27.
52. R. McKibbin, Classes and Cultures, 1998, p.269.
53. A. Sampson, Anatomy of Britain, 1962, p.177
54. Lord Wright obituary, *The Times*, 9 March 2020).
55. TES, 17 Oct 1952.
56. N. Hillman, 'Public Schools and the Fleming Report', Journal of the History of Education, 2011.

57. HMC Annual Meeting 1958.
58. J. Dancy, Public Schools and the Future, 1963, p.147.
59. J. Rae, Public School Revolution, 1981, p.85.
60. D. Sandbrook, Never Had it so Good, 1974, p.398.
61. R. McKibbin, Classes and Cultures, 1998, pp.242–3.
62. D. Sandbrook, Never Had it so Good, 1974, p.399.
63. D. Glass, Social Mobility in Britain, 1954, p.22.
64. D. Kynaston, Family Britain 1951–7, 2009, p.142.
65. P. Clarke, A Question of Leadership, 1991, p.30.
66. D.Turner, The Old Boys, 2015, p.194.
67. P. Addison in History of Oxford University, Vol 8, p.188.
68. The Times, 17 February 1964.
69. J. Rae, The Old Boys' Network, 2010, diary entry for 29 November 1979..
70. R.Verkaik, Posh Boys, 2018, p.99.
71. N. Hillman, 'The Public Schools Commission', Contemporary British History, Sept 2010, p.516
72. The figure of 36,000 came from the Public Schools Commission Report. About 15 per cent of boarders at public schools received assistance from the state, 10,000 from LEA bursaries and 10,000 through educational allowances paid to the armed forces and diplomats. The other 16,000 were supported to board at direct grant and maintained schools.
73. Public Schools Commission, First Report, 1968, p.1.
74. Beaumont College, a leading Roman Catholic school, closed in 1967.
75. N. Hillman, 'The Public Schools Commission', Contemporary British History, Sept 2010.
76. The Times, 12 March 1975.
77. D. Sandbrook, Seasons in the Sun, 2012, p.199.
78. D. Turner, The Old Boys, 2015, p.215.
79. A. Sampson, Anatomy of Britain, 1962, p.190.
80. D. Sandbrook, Seasons in the Sun, 2012, p.200.
81. C. Tyerman, Harrow School, 2000, p.416.
82. The 1989 Children Act firmly put the welfare of the child at the heart of educational philosophy and practice.
83. D. Cannadine, The Decline and Fall of the British Aristocracy, 1990, p.607.
84. P. Hennessy, Winds of Change, 2019, p.499.
85. A. Howard, RAB, 1987, p.122.
86. Note to author from Professor William Richardson, 17 July 2019.
87. Ibid.
88. L. McKinstry, Attlee and Churchill, 2019.
89. J. Colville,The Fringes of Power, 1985, p.613.
90. J. Bew, Citizen Clem, 2016, p.544.
91. R. Jenkins, Churchill, 2001, p.20.
92. John Colville diary, 1 December 1944, quoted in M. Gilbert, Road to Victory, 1986, p.1081.

Select Bibliography

Primary Sources
School WW2 Questionnaires
Questionnaires, giving statistical details and achievements, returned by the following eighty-nine schools: Abingdon, Ashford, Bablake, Bancrofts, Beaumont, Bedford, Bishop's Stortford, Bloxham, Bradfield, Brentwood, Bristol GS, Bromley HS, Canford, Charterhouse, Christ's (NZ), Christ's Hospital, Churchers, City of London Freemen's, Dean Close, Diocesan College (SA), Dulwich, Durham, Eastbourne, Elizabeth, Emanuel, Eton, Exeter, Framlingham, Giggleswick, Glenalmond, Gresham's, Haileybury, Hampton, Harrow, Highgate, Hulme GS (Boys), Hulme GS (Girls), Hurstpierpoint, Imperial Service College, KES Witley, King's Canterbury, King's Taunton, King William's IOM, King's Worcester, Kingswood, Lady Eleanor Holles, Latymer Upper, Leeds GS, Leighton Park, Loughborough GS, Magdalen CS, Malvern, Marlborough, Mill Hill, Monkton Combe, North London Collegiate, Nottingham HS, Oakham, Oundle, Perse, Portsmouth GS, Queen's Taunton, QEGS Wakefield, RGS Wolverhampton, Rendcomb, Robert Gordon's, Repton, Roedean, Rugby, Rydal/Penrhos, St Edmund's Canterbury, St Edmund's Ware, St Edward's Oxford, St Paul's Girls', St Peter's (Aus), Sevenoaks, Sherborne, Stowe, Taunton, Tonbridge, UCS, Uppingham, Warminster, Warwick, Wellington College, Westminster, Winchester, Woodbridge, Wycombe Abbey.

Headmasters' Conference
Reports from HMC Committee and Annual Meetings 1914–58.
HMC Membership Lists 1914–50.
HMC *Insight* magazine, December 2019.

Official Papers in School Archives
Eton College, Claude Elliott file.
King's School Canterbury Board of Education Report, 1930.
Marlborough College, Board of Education Report, 1934.
Marlborough College, George Turner papers.
Roedean School, Dame Emmeline Tanner report, July 1940.
Sherborne School, Board of Education Report, 1930.
Winchester College, Headmaster's Reports to Warden and Fellows 1939–46.

Unpublished letters and memoirs held in school archives
Bishop's Stortford, Letter from President, Old Stortfordian Club, 22 February
   1939.
Charterhouse, Frank Fletcher's scrapbook.
Charterhouse, address and other papers from Otto Fisher's memorial service,
   April 2016.
Charterhouse, Otto Fisher, 'Festschrift to Robert Birley', 1982.
Charterhouse, 'Charterhouse Miscellany'.
Christ's Hospital, H. Flecker, memoir of the war at Christ's Hospital.
Durham School, Rabbi John Rayner notes.
King's, Canterbury, Memoirs of wartime evacuation by N. Scarfe and J.
   Dalrymple.
Merchant Taylor's, N. Birley papers.
North London Collegiate School, P. Hobbs (ed), 'NLCS in Wartime 1939–45'.
Oundle School, M. Downes, 'Notable Old Oundelians'.
St Paul's Girls', W. Pasmore, memoir, 'The Night the School was Bombed'.
Sherborne School, 'Sherborne's Kindertransport children'.
Sherborne, R. Hassall, essay on Alan Turing.
Tonbridge School, Donald Birrell, diary 1940.
Winchester College, Letters to Malcolm Robertson.
Winchester College, John Dancy, memoir.
Wycombe Abbey, wartime correspondence.

School Magazines 1939–45
*Bradfield Chronicle, The Cantuarian, The Carthusian, The Diocesan, The
Elizabethan, The Harrovian, The Marlburian, The Shirburnian, The Stoic, The
Taylorian, The Tonbridgian, The Wykehamist.*

School War Memorial Books, Registers and Rolls of Honour
Bishops' Stortford Roll of Honour.
Du Croz, D. (ed), *Marlborough College and the Great War in 100 Stories*,
   Marlborough, 2018.
Henderson, P. *The King's School Canterbury in the Great War*, 2018.
Marlborough Register 1843–1952.
Marlborough Roll of Honour 1939–45.
Radley Register 1847–1947.
Records of the Old Girls Association, Hulme GS for Girls 1938/9.
Rendcomb College Roll of Honour 1939–45.
Roll and Record for Old Wykehamists, 1943.
Stowe Book of Remembrance.
Tonbridge Register 1861–1945.
Wearne, S., *To Our Brothers*, Helion, 2018.

Unpublished correspondence and conversations with authors

Conversations and/or correspondence with John Bew, Robin Brodhurst, John Dancy, Joe Davies, David Edgerton, Christopher Everett, Sir Brian Harrison, Peter Henderson, Nick Hillman, David Kynaston, William Richardson, Dominic Sandbrook, Alan Smithers, Richard Thorpe, David Turner.

Correspondence with those who experienced the war years: Graham Butler, David Brighton, Keith Jenkin, John Sievers, David McGregor, Christopher Wright, Desmond Vigors, Alan Loveless, Edmund Haviland.

Otto Hutter, letter and documents to author, October 2018.

Peter Briess, letter and documents to author, October 2018.

Correspondence with archivists, especially Angela Kenny (NLCS), David Jones (The Perse), John Weitzel (Loughborough GS), Suzanne Foster (Winchester), Catherine Smith (Charterhouse), Rachel Hassall (Sherborne), Peter Henderson (KSC), Carrie May (Wycombe Abbey), Jackie Sullivan (Roedean), Sarah Wearne (Abingdon).

Published Primary Sources

Ayer, A., *Part of My Life*, Harper Collins, 1977.

Bielenberg, C., *The Past is Myself*, Corgi, 1968.

Blunden, E., 'The Soldier Poets of 1914–18', in F. Brereton (ed), *An Anthology of War Poems*, 1930.

Bowlby, A., *The Recollections of Rifleman Bowlby*, Leo Cooper, 1969.

Briggs, A., *Secret Days*, Frontline, 2011.

Brodhurst, R. (ed), *The Bramall Papers*, Pen & Sword, 2018.

'Cato', *Guilty Men*, Faber, 1940.

Chapman, G., *A Passionate Prodigality*, Nicolson, 1933.

Churchill, W., *The Second World War*, Cassell, 1952.

Churchill, W. *War Speeches*, Cassell, 1951.

Colville, J., *The Fringes of Power*, Hodder & Stoughton, 1985.

Danchev, A. and Todman, D. (eds), *Alanbrooke War Diaries*, Phoenix, 2001.

Dilks, D. (ed), *Diaries of Sir Alexander Cadogan 1938–45*, Cassell, 1971.

Douglas, K., *Collected Poems*, Nicolson & Watson, 1951.

Douglas, K., *From Alamein to Zem Zem*, Nicolson & Watson, 1946.

Douie, C., *The Weary Road*, John Murray, 1929.

Duggan, M. (ed), *Padre in Colditz*, Hodder & Stoughton, 1978.

Dundas, H., *Flying Start*, Penguin, 1990.

Eberstadt, W., *Whence We Came, Where We Went*, WAE Books, 2002.

Elliott, W., *Esprit de Corps*, Michael Russell, 1996.

Feuchtwanger, E., *I Was Hitler's Neighbour*, Bretwalda, 2013.

Fletcher, F., *After Many Days*, Hale, 1937.

Gibson, G., *Enemy Coast Ahead*, Crecy, 1944.

Hart-Davis, D (ed), *King's Counsellor: Diaries of Sir Alan Lascelles*, Weidenfeld & Nicolson, 2006.

Hillary, R., *The Last Enemy*, Macmillan, 1943.

Hills, S., *By Tank into Normandy*, Orion, 2002.

James, B., *Moonless Night*, Pen & Sword, 1983.

Jary, S., *18 Platoon*, Light Infantry Office, 1987.

Kee, R., *A Crowd is not Company*, Eyre & Spottiswoode, 1947.

Leeson, S., *The Public Schools Question and Other Essays*, Longmans, 1948.

Lewis, C., *Sagittarius Rising*, Peter Davies, 1936.

MacDonald Fraser, G., *Quartered Safe out Here*, Harper Collins, 1993.

Macpherson, T., *Behind Enemy Lines*, Mainstream, 2010.

Masters J., *The Road Past Mandalay*, Cassell, 1961.

Masters, J., *Bugles and a Tiger*, Michael Joseph, 1956.

Mawson, S., *Arnhem Doctor*, Leo Cooper, 1981.

Mayfield, G., *Life and Death in the Battle of Britain*, IWM, 2018.

Montagu, E., *The Man Who Never Was*, Penguin, 1953.

Neave, A., *They Have their Exits*, Hodder, 1953.

Nicolson, N. (ed), *The Harold Nicolson Diaries 1907–64*, Weidenfeld, 2004.

Orwell, G., *The Lion and the Unicorn*, Penguin, 1941.

Piper, D., *I Am Well, Who Are You?*, Anne Piper, 1998.

Priestley, J., *Postscripts*, Heinemann, 1940.

Ranfurly, H., *To War with Whitaker*, Heinemann, 1994.

Reid, P., *The Colditz Story*, Pan, 1952.

Skinner, L., *The Man who worked on Sundays*, privately published, 1996.

Trevelyan, R., *The Fortress*, Faber, 1956.

Trevor-Roper, H., *The Wartime Journals*, R. Davenport-Hines (ed), Tauris, 2012.

Wellum, G., *First Light*, Viking, 2002.

Secondary Sources
School histories, biographies, war histories and books about public schools.
Allport, D. and Friskney, N., *Short History of Wilson's School*, 1987.

Annan, N., *Roxburgh of Stowe*, Longmans, 1965.

Bailes, H. (ed), *A Paulina Anthology*, 2004.

Bailes, H., *Once a Paulina*, Third Millennium, 2000.

Batten, S., *Shining Light: Bloxham School*, Third Millennium, 2010.

Beckett, M., *Wycombe Abbey Re-Visited*, 2016.

Blackie, J., *Bradfield 1850–1975*, 1976.

Brown, J., *Independent Witness*, Taunton School, 1997.

Burden, P., *The Lion and the Stars*, Coventry School, 1990.

Card, T., *Eton Renewed*, John Murray, 1994.

Christie, J., *A Great Teacher*, Plume, 1984.

Collenette, V., *Elizabeth College in Exile*, 1996.

Dancy J., *Walter Oakeshott*, Michael Russell, 1995.

Dancy, J., *The Public Schools and the Future*, Faber, 1963.

De Zouche, D., *Roedean School 1885–1955*, 1955.

Field, J., *The King's Nurseries*, James & James,1987.

Firth, J. *Winchester College*, Blackie, 1949.

Francis, P., *Old Yet Ever Young*, Sherborne School, 2020.

Green, F. and Kynaston, D., *Engines of Privilege*, Bloomsbury, 2019.

Hearnden, A., *Red Robert: Life of Robert Birley*, Hamish Hamilton, 1984.

Henderson, P., Exhibition catalogue on OKS Film Directors to mark King's Week, 1985.

Hinde, T., *Paths of Progress*, James & James, 1992.

Hinde, T., *Highgate School*, James & James, 1993.

Hobbs, P. (ed), *Memories of NLCS in Wartime*, 1995.

Hossain, E., *Grace and Integrity: Lady Eleanor Holles*, Third Millennium, 2011.

King, P., *Hurstpierpoint College 1849–1995*, 1996.

Lewis, R., *History of Brentwood School*, 1981.

McCulloch, G., *Cyril Norwood and the Ideal of Secondary Education*, Palgrave, 2007.

McDowell, D., *Carrying On: Fettes College, War and the World*, Matador, 2012.

Mileham, P., *Wellington College*, Third Millennium, 2008.

Newell, P. and Sankey, J., *Gresham's in Wartime*, 1987.

Newsome, D., *History of Wellington College*, John Murray, 1959.

Ogilvie, V., *The English Public School*, 1957.

Parker, B., *History of Elizabeth College, Guernsey*, Third Millennium, 2011.

Partridge, M., *Eastbourne College in the Second World War*, 2010.

Peel, M., *The Land of Lost Content*, Pentland, 1996.

Pigott, J., *Dulwich College 1616–2008*, 2008.

Quick, A., *Charterhouse*, James & James, 1990.

Rae, J., *The Public School Revolution*, Faber, 1981.

Rees, B., *Stowe*, John Murray, 2008.

Rice, K. (ed), *Garside's Wars*, Hampton School, 1993.

Rice, K., *Hampton GS in Wartime*, 2009.

Sabben-Clare, J., *Winchester College*, Cave, 1981.

Scragg, B., *Sevenoaks School*, 1993.

Seldon, A. and Walsh, D., *Public Schools and the Great War*, Pen & Sword, 2013.

Stephen, M., *The English Public School*, Metro, 2018.

Stranack, D., *Schools at War*, Phillimore, 2005.

Turner, D., *Be Grateful: Brighton College's Fallen 1939–45*, Shire, 2019.

Tyerman, C., *History of Harrow School 1324–1991*, OUP, 2000.

Verkaik, R., *Posh Boys*, One World, 2018.

Walsh, D., *A Duty to Serve: Tonbridge School and the 1939–45 War*, Third Millennium, 2011.

Watson, N., *The Family Album*, James & James, 2008.

White, B. and Wood, C., *History of Rendcomb College in Photographs*, Bosworth, 2012.

Wild, E. and Rice, K., (eds), *School by the Thames*, Third Millennium, 2011.

General Histories and Biographies
Addison, P., *The Road to 1945*, Pimlico, 1975.
Addison, P. and Calder, A. (eds), *Time to Kill*, Pimlico, 1997.
Addison, P., 'Oxford in the Second World War' in *The History of the University of Oxford*, Vol 8, OUP, 1994.
Alter, P., *Out of the Third Reich: Refugee Historians in Post-War Britain*, Tauris, 1998.
Andrew, C., *The Defence of the Realm*, Allen Lane, 2009.
Annan N., *Our Age*, Weidenfeld & Nicolson, 1990.
Barnett, C., *The Collapse of British Power*, Sutton, 1972.
Barnett, C., *The Lost Victory*, Pan, 1995.
Barnett C., *The Audit of War*, Macmillan, 1986.
Barker, R., *One Man's War*, Chatto & Windus, 1975.
Barker, R., *Education and Politics 1900–51*, OUP, 1972.
Beckett, I. and Simpson, K. (eds), *A Nation in Arms*, Pen & Sword, 1985.
Beevor, A., *Crete: The Battle and the Resistance*, John Murray, 1991.
Bew J., *Citizen Clem*, Riverrun, 2016.
Bishop, P., *Air Force Blue*, Collins, 2017.
Bishop, P., *Fighter Boys*, Harper, 2003.
Bishop, P., *Bomber Boys*, Harper, 2007.
Bond, B., *The Unquiet Western Front*, CUP, 2002.
Bond, B., *Britain's Two World Wars against Germany*, CUP, 2014.
Bungay, S., *The Most Dangerous Enemy*, Aurum, 2001.
Butler, R., *The Art of the Possible*, Penguin, 1973.
Calder, A., *The People's War*, Pimlico, 1969.
Cannadine D., *The Decline and Fall of the British Aristocracy*, Yale, 1990.
Cecil H., *The Flower of Battle*, Steerforth, 1996.
Chancellor, H., *Colditz*, OUP, 2001.
Chapman, J., *The British at War: Cinema, State and Propaganda, 1939–45*, Tauris, 1998.
Clarke, P., *A Question of Leadership: Gladstone to Thatcher*, Hamish Hamilton, 1991.
Colville, J., *Footprints in Time*, London, 1976.
Cooper, A., *Patrick Leigh Fermor*, John Murray, 2012.
Crang, J., *The British Army and the People's War*, MUP, 2000.
Davenport-Hines, R., *Enemies Within*, Collins, 2018.
Deakin, N. (ed), *Radiant Illusion*, Eden Valley, 2015.
Dent, H., *History of Education*, UTP, 1968.
Edgerton, D., *The Rise and Fall of the British Nation*, Allen Lane, 2018.
Edgerton, D., *Warfare State*, CUP, 2006.
Edgerton, D., *Britain's War Machine*, CUP, 2011.
Ellis, J., *The Sharp End*, Pimlico, 1980.
Ellis, J., *Cassino*, Andre Deutsch, 1984.

Elmes, J., *M-Mother*, History Press, 2015.

Faber, D., *Speaking for England*, Simon & Schuster, 2005.

Faulks, S., *The Fatal Englishman*, Vintage, 1997.

Foot, M., *SOE in France*, Routledge, 1966.

Foot, M., *SOE*, Bodley Head, 1984.

Foot, M. and Langley, J., *MI9: Escape and Evasion 1939–45*, Bodley Head, 1979.

Francis, M., *Ideas and Policies under Labour 1945–51*, Manchester UP, 1997.

French, D., *Raising Churchill's Army*, OUP, 2000.

Gilbert, M., *Winston Churchill*, Vols 5–7, Heinemann, 1976.

Gilbert, M., *Kristallnacht*, Harper, 2007.

Gore Langton, R., *Journey's End Explored*, Oberon, 2013.

Gosden, P., *Education in the Second World War*, Routledge, 1976.

Graham, D., *Keith Douglas 1920–44*, Faber, 2009.

Harrison, B. (ed), *History of the University of Oxford*, Vol 8, OUP, 1994.

Hastings M., *The Secret War*, Harper, 2015.

Hastings, M., *Bomber Command*, Michael Joseph, 1979.

Hastings, M., *Chastise*, Collins, 2019.

Hely-Hutchinson, H., *H.K. Marsden's War Dead*, Third Millennium, 2009.

Hennessy, P., *Whitehall*, Fontana, 1989.

Hennessy, P., *Never Again*, Jonathan Cape, 1992.

Hennessy, P., *Winds of Change*, Penguin, 2019.

Hichens, A., *Gunboat Command*, Pen & Sword, 2014.

Hoe, A., *David Stirling*, Little Brown, 1992.

Holland, J., *Heroes*, Harper, 2006.

Howard, A., *Crossman: The Pursuit of Power*, Pimlico, 1990.

Howard A., *RAB*, Jonathan Cape, 1987.

Howard, M., *British Intelligence in the Second World War*, Vol 5, HMSO, 1990.

Howarth, T. (ed), *Monty at Close Quarters*, Leo Cooper, 1985.

Jeffery, K., *MI6*, Bloomsbury, 2010.

Keegan, J., *The Battle for History*, Hutchinson, 1995.

Keegan, J., *Churchill's Generals*, Cassell, 1991.

Kendall, T., *Modern English War Poetry*, OUP, 2006.

Kennedy, L., *On My Way to the Club*, Collins, 1989.

Kynaston, D., *Austerity Britain*, Bloomsbury 2007.

Kynaston, D., *Modernity Britain*, Bloomsbury, 2013.

Leverton, B. (ed), *I Came Alone: Stories of the Kindertransport*, Book Guild, 1990.

Liddle, P., Bourne, J., and Whitehead, I. (eds), *The Great War 1914–45*, Harper Collins, 2000.

Longmate, N., *How We Lived Then*, Hutchinson, 1971.

Lyman, R., *Into the Jaws of Death*, Quercus, 2014.

McKibbin, R., *Classes and Cultures: England 1918–51*, OUP, 1998.

McKay, R., *John Leonard Wilson, Confessor of the Faith*, Hodder, 1973.

Macarthur, B., *Surviving the Sword*, Abacus, 2005.
Macintyre, B., *A Spy among Friends*, Bloomsbury, 2014.
Macintyre, B., *Operation Mincemeat*, Bloomsbury, 2010.
Macintyre, B., *SAS Rogue Heroes*, Penguin, 2016.
Mack, E., *The Public Schools and British Opinion*, Columbia, 1941.
Maxtone Graham, Y., *Terms and Conditions*, Abacus, 2016.
May, T., *The Victorian Public School*, Shire, 2011.
Mead, R., *Commando General*, Pen & Sword, 2016.
Messenger, C., *The Commandos*, Collins, 1985.
Milton, G., *Ministry of Ungentlemanly Warfare*, John Murray, 2016.
Molson, T., *The Millionaire's Squadron*, Pen & Sword, 2014.
Morris, R., *Cheshire*, Penguin, 2000.
Morris, R., *Guy Gibson*, Penguin, 1994.
Neave, A., *Saturday at MI9*, Hodder, 1969.
Overy, R., *Why the Allies Won*, Pimlico, 2006.
Parker, M., *The Battle of Britain*, Headline, 2000.
Parker, M., *Monte Cassino*, Headline, 2004.
Purcell, H., *A Very Private Celebrity*, Robson, 2015.
Ramsden, J., *The Dam Busters*, Tauris, 2003.
Ramsden, J., *Man of the Century, Winston Churchill and his Legend since 1945*, Harper Collins, 2003.
Reynolds, D., *In Command of History*, Penguin, 2004.
Reynolds, D., *The Long Shadow*, Simon & Schuster, 2013.
Roberts, A., *Churchill*, Allen Lane, 2018.
Roberts, A., *Holy Fox*, Zeus, 2014.
Ryan, M., *Running with Fire*, Robson, 2012.
Sampson, A., *Anatomy of Britain*, Hodder, 1962.
Sandford, K., *Mark of the Lion*, Penguin, 1962.
Saunders, H., *The Green Beret*, Michael Joseph, 1949.
Scannell, V., *Not Without Glory*, Woburn, 1976.
Seabrook, J., *The Refuge and the Fortress*, Palgrave, 2008.
Seldon, A., *The Cabinet Office 1916–206*, Biteback, 2016.
Shakespeare, N., *Six Minutes in May*, Vintage, 2017.
Simon, B., *The Politics of Educational Reform 1920–40*, Lawrence & Wishart, 1974.
Simon, B., *Education and the Social Order*, Lawrence & Wishart, 1991.
Sisman, A., *Hugh Trevor-Roper*, Weidenfeld & Nicolson, 2010.
Smith, M., *Secrets of Station X*, Biteback, 2011.
Smith, M., *Britain and 1940*, Routledge, 2000.
Stewart, I. (ed), *War, Culture and the Media*, Flicks, 2010.
Swift, D., *Bomber County*, Penguin, 2010.
Sykes, C., *Orde Wingate*, World, 1959.
Terraine, J., *The Right of the Line*, Hodder, 1985.

Thorpe, D.R., *Eden: The Life and Times of Anthony Eden*, Pimlico, 2003.
Townsend, P., *Time and Chance*, Harper Collins, 1978.
Tritton, P., *A Canterbury Tale*, Parkers, 2000.
Venning, A., *To War with the Walkers*, Hodder, 2019.
Wilmot, C., *The Struggle for Europe*, London, 1952.
Worsley, T., *Barbarians and Philistines*, Hale, 1940.
Wynn, K., *Men of the Battle of Britain*, CCB, 1999.

Other Journals
Bailey, R., 'Shellshock to Psychiatry', Gresham College lecture 2014.
Bramall, FM the Lord, interview *Daily Telegraph,* 2 June 2019.
Bramall, FM the Lord, interview *Sunday Times*, 28 July 2019.
Edgerton, D., 'Barnett's Audit of War: an Audit', *Contemporary British History*, November 1990.
Eley, G., 'Finding the People's War' in *American Historical Review*, June 2001.
Hennessy, P., 'Modern History in the Making' in *Director*, September 1992.
    Hillman, N., 'Public Schools and the Fleming Report', *History of Education*, Vol 41, No 2.
Hillman, N., 'Repton and HMC in the Second World War', *Conference and Common Room*, Spring 2012.
Hillman, N., 'The Parallels between Admissions to Independent Boarding Schools and Selective Universities', *Higher Education Review*, Vol 46, 2014.
Hillman, N., 'The Public Schools Commission', *Contemporary British History*, 2010.
Kidd, C., 'Britain's Twentieth Century Industrial Revolution', *New Statesman*, 11 July 2018.
Mahoney, R., 'Trenchard's Doctrine', *British Journal of Military History*, 2018.
Norwood, C., 'Public Schools and Social Service', *Spectator*, November 1926.
Otley, C., 'Public School and Army', *New Society*, November 1966.
Otley, C., 'The Educational Background of British Army Officers', *Sociology*, Vol 7, 1973.
Ramsden, J., 'British War Films of the 1950s', *Journal of Contemporary History*, January 1998.
Stevenson, J., review of *Audit of War*, *Historical Journal*, Vol 30, 1987.
Taylor, D., review of *Gilded Youth* by J. Brooke-Smith, *Guardian*, 6 April 2019.

Obituaries
Sir Harold Atcherley, *The Times*, February 2017.
Lord Bramall, *The Times*, November 2019.
John Dancy, *The Times*, February 2020.
Sydney Dowse, *Daily Telegraph*, April 2008.
Ronnie Harker, *The Times*, June 1999.
Norman Heatley, *Daily Telegraph*, January 2004.

Sir Michael Howard, *The Times* December 2019.
Rosemary Ince, *The Times*, May 2018.
Lord Moser, *Daily Telegraph* and *Guardian*, September 2015.
Dame Felicity Peake, *Guardian* November 2002.
Hermione, Countess of Ranfurly, *Daily Telegraph*, November 2016.
George Strauss, *Independent*, June 1993.
Geoffrey Wellum, *The Times*, July 2018.
Lord Whitelaw, *Independent*, July 1999.

Unpublished Dissertations
Holmes, R., 'A Moral Business: British Quaker Work with Refugees from Fascism 1933–45', Sussex University, December 2013.
Pillot, C., 'Public Schools 1939–45', Sorbonne University, 2019.
Romans, E., 'Selection and Early Career Education of Executive Officers in the Royal Navy 1902–39', Exeter University, March 2012.

Websites
Clifton College, Cranleigh School, King's School, Canterbury WW1 and WW2, Lancing College War Memorial, Marlborough College in WW1, Wellington College Digital Archive, Winchester at War, MI5, Nicholas Winton.

Selected Abbreviations

AAC	Academic Assistance Council
AAF	Auxiliary Air Force
ABCA	Army Bureau of Current Affairs
ACM	Air Chief Marshal
ARP	Air Raid Precautions
ATA	Air Transport Auxiliary
BEF	British Expeditionary Force
BUF	British Union of Fascists
CAS	Chief of the Air Staff
CCF	Combined Cadet Force
CIGS	Chief of the Imperial General Staff
CPGB	Communist Party of Great Britain
CSSAD	Committee for the Scientific Survey of Air Defence
CWGC/IWGC	Commonwealth/Imperial War Graves Commission
DFC	Distinguished Flying Cross
DSC	Distinguished Service Cross
DSO	Distinguished Service Order
FRS	Fellow of the Royal Society
GC&CS	Government Code and Cypher School
GBA	Governing Bodies Association
HMC	Headmasters' Conference
ICI	Imperial Chemical Industries
KRRC	King's Royal Rifle Corps
KSC	King's School Canterbury
LDV	Local Defence Volunteers (Home Guard)
LEA	Local Education Authority
LRDG	Long Range Desert Group
LSE	London School of Economics
MC	Military Cross
MGB	Motor Gun Boat
MI5	Military Intelligence 5 (Security Service)
NCO	Non-commissioned Officer
NLCS	North London Collegiate School
NZEF	New Zealand Expeditionary Force
OBE	Order of the British Empire

OCTU	Officer Cadets' Training Unit (Army)
OIC	Operational Intelligence Centre (Admiralty)
OTC	Officers' Training Corps
OTU	Operational Training Unit (RAF)
PIAT	Projector Infantry Anti-Tank
RAE	Royal Aircraft Establishment, Farnborough
RAFVR	Royal Air Force Volunteer Reserve
RAMC	Royal Army Medical Corps
RFC	Royal Flying Corps
RMC	Royal Military College (Woolwich)
RMA	Royal Military Academy (Sandhurst)
RNVR	Royal Naval Volunteer Reserve
SAS	Special Air Service
SBS	Special Boat Service
SIS	Secret Intelligence Service (MI6)
SOE	Special Operations Executive
STEM	Science, technology, engineering and maths
TLS	Times Literary Supplement
TRE	Telecommunications Research Establishment
TUC	Trades Union Congress
UAS	University Air Squadron
UCL	University College London
UCS	University College School, London
USAAF	United States Army Air Forces
VC	Victoria Cross
WAAF	Women's Auxiliary Air Force
WEA	Workers Educational Association
WRNS	Women's Royal Naval Service

Index

Public Schools Index

General Index

and direct grant schools, 9, 152, 275; and financial problems in public schools, xv, 23–4, 173–80; and the Fleming Committee, xix, 174, 180–4, 185–7, 191–4, 256–7, 261; foundation and growth, 8–9; and GBA, 178, 181; in the inter-war years, 8–26; and Jewish refugees, 208; and the 1945 Labour government, 250–61; and the OTC, 15; and overseas members, 25, 277; and political issues, 19, 22, 173–80; and the Public Schools Commission (1968), 265–7, 296; and the RAF, 67–9; and the Royal Navy, 66; and science, 151–3, 287; structure and membership of, 25, 275; wartime issues, 33, 45, 55, 173–80
Healey, Denis, 143–4, 267
Healey, Gray, 84–5, 88
Heath, Edward, 117, 263
Heatley, Norman, 167–8
Heinemann, Margot, 17
Hely-Hutchinson, Henry, 94
Henderson, Derek, 85–6
Henderson, Hamish, 293
Henderson, Ralph, 154
Hennessy, Peter, 38–9, 221, 269–70
Herivel, John, 138
Hichens, Robert, 73
Hiddleston, Tom, 292
Higgs-Walker, James, 25
Hill, Archibald, 200–1
Hill, M.D., 150, 168
Hillary, Richard, 18, 70; *The Last Enemy*, 70, 232, 276
Hills, Stuart, 103
Hinchingbrooke, Lord, 190
Hinsley, Harry, 119
Hoare, Samuel, 27–8, 34
Hobart, Percy, 164–5
Hodgkin, Alan, 161
Hoffman, Hans, 213
Hogg, Quintin (later Lord Hailsham), 35, 190, 261
Hollington, Gwen, 138
Hollis, Roger, 125
Holmes, Maurice, 20, 24, 34, 178; and the Fleming Committee, 179, 181–3, 192
Home Front, 269
Home Guard, 36, 164–5, 241, 269; and public schools, 41–4, 54, 56
Hone, Brian, 14
Hopgood, John, 18, 86, 88, 224
Hopkins, Richard, 39
Hopkinson, Tom, 226; *Picture Post*, 226

Hordern, Michael, 239–40
Hore-Belisha, Leslie, 34, 197
Horrocks, Brian, 106
Hough, J.F., 57
Howard, Michael, xiii–xiv, 170, 235–6
Howard, Peter, 36
Howard, Trevor, 221
Howarth, Tom, 265
Howlett, John, 264
Hudson, Bill, 130
Hughes, Glyn, 166
Hull, Caesar, 79
Hulton, Edward, 226; *Picture Post*, 226
Hutter, Otto, 205–6, 213
Huxley, Andrew, 169
Huxley, Julian, 150
Huxley, Leonard, 189

Ince, Rosemary, 139
Intelligence Services: Bletchley Park (GC&CS), 81, 118–19, 123–4, 136–40; 'Cambridge spies', 120, 122, 143–6; deception strategies, 126–7; Double Cross system, 122, 126–7; MI5, 122–8, 141–5; MI6 (SIS), 122–9, 142–5, 204; MI9, 127; Operation Mincemeat, 107, 127; Political Warfare Executive, 249; right-wing extremism, 141–3; and school and university networks, 119–23, 128; SOE, 119–20, 128–36, 164, 239
Ironside, Edmund, 43, 105
Isherwood, Christopher, 229
Ismay, 'Pug', xvii, 40

Jacob, Alaric, 237
James, David, 127, 285
James, Jimmy, 114–15
Jary, Sydney, 102
Jay, Douglas, 39, 188
Jebb, Gladwyn, 129
Jefferis, Millis, 163–4
Jellicoe, George, 108, 110
Jennings, Humphrey, 238; *Listen to Britain* (1942 film); *Fires Were Started* (1943 film); *Diary for Timothy* (1945 film)
Jewell, Bill, 127
Jews: anti–Semitism in public schools, 197–200, 202; as pupils in public schools, 197–200; and help from public schools to Jewish refugees, 200–12, 219–20; and *Kindertransport*, 203–12; and Nazi persecution, 200–12, 213–14; and wartime internment, 210, 212–13
Jones, Eric, 138

Jones, R.V., 154, 162
Johnson, Boris, xii, xxi, 263
Johnson, Celia, 81, 294
Johnson, Johnnie, 71–2, 79–80
*Journey's End (*play), 222–4, 292
Jowitt, William, 46, 250
Joyce, William, 142

Kay-Shuttleworth, Richard, 75
Kee, Robert, 112
Keegan, John, 235; *Six Armies in Normandy*, 235
Kell, Vernon, 123, 125
Kellett, Edward, 101–2
Kemp, Peter, 27
Kendall, Henry, 11
Kennedy, Ludovic, 13
Kennington, Eric, 225
Kempson, Eric, 71
Keynes, Geoffrey, 153
Keyes, Sidney, 13, 229, 275, 293
Keynes, J.M., 153, 174, 190–1, 269
Keynes, Richard, 153
Kenyon, Barbara, 42
Kettlewell, Marion, 81
Kidd, Colin, 148
Kingcome, Brian, 76
King George VI, 106, 161, 234
Kirby-Green, Tom, 104
Kirk, Ann, 219–20
Klugmann, James, 131
Knox, Dilly, 137
Kynaston, David, xi

Labour Party: and direct grant schools, 267, 275; and education, xix–xx,15, 21, 179–81, 185–6, 250–61, 265–7, 270, 275, 296; and the 1944 Education Act, 185–6, 253; and the Fleming Report, xx, 185, 253, 255–6, 260–1; and the 1945 General Election, xx, 248–50, 252; Labour governments (1945–51), xix–xx, 188, 194, 248, 250, 252–61; Labour governments (1964–70, 1974–79), 248, 265–8, 275, 296; and 'New Jerusalem', 155, 173, 185–6, 219, 269; and public schools, xix–xx, 14, 15, 179–81, 185, 250–61, 265–7, 270, 296; and the Wartime Coalition, 33, 173, 185
Lambert, Royston, 260
Langley, Jimmy, 127
Lascelles, Lord, 113
Lascelles, Tommy, 161–2, 252
Laski, Harold, 188

Latter, Algernon, 237
Lawrence, T.E., 107
Laycock, Robert, 107–9
Leach, Henry, 66
League of Nations, 15, 96, 143
Lean, David, 240; *The Bridge on the River Kwai*, 240
Lee, Jennie, 141
Leech, Richard, 224
Lees-Milne, James, 18
Lees-Smith, Hastings, 182
Leeson, Spencer, 23, 33, 175, 208, 217; and the Fleming Committee, 179–80, 182–3, 256, 260
Leigh, Vivien, 294
Leigh Fermor, Patrick, 18, 133–5
Leigh-Mallory, Trafford, 67
Le Mesurier, John, 16, 22, 241; *Dad's Army*, 241
Lever, Harold, 267
Lewes, Jock, 108–9, 284
Lewis, Alun, 293
Lewis, Cecil, 67, 232; *Sagittarius Rising*, 67, 232
Lidell, Alvar, 234
Lindemann, Frederick, 154, 156, 162
Lindsay, Martin, 130
Listowel, Lord, 250
Littledale, Ronnie, 114, 284
Littlewood, Joan, xiii, 223; *Oh! What a Lovely War*, xiii, 223
Lloyd, George, 35, 41
Local Education Authorities (LEAs),181, 186–7; and Fleming, 256–61; Hampshire, 256; Hertfordshire, 258, 265; London County Council, 183, 257; Middlesex, 258; Surrey, 193
London University, 39; Imperial College, 39, 150, 158, 160; King's College, 236; London School of Economics, 189, 200, 202; London University Air Squadron, 69–70; Medical schools, 166–7; University College, 39, 167, 169, 196, 203
Longden, Bobby, 60
Low, David, 37
Lowe, Arthur, 241; *Dad's Army*, 241
Lowndes, Ashley, 168, 288
Lowry, Charles, 19
Luce, Fritz, 208
Lyell, Lord Charles, 94
Lyon, Hugh, 6, 177
Lyttelton, Oliver, 38, 156

McCallum, David, 232
McKibbin, Ross, 253, 260